mod	other problems with modification (**19c**)
ns	*non sequitur*, "does not logically follow" (**5d, 5f, 5g**)
org	problem with organization (**6a**)
p	problem with punctuation (**23, 24**)
pl	plural needed (**15a.1**)
pred	problem with subject-predicate match (**19f**)
red	redundant; omit one of the redundant words or phrases (**20b.2**)
ref	pronoun reference unclear (**12c.2**)
rep	unnecessary or ineffective repetition (**18e**)
shift	shift in person or tense (**12c.1, 14g**)
sp	problem with spelling; check dictionary (**22**)
sub	problem with subordination (**19b**)
sup	superlative form of adjective needed (**17b, 17c, 17d**)
th	thesis absent or unclear (**3a**)
trans	transition absent or unclear (**12b**)
ts	topic sentence absent or unclear (**11b**)
v	problem with voice; change active to passive or vice-versa (**18g.1, 19d**)
vb	problem with verb form (**14**)
tense	problem with verb tense (**14a**)
w	wordy (**20b.2**)
wo	problem with word order (**18g, 19e**)
∧	insert; may be used in margin as well as in the writing
ℓ⌐, [ ]	omit—wordy, unnecessary, or distracting; sometimes brackets are also put around material to be omitted (**20b.2**)
¶	paragraph division needed (**11c**)
//	problem with parallel structure (**19g**)
?	something missing or not clear
#	space(s) needed

THE CONFIDENT
WRITER
A NORTON HANDBOOK

Second Edition

THE CONFIDENT WRITER
A NORTON HANDBOOK

Constance J. Gefvert

Second Edition

W·W·NORTON & COMPANY·NEW YORK·LONDON

Published simultaneously in Canada by Penguin Books Canada Ltd., 2801
John Street, Markham, Ontario L3R 1B4
Printed in the United States of America.

The text of this book is composed in Sabon, with display type set in Bembo.
Composition by Vail-Ballou. Manufacturing by The Maple-Vail Book Group.
Book design by Jacques Chazaud

Library of Congress Cataloging in Publication Data

ISBN 0-393-95618-0

W. W. Norton & Company, Inc., 500 Fifth Avenue, New York, N.Y. 10110
W. W. Norton & Company Ltd., 37 Great Russell Street, London WC1B
3NU

2 3 4 5 6 7 8 9 0

Nancy Bubel: "How to Make a Terrarium" reprinted by permission from
Blair & Ketchum's Country Journal. Copyright © December 1978, His-
torical Times, Inc.
Anthony Burgess: Selections from "Is America Falling Apart?" Copyright ©
1971 by the New York Times Company. Reprinted by permission.
Annie Dillard: "Death of a Moth." Copyright © 1976 by Annie Dillard.
Reprinted by permission of the author and her agent Blanche C. Gregory,
Inc.
F. Scott Fitzgerald: "Letter to Scottie" from *The Letters of F. Scott Fitzgerald,*
edited by Andrew Turnbull. Copyright © 1963, Frances Scott Fitzgerald
Lanahan. Reprinted with the permission of Charles Scribner's Sons.
Garrison Keillor: "Re the Tower Project" from *Happy to Be Here.* Copyright
© 1982 Garrison Keillor. Reprinted with the permission of Atheneum Publishers, a division of Macmillan, Inc.
Archibald MacLeish: Excerpt from "The Conquest of America." Copyright
© 1980 by Archibald MacLeish as first published in *The Atlantic.* Reprinted
with permission.
Marianne Moore: "The Mind is an Enchanting Thing." Copyright 1944, and
renewed 1972, by Marianne Moore. Reprinted with permission of Macmillan Publishing Company.
E. B. White: "Democracy" from *The Wild Flag* (Houghton Mifflin). © 1943,
1971 by E. B. White. Originally in *The New Yorker.*

CONTENTS

PREFACE

As a teacher of composition, linguistics, and literature for twenty years, and as director of a large writing program for eight years, I have seen more handbooks than I could ever have imagined existing when I took my own freshman composition course in 1959. I have reviewed handbooks for other publishers, I have evaluated them for use in my own teaching, and I have debated within composition committees about the virtues and vices of various handbooks we have considered for use in our writing programs. As a teacher of linguistics, I have been appalled at the unrelieved prescriptivism of many handbooks, and as a teacher of literature and composition, I have been distressed at the unwillingness of many linguistically oriented texts to tell students how modern readers react to certain variations in style and grammatical usage.

Like many enthusiastic composition teachers, I dreamed as far back as graduate school of writing my own handbook—one which would be the perfect compromise between the purely prescriptive and the purely descriptive, one which would be *rhetorical* in nature, recognizing that while one cannot make absolute judgments about good and bad in language, one must be able to judge how a particular usage will affect a particular audience. A course in American Social Dialects, which I took from Harold Allen at the University of Minnesota, gave me my first insight into how inadequate most handbooks were; a paper I had to write for Professor Allen evaluating one particular handbook provided the first systematic attempt I made to formulate my own idea of what a handbook should be.

During my years of teaching composition at Minnesota and at Wayne State University, I continued to do some serious thinking about the relationship between language as it is and language as people expect it to be, and I kept trying to find the handbook that would give students a realistic understanding of that relationship. When I moved to Virginia Tech from Wayne State in 1976 and attended my first SAMLA meeting, I had a helpful conversation with Barry Wade from Norton, who listened with interest to my description of the "ideal" handbook and encouraged me to try writing it. That was the beginning of a long process of exploration, writing, and rewriting.

An important part of the process was the Usage Survey, which Norton generously supported because they agreed with me that a useful handbook for today's students would give accurate information about how people other than linguists and English professors feel about usage. In the survey, therefore, we went to people in business, industry, and government, as well as education—to the people students will be working with when they graduate from college—and asked their opinions about which controversial usages they find acceptable in different circumstances. The usage advice in this handbook is based on that survey (which is described in more detail both in the Introduction and in the Instructor's Manual; a more thorough description of the survey is in preparation for separate publication). We believe that because of the survey, students can be confident that this handbook does not merely reflect the prejudices of the author or publisher or, indeed, of English professors in general.

The purpose of *The Confident Writer: A Norton Handbook* is to give students and other writers the help they need to write with confidence and therefore with persuasive power. From the beginnings of the writing process through the final editing stages, this handbook will help students make the choices—of thesis, supporting arguments and details, order, paragraph structure, sentence structure, words, and grammatical forms—that will allow them to achieve their purpose. The book is based on two major assumptions: 1) that effective writing speaks to a particular audience for a particular purpose and 2) that students need a repertoire of techniques as well as a knowledge of what grammatical forms are appropriate for what situations and audiences, so they can make the choices that will make their writing effective.

This handbook can be used in a variety of ways: as a reference handbook for any writer, whether apprentice or experienced; as a self-study guide for students and others who want to make their writing more effective; as a revision guide to which teachers can direct their students; and as a classroom text. I have organized the handbook so it will be useful in any of these situations. If the book is used as a writing text in the classroom or for self-study, the chapters can be used in the order they are arranged in the book. The writing process is placed first so that all matters of grammatical usage may be placed in a rhetorical context; that is, every choice a writer must make about sentence structure, word choice, and punctuation makes sense only in terms of the purpose of a piece of writing, its audience, and the medium in which it is written.

If the book is used primarily for reference, the Table of Contents, Index, organizational chart on the back endpapers, and index of correction symbols on the front endpaper can all be used to find things easily. A more detailed explanation of how to use the book is included at the end of the Introduction. The answers to exercises, approaches to teaching composition, suggestions for writing, and ideas for using the book are included in an Instructor's Manual written by my colleague Carol Domblewski, who is a seasoned composition instructor and who has helped with this handbook at various stages of its evolution. The workbook that accompanies the handbook was written by Amy Richards, a veteran professor and administrator of composition programs at Wayne State University. Answers to the workbook exercises are also included in the Instructor's Manual.

When I undertook the job of writing a new handbook, I knew I would need to defend placing yet another handbook on the market. The features that made the first edition distinctive have been retained in the second edition, among them the following:

- All of the usage advice in *The Confident Writer* is based on actual data collected in a survey of over 250 people from across the country in a variety of professions. Students are often skeptical of advice in English handbooks because they believe English teachers are fussier than other people about the niceties of writing. They will find in this handbook, however, that the majority of people in my Usage Survey were as conservative as most English teachers. More importantly, however, they will find the advice based on the opinions of people who are responsible for writing in the places most of them will be working after college graduation—in business, industry, government, and education.

- The exercises in *The Confident Writer* ask students to write, not just analyze and identify, even though ample traditional exercises are provided for students who need that kind of practice.
- The rhetoric chapters (Part One) in *The Confident Writer* are based on contemporary theory and research, but in a manner useful for real students writing real papers; they include material on overcoming writing anxiety, based on recent research in that area.
- The rhetoric chapters in *The Confident Writer* include a number of different approaches to invention (informal ones like brainstorming and looping; formal ones like the grid, the pentad, and the common topics); the idea is to give students a repertoire of possibilities from which they can choose the techniques most helpful to them in particular kinds of writing situations.
- Students are encouraged to make rhetorical choices according to the constraints of purpose, medium, and audience; sentence structure, word choice, grammatical usage, and even punctuation and spelling are placed in a context of audience, medium, and purpose.
- Paragraphing is taught as a process; students are shown the many different reasons for paragraphing rather than thinking of paragraphs merely as building blocks.
- The section on words includes a brief history of the English language, so that students can understand apparent inconsistencies in the language from a historical perspective. The section on words is also useful for vocabulary building and includes a treatment of Greek and Latin roots.
- The problems of sexism and racism in language are treated in detail, with helpful alternative suggestions and ways of getting around the cumbersome *his/her* difficulty.
- The punctuation chapters summarize rules already explained in the appropriate context in other chapters, so that punctuation is not seen as an isolated list of arbitrary rules. Comma splices and sentence fragments are dealt with in the context of punc-

tuation appropriate for independent and dependent clauses, rather than being treated as isolated "grammatical" problems.

- The research paper section was originally written by Donald Kenney, head of the General Reference Department at Virginia Tech's Newman Library, and George Hayhoe, Director of Virginia Tech's Writing Center. I have revised the chapter, but it owes its strength to the experience of Kenney and Hayhoe, who developed their method of teaching research strategies and the process of writing the research paper over several years, during which they conducted term paper workshops for students across the university as part of the library's outreach program. It represents an effective partnership between English professor and librarian.
- The appendix on Professional Writing, which I have revised for this edition, was written by an expert in that area, Donna Hudelson, who is an experienced teacher of business writing as well as an experienced free-lance writer.

The second edition has drawn on the experience of teachers and students who have used the book, and who have suggested many changes that will make this edition more useful:

1. The chapter on persuasion has been moved to Part 1, in order to emphasize that techniques of persuasion such as argumentation and special appeals are part of the total writing process. In addition, the chapter has been revised to emphasize techniques of *writing* persuasive prose rather than merely analyzing the persuasive techniques of other writers.

2. The chapter on using the dictionary has been combined with the chapter on sources of English words, to produce one chapter that emphasizes choice of words in a rhetorical context. The background information on sources of words and use of dictionaries is still there, but the emphasis has been made more rhetorical.

3. The chapters on researched writing have been moved to follow the rhetoric chapters in Part 1, and have been shortened by omitting unnecessary duplication with treatment of the writing process. Also, changes that occurred in the MLA *Handbook* since *The Confident Writer* was published have been included in this second edition of *The Confident Writer*.

4. The brief section on drafting and revising with a word processor has been eliminated; instead, references to writing with a word processor have been vastly expanded and integrated into the text.
5. The new edition has been made almost 100 pages briefer, mainly by eliminating unnecessary repetition; the handbook remains shorter than many standard handbooks, even though it is equally thorough in its coverage.
6. The chapter on Professional Writing has been shortened slightly and placed in an Appendix at the end of the book.
7. The chapter on problems with sentence punctuation has been combined with the chapter on punctuating sentences, and both have been shortened by eliminating repetition.
8. The treatment of apostrophes has been expanded and clarified, both in the chapter on punctuation of words and in the sections on possessive case of nouns and pronouns.

Writing is always a collaborative process. Just as I encourage students in this book to get helpful feedback from peers and teachers, so I have had a great deal of assistance in writing this book. My invaluable mentor, critic, and helper has been my editor, Barry Wade, without whom I would never have begun or completed this book. From his initial enthusiasm about my proposal to write a handbook almost twelve years ago to his artful editing of both editions, he has done more than anyone could expect of an editor. His poetic soul, disciplined mind, and fine sense of what students need have made the book far richer than it would otherwise have been. And without his sense of humor, patience, tact, and sheer doggedness, I might have quit long before this project was completed.

Many of my students were invaluable in helping me revise earlier drafts of this book. In particular, the students in my fall and winter sections of freshman English in 1980–81 worked through a trial edition, and many of them contributed writing to this book; they are cited after their contributions.

To the many reviewers of various drafts of the first edition, I can hardly say thank you enthusiastically enough. They are the ones who allowed me to put my own advice into practice, making me sensitive to the needs of my audience: Jean Brenkman,

University of Wisconsin—Madison; Harry Brent, Baruch College; Alma G. Bryant, University of South Florida; Forrest D. Burt, Texas A & M University; Jon C. Burton, Northern Virginia Community College; Robert J. Connor, Louisiana State University; Timothy W. Crusius, Texas A & M University; Kenneth W. Davis, University of Kentucky; Mary Jane Dickerson, The University of Vermont; Kim Flachmann, California State College, Bakersfield; Ron Fortune, Illinois State University; J. L. Funston, James Madison University; Barbara Munson Goff, Rutgers University—Cook College; Paul T. Graham, University of Missouri; Winifred B. Horner, University of Missouri; Francis Hubbard, California State University, Sacramento; James Kinneavy, The University of Texas at Austin; Jake Kobler, North Texas State University; Andrea A. Lunsford, University of British Columbia; Richard McLain, State University of New York—Binghamton; Michael J. Marcuse, University of Maryland; Jeanette Morgan, University of Houston; Catherine E. Moore, North Carolina State University at Raleigh; E. J. Murphy, California State University Hayward; Frank O'Hare, Ohio State University; Maurice Scharton, Illinois State University; Ann Sharp, Furman University; Charles Schuster, University of Washington; Lynne M. Shuster, Erie Community College—Buffalo; Daniel R. Thomas, Shelby State Community College; Peter T. Zoller, Wichita State University.

In addition, I am grateful to those who have helped in various ways with the second edition:

Amy Richards, author of the workbook to accompany *The Confident Writer,* who contributed many helpful ideas for the second edition of the handbook; she has also prepared a second edition of the workbook which is more concise and reflects changes in the handbook.

Carol Domblewski, who contributed so much to the first edition as well as writing the Instructor's Manual.

And the instructors who gave helpful suggestions in written reviews and telephone interviews: Gail Bounds, Chesapeake College; Janet Byron, Cleveland State University; Richard Denham, Houston Baptist University; Norbert Eliot, East Texas State University; Gwendolyn Gong, Texas A & M; Patricia Hernlund, Wayne State University; Sheila Juba, Lane Community College; Nancy McGrath, Sacramento City College; Margaret Nearing,

Sacramento City College; Edward Nolte, Norfolk State College; Shirley Thompson, Chesapeake College.

I would like to thank especially my sisters at St. John's Convent in Willowdale (Metropolitan Toronto), who generously allowed me the time to revise the book for the second edition and supported me in every way, including taking on many duties that I would otherwise have done.

I dedicate this book in loving memory of my mother Florence, whose happy confidence helped bring it to birth.

THE CONFIDENT WRITER

A NORTON HANDBOOK

Second Edition

INTRODUCTION

Handbooks are among the most common books in our society. In almost any bookstore you will find handbooks for car repair, handbooks of stereo equipment or musical terms, football or chemistry or computer handbooks. Some handbooks provide a compendium of the knowledge in a certain field: a handbook of astronomy, for instance, will give the basic facts about stars, planets, their movements, and the way heavenly bodies affect the earth; a handbook of old 45-rpm records will list labels, composers, and artists, along with acceptable prices. But most handbooks are more than collections of information; they are also how-to books, explaining how, for instance, to identify the constellations or how to shop for collectable records.

The Confident Writer is both a collection of information and a how-to book. It contains information about our language, including grammar, punctuation, and spelling. But it also contains some how-tos: how to get started writing a paper, how to revise your writing so it satisfies your needs and the needs of your audience, how to tell effective writing from ineffective. Most people tend to think first of grammar when they think of handbooks, but rhetoric (which involves the how-to) is also an important part of an English handbook. While grammar has to do with what is possible in the language, rhetoric involves the choices a writer can make from among many possible options.

Rhetoric

Rhetoric comes from the Greek word *rhetor,* which means "orator" or "public speaker." In classical Greece, *rhetors* were specially trained to speak in the Greek senate, in courts of law, and on other public occasions. They were expected to be skilled at explaining themselves, laying out an argument clearly, and persuading their audience to adopt their point of view or to follow a specific course of action. Learning those skills involved learning to choose the words, ideas, and examples that would best accomplish their purpose. Most of the principles taught to apprentice or student *rhetors* in ancient Greece still apply to the writing of speeches and essays today.

Because rhetorical choices depend on your purpose for writing, this handbook begins with a discussion of the processes successful writers follow when they sit down to address a particular audience for a particular purpose. Based on what is known about their writing processes, *The Confident Writer* offers some suggestions to help you when you have to write a college paper, a business or technical report, or any other kind of writing in school or on the job.

An important part of the writing process for skillful writers is revision—both rewriting and editing; and in order to revise effectively, you need to know something about grammar as well as rhetoric.

Grammar

The word *grammar* comes from another Greek word, *grammatikos,* which means "knowing one's language." Many people think of grammar as a mere list of dos and don'ts, rules that do not seem related to the way we really use the language. Grammar is, however, much more than a list of rules, and it does have a great deal to do with the way we use our language—both in speech and in writing. In modern English, the word *grammar* has at least three different meanings:

Grammar as Structure
In its most basic sense, the word *grammar* means "the structure of a language," including the forms of words and the ways in

which they are arranged in sentences, as well as certain oral and written signals we use to convey meaning.

The *forms* of words (including their spelling and added letters or syllables) are important in conveying the meaning we want. Consider, for example, the following sentences:

> Friends are willing to help.
> Friendship is willingness to help.

When we change the form of *friends* to *friendship,* *are* to *is,* and *willing* to *willingness,* we change the meaning of the sentence. The first sentence is a general statement about friends; the second is a definition of friendship.

The meaning of a sentence also depends on the *order* of words. "Children like dogs," for example, is quite different from "Dogs like children," and "light green" has a meaning different from "green light."

Finally, we use certain oral or written *signals* to convey meanings. The sentence "Jane graduated from college," for instance, could have a number of different meanings, which we would understand in speech by listening to stress and intonation, or in writing by observing punctuation and stress markings. We can understand the different meanings clearly by imagining what the speaker would say next in each case; notice the stress markings (shown by italic type) and the punctuation marks:

> Jane graduated from *college?* I thought she was still in high school.
> *Jane* graduated from college? I thought Ellen had all the brains in the family.
> Jane graduated from college! Hooray!

These characteristics of English structure—form, word order, and verbal signals—exemplify an important fact about all languages: they are *conventional;* certain expectations are set up that all native speakers will follow.

How do we learn the grammar of our native language? Scholars of language do not all agree, but probably through a combination of hearing the language spoken and making generalizations about its patterns, we assimilate those patterns into our own speech without consciously thinking about them. By the time we are five or six years old, we have learned most of the grammar of our native language. We do not, for example, have to be taught that adjectives come before nouns if English is our native language. Why, then, is it necessary to teach grammar?

First, at home and in school we are taught the many exceptions to the conventions of English that we learn subconsciously. We learn on our own how to make the past tense of verbs by adding -*ed* to the end (walk*ed*, play*ed*, jump*ed*, etc), but we often have to be taught that the past tense of *think*, for example, is not think*ed* but *thought*.

Second, in school we learn the differences between the "standard" dialect and the variety of English some children learn at home or speak with friends. A child might learn, for example, that in the standard dialect "I ain't" is replaced by "I'm not."

Third, when we study grammar in school, we learn how to *analyze* language: to classify, identify, name, and define those structures we have already learned.

Grammar as Description

If the first meaning of *grammar* is the *structure* of language, then the second meaning is a *description* of that structure, or a description of the conventions that we follow when we speak or write about our language. People have always been fascinated by trying to make order out of their universe. Philosophers and chemists, theologians and physicists—all have tried to explain the way our language works. Many different descriptions of English are possible, depending on *how* one describes it (in terms of traditional or modern grammar, for instance) and *what* one describes. This handbook uses a combination of traditional and modern approaches to describe one variety of our language, the so-called "standard" dialect.

Grammar as Prescription

Finally, the word *grammar* often refers to the "correct" way to use the language or the most appropriate choice of language in given circumstances. It is the etiquette of our language, a set of rules about what is appropriate and inappropriate in speech and writing. A *descriptive* grammar explains the conventions of our language and describes how native speakers of English use it. A *prescriptive* grammar explains not what we do, but what we *ought* to do. As you will see below, this handbook is both descriptive and prescriptive.

Varieties of English

English comes in many varieties, often called *dialects*, which are spoken by definable groups of people—those from a certain geographical region, like New England or the Appalachian mountains for example, or those from a particular social or ethnic group. Most modern linguists consider that what is traditionally called "standard English" is one dialect among many others; it has become standard because the people who use it—largely college-educated people of upper socioeconomic levels—give it status, not because it has any innate linguistic superiority.

To illustrate: suppose you knocked on the door of a close friend and he called, "Who is it?" You would most likely reply without hesitation, "It's me." That response would not be appropriate in some circumstances, but if your friend opened the door and said, "Good to see you—come on in," you would know that no other answer could have been more appropriate in that situation. The more formally correct "It is I" would sound stilted, even unfriendly. On the other hand, suppose a potential employer who has interviewed you for a job should call and say, "I'd like to speak to Joan Davis." You might stumble or hesitate, finally deciding to say, "This is she," being aware that that response is not inherently *better* than "It's me," but more *appropriate* in that situation because it fits certain expectations.

We all know how to talk and write to our friends; when we do so, nonstandard or informal usage is often appropriate. But we are not always sure what is considered standard and, especially, what is appropriate to use in more formal situations. In this handbook, therefore, the grammatical descriptions are based on those forms of the language usually recognized as standard and generally accepted as the norm for educated users of the language in America.

The term *standard English*, however, must be used cautiously, because no single standard exists throughout America. For one thing, there are regional differences: standard speech in Atlanta varies somewhat from the standard in Boston or Los Angeles. Further, there are differences throughout the country between spoken and written English: we tend to be more conservative in writing than in speech, preserving older grammatical forms (like the distinction between *who* and *whom*). Differences also exist that we may call historical. Our language is always changing, and people vary in their willingness to accept new forms into the language; so what some people consider nonstandard today may be considered standard in a few years. Finally, standard English varies depending on the formality or informality of the context in which it is used. In a formal letter, I might ask, "To whom shall I send the report?" In an informal or casual situation, I would be more likely to write, "Who should I send the report to?" The two versions are different in pronoun form (*whom/who*), auxiliary verb form (*shall/should*), and position of the preposition (*to* at the beginning/end of sentence). But both versions are written in standard English.

Range of Usage

Within the scope of standard English, we can identify three styles of language use, whether in speech or in writing—*formal, informal,* and *casual.* When grammatical usage is described in this handbook, all three labels will refer to usage that is *standard*— that is, accepted by most educated writers and speakers. Formal and informal writing and speech are not only standard but also *edited*: the writer consciously considers the form of the writing, including the grammar, and often changes whatever seems inappropriate for the audience and occasion. In casual writing and speech, on the other hand, editing is not normally important; writers say what they have to say spontaneously, without worrying about the choices they have made.

One way to get a picture of the differences among formal, informal, and casual usage is to compare the language you use to the way you dress for different occasions. Job interviews, religious services, and weddings, for instances, are often *formal,* and on such occasions you may be concerned not only with the form of dress but with the kind of language you use. In formal situations, you may not know all the other people involved very well (in fact, many might be strangers), and you probably share little common knowledge with them. In formal writing, like research reports, campaign speeches, and legal briefs, you must consider your grammatical choices carefully and edit your writing to suit the occasion and audience.

In *informal* situations, the form of both dress and speech is less important than in formal ones, but important enough that you think twice about what you want to wear or say or write. On occasions like a college dance or a committee meeting, you usually know the people involved to some extent, and you often share a fair amount of common knowledge with them. In writing a newspaper article or a letter to the editor, you would be acquainted with the general audience if not with specific readers, and you would be concerned enough about your audience to edit your writing, but without necessarily choosing the most formal options.

In *casual* situations, form is usually irrelevant. On occasions like picnics and parties with friends and family or in dormitory bull sessions, how you dress or speak is less important than the relationships with the people involved, whom you usually know very well and with whom you share a great deal of background knowledge. Because form is not important in casual situations, casual speech and writing, like conversations with friends or letters to your family, are usually not edited; in such situations, you may use both standard and nonstandard forms, and you do not usually stop to consider whether you have used the "correct" word or appropriate grammar because you are more interested in what you say than in how you say it.

Although these three labels are used throughout the book to guide you in making grammatical choices, they are not absolutes. They describe a wide *range* of usage that can vary from situation to situation. It is up to you, as the writer, to be sensitive to the needs of your audience and to choose expressions that will not offend your readers by being too casual on formal occasions or too stuffy or stilted on less formal occasions. This matter of choice is something that sounds complicated, but it comes more easily as you get practice and as you develop sensitivity to your audience.

Since formal, informal, and casual are all varieties of standard English, the label standard is not used in this book except to distinguish such usage from *nonstandard*: usage that is unacceptable in edited writing for an educated audience.

You will see other labels in this book too, like the distinction between *confusing* and *clear*. These labels refer to sentences written in standard English, but with problems that affect how effectively the sentences carry their messages across to readers. In addition, since spelling and punctuation are not matters of grammar but rather of how the language is transcribed into speech, *unconventional* will indicate spelling and punctuation that are not normally used in published books and magazines (which follow *conventional* spelling and punctuation) and that may therefore be confusing to your reader.

The Usage Survey

Conventions of grammar and punctuation are often debatable and change frequently. In order to be as useful as possible to current students who are preparing for careers in a variety of occupations, a handbook like this one has to be up to date, and it must also reflect attitudes toward usage that are prevalent in the working world most students are preparing to enter. In order to be sure this handbook achieved those two goals, I conducted a major survey of people who are responsible for the quality of writing in their places of employment. I asked these writers and editors—in business, industry, government, education, and other fields—to give their opinions about edited usage, to tell whether they would accept a certain item of grammar or punctuation if they were editing the writing in which it appeared.

Whenever you see labels like *formal / informal / casual, standard / nonstandard, conventional / unconventional* you should keep in mind that they are not merely the preference of the writer of this handbook, nor the preference of English teachers or book publishers. Rather, the advice in this handbook is based on several sources of information. Whenever usage is controversial (that is, where other handbooks as well as dictionaries disagree), the advice in *The Confident Writer* is based on the results of the usage survey. For usage that is not particularly controversial, the advice is largely consistent with that in the major college dictionaries and in handbooks of usage.

Using this Book

In addition to assignments your instructor makes in *The Confident Writer,* you will sometimes want to use the book for reference yourself, and sometimes you will want to find something your instructor has sent you to look for. In either case, you need to know how to use this book as a reference tool. Following are some tips for finding your way around in *The Confident Writer*:

1. Become familiar with the organization of the book. Notice how the writing process is described first, then how various elements of grammar, sentence structure, word choice, spelling, and punctuation follow, with the sections on special assignments and the Glossary of Usage last. Skim through the Table of Contents to see what subtopics are included in each chapter, and examine the Organizational Chart on the back endpapers of the book, to see a schematic arrangement of the book's contents. Notice that chapters are divided into sections, and sections into subsections. Chapters are numbered, sections are lettered, and subsections are numbered. The smallest unit, a subsection, will be labelled with the chapter number, followed by the section letter, followed by a period and the subsection number. For instance, 20b.7 refers to the subsection on "Clichés and Trite Expressions" in section b (Choosing Words for Emphasis) of chapter 20 (Choosing Effective Words).

2. Become as familiar as you can with the content of the book by reading through any sections that seem particularly useful to you and by skimming the other parts so you know what is there.

3. If you have followed the first two steps, then when you need to use *The Confident Writer* for reference, you will be able to do so with ease. Suppose you need advice about which case of pronouns to use after linking verbs in formal and informal usage. You could skim through the Table of Contents, find the chapter entitled "Problems with Nouns and Pronouns," and then look for something about case forms and linking verbs. As it turns out, section 15b is entitled "Personal Pronouns and Case Forms," and subsection 15b.1 is entitled "After Linking Verbs." The blue index tabs along the outer margins of each page will help you find the sections easily.

A quicker way to find what you need might be to look at the organization chart on the endpapers, and an even quicker way would be to go to the alphabetical index. If you checked under "pronouns" first, you would find a subheading, "after linking verbs." If you looked under "case" first, you would find a cross-reference, "See Pronouns." Most people find the index the best and quickest route to what they need.

When you want advice on a controversial item of usage, you may find it in an alphabetical list in the Glossary of Usage (and glossary items are included in the index as well), or you may find it in one of the grammatical chapters of the book. If it is a grammatical principle that involves many different words, it will be in the chapter dealing with that principle, like the example above about the case of pronouns after linking verbs. If your question is about a particular word, like *impact*, for instance, you should check in the Glossary of Usage. Sometimes a question about a particular word (the use of *whom* versus *who*, for instance) will lead you to an item in the Glossary of Usage that will in turn send you to another section of the handbook (the section on relative pronouns, 15e, for instance). Or a discussion in one part of the handbook (on principal parts of verbs, for instance, in 14a.5) will refer you to questions about specific words in the Glossary of Usage (for instance, the different past forms of the verb *dive*).

In short, no matter where you start in the book, you should find ample cross-references to other sections. If you follow through the various cross-references you find, you will discover much more about the item you were looking up than you expected, and by seeing it discussed in various contexts, you should find yourself becoming more confident in your ability to choose the right words and expressions for your audience.

Part One

WRITING
AS A PROCESS

1

AN OVERVIEW

1a   What Is the Process?

Many people think that good writing emerges full-blown from
the writer's pen, like a genie from Aladdin's lamp. But an essay,
a report, or a research paper does not appear by magic. Even
professional writers go through a long, complex process to get to
the end product.

Like any process, writing involves certain steps, but it differs
from some other processes. When good cooks set out to make an
omelet, they have a pretty good idea of what the omelet will look
like when it is finished and the steps they must follow to produce
it. Likewise, when contractors build houses, they usually begin
with carefully drawn architectural plans and know the steps they
must perform in a certain order.

In writing, by contrast, you often discover what you are making only in the process of making it, and the various activities are
performed in different orders by different people—or even by one
person for different writing tasks. Some writers think through
their ideas, plan carefully, and write a formal outline before ever
starting an essay. Other writers begin writing immediately in order
to get the ideas to flow; when these ideas do not occur where
they will be most helpful to the reader, such writers cut the pages
and rearrange them, putting them together with tape or stapler.
Or if they write with a word processor, they can move paragraphs, pages, even sections around on the computer screen.

Even though such variations are common among successful
writers, certain activities occur in the process of all good writing.
They do not always follow the order below, and they often over-

lap and recur. But it is helpful to consider each part of the process separately.

1. *A Starting Point*: In any writing, you must have a starting point—a question to answer, a problem to solve, an interesting idea to develop. Sometimes the starting point is entirely up to you. More often the topic itself is given, although you might have to narrow the subject to manageable proportions or find your own angle or point of view.

2. *Discovery*: The invention or discovery of ideas and facts is a part of every writing process. The amount of discovery in the writing process depends on how much of the assignment is already specified. If your boss asks you to write up a year-end sales report, for example, you are given a starting point, and most of the supporting material is already available in the form of statistics; your job is to arrange those statistics in the clearest and most readable way. At the other extreme, your English professor may give you an essay assignment in which you can choose the topic; then you have a great deal more freedom to discover your own ideas.

3. *Incubation and Illumination*: Almost all writers (including those who write for their employers) find it necessary to leave some time for gestation or incubation, some time when the conscious mind is resting and the subconscious mind can "work" on the problems in the writing; illumination is the result of that subconscious activity.

4. *Selecting*: As you think about the subject of your writing, and after you have discovered as many ideas as possible, you will have to decide what your thesis or central idea is and which ideas and supporting details you will use to develop that thesis.

5. *Planning and Arranging*: During this part of the writing process, you decide which method of writing is the best to accomplish your purpose and in which order you will choose to present your material. It may or may not include traditional outlining; many writers do some informal planning, write the first draft, and then use an outline to check the organization. But however you do it, all writing involves planning the shape you want the finished product to take.

6. *Writing a First Draft*: Writing a first draft may come before or after selecting and arranging, since it sometimes happens that writers will prune, select, and rearrange after the first draft (or before, during, *and* after it). Likewise, the first draft may come after the discovery of ideas or along with it (for those who find that writing the draft is itself a way to generate ideas). But at some point you will arrange your notes into a logical order, put your ideas into words, and produce a preliminary version of the whole paper. This is not usually the time to worry about grammar, style, punctuation, spelling, or even finding just the right word. Usually you will be able to write a draft more easily, without blocking your creative ideas, if you let all those other matters wait until a later stage.

7. *Revising*: To revise is to "look again" at what you have written, to see it through fresh eyes. Revision includes two activities:

   a. When you *rewrite*, you consider your thesis or main point, the supporting details, their arrangement, your choice of words, and in general how clearly and effectively you have gotten your message across. This is the time most writers consider the effectiveness of their sentences and the best choice of words. If you try to rewrite while you are still writing the first draft, sentence by sentence, you may find you cannot write as easily.

   b. When you *edit*, you consider the surface features of writing—grammar, usage, spelling, and mechanics. Editing is the one activity that should almost always come last, and for two reasons it is best done after the major rewriting. First, to fuss too much too early about grammar and punctuation may be wasted effort, since in the process of rewriting, sentences are often deleted or totally rewritten. Second, you should not let questions of grammar and mechanics interfere with the creative energy at work when you are writing and rewriting.

In the chapters that follow, we will look in detail at what is involved in each stage of the writing process. Remember that writing is a highly individual process, and while certain activities are a part of almost everyone's writing habits, they are not emphasized equally, nor do they always occur in the same order. Try out the practical suggestions in the rest of this chapter and the chapters that follow, but if some suggestions do not work for you or seem alien or mechanical, more trouble than they are worth, then drop them and use the ones that fit your writing personality the best. Do not give up before you have given them a fair try, however; sometimes what seems most difficult at first turns out to be the most helpful.

1b   Overcoming Writing Anxiety

Students often think that writing comes easily to English teachers or to professional writers, that students alone have a difficult time. But writing is difficult for almost everyone. The person who seems to write so easily has probably struggled through many starts and stops, revisions and rewrites, and those psychological blocks from which almost everyone suffers: the procrastination that not only puts off the writer's task but increases anxiety and causes further procrastination; the mind that seems as blank as a clean sheet of paper; the sudden need to balance the checkbook, call a friend, review the contents of the refrigerator—to do anything but write.

What causes this fear of putting pen to paper? Why is writing so much more difficult than talking?

For one thing, writing is a less "natural" activity than speech. Speaking comes first not only in the history of the human race but also in your own personal history. You learn to speak long before you learn to put your thoughts in writing. Speaking becomes almost second nature—like walking, breathing, or eating—while writing seldom becomes that automatic.

Second, writing is difficult because you have no immediate audience. In speaking, you have the advantage of seeing how your listeners react to what you are saying. If their facial expressions, gestures, or postures indicate disagreement or disapproval, you can usually clear up any misunderstandings immediately. Even in telephone conversations, you use "verbal gestures" like *yes, no, uh-huh, hmmm*. Listeners ask you questions that you can answer on the spot. But if a reader disagrees with you, you cannot immediately clarify or restate or try another argument. Instead, you have to try to anticipate your readers' responses and "answer" them before the readers have a chance to pose them in their own minds.

Third, speaking is more comfortable than writing because it is usually tentative: if you do not like what you have said, you can back up and start over again. But when you present someone with something you have written, you commit yourself in a way that is difficult to undo.

Finally, writing, unlike speaking, is often assigned—not only in college classes but on the job as well. Most academic and professional writing is writing-on-demand: essays, lab reports, research papers, business letters, memos, technical reports, press releases, grant proposals. Almost all of this assigned writing will be evaluated, and the fear of failure is common to us all.

In short, writing is hard work. To take what is within us, to conceive a new idea or a new approach to an old idea, and to give birth to it in writing takes time and sweat and commitment. It is no wonder we often try to put writing assignments off. There are, however, some things you can do to make writing less painful and difficult.

1. *Get Used to Writing*: As with any skill, the best way to achieve greater ease in writing is to practice, even when you do *not* have an assignment. (A musician would never dream of not practicing between concerts.) Keep a journal or daily log. Write letters to family or friends instead of picking up the telephone. Try the ten-minute "nonstop" (often called "freewriting"): set a timer or alarm clock for ten minutes and write continuousiy during that time about anything at all that comes to your mind, with no editing, no worrying about grammar or spelling. (See exercise 3 below.) The results of these nonstops should be read by no one except you, so be as uninhibited as you like. If you find you have nothing to say at first, try copying something out of a book or writing over and over again "I want to find something to say . . ." The whole point is to *exercise*—your writing (or typing) hands as well as your brain—in order to make hand and brain more familiar and therefore more comfortable with the written language. Then, when you are confronted with a writing assignment, you will be able to put pen to paper with greater ease.

If you have a word processor, you will find nonstops especially useful. You can ignore the screen (or turn it off) so that you are not inhibited by what you have already written. Or, if you are not the kind to type "blindly," the sight of the cursor steadily moving across the screen might be just what you need to keep your thoughts following behind. And if you are the kind who thinks faster than you can write, using a keyboard (even on a typewriter) will help you hold on to your thoughts in the process of writing.

Another advantage to doing nonstops on a computer is that you can conveniently save what you have written, in case it should prove helpful, and later you can revise, edit, and incorporate something from the nonstop into another piece of writing. Be cautious, though: if you do any nonstop (including a handwritten one) with the intention of using it later in a finished essay, you may inhibit the purpose of the nonstop, whose real goal is to loosen up your writing. If it also gives you material you can use later, that is a happy by-product.

2. *Talk Your Way to Writing*: Try talking out an assignment with a friend or colleague who understands the subject. Get him to jot down notes while you talk, and you might do the same about his responses. Use his help to clarify several things: the main point of your essay or report or memo; the supporting points; the best order in which to present them. Try using a tape recorder to work out your ideas, jotting down notes when you play it back. Draw up an informal outline or sketch or blueprint of what you are about to write, drawing on the written notes from the conversation or the tape recording.

3. *Separate Writing from Editing*: If grammar, spelling, and punctuation worry you, forget about them for the first draft—the first ten drafts, if need be. Think about what you have to say and say it as clearly as possible. The polishing up can be done in the editing stage, when you have gotten all your thoughts down and you need not worry about losing your train of thought while thinking through a grammatical problem.

Again, this advice is easier to follow if you use a word processor. The final editing would be done on the computer screen and would not involve retyping the whole paper (the computer's printer will do that for you!), so there is no penalty at all for not editing earlier, and there are many advantages to leaving the editing until the very last stage.

1b

4. *Know Your Audience*: One reason writing is so much more difficult than speaking is the lack of a visible audience. You can make up for that in part by learning as much as possible about your audience and their expectations of you. If you do not know who your audience will be, try imagining a real person, or group of people, who will be reading what you write. (See also **3d**.) Not only will that make the writing flow more easily, but it will also make you a more effective writer; the sense of a real person writing to real people will come through in a way it cannot when you are writing for nobody.

5. *Consider Writing as a Process*: The suggestions in the following chapters on the writing process will also help you overcome anxiety and writing blocks. If you think about writing as a step-by-step process rather than as a magically produced, perfect end product, you will get a feeling of control over your writing; that sense of control will go a long way toward giving you confidence and momentum.

EXERCISES

1. Read the following two passages—one from a professional writer and one from a student. Both express a sense of powerlessness and frustration that is common to all writers. Write a short essay in which you describe how *you* feel when confronted with a writing assignment. Try using a metaphor or analogy, as Kazantzakis uses the metaphor of the inkwell and letters and as Bakel uses the analogy of a battle.

   a. I had taken up my quill to begin writing many times before now, but I always abandoned it quickly: each time I was overcome with fear. Yes, may God forgive me, but the letters of the alphabet frighten me terribly. They are sly, shameless demons—and dangerous! You open the inkwell, release them: they run off—and how will you ever get control of them again! They come to life, join, separate, ignore your commands, arrange themselves as they like on the paper—black, with tails and horns. You scream at them and implore them in vain: they do as they please. Prancing, pairing up shamelessly before you, they deceitfully expose what you did not wish to reveal and they refuse to give voice to what is struggling, deep within your bowels, to come forth and speak to mankind.   —Nikos Kazantzakis, *Saint Francis*

   b. As I stand poised, weapon uncontrollable in hand, the same weapon

1b

that has caused the death and destruction of many before me, I desperately search for the avenue of escape that will end the dreadful struggle. This relentless battle is not of mortal combat but writing the feared English essay. It is a struggle begun many years before, that will continue for many years to come.

—Joseph Bakel

2. Consider a heated discussion you have had lately that you would like to "rewrite." Describe what started it (the starting point), the conversation itself (the first draft), the process during which you gained new perspective on it (discovery and incubation), how and when you discovered what you ought to have said or how you ought to have handled it (illumination), how you would replay the conversation (selection and arrangement of details), and how you would rewrite and edit it to suit yourself.

   You need not discuss these steps or stages in any particular order; however, you should strive to make your reader aware of the way one thought led to the next and all the thinking, planning, and rearranging that went into making the conversation suit you. Place your emphasis on the process that went on in your head.

3. Try some nonstops (or "freewriting"). Set a timer for ten or fifteen minutes. Begin with one of the following phrases, or pick your own beginning. But remember, do not stop; just let one idea suggest the next, however incoherent they may seem.

   "As I write, . . ."
   "Looking at my [fill in the blank: shoe, paper, hand, desk, etc.], . . ."
   "When I think of myself as a writer, . . ."
   "I am thankful that . . ."
   "I am worried that . . ."
   "I wonder . . ."

4. Try writing a paper in one of the following ways. Either should be especially helpful to you if you do not do well with the traditional outlining approach.

   a. Write each paragraph on a separate piece of paper or large index card. While you do this, keep in mind the central point at all times, but write the paragraphs as though each were a self-contained unit. Then reread the paragraphs in various orders, arranging them until you have achieved the most effective presentation of the material. At this stage, you might add some transitional paragraphs or delete material, as you see fit.

      If you have a word processor, do this exercise by typing each paragraph on the screen without regard for the order you will put the paragraphs in. Then use your "Move" command to rearrange the paragraphs in several different ways (you can print the most likely alternatives). Select the most effective.

b. Compose a rough draft of an essay without worrying about the order of your ideas. Write on only one side of the page. Then use a scissors to cut apart the various paragraphs or sections, and try rearranging them. You may find that your first supporting point works better toward the end of your essay or that your conclusion works better as an introduction. However you finally decide to arrange the parts, when you are relatively satisfied, tape or staple them to clean sheets of paper, adding transitions or deleting material until it all flows smoothly. Then you are ready to copy over to make a clean draft.

A word processor will allow you to do this exercise even more easily, by using your "Move" command instead of a literal pair of scissors and by using your computer printer to give you a clean copy of the newly arranged draft.

5. Imagine that you are writing a pamphlet for incoming students at your school. Your assignment is to tell high school students what writing papers in college will be like and to give them some helpful suggestions about the process of writing a paper. Include some techniques that you have found helpful and offer them some way to look at the task without too much anxiety.

2

DISCOVERING IDEAS

2a The Starting Point

Finding a starting point for your writing is one of the most important things to do, whether you have been assigned a writing task or can write on something you choose. Many people believe it is easiest to begin with an idea, happening, or object that you feel particularly comfortable with and know well; other writers believe you can get started more easily if you write about something you do *not* know much about or feel comfortable with. You will discover which of these approaches works best for you.

2a.1 Starting with What You Already Know

In most writing tasks, you will know something about the topic but not everything. Clarifying what you already know will make it easier for you to move on to what you do not yet know. Suppose, for example, your employer asks you to write a proposal arguing for a new administrative assistant in your sales office. First, you might write down all the things you know such an assistant could do to help the sales staff, like making initial contact with clients, organizing monthly sales meetings, and writing preliminary drafts of sales reports. Next you would find ways to fill in the gaps of your knowledge—you could talk to the rest of the sales staff to get their suggestions, and you could check with other firms to see what their administrative assistants do. The information you receive from these contacts might be the best place to begin writing, but you will want to work through these ideas yourself, putting them in your own words and in the context of your own thinking.

If you are asked to choose your own topic, as in an English course, try picking a subject you know something about—like your major, a favorite writer or musician, a TV series, jogging, football, a current event of national importance—and then going beyond what you already know. First, list some facts you know from personal experience as well as what you have learned from friends, books, and the media. Then write out several questions about what you still need to know and go looking for some answers, whether from books or from other people. Here, too, the least obvious material—something you did not know when you began—might make the best starting point for your writing.

2a.2   Starting with Something That Disturbs You

The psychologist Jean Piaget has suggested that the starting point for any mental growth is a sense of "dissonance"—that is, something puzzling, unsettling, or disturbing, something we cannot account for in our ordinary understanding of things. We are set off balance by new information, new experiences, or new perspectives, and our minds struggle to put things right. Many writers believe the best starting point for writing is this sense of mental dissonance. If you are asked to choose your own topic, another approach is to pick a subject or issue that disturbs or unsettles you. If you are assigned a topic, think of some issue concerning that topic that might raise questions for you. (Why do you dislike jogging—or any activity that other people enjoy? Why are you angry about something you read in the paper recently that seemed to please others? Do you really need an administrative assistant in the office, or is your boss simply trying to get a bigger share of the corporate pie?) Sit down for fifteen minutes and write down everything that comes into your head about that issue or question—including facts, opinions, questions, puzzlements. Then look back at what you have written and see if it contains the germ of an idea for an essay.

2a

2a.3 Using Reference Books

Reading more about your chosen or assigned topic will give you new ideas for approaching your writing assignment. Perhaps you learn that jogging had a counterpart in ancient Rome or that administrative assistants are status symbols of middle managers in corporations. If you have complete freedom of choice about your topic, you might look through a book of quotations or proverbs and find a couple that are particularly intriguing. Proverbs, like those from the Bible or *Poor Richard's Almanack*, are an especially good source of ideas, because they frequently contain a note of mental dissonance. Reference books of facts might also offer you some interesting suggestions. Almost any of the books listed in chapter 8 could be useful. The *Guinness Book of World Records*, the *World Almanac and Book of Facts*, and similar resources will serve to remind you of all kinds of things interesting enough to write a paper about; they also will help you discover some ideas and facts you did not know before.

EXERCISES

Choose one of the paths below to lead you to a starting point.

1. Choose a proverb that creates a sense of cognitive dissonance for you—one of those listed below or another that you might find in a source like *Bartlett's Familiar Quotations* or the book of Proverbs in the Bible. Write down one or two ideas for starting points for an essay.

   a. If you would not be forgotten,
      As soon as you are dead and rotten,
      Either write things worthy reading,
      Or do things worth the writing.   —Benjamin Franklin

   b. Little strokes,
      Fell great oaks.   —Benjamin Frankin

   c. Go to the ant, thou sluggard; consider her ways, and be wise.
         —Bible, Proverbs 6:6

   d. The thing I fear most is fear.   —Michel de Montaigne

   e. I want death to find me planting my cabbages.
         —Michel de Montaigne

2. Consult one of the volumes of the *Handbook of American Popular Culture*, edited by M. Thomas Inge. Choose one topic that interests you in the table of contents. In volume 3, for example, you might be intrigued by the chapter on jazz, or magic and magicians, or pornography, or physical fitness. Make a photocopy of the historic outline of

the subject; skim it and underline everything in it that interests you. Then list a few of the most intriguing ideas that might serve as starting points for writing.

3. Thumb through Alberto Manguel and Gianni Guadalupi's fascinating *Dictionary of Imaginary Places*. Find a place you have already visited in literature or film, such as Dracula's castle or Sleepy Hollow, and see how clearly the dictionary recreates it for you. Or read the description of a place with an alluring name, such as "Herland" or "Narnia," that may be new to you. Think of an imaginary place not listed in the dictionary, or make up one of your own to attract tourists to.

4. Skim Lillian Roxon's *Rock Encyclopedia* (or a similar volume). Flip through its pages and read a few entries on musicians who interest you. Come up with a starting point by deciding what type of entry most consistently draws your attention—female vocalists, 1960s heavy metal, enduring groups like the Rolling Stones and the Grateful Dead, or superstars like John Lennon and Elvis Presley.

2b   Informal Discovery Techniques

Like every creative activity, writing involves discovery of ideas and facts that are new to you as well as those dormant within you. You may discover what you want to say in the very process of writing, but if you cannot seem to get started, if you stare blankly at a sheet of paper, and if you continually cast off every idea as useless, the techniques described in this section can help you overcome writer's block and inertia. They are based on the principle that once you turn off your mental "censors," and once the creative process begins, one idea generates another and one possibility leads to the next.

You will profit most from these procedures if you *write* your responses to them. Just as painters often do pen-and-ink or pencil drawings to sketch out ideas they later transfer to paint and canvas, so writers usually profit from thinking out their ideas on paper or on a computer screen.

At first you may worry that these techniques involve much jotting or writing that ultimately gets discarded. But even though you may throw a lot away, you will end up with more, because brainstorming and looping are meant to block out the internal censors which so often prevent us from making associations and getting new ideas. You will also spend less time in these activities than most uptight writers spend thinking and stewing. (For another informal discovery technique, see **6c,** exercise 1.)

2b.1 Brainstorming

In brainstorming you make a list of everything you can think of about your topic, without discriminating between the important and unimportant. When you have the ideas all down on paper or on your computer screen, then you can begin looking for a central idea or generalization that you want to write about, and you can start to sort out the important from the trivial, the stronger arguments from the weaker, the useful details you want to use in your paper from those you do not find useful.

Here are some rules to make brainstorming work effectively for you:

1. Choose a block of *uninterrupted* time—anywhere from five minutes to an hour, depending on how complex your topic is and how long the writing assignment is.

2. Start with a *large* clean sheet of paper or a clean computer screen. As you begin to record your thoughts one idea will suggest another much more easily if you can see what you have already written.

3. Write down *everything* that comes to mind. Do not stop to think whether it is useful; you can do the selecting later, when you have got all your ideas down.

4. *Never erase* or delete anything. You should only be thinking of new things to write down, not reconsidering something you have already recorded.

5. Let one idea suggest another. *Never stop* the free association of ideas.

6. Do not worry about *where* to write something down; do not try to classify and group items while brainstorming. If you think you have already written an idea down in slightly different words or from a different point of view, just write it down again as it occurs to you now. If one idea seems to be a specific example of another more general one you already wrote down, write it down anywhere for now. If you use a word processor, just list the ideas one after another; you can easily do the sorting later with your "Move" command.

7. The point of brainstorming is to "storm the brain"—march in and take over its critical function while you let the creative faculties free. Only *after* you have finished brainstorming, when you have no ideas left, should you bring your critical brain back into play. Then you can sort out the useful items from the less useful, group similar ideas together, classify more specific examples under more general ideas, and begin to look for a focus for your essay.

Figure 2.1 is an example of brainstorming done by one student who had been asked to write a review of two seemingly dissimilar films: *Modern Times*, starring Charlie Chaplin, and *Waiting for Godot*, starring Zero Mostel and Burgess Meredith. You will notice evidence of her having followed closely the "rules" of good brainstorming—the order suggested by free association; the repetition of details and ideas, sometimes stated in somewhat different words; the mixture of items relating to each film; the mixture of general ideas and specific, concrete examples. She has a rich supply of ideas and details from which she will eventually draw a thesis and form an essay (see 3e for the finished essay).

Brainstorming also works well with a group of people when the subject is something everyone has some knowledge about. Everyone calls out everything that comes to mind about a particular subject while someone else writes the ideas down, preferably on a blackboard or other place where everyone can see and where the suggestions already made will stimulate further ones. The rules for group brainstorming are the same as for individual brainstorming: no one in the group can be critical or act as a censor during this activity; its purpose is to get out as many ideas as possible; the selectivity comes later.

2b.2 Looping

Looping is a special application of the nonstop† (see **1b,** suggestion 1) that works particularly well with fairly open topics. For example, suppose you have been assigned to write about an experience that has changed your life. You might start by writing about anything that comes to mind on the topic. Write for a set length

---

†I am indebted to Peter Elbow for the idea of exploring through nonstops and to Elizabeth and Gregory Cowan for the term "looping."

Charlie Chaplin - comedy
  arrest/flag   jail/communism
    Didi & Gogo
    gloomy & funny
    traveler
    helplessness
    suffering, despair
      SUICIDE wish
failure of suicide
Chaplin hopeful in spite of failure
  poor girlfriend
        GODOT = GOD?
  existentialism
rave reviews
  director and producer
    fast scene changes — factory, jail, house,
      street, waterfront, bar
  GoDoT - desert or prairie?
  ditches, shack, state rooms
  poor food - turnips and bananas
      social outcasts - VICTIMS
dates of films? Modern Times - faith in future
      poor jobs, meager wages
      Waiting for Godot - idleness & stagnation
experiments (new machines)
unjust accusations
    poor
      illogical thinking
  Modern Times - American spirit, individualism,
      dehumanization
    hope/despair
  Modern Times - fast moving & fast talking.
    Waiting for Godot — inaction, emptiness

FIGURE 2.1. Example of Brainstorming: *Modern Times* and *Waiting for Godot*

of time (perhaps ten or fifteen minutes). Never stop to think about what you want to say: it is the actual writing that produces ideas in this activity, not the other way around. When you finish, find a phrase or sentence that seems to be the most important point and to which many others seem related; that is the "center of gravity" of your first loop. Underline it. Use that phrase or sentence as the beginning of a second loop; then find the new center of gravity, and underline it. Use that phrase or sentence as the beginning of a third loop; look for its center of gravity, and you will probably have a starting point or even a thesis (see **3a**) for your essay. If you are not yet satisfied, do another loop. If you really keep writing and do not spend time chewing the end of your pencil or gazing at the computer screen, looping will eventually produce an idea for your paper, and you will find that some of the material you produced in the loops can be used in your essay.

Following is an unedited example of looping done by a student who used the final center of gravity as the starting point of an essay and some of the material from the loops to develop the essay. The center of gravity is italicized in each loop and becomes the beginning of the next loop. Notice that each loop brings the writer to see the connection between learning to write and learning to be an engineer.

Loop 1:
    As a writer, I am not very competent comparatively speaking. In high school my English teachers thought I did very well, but even then I realized I was not totally prepared for college. I did things in my high school writing that this class has already shown to be unacceptable. Some of these things can probably be found even in this short writing. *Writing is very difficult for me, but I realize I must learn to write well even though I am going to be an engineer* (assuming I don't flunk out of freshman English and get sent home in disgrace). Sometimes I enjoy writing but usually it's a chore. I've always felt that if I had an inspiration, that is, some new idea on a topic, my paper would turn out well. If I did not have an instant inspiration, I assumed that particular writing assignment was destined to be a flop, not matter.

Loop 2:
    Writing is very difficult for me, but I realize I must learn to write well even though I'm going to be an engineer. As a matter of fact,

2b

it's very important for engineers to have good writing skills. Engineers must be able to present their ideas in a way their colleagues can understand. *Clear, concise writing implies clear, concise thought.* This is another reason why engineers should learn to write well. Writing logically can help one to think logically. No matter what one's profession is, he should develop his writing skills. Writing well is difficult to do, but once learned it can serve a person well.

Loop 3:

Clear, concise writing implies clear, concise thought. In these times of complex events, it's important for people to write clearly. Newspaper reporters must learn to write in such a way that the general population can understand what is happening. People who write textbooks must write clearly so students do not have to spend hours trying to comprehend a particular concept. *It is also important for the engineer to write clearly. If an engineer cannot write well, he will have difficulty applying for jobs, applying for grants, and getting his projects approved.* This is my main motivation for learning to write. It is easy for me to become motivated when I see that something will be of use to me in the future. It is hard for me to become motivated to write if I think of it on the basis of having to do a paper for English class. Instead, I think of it as practice for a skill I will use all through my career.

—Victoria Webber

EXERCISES

Use one of the topics listed below to practice brainstorming and looping. Brainstorm with your class, or with a small group from your class, on one of the topics; then at home on your own, try looping on the same topic. See which method generates the most helpful ideas. (Because your looping may be influenced by the group brainstorming, you might want to do the exercise a second time, reversing the procedure: do the looping first on your own, and then try brainstorming with the class.)

1. You have been asked to write an editorial for your college newspaper on the subject of campus crime and what can be done to combat it.
2. Your sociology professor has asked you to write an analysis of the different social groups on your campus and their effect on campus social life.
3. Your roommate wants your help in writing a letter home, persuading his or her parents that he or she should be allowed to move off campus next year.
4. You have been asked to write a "campus tour" for next year's student

handbook, in which you describe the important buildings on campus and their various uses.

2c The Grid

A number of writers, both ancient and modern, have developed more systematic procedures for exploring a subject. The grid† is one of these, along with the pentad (2d) and the classical "topics" (2e). You will profit from trying some of these formal techniques, especially if you find that the informal ones do not work well for you. Remember, though, that all of them are meant to be exploratory only. They should generate ideas and material for your writing, but they should not dictate the final form of your essay.

The nine-square *grid* brings together the insights of physics and linguistics; it can be superimposed on any object, event, or idea in order to help you discover ideas about it. From physics comes the idea that we can see everything in our experience from one of three points of view: as a *particle* (a static object seen at one moment), a *wave* (a dynamic process, moving and changing through time), and a *field* (a system, composed of subsystems or interdependent parts). A city, for example, can be viewed *statically*, as an object before your eyes, with dimension, color, and texture; or *dynamically*, as something constantly growing and changing; or as a *system*: it is part of a larger system (a state, for instance, which is both a political and a geographic system); and it comprises a number of subsystems (wards, districts, or neighborhoods, for instance).

The grid further suggests that a subject can be seen in relation to other things: what *class* it belongs in, how it *contrasts* with other members of the class, and what *context* it appears in. And these three considerations—class, contrast, and context—can be applied to each of the other three ways of looking at the city—statically, dynamically, and as a system.

The chart in figure 2.2 contains a summary of the discovery

†The grid was developed by Richard Young, Alton Becker, and Kenneth Pike, all of the University of Michigan.

Object, event, idea viewed	AS A CLASS:	IN CONTRAST:	IN CONTEXT:
STATICALLY:	What larger class and subclass is it part of? What does it have in common with other members of that class?	How does it contrast with other members of its class? with things outside its class?	Where is it usually found?
DYNAMICALLY:	What group of processes is it part of? Or what processes does it have in common with similar things?	How does it contrast with other kinds of processes? with itself at different times and places?	When do the processes usually occur?
AS A SYSTEM:	What kind of system is it (organic, mechanical, or abstract)?	How does it contrast with other systems?	What context is this system part of? What effects does this system have on the environment?

FIGURE 2.2. The Grid

procedure. Each of the nine points of view is formulated as a question that you can ask about any topic you may be writing on.

Here is a student example of how the grid can be used to generate ideas for an essay:

GEORGE GERSHWIN

Viewed statically as a class: George Gershwin is a composer and belongs to a subclass of American composers of the twentieth century, specifically those who wrote popular music. Popular music composers write for the immediate enjoyment of the masses.

Viewed statically in contrast: Gershwin was different from other American popular composers beause he was also a serious composer who wrote operas and full symphonic works besides popular tunes.

Viewed statically in context: A composer in America is usually found in major cultural and business centers. Gershwin worked primarily in New York City and sometimes in Hollywood.

Viewed dynamically as a class: He was part of a rapidly changing music industry, specifically that of Broadway in the 1920s and 1930s, and as such he was affected by contact with the composers, performers, lyricists, and producers who were part of that industry.

Viewed dynamically in contrast: Gershwin was part of the American music business which later in his career became geared toward record selling via radio airplay. Earlier composers relied on having their music heard at live performances. Gershwin contrasts with other American composers because he was successful before and after the advent of radio, which occurred in the middle years of his career.

Viewed dynamically in context: Gershwin's career as a composer ran from about 1916 to 1937. Broadway as we know it was just beginning at the start of Gershwin's career, as was Tin Pan Alley. So Gershwin came out of a time and place conducive to aspiring songwriters like him.

Viewed as part of a class of systems: George Gershwin and his music were part of the rebirth of American culture after the end of World War I and during the prosperity of the 1920s.

Viewed as a system in contrast: The American music scene during Gershwin's career was different from that of Europe. American popular music was a new form comprised of many styles both native and foreign.

2d

Viewed as a system in context: Gershwin is part of our musical heritage. He has affected our musical tastes and styles in many ways. Even though he died over forty years ago, his music is increasing in popularity, indicating that his music is still a catalyst for others.

—Thomas Chmill

2d The Pentad

Another formal discovery technique, called the *pentad*,† sees all human experience in terms of a drama that involves five elements (hence *pentad*). The five elements involved in any action or relationship are *action* (what happened), *agent* (the person or thing that caused the action), *scene* (where it happened), *agency* (the means or instrument used to accomplish the action), and *purpose* (why the action occurred).

Ratios (the various combinations of the five elements) describe the motives and causes of human relationships. The scene-action ratio, for example, suggests that a particular action was influenced mainly by the scene (the time or place in which something happened); the agent-action ratio implies that the action was caused primarily by the person (agent) who performed it. In addition, the *circumference* (the context in which something happened) has an important effect on the action, and *attitude* describes how the agent felt about the scene and action.

In order to use the pentad to generate ideas for writing, it is helpful to turn the five categories, ratios, circumference, and attitude into a series of questions:

ACTION: What was it? What happened? Who or what was affected or changed? Was the action physical or mental?

AGENT: Was the primary actor human? Was some nonhuman agent the cause of the action (nature, technology)?

SCENE: When did it happen (what time in history, what time of the year, what time of day, etc.)?

AGENCY: What did the agent use to accomplish the action? Was the

---

†The pentad and related concepts were developed by the philosopher Kenneth Burke as a method of analyzing human behavior and relationships. The description here is an adaptation of Burke and William Irmscher, who was the first to suggest using the pentad as a discovery technique.

action purposeful and planned, or spontaneous? How did the attitude of the agent affect the action?

PURPOSE: Why did it happen? Was there a broader purpose, reason, or explanation than one could see from the action alone?

RATIOS: Which combination of the five categories seems to account most adequately for the subject you are considering?

action-agent	action-scene	action-agency	action-purpose
agent-scene	agent-agency	agent-purpose	
scene-agency	scene-purpose		
agency-purpose			

CIRCUMFERENCE: What is the wider context (historical, geographic, ideological, or circumstantial) in which the subject is found?

ATTITUDE: What was the agent's attitude toward the action? toward the scene? How did that attitude affect the action?

Following is the work of a student who applied the pentad, with a note of understated humor, to the subject of going to college. (The student refers to himself as "the protagonist," the hero of a drama.) It could lead to a humorous or ironic essay on the subject.

COLLEGE LIFE

ACTION:

What was it? Going to college, partying, and flunking out.

What happened? The protagonist had too much freedom and neglected his responsibilities.

Who was affected? The protagonist, through his grades.

Was the action physical or mental? Both: what he was doing (partying) was physical, but it was related to a mental attitude that made "college life" more important than studying.

AGENT:

Was the primary actor human? Yes, I'll call him Mike.

Was some nonhuman agent the cause? Indirectly—his newfound freedom allowed him to do what he did.

SCENE:

When did it happen? This year.

Where did it happen? Fishburn College (fictional institution).

What was the larger context? The conflicts present in American college life.

AGENCY:

What means were used by the agent? He took advantage of his freedom and of the diversions offered at his college—for example, drinking and playing electronic games instead of studying.

Was the action planned or spontaneous? The action itself was deliberate, but the results were not planned.

How did the attitude of the agent affect the action? His attitude toward college as just a place to have a good time was the cause of his actions.

PURPOSE:

Why did it happen? His parents were strict with him, and he didn't know how to handle his freedom.

Was there a broader reason? Mike's immaturity and the prevailing student temper caused his downfall.

RATIO:

The scene/action ratio would apply because Mike's actions were precipitated by the environment in which he was placed.

CIRCUMFERENCE:

What is the wider context? Growing up.

ATTITUDE:

Whose attitude caused Mike's downfall? Mike, with his bad attitude toward studying and his good attitude toward having fun, undoubtedly contributed to his problems, but so did his professors, who had a bad attitude toward Mike's bad attitude.

—Michael Martineau

The pentad of questions and ratios can be applied to an idea, person, or object as well as to an event. Since Burke's philosophy is based on the idea that all of life is "dramatistic," the pentad is not restricted to obviously dramatic events.

2e   The Topics

While the grid forces us primarily to look at something, and the pentad encourages us to dramatize it, the *topics* emphasize mental relationships, even though the visual and the dramatic play a role too.

As Aristotle† explained them, the topics are places or regions in the mind where you can go to look for ideas about a subject for writing. (Used as a discovery technique, the word *topic* comes from a Greek word meaning "place" and has a rather different meaning than it does when we speak of a topic as a "subject" to write about.) Cicero and Quintilian systematized the topics into five groups with several subtopics that can be used for developing ideas on any subject:

TOPIC OF DEFINITION

Definition by Classification: What larger class is x in? How is it differentiated from other members of the same class?

Definition by Division: What are the parts that make up x? What are the subclasses of x?

TOPIC OF COMPARISON

Comparison by Similarity: How is x similar to y? What characteristics does x have in common with y? How is y an analogy for x?

Comparison by Difference: How is x different from y? (How does it contrast with y?)

Comparison by Degree (Comparison of Value): How is x ——— than y? (Fill in the blank with comparative words like better, worse, larger, smaller, more/less valuable, more/less important, more/less useful, etc.).

TOPIC OF RELATIONSHIP

Relationship of Cause and Effect: What is the cause (or causes) of x? What is the effect (or effects) of x?

Relationship of Antecedent and Consequent: If x happens, what will follow? What must have preceded?

Relationship of Contraries and Contradictories: What is opposite to, contrary to, or incompatible with x? If x is true, what must be false? (Or if x is false, what must be true?)

TOPIC OF CIRCUMSTANCE

Circumstance—the Possible and Impossible: What is possible in a given circumstance? What is impossible?

---

†Aristotle, Quintilian, and Cicero were three teachers of Greek and Roman antiquity who developed the system of topics as it was used in the schools and universities from classical times until the Renaissance. It has seen a revival in universities in the 1970s and 1980s.

Circumstance—Past Fact and Future Fact: What happened to x in the past? What will probably happen to x in the future?

TOPIC OF EVIDENCE

Evidence of Authority: What do authorities on x say about it? Who are the authorities and what are their credentials?

Evidence of Testimonial: What has been said by people who are not authorities but have some experience with x or have said something related to x?

Evidence of Statistics: What are the statistics in support of x (or in refutatation of x)? How reliable are they? (See **5c.1** for a discussion of reliability.)

Evidence of Maxims and Proverbs: What famous sayings can be applied to x?

Evidence of Law: What laws support (or prohibit) x?

Evidence of Precedent: What previous examples of similar situations can be applied to x? How valid is the precedent?

Following is an example of a student's application of the topics to the general subject of jazz:

JAZZ

TOPIC OF DEFINITION

Definition by Classification: In larger class of music. Distinctive in that it is an American phenomenon; it arose largely from black American origins, that is, from a subculture.

Definition by Division: Parts that make it up, subclasses—blues, ragtime, New Orleans style, swing, bop or bebop, cool or progressive.

TOPIC OF COMPARISON

Comparison by Similarity: Jazz and classical music can be similar in the degree of technical sophistication required; both can call on the talents of virtuoso performers. Sometimes jazz and classical are blended to fuse the emotional appeal of jazz with the intellectual appeal of classical.

Comparison by Difference: Lots of jazz is improvised and spontaneous; many of its more famous musicians have no formal training. We hear classical in the concert hall, jazz on the street and in smoke-filled bars. Jazz is sensual and sometimes narcotic in its effect; classical is often contrived and highly intellectual.

Comparison by Degree: Jazz is easier to listen to; it requires less sophistication from the listener. It is far more exciting in its emphasis on rhythm and beat and its diversity of sounds. It is also more narrowly percussive and primal. To me jazz is more real.

TOPIC OF RELATIONSHIP

Relationship of Cause and Effect: Cause—came out of a repressed population with a need like any other to express itself fully and forcefully. Effect—not only accepted but appreciated by the mainstream, worldwide, less than one hundred years after its beginnings.

Relationship of Antecedent and Consequent: What will follow is anyone's guess since jazz has developed so quickly and in so many directions in the twentieth century. Effects of jazz can be seen in rock as artists incorporate characteristic rhythms, syncopations, sounds. The blues especially has affected popular music in both its themes and style.

Relationship of Contraries and Contradictories: Incompatible with jazz are authoritarian schoolteachers, Wall Street, and sewing circles.

TOPIC OF CIRCUMSTANCE

The Possible and Impossible: If jazz is being performed, any improvisation is possible, whether in the singing, the playing of the instruments, or the words or actions of the performer. Nothing seems impossible with jazz. There have even been jazz "prayers," e.g., Coltrane's "A Love Supreme."

Past Fact and Future Fact: Ragtime was the earliest form of jazz to have a broad appeal; Scott Joplin was a key figure in its popular success. Jazz appears to be headed away from mass appeal, however, except perhaps for the increasing interest in the enduring blues.

TOPIC OF EVIDENCE

Authorities: Consult *Encyclopedia of Jazz* or other source.

Testimonial: Record sales and profiles of jazz fans attest to a small, devoted group of followers. Occasionally, a middle-of-the-road jazz artist like George Winston or John Klemmer draws fans from outside the normal circle.

Law: It is hard to separate jazz from associations with the drug culture. Of course, the same is true for rock. Respectable, everyday citizens and jazz seem vaguely incompatible. —Carol Dumfries

As you apply the topics to various writing subjects, you will find that certain of the topics are inherently more productive for you than others are. You might find, for example, that you like to think in terms of comparison and analogy; in that case, the three topics of Comparison would be especially helpful in generating ideas for a suitable approach. If you are intrigued by proverbs and witty sayings, you would use the topic Evidence of Maxims and Proverbs (which works particularly well as a starting point for nonstops). At other times, certain topics will be necessary because of the given assignment. If a professor asked you to write an essay examining the causes of the Civil War, for example, you would naturally use the topics of Relationship; if an employer asked you to write a sales report, you would likely think about the topics of Evidence.

2f   Incubation

Psychologists who have studied the creative process have found that it is necessary to allow some time when the conscious mind is not thinking about a subject, in order for the subconscious mind to work creatively. Some people find it hard to do this when writing, both because procrastination often does not leave enough time for the incubation stage and because people just do not believe that something creative can be happening when they are not consciously working at it. But in fact something *does* happen.

While psychologists do not know much about how the subconscious mind works, they do know that it allows the mind to mix and match ideas, to see new relationships, to discover new ideas, and to solve problems. Many times a problem in writing that cannot be solved by conscious concentration will be resolved if you deliberately avoid thinking about it for a day or so (at least overnight). You may find your subconscious mind will suddenly deliver an insight to your conscious mind and the problem will be solved—a process Isaac Asimov calls the "eureka phenomenon" (see exercise 4 below).

Incubation time, then, is one of the most important parts of the writing process. It can occur at many points, but it seems to be particularly fruitful after (or even during) the discovery stage. Try leaving some incubation time after you have used one of the discovery procedures and before you formulate your thesis. Or if you are working on a discovery technique and hit a mental roadblock, let it incubate for a while. One of the best uses of incubation is to leave time between a preliminary draft of your essay and the final draft. Sometimes, of course, you need to let your conscious mind play with ideas, even struggle with them; but in all creative work, you must sometimes give up the conscious effort and accept some help from the silent partner, your subconscious mind.

EXERCISES

1. Most of us have conflicting emotions about horror. While many people might choose to attend a scary movie on Saturday night and later rave about the chills it gave them, few would be delighted to find a werewolf or an escaped convict in their backyards.

   What is horror? What makes a good horror story wonderful and a horrifying experience terrible? How can the same thing that could impair or injure us in person thrill us on the screen? Apply the grid, the pentad, or the classical topics to the subject of horror, choosing as many of the categories or questions as will be helpful to you. You may start with the idea of horror or fright, the event of being terrified or in a state of shock, or the object of a haunted house, graveyard, late night city street, or any other frightening situation or place.

   Remember that the purpose of the discovery technique you choose is not to generate a story or an essay but to help you retrieve all the stored associations you have with your topic that might otherwise remain locked in memory.

2. A student suggested the following exercise:

   Choose a particular aspect of your life that is different at different times. The time frame is up to you. It could be in one day, like your moods; in a year, like the effects of weather on you; or in a lifetime, like the way you are affected by living in different places. Then apply the pentad, the grid, or the classical topics to generate ideas for an essay on how you change during the time frame you have chosen.

   —Debbie McKenna

3. Read the following excerpt from Isaac Asimov's description of the "eureka phenomenon." Then write a brief essay in which you describe an experience you have had in which your subconscious mind solved a problem while you and your conscious mind were engaged in something entirely different.

   In the old days, when I was writing a great deal of fiction, there would come, once in a while, moments when I was stymied. Suddenly, I would find I had written myself into a hole and could see no way out. To take care of that, I developed a technique which invariably worked.

   It was simply this—I went to the movies. Not just any movie. I had to pick a move which was loaded with action but which made no demands on the intellect. As I watched, I did my best to avoid

2f

any conscious thinking concerning my problem, and when I came out of the movie I knew exactly what I would have to do to put the story back on the track.

It never failed.

In fact, when I was working on my doctoral dissertation, too many years ago, I suddenly came across a flaw in my logic that I had not noticed before and that knocked out everything I had done. In utter panic, I made my way to a Bob Hope movie—and came out with the necessary change in point of view.

—Isaac Asimov, "The Eureka Phenomenon"

3

MAKING CHOICES

3a Finding a Thesis

At some point, whether during or after the discovery process, you need to formulate a thesis for most kinds of writing. A *thesis* is an assertion or proposition that says in capsule form exactly what the point or focus of your writing will be. When you formulate a thesis, you take the subject of your paper and make an assertion about it. Because a thesis is an assertion, it is usually expressed in a sentence (or two). A thesis has a subject (the subject of your paper) and a predicate (the assertion you make about that subject), and a second sentence may be used to make the thesis more specific. Take, for example, two of the subjects we discussed in the previous section on discovery:

> George Gershwin
> *Modern Times* and *Waiting for Godot*

If you add a predicate to each of those phrases to make them into sentences, you will change each subject into a thesis. How useful each thesis is will depend on how *specific* it is; how well it fits the *scope* of the assignment; whether it shows the *focus, point of view*, or *angle* you have on the subject; and whether it provides some clue to the *organization* of your paper. Consider the following thesis statements:

> George Gershwin is a famous composer.
> *Modern Times* and *Waiting for Godot* have similar themes.

Neither of these theses is very informative. Each of the statements makes an assertion about the subject, true; but neither is

45

specific, neither fits the *scope* of a short essay, and neither provides a clue to the *focus* or *organization* of the essay.

If you look back at the sample applications of grid, pentad, and classical topics, you will find, in the material the authors generated, many possible approaches to the subjects that can be expressed in more specific, more focused thesis statements:

> George Gershwin is a famous American composer.

> George Gershwin has played an important part in our American musical heritage.

> George Gershwin has played an important part in our American musical heritage because he has influenced all subsequent popular music.

> George Gershwin has made a unique contribution to our American musical heritage, because he not only influenced the style of popular music in this country but was a great classical composer as well.

Each thesis is successively more specific, but the last one will create the best essay because it provides a focus and a point of view. The *because* clause emphasizes Gershwin's real uniqueness, and the main clause makes a claim that he made the "most important contribution" to American music. A possible organization is also suggested: the author will probably discuss Gershwin's contribution to popular music first, then his contribution to classical.

> Although *Modern Times* and *Waiting for Godot* have similar themes, they approach those themes in very different ways.

> Although *Modern Times* and *Waiting for Godot* both center on the dehumanization of an "endangered species"—the individual—the attitudes toward those themes are different in each film.

> Although *Modern Times* and *Waiting for Godot* both center on the dehumanization of an "endangered species"—the individual—*Modern Times* is full of hope, while Didi and Gogo in *Waiting for Godot* endlessly despair over their situations.

Although *Modern Times* and *Waiting for Godot* both center
on the dehumanization of an "endangered species"—the
individual—*Modern Times* is full of hope, while Didi and
Gogo in *Waiting for Godot* endlessly despair over their situations. The differences can be seen in the way the two films
use humor, the way they depict human suffering, and the
contrast betweeen action and inaction.

Again, each successive version is more specific; the last version
not only is the most specific but suggests the focus and direction
of the essay by telling us that the differences in theme are viewed
through humor, suffering, and action/inaction. (Notice that the
last thesis is stated in two sentences.)

A thesis can be stated at the beginning or end or somewhere in
the middle of your finished essay. Or it might simply be implied.
In any case, you should know what your thesis is; if it is clear in
your mind, it will likely come across clearly to your reader, even
if it is not expressed in so many words.

Not all kinds of writing have a thesis. An essay whose main
purpose is to narrate a story or to describe something may not
have a central assertion to be supported. Instead, such an essay
aims to create a *dominant impression*, which all the details in the
essay are meant to support. In essays whose purpose is to explain
something or argue a point, however, the thesis will always be
important and will usually be stated explicitly in the introduction
or the conclusion or both.

A thesis often develops during the discovery process, even after
most of the exploration is finished. At other times, however, the
thesis comes first and provides the starting point for discovery.
On an essay exam, for instance, your professor might say, "Argue
for or against the following position: . . ." Or your boss might
request that you write a proposal arguing that a new product be
purchased, that a new employee position be established, or that
funds be allocated for a particular project. In cases like these, the
thesis—the proposition to be supported—is given to the writer,
who needs to find the best evidence to support that proposition.
The thesis, then, may become *the starting point* of the writing
process.

No matter at what point you first formulate your thesis, you

3b

should be open to changing it. Even if you think you know exactly what point you want to argue, the act of writing the argument may change your point of view.

EXERCISES _____

1. Following is a list of general subjects. Choose five and write three possible thesis statements for each subject. First take a specific instance of the general subject (name your favorite film, your hometown, the vacation spot, etc.). Then add predicates that assert something about the subject. Do not begin by simply asserting what the specific subject is ("My least favorite teacher is Professor Windy") but by making an assertion *about* the specific subject ("Professor Windy bores me because . . .").

   a. your favorite film
   b. your favorite book
   c. your hometown
   d. a vacation spot you have always wanted to visit
   e. your best friend or spouse
   f. your favorite (or least favorite) class
   g. your favorite (or least favorite) teacher
   h. your favorite (or least favorite) sport
   i. a hobby you particularly enjoy
   j. a controversial subject currently in the news

2. Choose one of the subjects you explored in exercises 1-3 at the end of chapter 2, and assume you have been asked to write an article of general interest for your college newspaper or magazine. Formulate a thesis statement that you could use as the starting point of that article. Selecting from the facts and ideas you generated with the discovery procedure, list a few major points you could use to develop your thesis if you were going to write an essay.

_____

3b Purpose, Medium, and Audience

The thesis is not the only—nor the most important—constraint on your writing. You must also be aware of three variables that affect the decisions any writer makes: the purpose, the medium, and the audience.

The *purpose*† of a piece of writing is the goal or aim you want

†The scholar James Kinneavy has developed this fourfold classification of the aims of discourse.

your writing to achieve: to *inform* someone (as in instructions for using a certain kind of machine or as in a scientific explanation of genes and their functions); to *persuade* others (as in advertising copy, proposals, or letters to editors); to *express* for yourself what you think or how you feel (as in diaries and certain kinds of literature, especially lyric poetry); or to create a *literary* work (as in novels, plays, and narrative poetry). Since this handbook is concerned with practical forms of prose, we will concentrate on the two aims used most often in college writing and on the job: *informative* and *persuasive* writing.

The *medium* of communication is the form in which the message is conveyed. A newspaper, for instance, is a medium of communication, as are the more specific kinds of writing within a newspaper: a letter to the editor, a news story, a feature article, a sports summary, the comics, help columns like "Dear Abby," even the want ads—all of these are different ways of conveying a message, and they demand different kinds of writing.

The *audience* is the person or group to whom the writing is addressed. A certain medium often implies a specific kind of audience—in a newspaper, for instance, the audience of a "Dear Abby" column or the audience of the opinion/editorial page. While the same person may read both, the collective audience of each will be different (many newspaper readers never read editorials, and many never read "Dear Abby"). Different readers may also read the same thing for different reasons: some may read "Dear Abby," for instance, because they are seriously seeking help in daily living and human relationships, others because they like to see the humor in the foibles of human nature. Often in college writing, your instructor will be your audience and will read what you have written to find out either how well you are learning to write (if it is a writing course) or how much you know about the subject of the course. Sometimes a writing instructor will ask you to write for various "real life" audiences, but just as frequently the instructor will be the audience.

All three of these variables—purpose, medium, and audience—are interrelated, and they all affect the choices that a sensitive writer will make. For example, if you were asked by your employer to write up a year-end sales report, you would be constrained by your audience, the company's board of directors; by your purpose, to inform them of the sales patterns and, perhaps, also to

3c

persuade them of the good job done by the sales representatives; and by your medium, the sales report, which takes a definite form usually specified by the company.

To consider another example, recall the last thesis we arrived at for *Modern Times* and *Waiting for Godot* (see **3a**). The student who did the brainstorming on the two films went on to write a film review for her local newspaper. The purpose of her medium, the film review, was to evaluate the films for her readers, help them decide whether or not to see the films, and give them some idea of what to expect and how to interpret the films. As you will see later (**3e**), her purpose, medium, and audience determined how she developed the review.

3c   Levels of Formality

Some of the choices you must make as a writer can be classified according to a principle of *formality*: that is, how much the form of your writing is constrained by the demands of audience, purpose, and medium. We can describe three different levels of formality: formal, informal, and casual. They are not so much discrete categories as points on a continuum: formal writing merges into informal and informal into casual. The descriptions below include examples of specific media, or forms, of writing that are common at each level. Generally speaking, the more constraints there are on the format of the writing, the more formal and conservative will be the choices you make of grammatical forms and punctuation. (The discussions of grammar and usage in Part 4 and in the Glossary of Usage make suggestions about when a particular usage is appropriate, in situations ranging from formal to casual.)

Formal writing† is addressed to an unknown or general audience on a serious occasion. The audience may be a single person or a small group that the writer does not know personally; or it may be a large group with a variety of interests, a range of knowledge, and values different from each other's and from the writer's. Examples include a business letter to a potential client, a news article or editorial, a report to stockholders, a letter or

---

†Formal writing also includes two specialized areas: *scholarly* or *technical* writing, addressed to a largely unknown audience with technical expertise; and *literary* works, which also address a largely unknown audience.

memo to a superior about an important matter, a political manifesto or religious credo, an encyclopedia article, the script of a sermon or political speech, and some college textbooks.

Informal writing is addressed to an unknown or general audience on a less serious occasion. Examples include a business form letter to a general audience, a feature article in a magazine or newspaper, instructions for a hobby or leisure-time activity printed in a consumer brochure or in a magazine or newspaper, a consumer newsletter (like the pamphlets put out with monthly bills by public utilities), or an interdivisional memo or letter to someone (a superior or a group) with whom the writer is not familar.

Casual writing† is produced for a known audience or an audience one wants to pretend to know, as in much advertising copy. Examples include advertising copy or promotional material aimed at consumers, an intradivisional memo to someone the writer knows fairly well, a business letter or memo to a familiar client or friendly competitor, an internal company newsletter, some scripts of political speeches, and some political advertising.

The following examples will show how levels of formality affect your writing:

FORMAL: If you were composing an article on the Civil War for professional historians, to be published in a scholarly journal, you would assume a great deal of knowledge on the part of your audience, and you could safely use the technical vocabulary of historians without having to define terms.

FORMAL/INFORMAL: If you were writing a research paper on the Civil War for your history professor, you would assume a knowledge of the subject, but you would also define terms and give common facts in order to show your professor what you had learned.

INFORMAL: If you were writing an article on the Civil War for a popular magazine, you would spend time discussing the details and events that would particularly interest your audience (which

---

†Casual writing also includes *intimate writing* (for example, love letters, diaries, and prayers), which is addressed to someone the writer knows so well—including the writer himself—that it is possible to convey a great deal with very few words.

might be different for a southern audience than for a northern one, for instance).

CASUAL: If you wanted to write a fictionalized firsthand account of the Civil War, you might write from the point of view of a soldier in the war writing a letter home to his family. You would assume that your audience (the soldier's family) understood personally the issues for which he was fighting.

3d Making Rhetorical Choices

How formal or casual your writing is will depend on your audience, your purpose, and the medium in which you write. Together with your thesis, they are important influences on the choices you make in your writing. Following are some questions you can ask to help you decide how to select and arrange the details, arguments, and other supporting material you use to develop your thesis:

1. *Audience*:
   a. How much do you know about the members of your audience?
   b. What kind of relationship do you have with your audience? Are they close friends, peers, subordinates, superiors?
   c. How much do the members of your audience have in common? Are they diverse, like the audience of a national news magazine, with varied interests, levels of knowledge and education, abilities, and attitudes; or are they pretty much alike?
   d. Does your audience include a special-interest group? If so, what attitude will its members have toward your subject?
   e. How much do they know about your subject?
   f. Do you want to aim at readers with the least knowledge, the most, or the average amount?
   g. On what points are they likely to agree with you? disagree with you?
   h. If you are assigned a paper by a professor who asks you to write for a "fictional" audience, can you ignore the professor as a "hidden" audience? What choices might you make that would be different if you were *really* writing for the fictional audience?

3d

2. *Purpose*:
   a. Why are you writing this? If it is because you "have to" (because your teacher has assigned it, for instance), what should your writing itself demonstrate? What do you want your thesis to do?
   b. Is the occasion a formal, informal, or casual one?
   c. Is the occasion a special one, or are you simply commenting on a subject of general interest?

3. *Medium*:
   a. What form will your writing take—essay, report, letter, proposal, article?
   b. What are the requirements of your medium? A set form, as in a memorandum? Very short paragraphs, as in a newspaper article? An essay form set by your professor?

4. *Thesis*:
   What structure and what choice of details are suggested by your thesis?

EXERCISES

1. Read the following passages, decide which level of formality they illustrate (formal, informal, or casual), and answer the following questions about each:

What is the writer's purpose? In what medium is each written? Who is the audience?
What is the relationship between writer and audience? Are the writers specialists in their fields? How much knowledge do they assume their readers already have?
What is the vocabulary like in each passage? Are the writers very specific and detailed? Do they use many words whose meaning would be known only by a specialist, or can the reader of average education understand?
What is the tone of each passage? Serious? Ironic? Argumentative? Sarcastic? Condescending? Do the writers sound chatty, as though they knew their readers well, or do they maintain a formal distance? Do they sound very objective about their subjects or are they personally involved?

   a. REACH OUT. REACH OUT AND TOUCH SOMEONE. Your sister's big day is only weeks away. You've always been close. And when you found out you couldn't make that shower, you knew it could spoil her day. So you call, and a family heirloom changes hands. With love. Wonderful, isn't it, how a simple phone call from far away can make everything just great. Reach out and touch someone who's waiting to share her day.   —Bell System ad

b. Never in the history of the world was one people as completely dominated, intellectually and morally, by another as the people of the United States by the people of Russia in the four years from 1946 through 1949. American foreign policy was a mirror image of Russian foreign policy: whatever the Russians did, we did in reverse. American domestic politics were conducted under a kind of upside-down Russian veto; no man could be elected to public office unless he was on record as detesting the Russians, and no proposal could be enacted, from a peace plan at one end to a military budget at the other, unless it could be demonstrated that the Russians wouldn't like it. American political controversy was controversy sung to the Russian tune; left-wing movements attacked right-wing movements not on American issues but on Russian issues, and right-wing movements replied with the same arguments turned round about.

—Archibald MacLeish, "The Conquest of America," *The Atlantic*

c. The insured or other person making claim for damage to property shall file proof of loss with the company within sixty days after the occurrence of loss, unless such time is extended in writing by the company, in the form of a sworn statement setting forth the interest of the insured and of all others in the property affected, any encumbrances thereon, the actual cash value thereof at time of loss, the amount, place, time and cause of such loss, and the description and amounts of all other insurance covering such property. Upon the company's request, the insured shall exhibit the damaged property to the company.

—automobile insurance policy

2. Choose one or two of the passages above and rewrite them, using a level of formality different from the original but keeping the content generally the same. Before rewriting, consider what words will have to be changed, what details added or deleted (you can make up anything you need to), and whether you will have to change the tone.

3. Pick a magazine you regularly read and analyze its contents, including the advertisements. Skim some of the articles, and consider the following questions:

a. What kind of audience usually reads this magazine? (The ads will give you clues as well as the articles.)

b. What do you have in common with them?

c. What can you conclude about the overall purpose of the magazine?

Now write a brief essay in which you summarize your analysis.

3e   Selecting

Once you have clear in your mind what your thesis is, who your audience is, and what the purpose and medium are, you need to decide which details, examples, and other material you will use in developing your thesis. Some writers examine all the details they have gathered from the discovery stage, decide which are appropriate and which not, and then sort them into groups of similar details, ultimately deriving the plan of their essay from the raw material. Other writers work in the opposite direction: they draw up an abstract plan with categories for different parts of their subject and then find the details that fit each category. Still other writers "discover" the specific details in the process of drafting the essay and then amplify them in rewriting.

As an illustration of the first process, recall the thesis about *Modern Times* and *Waiting for Godot*, reprinted below. The first part of the thesis came to the writer as a general impression created by the discovery process; the second part came after sorting through the details, when she found they fell rather naturally into the three groups mentioned at the end of the thesis—humor, suffering, and action/inaction. Following is a brief sketch she made of the shape of her essay:

INTRODUCTION:

1. General information about the themes of the two films; how they focus on individuals, their problems, and their dehumanization.

2. Thesis: Although *Modern Times* and *Waiting for Godot* both center on the dehumanization of an "endangered species"—the individual—*Modern Times* is full of hope, while the characters in *Waiting for Godot* endlessly despair over their situations. The differences can be seen in the way the two films use humor, the way they depict suffering, and the contrast between action and inaction.

SUPPORT:

1. Humor as relief from somber theme
   —descriptions
   —examples
2. Suffering by characters in both films
   —their situations in life
   —hope of one versus the hopelessness of the other
3. How action and inaction affect tone of film
   —action in *Modern Times*

3e

—stagnation in *Waiting for Godot*
—action vs. idleness

CONCLUSION: Summation of the similarities in themes, ending with a sharply defined contrast of how the two films deal with the one theme of the individual.

To illustrate how the author used the details she selected, her article is reprinted below. Notice several things she did when she actually wrote the article: 1) she included all the ideas from the thesis in the introduction to the article, but in amplified form; 2) she saved the notion of the "endangered species" for the end, where it makes an effective closing; 3) she deliberately chose to develop the supporting paragraphs in the order she did: the movement is from the most *obvious* contrast—humor—to the most subtle—action and inaction. The latter point is the strongest in her essay, the one she wants to leave with her readers. (You may recall that her medium was a film review for a newspaper, her audience the readers of the arts section of the paper, and her purpose to convince her audience to see the two films together.)

TWO VIEWPOINTS ON THE INDIVIDUAL

Modern Times and *Waiting for Godot* are two films that center on individuals: the problems of identity, their domination by a greater power, and their ultimate dehumanization. These films are meaningful pieces of art that should be seen together by anyone concerned about the human predicament; though their themes are parallel, they approach their subjects in vastly different ways. Charlie Chaplin of *Modern Times* and Didi (Burgess Meredith) and Gogo (Zero Mostel) of *Waiting for Godot* are all depicted as clown types; but Chaplin is full of hope while Didi and Gogo endlessly despair over their situation. Chaplin never ceases to pursue the happy way of life, unlike the other two, who have accepted their situation. The differences can be seen in the way the two films use humor, the way they depict suffering, and the contrast between action and inaction.

Baggy pants, vests, oversized jackets, and bowler hats are all symbols of a clown. The characters in both films are dressed this way for a comic effect, but also to exemplify the state of poverty they are in. While watching these films, I could easily hear the laughter, and then the quick catch of breath, as the audience found themselves feeling guilty over indulging in humor at the predicaments the characters unknowingly get themselves into. On one occasion Chaplin is arrested for leading striking workers because he picks up a flag that had fallen off a construction truck just as the workers came marching up behind him. The police arrive at the scene at this precise moment and carry Chaplin off to jail on suspicion of being a communist. Didi and Gogo strike a note of humor and pain, also, as they attempt to help a fallen traveler; both of them, being rather old and helpless themselves, fall down on the traveler and none of them is able to get up. This all seemed hilariously funny until I stopped to think about the condition the actors were in and the hopelessness of the whole situation.

Humor is not, however, one of the dominant characteristics of either film. It exists to relieve the viewers of the constant suffering that is evident throughout. In both films, the shabby living conditions—abandoned shacks, ditches, and storerooms; the food they eat—bread, bananas, turnips, and radishes; their working conditions (when they're employed)—long hours, no safety, and meager wages; and the way others in the films treat them—making unjust accusations, using them for experiments with new machines, and shunning their very existence: these are all pains the players suffer each day of their lives.

All the characters have similar problems, but how each deals with the situation is sharply contrasted. Chaplin maintains an unending, unfaltering hope. He endures failure after failure; he loses jobs, goes in and out of jail, gets a job only to find the workers on strike ten minutes after starting time, loses his home, and repeatedly tangles himself in tight situations quite by accident. His faith in himself and in the future never falters and he continues to plod his way through life with his equally impoverished girlfriend. Didi and Gogo, on the other hand, are full of despair. They have allowed their hopes to be dashed long ago by the forces of society. They continually contemplate suicide but never really attempt it for lack of a strong piece of rope to hang themselves with. Didi's and Gogo's lives are void of love. There may be no love because there is no hope, or there may be no hope for lack of love; even they do not know which.

The outstanding feature of the two films is the swift action in *Modern Times* that contrasts with the idleness, almost stagnation, in *Waiting for Godot*. The characters in *Modern Times* are constantly moving—working, playing, walking. The scenery changes frequently: one minute Chaplin is on a crowded city street; the next, he is in a factory; a few minutes later he may be in a bar, a jail, or on the waterfront. On the contrary, the whole essence of *Waiting for Godot* is immobility. The scene never changes. The scenery itself resembles a desert, but not exactly; a prairie, but not exactly. The place could be anywhere, but looks like nowhere in particular. In *Modern Times* Chaplin himself is always in motion. His thoughts progress and his mind reacts to the given situation. He decides to act and he completes the motion. Didi and Gogo travel on no logical train of thought. Their minds wander, their bodies stay still. In the end of the film they agree to leave the spot and return the next day, yet they never move. No motion is carried out, no thought completed.

Both tales depict socially victimized people. They both use comic relief to hold interest. They both also deal with the search for meaning and happiness. *Modern Times*, though, can be described as a film of action driven by optimism, while *Waiting for Godot* is a film of inaction resulting from hopelessness and discouragement. The individual who fights back, never gives up, and has the American spirit creates an uplifting tone and a smiling audience. Dejection, stagnation, and lack of motivation blacken the tone and leave a bad taste in one's mouth. The two films enlighten the audience to two very different viewpoints on a controversial, and constantly changing, endangered species—the individual.   —Kimberly Barger

EXERCISES

1. Answer the following questions about "Two Viewpoints on the Individual":
   a. Did the author include all the details from her brainstorming (see figure 2.1 on page 30)? If not, why did she leave out what she did?
   b. Recalling that her audience is made up of the readers of the arts section of a daily newspaper, describe her readers as specifically as possible, considering the questions in **3d**.
   c. Imagine a different audience, medium, and purpose: suppose she had written an essay for her English professor comparing the two films—the audience her professor, the medium an English essay, and the purpose to show the professor that she has some understanding of drama and the ability to analyze it. How would you rewrite the article? What language would you change? What details would you add or delete? What changes would you make in the structure of the essay?
   d. Now go ahead and write the "English essay" version.
2. Go back to one of the subjects you worked with in exercise 2 at the end of **3a**. Draw up a simple "blueprint" similar to the one for "Two Viewpoints." Your medium, remember, is an article in your college newspaper; your audience includes the students and faculty who read the newspaper; your thesis was determined by you in the earlier exercise. You will have to decide on a purpose appropriate to your subject and audience.
3. Now write the essay based on the blueprint you just designed.

4

DEVELOPING THE THESIS

In the article "Two Viewpoints" (3e), the author used a variety of methods to develop her ideas. She *compared* the films (showing their similar points), *contrasted* them (showing the different ways the themes were developed), *described* them, *narrated* some incidents, *divided* (analyzed) her thesis into three parts (humor, suffering, and action/inaction), and supported each idea with *examples* (including details and illustrations). Most kinds of writing use these methods as well as others: some essays explain a *process*; some analyze the *causes* or *effects* of an event; some *classify* events, people, or things into groups; and some use *analogies* to explain something or to persuade someone. All of these methods are used to develop the thesis and the *general* aim (informative, persuasive, expressive, or literary—see 3b). They are, in fact, more *specific* aims. In "Two Viewpoints," for instance, the author's specific aim is to *compare* and *contrast* the two films in order to achieve her more general aim, to *persuade* the reader to see the films (and to see them together).

Note that the methods of development are not used in isolation; they are not discrete categories, but rather work together to achieve the author's general aim. Every piece of writing has a *dominant* method as well as various *supporting* ones, and various parts of a longer work will in turn have dominant and subordinate methods.

4a Description

Description is a method we tend to think of primarily in connection with literature, but it is widely used in all kinds of other writing as well. In fact, one of the marks of a good writer is the ability to *see* clearly what other people miss and then to present it in such a way that they can see it as clearly as the writer does. Description appears frequently as a supporting method (in "Two Viewpoints," for instance). When it is a dominant method, it is usually presented through *spatial* order (**6a.1**) or through order of *specificity* (**6a.3**).

The following paragraph argues that the great composer Richard Wagner was "a monster of conceit." The author supports the description with examples, presented in a general-to-specific order: from a general statement of Wagner's egocentricity, to details about how he thought about himself, to details about his conversation and how others reacted to him.

> He was a monster of conceit. Never for one minute did he look at the world or at people, except in relation to himself. He was not only the most important person in the world, to himself; in his own eyes he was the only person who existed. He believed himself to be one of the greatest dramatists in the world, one of the greatest thinkers, and one of the greatest composers. To hear him talk, he was Shakespeare, and Beethoven, and Plato, rolled into one. And you would have had no difficulty in hearing him talk. He was one of the most exhausting conversationalists that ever lived. An evening with him was an evening spent in listening to a monologue. Sometimes he was brilliant, sometimes he was maddeningly tiresome. But whether he was being brilliant or dull, he had one sole topic of conversation: himself. What *he* thought and what *he* did.
>
> —Deems Taylor, *Of Men and Music*

4b Narration

Narration, relating a series of events through time, is another method that we tend to associate with fiction. But it is also used as a dominant method in, for example, biography and autobiography, as well as a supporting method in all kinds of situations. Anecdotes, parables, or fables, for instance, are narrative forms used to illustrate a point. Narration almost always follows a *chronological* order or some variation of it (**6a.2**).

In the following example, taken from a famous writer's letter to his daughter, contrast is used as a supporting method—a contrast between his life before marriage and his life after. The order is chronological.

> When I was your age I lived with a great dream. The dream grew and I learned how to speak of it and make people listen. Then the dream divided one day when I decided to marry your mother after all, even though I knew she was spoiled and meant no good to me. I was sorry immediately I had married her but, being patient in those days, made the best of it and got to love her in another way. You came along, and for a long time we made quite a lot of happiness out of our lives. But I was a man divided—she wanted me to work too much for *her* and not enough for my dream. She realized too late that work was dignity, and the only dignity, and tried to atone for it by working herself, but it was too late and she broke and is broken forever.   —F. Scott Fitzgerald, "Letter to Scottie"

4c Process Analysis

When process analysis is used as a dominant method, the purpose is to show readers how to do something, how something works, or how something was done. While the latter sometimes seems similar to narration, the difference is in the purpose. If I were to tell you how I went about writing this book, for example, I might treat it as a process analysis if I wanted you to learn from my experience how to write a book yourself; but if I were writing an account of a period of my own life, for autobiographical or entertainment purposes, I would treat it as narration, and of course my manner of telling it and my choice of details would be somewhat different. Process analysis usually follows a *chronological* order (**6a.2**), since the easiest way to show people how to do something is to tell them step by step.

The following example is from an article on making terrariums, and this passage follows a description of how to gather the plants and other materials. The supporting method is division, as the writer divides the process into discrete steps; and the order is chronological.

> Begin by putting down a base composed of several layers, as follows, remembering that each layer serves a purpose. First, put down a mat of moss to absorb moisture and form an attractive lining.

Then pour a layer of sand or fine gravel over the moss to promote drainage and prevent waterlogging. Next scatter a handful of charcoal pieces over the gravel to prevent souring of the soil.

Now add the final layer—soil. Bagged sterilized soil is fine, but if you want to mix your own, aim for the following proportions:

    2 parts topsoil
    1 part sand
    1 part leafmold or compost

Put in a thin layer, just covering the charcoal. Then set the plants in place and firm the remainder of the soil around their roots. Much of this soil will later settle lower around the roots. . . .

—Nancy Bubel, "How to Make a Terrarium"

4d Definition

Definition is more commonly used as a supporting method than as a dominant method, but essays and even books have been written with the primary purpose of defining. When you write definition, you almost always begin by putting the concept or thing to be defined in a large class (in the following example, *omelet* is placed in the class of "egg dishes") and then by explaining what makes it different from other members of its class (for instance, what makes an egg dish an omelet rather than a soufflé or scrambled eggs). A basic definition can often be stated in one sentence, in the following form (where x represents the word you are defining):

X is a _____ which _____ .

In the first blank, fill in the class the word belongs to; in the second, the characteristics that distinguish it from other members of its class. In the following example, you actually get three different endings for that formula:

An omelet is an egg dish which (in America) . . .
                              (in France) . . .
                              (in Italy) . . .

The bulk of discourse based on a dominant method of definition is given over to elaborating on the second blank—describing the item being defined. The most common order when definition is the dominant method is *specificity* (6a.3)—from general (the definition) to specific (the description and particular examples).

The supporting methods in the following example are division (three kinds of omelets) and description (the concrete details that describe the omelets so vividly). The order is general to specific, as the authors first define omelets in general and then discuss the three kinds (American, French, and Italian).

The name "omelet" is loosely applied to many kinds of egg dishes. In America, you often get a great puffy, soufflélike, rather dry dish in which the egg whites have been beaten separately and folded into the yolks. In France an entire mystique surrounds a single process in which the egg is combined as unobtrusively as possible to avoid incorporating air and this marbleized mixture quickly turned into a three-fold delicacy, filled or unfilled. In an Italian frittata, the food is often mixed at once with the stirred egg and this thin pancake-like mixture is cooked in a little oil, first on one side and then on the other, with a result not unlike a large edition of Eggs Foo Yung.

—Irma S. Rombauer and Marion Rombauer Becker,
The Joy of Cooking

4e Comparison and Contrast

Comparison and contrast are closely related, but comparison emphasizes the *similarities* among things while contrast emphasizes the *differences*. Whichever is the dominant method, the other is always a supporting method.

Contrast requires a basis of *similarity* or comparison—otherwise the things you compare would bear no relationship to each other. For instance, if you want to contrast a liberal arts college with a university, you must first establish what they have in common (they are both institutions of higher education).

Likewise, comparison requires a basis of *difference* or contrast. For example, if you want to compare colleges and universities, you would have to establish some points of contrast—difference in size, difference in emphasis on teaching and research, and so on.

Comparison and contrast usually follow an *alternating* order (see **6a.4**), in which you first discuss each point of comparison (or contrast) about Item A and then each point about B, in the same order; or you alternate point-by-point, discussing one point about A and B, then another point about A and B, and so on.

In the following example, the dominant method is contrast—between history textbooks of the 1950s and those of the 1970s. (The *basis* for the contrast is in the comparison of the two groups—both are history textbooks.) A supporting method is example, as the author uses specific examples to show how the books differ. The order is alternating; the author uses two main divisions—first, textbooks of the 1950s and second, textbooks of the 1970s. In each division, she discusses two points of contrast—the books' attitudes toward American society first, and their portrayal of the political system second.

> Ideologically speaking, the histories of the fifties were implacable, seamless. Inside their covers, America was perfect: the greatest nation in the world, and the embodiment of democracy, freedom, and technological progress. For them, the country never changed in any important way: its values and its political institutions remained constant from the time of the American Revolution. . . .
>
> But now the texts have changed, and with them the country that American children are growing up into. The society that was once uniform is now a patchwork of rich and poor, old and young, men and women, blacks, whites, Hispanics, and Indians. The system that ran so smoothly by means of the Constitution under the guidance of benevolent conductor Presidents is now a rattletrap affair.
>
> —Frances FitzGerald, *America Revised*

4f   Analogy

Analogy is a special kind of comparison in which you compare one thing to another in order to illuminate something about the second. For instance, if you want to help someone understand sound waves, you might compare them to waves on a beach.

Analogy is frequently used as a supporting method for cause-effect analysis or definition. It generally follows an *alternating* order (**6a.4**). In the following paragraph, Freud uses an analogy to accomplish his primary purpose—to define the relationship between the ego and the id. The ideal situation, in which the ego controls the id, is followed by the more negative situation, in which the id is in control, so the order is alternating.

> One might compare the relation of the ego to the id with that between a rider and his horse. The horse provides the locomotor energy, and the rider has the prerogative of determining the goal and of guiding

the movements of his powerful mount towards it. But all too often in the relations between the ego and the id we find a picture of the less ideal situation in which the rider is obliged to guide his horse in the direction in which it itself wants to go.

—Sigmund Freud, *The Anatomy of the Mental Personality*

4g Division and Classification

Division and classification are closely related methods. In division (or *analysis*), the purpose is to break something up into its constituent parts (analyze it) in order to help your readers understand it more clearly. In classification, you put individuals (people, things, ideas) into classes or categories in order to help your readers see the relationships and differences among them more clearly.

Division is usually a supporting method for classification. Before you can classify a variety of individuals into classes or groups, you must identify the groups by dividing a larger unit. For instance, in order to discuss the way words work in our language, books on grammar (including this one) divide our language into several classes or categories often called "parts of speech," and then classify various words, or various uses of those words, into the classes they have established (nouns, verbs, etc.).

Division is also used as a supporting method for process analysis, and classification is an essential supporting method for comparison and contrast and for definition.

When division or classification is the dominant method in a piece of writing, the order in which the writer presents the groups will most likely be an order of *climax* (**6a.5**) or *familiarity* (**6a.6**).

In the following example, a famous composer introduces his subject, listening to music, by dividing it into three parts, using both a climactic order to impress the readers with the point he wants to leave with them, and an order of familiarity (most listeners listen on the sensuous plane, some on an expressive plane, but only a few on the purely musical plane).

We all listen to music according to our separate capacities. But, for the sake of analysis, the whole listening process may become clearer if we break it up into its component parts. In a certain sense we all listen to music on three separate planes. For lack of a better terminology, one might name these (1) the sensuous plane, (2) the expressive plane, (3) the sheerly musical plane. The only advantage to be gained from mechanically splitting up the listening process into these hypothetical planes is the clearer view to be had of the way in which we listen.   —Aaron Copland, "How We Listen to Music"

4h Examples

Examples will be the dominant method when your thesis states a generalization that needs to be supported. Examples are usually presented in an order of *climax* (**6a.5**) or *familiarity* (**6a.6**).

In the following illustration, the primary purpose is to show readers the horrors of the atomic bomb by presenting examples of specific details, but narration and description are used as supporting methods. The order is general to specific; the author first gives us a general statement about what happened on that day and then goes on to give specific examples of events that happened.

> A doctor who was at a military hospital outside Hiroshima said that about an hour after the bomb went off, "many, many people came rushing to my clinic. They were rushing in all directions of the compass from the city. Many were stretcher cases. Some had their hair burned off, were injured in the back, had broken legs, arms, and thighs. The majority of the cases were those injured from glass; many had glass imbedded in the body. Next to the glass injuries, the most frequent were those who had their faces and hands burned, and also the chest and back. Most of the people arrived barefooted; many had their clothes burned off. Women were wearing men's clothing and men were wearing women's. They had put on anything they could pick up along the way."
>
> —Alexander Leighton, "That Day at Hiroshima"

4i Cause-Effect Analysis

Cause-effect analysis is frequently a dominant method in historical writing, where the purpose is often to show the reasons (causes) for certain events, as well as their results (effects). Likewise, in much scientific writing, the relationship between cause and effect is often the major method of presenting the results of experiments. The order may be *chronological* (see **6a.2**), where the events are described as they happened—causes first, effects second—or an order of *specificity* (**6a.3**), where a general cause or effect is followed by specific effects or causes (or vice versa).

In the following example, the author moves from the effects (four kinds of pressure on college students) to the causes of those pressures (four "villains"):

> I see four kinds of pressure working on college students today: economic pressure, parental pressure, peer pressure, and self-induced pressure. It is easy to look around for villains—to blame the colleges for charging too much money, the professors for assigning too much work, the parents for pushing their children too far, the students for driving themselves too hard. But there are no villains; only victims.
>
> —William Zinsser, "College Pressures"

EXERCISES

1. Discuss the following passages. What is the dominant method of each? What are the supporting methods? What can you tell about the purpose and audience of the whole work from each excerpt? How are the methods appropriate to the author's purpose and audience?

a. There was that blindly adoring period of childhood when my father was the strongest and wisest of men. He would scare off the bears my young imagination feared as they prowled the night outside our Texas farmhouse, provide sunshine and peanut butter, make the world go away. I brought him my broken toys and my skinned knees. He did imitations of all the barnyard animals; when we boxed he saw to it that I won by knockouts. After his predawn winter milkings, shivering and stomping his numb feet while rushing to throw more wood on the fire, he warned that tomorrow morning, by gosh, he planned to laze abed and eat peach cobbler while his youngest son performed the icy chores.

   —Larry King, "The Old Man," *The Washington Post*

b. In post-Renaissance Europe two overriding fears dominated thinking on women's education: the fear that learning would unfit women for their social role, defined as service to husband and children and obedience to the church; and, a corollary of the first, that open access to education would endanger women's sexual purity. For while humanist philosophy taught that education led to virtue, writers on education were at once conflicted when they applied the premise to women. Nearly all, beginning with the influential sixteenty-century Juan Luis Vives, opted for restricting women's learning. Only a few radical thinkers—some men, such as Richard Mulcaster in Tudor England and the extraordinary Poullain de la Barre in seventeenth-century France, some women, like the feisty Bathsua Makin and revolutionary Mary Wollstonecraft—spoke out for the full development of women's intellectual potential.   —Dorothy Gies McGuigan, "To Be a Woman Scholar"

4i

c. Choosing the land and siting the house on the land deserve as much care as the floor plan, especially for a house that will depend on the sun and the wind for heating and cooling. Designing a house as a solar collector, which is what passive solar is all about, requires getting to know how the sun travels across your land through each season of the year; which trees provide summer shading and which block the warmth of the winter sun. Familiarity with air paths around your structure is also essential, so you will know how to ward off the cold winter winds and invite the cool summer breezes in.

—Barbara Flanagan, "Ecological Home Building," *New Age*

d. Amy works as a word-processing operator for a major industrial firm in Cincinnati. One day, she paused briefly from word processing just as her manager walked in. "What are you doing?" he demanded. "Oh, I'm just thinking for a minute," she replied. "Well, get back to work," he snapped. "You're not paid to think. I am."

Amy's experience is typical of the problems that are made worse by the rapid introduction of office automation, and by the attitude of her manager. "Get back to work. You're not paid to think," is at the core of the creation of the electronic sweatshop. Yet, in business and trade journals, we read rave reviews of the wonders that the new office technology is bringing us.

—Judith Gregory, "The Electronic Sweatshop"

e. European beers are easily distinguished from American beers because they are usually darker in color, heavier in consistency, and higher in alcohol content. Even the pilsner and "Weiss" beers, which are lighter in color, are much stronger than American beers. A European beer will also have a thick, creamy head, not just bubbles. On the other hand, American beers are brewed to be more dilute. A beer such as Miller is pale and uniform enough to be sold in an untinted bottle, and light beers appeal to Americans who want an even more watered-down beer. American beers are also restricted as to their alcohol content, according to statutes which vary from state to state.　　　　—Michael Martineau

2. Choose one of the examples above: write on a different subject, but use a similar structure and write for a similar audience and purpose (as you identified them in the previous exercise).

5

PERSUADING YOUR READER

5a What Is Persuasion?

When your primary aim (see **3b**) is to *persuade* rather than *inform*, you place major emphasis on your readers, on presenting your point of view as convincingly as possible, so that they will be moved to adopt the belief or course of action you want them to. In one sense, of course, all writing is persuasive. If your primary aim is to inform your readers of something, your secondary aim must be to persuade them that your information is trustworthy. And, of course, the best persuasive writing is also informative. The Declaration of Independence, a masterpiece of persuasive writing, includes a long catalog of the wrongs done the colonists by the king of England: informing the people of the wrongs done them (even though some of these wrongs were imagined or exaggerated) was a way of persuading them that certain actions had to be taken.

While these two aims—informing and persuading—overlap to some extent, we will use the term *persuasive writing* to mean writing whose *primary* purpose is to convince people with argument, to persuade them of the truth of something, or to move them to action.

Persuasive writing relies on all the writing techniques discussed in chapters 1–4, but it also uses both argument and special appeals to achieve its purpose. This chapter will discuss some techniques that will be especially helpful when you are writing something whose primary aim is to persuade.

5b What Is Argument?

Argument is a method of logical reasoning in which you present your reasons for believing something to be true (your conclusion, or the *thesis* of your argument) and try to persuade your readers to accept your beliefs or adopt a particular course of action based on those beliefs. In a more technical sense, an *argument* is the form in which you present your thesis and the reasons for believing it or acting upon it. It is a set of propositions in which one or more are affirmed to be reasons for others.

A *proposition* is a statement in an argument that can be affirmed or denied. For example, "The door is shut" is a proposition: by looking at the door, we can either affirm or deny that it is shut. But "Please shut the door" or "Who is at the door?" are not propositions; because nothing has been asserted, nothing can be affirmed or denied.

"It is raining" and "A low-pressure front has moved in" are both propositions. Asserting (or implying) that one is the cause of or a reason for the other creates an argument: "It is raining *because* a low-pressure front has moved in." It is possible not only to affirm or deny each proposition in an argument, but also to affirm or deny the connection between them. For example, we might agree that "It is raining" and that "The door is shut," but we might not agree with the argument that the door is shut *because* it is raining.

When we affirm or deny a proposition, we affirm or deny its *truth*—that is, whether it corresponds to reality. A proposition is true, not true, or *probably* true. If we affirm or deny an argument, we may be thinking of truth (*is* it raining because a low-pressure front moved in?), but most often we are thinking of whether the argument is logical or reasonable. Then we are dealing not with truth, but with *validity*, which concerns the method of an argument, not the truth of its propositions. For example, we could state as propositions that "Athletes don't smoke" and "John doesn't smoke." If we concluded that therefore John is an athlete, we would have an invalid argument. The propositions might both be true, yet the reasoning is invalid. Whether the conclusion is true or false is incidental: if John is an athlete, it is not because of any connection in that argument.

When we sense that something is wrong with an argument, like this one, we often say that it is "illogical," whether or not we can explain exactly what we mean. *Logic* is the system of reasoning that produces valid conclusions. It is the structure of an argument, just as grammar is the structure of the language. Logic, then, is both a way to structure an argument and a tool to help us evaluate an argument. An *invalid* argument is one that violates the rules of logic.

The most common forms of logical reasoning are induction and deduction. *Induction* is the process of drawing a conclusion (usually a generalization) from particular instances or evidence. For example, if a professor notices that some of his students come to class every day unprepared and that those students are all sophomores, he may conclude that sophomores are lazy. If he does not take into account those sophomores who *do* come to class prepared, he may arrive at an invalid and probably false conclusion (about all sophomores) based on an *unreliable* sample. The word *reliability* has a rather specialized meaning in statistics, but we will use it here in a more general sense to mean the quality of evidence from which an inductive conclusion is drawn.

Deduction takes a general statement about a class and applies it to particular members of the class, or to subclasses. For example, if the professor believes that all sophomores are lazy and knows that his student Ray is a sophomore, he may deduce that Ray is lazy. This conclusion would be *valid* because, as we will see later, it follows the rules of deductive logic; but it may not be *true* because one of the propositions on which it is based is untrue (that is, that all sophomores are lazy). *Validity*, therefore, has to do with the structure of a deductive argument and, like reliability, it should not be confused with truth.

Inductive and deductive methods of thinking are often used together, as in the case of the professor who concluded that "Ray is lazy." The scientific method works by a combination of inductive and deductive thinking. Galileo, for example, noticed that objects seem to fall to the ground at an equal rate, regardless of how heavy they are. He reasoned (inductively) that objects do not fall to the earth by their own mass, but rather are pulled by the force of gravity. This proposition, the *conclusion* of an induc-

5b

tive thinking process, then became a theory that could be tested by Galileo and other scientists deductively.

EXERCISES

1. Determine whether each of the following examples contains an argument; if it does, determine whether the argument is deductive or inductive, and state the conclusion.

   a. When we run, some remarkable things happen. We feel better, look better, have more energy, and think more clearly. We lose weight, increase our resistance to heart attack and alter our blood chemistry for the better. We even delay certain of the body's aging processes and, some researchers say, probably live longer than we would if we didn't run.   —James Fixx

   b. If, from reading the hierarchy of facts about the machine, the mechanic knows the horn of the cycle is powered exclusively by electricity from the battery, then he can logically infer that if the battery is dead the horn will not work.   —Robert M. Pirsig

   c. To a worker, leisure means simply the hours he needs to relax and rest in order to work efficiently. He is therefore more likely to take too little leisure than too much; workers die of coronaries and forget their wives' birthdays.   —W. H. Auden

   d. I know of no Medicine fit to diminish the violent natural inclinations you mention; and if I did, I think I should not communicate it to you. Marriage is the proper remedy. It is the most natural state of Man, and therefore the state in which you are most likely to find solid Happiness.   —Benjamin Franklin

   e. I have found repeatedly, of late years, that I cannot fish without falling a little in self-respect. I have tried it again and again. I have skill at it, and like many of my fellows, a certain instinct for it, which revives from time to time, but always when I have done I feel that it would have been better if I had not fished.

   —Henry David Thoreau

2. The following sentences are all propositions. Use each one in an argument in which you try to convince your readers of the truth of the proposition.

   a. A college education is an absolute necessity today.
   b. Real coffee lovers would never touch a cup of instant coffee.
   c. Food prices are rising too fast.
   d. The world would be better off without modern technology.
   e. Computers are rapidly overtaking microwave ovens as the number one Christmas gift item.

5c Inductive Argument

5c.1 Reliability and Probability

An inductive argument is one that draws a general conclusion on the basis of specific data or evidence. Sound inductive reasoning is based on *reliable* evidence: evidence that is *representative*, *unbiased*, and *sufficient*. Reliable generalizations, for instance, are often made by agencies who want to poll the American public concerning their points of view on a certain issue. If such agencies take a representative sample of the population, if they are careful to be unbiased (by sampling members of all the political parties, for instance), and if the sample is sufficiently large, there is a high probability that the conclusion will be true. A reliable sample could be chosen either by *representative sampling* (choosing precincts whose populations are roughly in the same proportions as the whole state in regard to political affiliation, income level, education level, sex, and so on) or by *random sampling*. A random sample is one chosen purely by chance—by using a table of random numbers, for example, or by choosing every 250th name from the telephone book of a large city. If the sample is large enough and if it is representative and unbiased (whether chosen randomly or by certain representative factors), then the predicted results will likely occur—or, to put it another way, the survey will have *predictive validity*.

Although data collected in such surveys are said to be *reliable*, the conclusion of the survey may or may not turn out to be true, because reliability refers to the methods used, not to the truth of the conclusion drawn from them. The more reliable an inductive survey is, the more likely are its results to reflect the truth, but there is always room for error. Induction deals with the *probability* of something being true, not with absolutes. It is probable that since the sun has come up every day of my life, it will do so tomorrow. But something could, of course, happen tomorrow to prevent the sun coming up (as fantasized in the science fiction film *The Day the Earth Stood Still*).

5c.2 Reports, Inferences, and Judgments

When we look at various propositions in an inductive argument, it is useful to distinguish three types: reports, inferences, and

5c

judgments. These are all types of propositions and therefore can all be affirmed or denied, but there are important differences among them.

A *report* is a proposition that can be verified. If I tell you it is 3,050 miles from New York to San Francisco, you could get in your car, drive from New York to San Francisco, and check the mileage (*primary verification*). Or you could check a map that gives mileage between cities (*secondary verification*).

An *inference* is a conclusion drawn from a report. "It will take six days to drive from New York to San Francisco," is an inference drawn from certain facts—namely, the number of miles from New York to San Francisco and an average driving time.

A *judgment* is an inference that states an opinion of *value*: "It's not worth driving from New York to San Francisco." For the professor to say that all his sophomores are lazy is to make an inference why they are unprepared and to judge them negatively. Some words, like *lazy*, have built-in judgments (connotations), so that any proposition in which they are found will be a value judgment (see **5g.12**).

The soundest inductive arguments are those whose inferences (conclusions) are based on reports of reliable evidence and whose judgments are not misrepresented as reports. An argument that sophomores are lazy will be more effective if the professor clearly states that he is making a judgment and if he has reliable evidence to support it.

EXERCISES

The following statements exemplify the mixture of reports, inferences, and judgments that we see daily. Try to classify each statement, noting that most are not pure examples of a single category.

1. As recent accidents have shown, the likelihood of widespread pollution of the sea surface and beaches by the wrecking of the new large tankers is rapidly increasing with the growth of ocean oil transport.
   —Herbert J. Muller

2. When Ella Wheeler Wilcox died in 1919, more people were reading her verses than Shakespeare's; yet in a few years her work was dead. It had been buried by its poverty of emotions and its trivialness of thought.   —John Cheever

3. The Rolling Stones were not boys our mothers would like—which made them more appealing, of course.   —Richard Goldstein

4. Travel means going away from home and staying away from home; it is an antidote to the humdrum activities of everyday life, a prelude to a holiday one is entitled to enjoy after months of dulness.
—Margaret Mead

5. . . . . Saturn's day, the Sun's day, and the Moon's day are clearly recognizable in their English names of Saturday, Sunday, and Monday.
—John Livingston Lowes

5d Pitfalls in Inductive Argument

When you use statistics and other kinds of evidence to support an inductive argument, it is easy to forget to present all sides of the issue objectively. Some writers, assuming their readers are not very critical, may deliberately manipulate statistics and other kinds of evidence to support their arguments. While you might persuade some people with unsound arguments, however, you will not persuade a critical reader, and in fact you can damage your cause if you present an argument that is easy to discredit. You should try to avoid pitfalls in your reasoning that might lead you inadvertently to present an unreliable argument.

5d.1 Manipulation of Statistics

Statistics can be persuasive evidence in supporting a proposition, if they are not altered, distorted, misinterpreted, or partially suppressed. Suppose, for example, that a math professor writes an editorial in the college newspaper trying to persuade students to study more in order to get better grades. As evidence, he reports that seventy-five percent of the students who failed the course had studied for it three hours or less per week. But how do we know that lack of study caused students to fail the course? What if seventy-five percent of the students who passed also studied three hours or less a week? If statistics concerning the passing students are suppressed (or never researched) we are not likely to be persuaded by his argument.

A critical reader will judge the reliability of a statistical inference by comparing it with other statistical reports on the same subject, will consider the reputation of the person or organization who did the statistical survey and report, and will ask these questions: Is the data-gathering method extensive enough? Is there missing evidence? Could the sample have been deliberately biased to produce the desired statistics?

5d.2 Special Pleading (Slanting)

When you present an argument that uses factual reports to support a proposition, you need to be careful not to bias your readers unfairly. Your presentation of the evidence may contain only reports and no explicit judgments, yet it may *imply* a judgment by the selection of details.

In reporting a murder, for example, a journalist might report past crimes or attempted crimes of the murderer, his estrangement from his family because of his violent temper, his frequent arrests for drunkenness, and his having been cheated out of a large sum of money by the murdered man (the last providing a possible motive for the crime). Or she might ignore all these details and dwell instead on certain misfortunes in the life of the murderer and on certain actions of the victim that give the impression he was a hateful person who drove the murderer to the crime. In either case, she would provide nothing but reports—all of which might be true—but her decision to exclude certain other reports would manipulate the reader's attitude toward the murderer.

Such presentation of information is called by a variety of names: *special pleading* (because the report includes an implied plea for a special cause), *bias*, or *slanting*. Newspaper reporters are not, of course, the only people who use slanted reports. Trial lawyers slant their pleas in favor of their clients. When you apply for a job, you probably include all the positive facts about yourself and exclude all the negative ones. Every time we present reports for the purpose of persuading, we are likely to slant those reports toward the point we want to persuade people about.

But your readers are not likely to be convinced if everything you say about one side of an issue is positive and everything you say about the other side is negative; very few things in our world are all good or all bad, and a discerning reader will recognize that.

5d.3 False Cause

A man who falls and breaks his arm after walking under a ladder is superstitious if he believes walking under the ladder caused his fall. Just because two things occur consecutively, the first is not necessarily the cause of the second; in order to write persuasively, you must establish a causal connection between two events.

5d

Magazine or TV advertisements often imply that if you use a certain brand of deodorant or mouthwash, you will have more friends or lovers. Bad breath and body odor can keep people away from you, but eliminating them will not by itself bring people to you (unless they are the *only* things keeping people away); and even if there were a causal connection between getting rid of body odor and making new friends, there would not necessarily be a connection between the particular brand of deodorant you used and the eliminated body odor. The persuasiveness of these ads does not result from logic.

EXERCISES

1. Identify and be prepared to discuss the distortions in the following examples (including unrepresentative or misleading samples, manipulation of statistics, special pleading, and false cause).

   a. Probably the most extensive survey on sexual harassment was conducted by *Redbook* magazine in 1976. Nine thousand women responded to the magazine's questionnaire; the majority of them were in their 20s and early 30s and earned between $5,000 and $10,000 per year in white-collar jobs. Nine out of ten respondents said they had experienced unwanted sexual attention at work, ranging from leers and remarks to overt requests for sexual favors with the implied threat of retaliation. Seventy percent of the women said they found these situations embarrassing and demeaning. The problem, *Redbook* concluded, is not epidemic—it is pandemic.
      —*Mother Jones*, June 1978

   b. But now there's good news—exciting news—from one of the world's leading medical institutions:
      Researchers there, treating 4,000 hypertensive men and women, succeeded in reversing 85% of the mild cases and 51% of the severe cases—*all without using any drugs!*
      —ad for *Prevention* magazine

   c. Jeannette Harris, a nutritionist who has worked with overweight women at Gurney's Health Spa in Montauk, L.I., and who now teaches nutrition classes at East Hampton's Body Shop, says a majority of women are consumed by the perpetual need to shed that last 5 or 10 extra pounds, even though in many cases nature has deemed otherwise.
      —Deborah Blumenthal, "Body Image," *New York Times Magazine*

   d. The University of California and the University of Nebraska have just released two independent studies that have been published in the Entomological Society of America Journal. In the studies, thirty-one well known consumer and commercial insecticide products were tested in heavily roach infested homes and apartments. Confirming an earlier University of California published report, ROACH PRUFE'S patented formula again took the **#1 spot as the most effective roach killer.**   —Roach Prufe ad

2. From your daily newspaper, choose a short article that is slanted either positively or negatively toward its subject. Then rewrite the article, making up additional facts that could have been left out of the original article, in order to slant it in the opposite direction.

3. Now rewrite the article once more, this time presenting a balanced view of the subject.

4. Choose an article in a recent newspaper or magazine that relies heavily on statistics. Write an essay in which you analyze the problems in the article and evaluate the reliability of its conclusions.

5e   Deductive Argument

In a deductive argument, a conclusion is drawn (*deduced*) from previous, usually more general propositions. Deductive arguments follow formal rules of logic that can be expressed in the form of a *syllogism*.

5e.1   Syllogisms

A *categorical syllogism*† includes three kinds of propositions, each of which makes a statement about certain *categories* (classes) and some of which are said to be reasons for others, thus creating an argument. A syllogism contains three propositions: a *major premise*, a *minor premise*, and a *conclusion*. Below is a variation of a famous example:

	MIDDLE TERM		MAJOR TERM
MAJOR PREMISE:	All humans	are	mortal.
	MINOR TERM		MIDDLE TERM
MINOR PREMISE:	Socrates	is	a human.
	MINOR TERM		MAJOR TERM
CONCLUSION:	Socrates	is	mortal.

†While there are other kinds of syllogisms, the categorical syllogism is the one most often used in persuasive writing.

The major premise puts one class of things (humans) into a larger class (mortals). The minor premise puts a particular individual (Socrates) into the smaller of the two classes (humans) in the major premise. The argument concludes that Socrates is mortal because, by virtue of his being in the smaller class of humans, he is also in the larger class of mortals.

Notice that there are just three classes or *terms* in a syllogism. The *minor term* is in the minor premise as well as in the conclusion. The *major term* is in the major premise as well as in the conclusion. The *middle* term connects the major and minor terms; it appears in the premises but not in the conclusion.

5e.2 Rules of Validity

Certain rules of logic must be followed in order to produce a *valid* argument. If the reasoning is valid *and* the premises are true, then a categorical syllogism produces a *sound* argument in which the conclusion will necessarily be true. While there are many complex rules in formal logic, the ones we need to know for persuasive writing can be stated simply, and they can be classified into two groups: rules about the *number* and *distribution* of terms, and rules about *negative* terms.

a. Number and Distribution of Terms:

We say that a term is *distributed* if it refers to the entire category. In the major premise of our previous example, the middle term (*humans*) is distributed: *all* humans—the entire category—are mortal. (The words *all* and *no* will always signal distribution.)

In the minor premise, however, *humans* is not distributed, since it refers not to the whole class of humans, but only to one person—Socrates. (The fact that *human* is preceded by *a* indicates that we are talking of only one member of the class.) *Socrates*, the minor term, is distributed because it is a class of its own (Socrates is the only member).

Our example illustrates three rules that a valid syllogism must follow: First, *there must be three and only three terms* (here *mortal*, *human*, and *Socrates*). If the major premise has two terms and the minor premise two different terms, there will be no way to connect the two and therefore no way to draw a valid conclusion.

Second, *the middle term must be distributed in at least one of the premises.* If it is not, no conclusion can be drawn. Consider, for example, the following invalid syllogism:

> Some humans are mortal.
> Socrates is a human.
> *Therefore, Socrates is mortal.

Since the middle term refers to *some* humans (the word *some*, like *a*, always means the term is undistributed), it follows that there may be some humans who are *not* mortal; therefore, Socrates is not necessarily mortal.

Third, *if a term is not distributed in the premise, it cannot be distributed in the conclusion.* In other words, the conclusion cannot claim more than the premises imply. Consider the following invalid syllogism:

> All people born in the U.S. are mortal.
> All people born in the U.S. are American citizens.
> *Therefore, all mortals are American citizens.

Even though both premises are true, they do not imply the conclusion. Since the major premise does not refer to *all* mortals (*mortals* is not distributed), the conclusion cannot make a valid statement about all mortals. We can, of course, infer that some mortals are American citizens and some American citizens are mortal, but the premises do not necessarily imply either that all American citizens are mortal or that all mortals are American citizens.

b. Negative Terms:
If one of the premises is negative, the conclusion must also be negative.

> No angels are mortal.
> Gabriel is an angel.
> Therefore, Gabriel is not a mortal.

The word *no*, like *all*, indicates that a term is distributed; that is, "no angels" refers to the entire class of angels. Since no angels are mortal, the entire class of angels must be entirely separate

---

*The asterisk in front of a conclusion indicates that the conclusion is invalid.

from the class of mortals. Therefore Gabriel, being an angel, cannot be in the class of mortals.

If both premises are negative, no valid conclusion can be drawn. Consider the following syllogism:

> No angels are mortal.
> Jennifer is not an angel.
> *Therefore, Jennifer is a mortal.

All we can tell from the premises is that Jennifer is not an angel; she may or may not be a mortal; that is, there may be classes of beings that are neither angel nor mortal, and Jennifer may be one of those.

EXERCISES

1. Put the following statements into standard categorical form. (First find the subject and predicate of the conclusion so that you can identify the major and minor terms.) Then determine if the syllogism is valid.
   a. Vegetarians are people who do not eat meat, but people who do eat meat are normal; therefore, vegetarians are abnormal.
   b. Coal Industry lobbyists fought legislation to increase retirement payments to miners. The payments would help miners become self-sufficient. The coal industry always opposes legislation designed to increase miner self-sufficience.
   c. The Concorde should not be allowed into any American airport because nothing that makes noise in excess of EPA standards should be allowed to land in American airports. The Concorde makes noise far in excess of EPA standards.
   d. Every famous rock group is fantastic in concert and cooperates with the press during interviews. If the greatness of their recent concert tour is any indication, "The Electric Lights" are destined to become one of the most famous rock groups of the decade. Their concerts were widely appreciated by every one of the nearly fifty thousand enthusiastic fans who came to see them, and each concert was followed by a press conference during which band members answered questions fully and cooperatively.
   e. The students are the ones who cause damage in the dining hall. Anyone who causes damage should have to pay for it; therefore, students should pay for damage in the dining hall.
2. First identify the following arguments as valid or invalid. Second, identify (where possible) the truth or falsity of the conclusions.

a. All fish have fins, and all sharks have fins. Therefore, all sharks are fish.

b. All bicycles have wheels, and all roller skates have wheels. Therefore, all roller skates are bicycles.

c. All birds are canines, and all dogs are birds. Therefore, all dogs are canines.

d. Every football team must have at least eleven players. The Anteaters have at least eleven players. Therefore, the Anteaters are a football team.

e. All students are lazy, and all teenagers are lazy. Therefore, all teenagers are students.

5e.3   Deductive Arguments in Ordinary Language

The syllogisms we have examined are stated very formally. Rarely in written or spoken arguments are things expressed so neatly. Instead, when you analyze an argument, you often must abstract its underlying structure from the prose in which it is expressed. And when you use an argument in writing, you need to know how to express it fluently. Here we will examine some ways in which formal syllogisms are translated into ordinary language, and vice-versa.

a. Signals of Distribution:

The signals we have been using to indicate whether or not a term is distributed include words like *all* and *no* with distributed terms, *some* and *a* with undistributed terms. Frequently, however, these words are omitted or other words are substituted. For example, it would be more common in ordinary conversation to say "Humans are mortal." The sense of the sentence tells us that "humans" means *all* humans, even though the word *all* is omitted. Similarly, the word *not* before a predicate has the same meaning as *no* before a subject: "No angels are mortal" might be restated "Angels are not mortal." The word *only* is often used as an implied negative: "Only humans are mortal" implies "Angels are not mortal." Also notice that negatives may be expressed in positive form, or vice versa. For instance, "Russia is ahead in the arms race" might imply "The U.S. is behind in the arms race." Arguments in ordinary language, then, can be translated into formal syllogistic language in order to test their validity.

b. Abbreviated Syllogisms:

The three propositions of a categorical syllogism are seldom all stated explicitly. More often than not, one of the three is only implied, and the reader must mentally supply it. Such syllogisms are *abbreviated*.

A syllogism with an implied major premise:

> George must be physically fit, because he runs every day.

The first clause of this sentence is the conclusion; the second is the minor premise. In order to have a middle term that will link George with the physically fit, we have to supply the implied major premise: People who run every day are physically fit. The syllogism would then look like this:

MAJOR PREMISE (implied):	People who run every day are physically fit.
MINOR PREMISE:	George runs every day.
CONCLUSION:	Therefore, George is physically fit.

Once we have supplied the major premise, we can determine the validity of the syllogism.

A syllogism with an implied minor premise:

> Freshmen have to take English, so Henry must be taking English.

The missing minor premise is that Henry is a freshman.

A syllogism with an implied conclusion:

> A student who is doing well in the course would not cheat, but Julia cheated on her math exam.

The missing conclusion is that Julia is not doing well in the course.

c. Extended Arguments:

Arguments in ordinary language will often be found linked together in a series of premises leading to a conclusion that in turn becomes a premise of the next syllogism, and so on. In order to determine the validity of such arguments, it is necessary to sort out the var-

5e

ious syllogisms. For example, I might argue that Professor Dormey should not be a college professor because he prefers research to teaching, and people who prefer research to teaching, because they do not make good teachers, should not be college professors. If we sort out this argument, we will find two syllogisms underlying it; the conclusion of the first becomes the major premise of the second:

SYLLOGISM 1

MAJOR PREMISE:	People who do not make good teachers should not be professors.
MINOR PREMISE:	People who prefer research to teaching do not make good teachers.
CONCLUSION:	People who prefer research to teaching should not be professors.

SYLLOGISM 2

MAJOR PREMISE:	People who prefer research to teaching should not be professors.
MINOR PREMISE:	Professor Dormey prefers research to teaching.
CONCLUSION:	Therefore, Professor Dormey should not be a professor.

When you write an argument, of course, you will not usually work it out in syllogistic form first, because the argument will usually develop in reverse: that is, most writers begin with their conclusions and then work backward to present the premises that will convince their readers. You will find that the syllogism is most helpful when you want to analyze the strength of your own arguments. Just as an outline of your essay is often most useful after you have written a draft, so a syllogism will allow you to check the validity of your argument.

d. Enthymemes:

While formal arguments often depend on the logic of syllogisms, much of the arguing we do is based on the *enthymeme*. A valid syllogism will lead to a *necessary* conclusion because it is based on provable premises; an enthymeme will lead to a *probable* conclusion because it is based on premises that may not be provable.

Circumstantial evidence used in a courtroom provides a good

example of an enthymeme. When the prosecuting attorney argues that the defendant is guilty because she has committed prior crimes, is known to lie, and was seen at the scene of the crime, his argument is based on an enthymeme rather than a categorical syllogism. Similarly, premises are not always absolutely true or false but may be generally or usually true. If a father tells his daughter, "Don't cross the street alone; you'll get hit by a car," he is using an implied premise that is *probably* but not necessarily true: that children who cross the street alone will get hit.

The enthymeme cannot convince anyone absolutely; because the premises are only probable, so is the conclusion. But the enthymeme is a powerful rhetorical tool to *persuade* an audience if not convince them absolutely.

Enthymemes are usually expressed in abbreviated form:

> *Most* people who run every day are physically fit; therefore, George is *probably* physically fit.
>
> *Most* freshmen have to take English, so Henry is *probably* taking English.
>
> *Usually* the people who cheat are not doing well in the course; consequently, Julia is *probably* not doing well in the course.

In evaluating an abbreviated enthymeme, it is a good idea to reconstruct the full form, because it is often the missing (implied) premise that is most open to debate. Consider the following enthymeme:

> Bev will do poorly on the exam because she didn't get enough sleep last night

If we reconstruct the syllogism, we see that the conclusion is "Bev will do poorly on the exam" and one of the premises is "She didn't get enough sleep last night." We know that one is the minor premise because the subject is the minor term (she/Bev). That means the missing major premise could be "Students who didn't get enough sleep last night will do poorly on the exam." Or it might be "Students who will do poorly on the exam didn't get enough sleep last night." If the writer intended the latter, we could argue that the enthymeme is not valid:

> Students who will do poorly on the exam didn't get enought sleep last night.

Bev didn't get enough sleep last night.

*Therefore, Bev will do poorly on the exam.

This syllogism displays the fallacy of the undistributed middle term, and therefore we cannot conclude that Bev will do poorly.

If we choose the other possible major premise, we will have a valid syllogism:

People who didn't get enough sleep last night will do poorly on the exam.

Bev didn't get enough sleep last night.

Therefore, Bev will do poorly on the exam.

But notice that while this is a *valid* argument, its conclusion is probable, not necessary, because the premises are not absolute. For one thing, *enough* and *poorly* are open to dispute (how much is enough and how bad is poor?). For another, while it is *generally* true that people who do not sleep enough do poorly, it is not *categorically* (in every case) true.

Enthymemes, especially in abbreviated form, are crucial for effective writing. Since most of our writing is about human beings and human affairs, subjects about which little is absolute, your most effective tool in deductive argument will be the enthymeme.

EXERCISES

1. For each of the following abbreviated enthymemes, supply the premise or conclusion that would make the argument valid and state whether the conclusion is *probably* true.

   a. The U.S. is bound to lose in a nuclear war because it has a smaller store of weapons than Russia.

   b. Like all runners, he's in excellent shape.

   c. Everybody who fails Professor Nervy's midterm fails the course, and I just failed the midterm.

   d. Thelma Brown is doing a good job as the new university president; just think about it: she's been in office for nearly a year and hasn't raised tuition.

   e. Of course he can figure out his income tax forms; he's an accountant.

2. Analyze the following arguments by extracting the categorical syllogisms or enthymemes that structure them. Put each step of the argu-

ment into standard categorical form, so that the conclusion of one syllogism becomes a premise of the next. For those that are abbreviated, supply the missing premises.

a. My unnerving conclusion is that students are sad because they are not needed. Somewhere between the nursery and the employment office, they become unwanted adults. No one has anything in particular against them. But no one knows what to do with them either. We already have too many people in the world of the 1970s, and there is no room for so many newly minted 18-year-olds. So we temporarily get them out of the way by sending them to college where in fact only a few belong.

—Caroline Bird, *The Case Against College*

b. I think there are many reasons for this flight away from facing death calmly. One of the most important facts is that dying nowadays is more gruesome in many ways, namely, more lonely, mechanical, and dehumanized; at times it is even difficult to determine technically when the time of death has occurred.

—Elizabeth Kübler-Ross, *On Death and Dying*

c. When religion was the topic of discussion, the morals of the people became more pure.   —Alexis de Tocqueville, *Democracy in American*

d. Dream is the personalized myth; myth the depersonalized dream.

—Joseph Campbell, *The Hero with a Thousand Faces*

e. Anatomy is not destiny, but it is not irrelevant either.

—Carl Sagan, *The Dragons of Eden*

5f Fallacies of Deductive Argument

Just as there may be pitfalls in inductive arguments, so there are sometimes fallacies in deductive arguments. If you want to persuade a critical audience, you should be sure the form of your argument is valid.

5f.1 The Undistributed Middle

The most common fallacy people make when arguing deductively is called the fallacy of the undistributed middle term. You may recall the example we used in **5b** about athletes:

MAJOR PREMISE: All athletes are people who don't smoke.
MINOR PREMISE: John is a person who doesn't smoke.
CONCLUSION: Therefore, John is an athlete.

The middle term, "people who don't smoke," is not distributed in either premise: neither premise makes an assertion about *all* people who don't smoke. Athletes don't smoke and John doesn't smoke, but John is not necessarily an athlete.

5f.2   The Ambiguous Middle (Four-Term Fallacy)

A valid categorical syllogism can have only three terms. If the middle term is ambiguous (that is, if it has more than one meaning), it must be considered two different terms, and the syllogism would thus have four terms. Without a middle term to join the major and minor premises, it is impossible to draw a valid conclusion. Good examples of this fallacy can be found in many newspaper editorials and letters-to-the-editor.

Suppose, for example, someone writes an editorial arguing that restaurants should provide special seating for nonsmokers. She states that restaurants can be dangerous to your health because many restaurants make you sit at a table next to smokers, and smoking can be dangerous to your health. There are really four terms in this argument (each term is in italic type):

MAJOR PREMISE:	*Smoking* can be *dangerous to your health.*
MINOR PREMISE:	*Many restaurants* cause you to *sit at a table next to smokers.*
CONCLUSION:	*Many restaurants* can be *dangerous to your health.*

What appears to be the middle term is really two terms: *smoking* and *sit[ting] at a table next to smokers.* While much research has shown that health dangers can come from being around smoke blown from other peoples' cigarettes, this argument merely confuses the two activities (smoking and sitting at a table next to smokers). Because there is no *single* middle term to connect the major and minor terms, the argument proves nothing.

5f.3   Circular Argument (Two-Term Fallacy)

Some categorical syllogisms are invalid because they do not really have three terms; two of the terms may appear to be different, but in fact refer to the same thing, resulting in an argument whose conclusion is merely a restatement of the premises. The fallacy in such arguments is not always easy to spot because the terms are couched in enough rhetoric to give the appearance of a valid argument. The following quotation contains a premise and conclusion that assert the same thing in different words:

> To allow every man unbounded freedom of speech must always be, on the whole, advantageous to the state; for it is highly conducive to the interests of the community that each individual should enjoy a liberty, perfectly unlimited, of expressing his sentiments.
> —Richard Whately, *Elements of Logic*, London, 1826

This argument really has only two terms. Put more simply, the first clause says, "Freedom of speech is advantageous to the state," and the second clause, "It is advantageous to the community [state] that individuals have liberty of expressing sentiments [freedom of speech]."

EXERCISES

Identify the fallacies in the following syllogisms; then rewrite each as a valid syllogism.

1. Most presidential candidates are verbose, and my uncle jabbers all the time, so I guess he's running for president.
2. Sally must be a mother because she bakes cookies and lots of mothers bake cookies.
3. Most A students work hard, and I work very hard, so I must be an A student.
4. Professional athletes are those who are paid to play. Many college athletes are paid to play; therefore they must be considered professionals.
5. The situation in Northern Ireland must be the result of a slow economy, because internal disagreements are often the result of a slow economy and the situation in Northern Ireland is an internal disagreement.

5g Special Appeals and Doublespeak

In addition to formal argument, there is a whole range of techniques used for persuasion that include appeals to various emotions and values to which people are often vulnerable. It is undeniable that they are often effective in political rhetoric, advertisements, and other kinds of writing. But if you want to persuade a critical audience, you should rely on logic, not on easily refutable appeals.

5g.1   Appeal to Authority

In all kinds of research, authorities are quoted and paraphrased to give weight to opinions. In commercial advertising, the technique is often abused by having actors portray doctors, dentists, and scientists who attest to the value of certain products. Sometimes the testimony of a particular person is used to manipulate our feelings: the testimony of a rock star might be relevant if someone is trying to sell sound equipment, but a rock star is no more qualified to comment on the worth of one cigarette brand than is any other citizen.

5g.2   Appeal to Ignorance

The appeal to ignorance occurs when one argues that something is true because it has not been proved false, or false because it has not been proved true. Some people argue fallaciously, for example, that UFOs must exist because no one has proved they do not exist. Others argue that God must not exist because no one has ever proved that God does exist. Both arguments are faulty because they depend on assertions about the unknown.

5g.3   Appeal to Force

When other appeals fail, the appeal to force is often very convincing. A lobbyist in Congress may threaten his representative with a loss of votes from his constituency if she does not vote as the lobbyist wants; a kidnapper may write a powerful letter persuading parents to turn over money if they do not want the child to be killed; or a terrorist may persuade an entire government to take a certain action by threatening reprisals against hostages.

5g.4   Appeal to the People

Many writers and speakers attempt to win popular support by appealing to the emotions associated with belonging to a particular group. Hitler, for example, convinced many Germans that Jews were the source of Germany's economic problems and that as a non-Christian and non-Aryan people they were a threat to German culture.

In a less lofty way, advertisers appeal to the people. In magazine ads, for instance, we see highly sophisticated, glamorous people smoking the right cigarette, driving the right car, or drinking the right scotch. Ad writers encourage us to jump on the bandwagon to join the "Pepsi generation," to wear alligators on our shirts and signatures on our jeans. Book advertisers use bestseller lists to promote new books, and record companies use the Top 40. While these popular advertising appeals seem far removed from Hitler, they all appeal to our desire to protect ourselves from people we think are hostile and associate ourselves with the emotions and actions that our peers approve.

5g.5 Appeal to Pity
The appeal to pity, like the appeal to the people, is often used in place of a reasoned argument. Consider, for instance, the student who argues that his professor cannot fail him in freshman English because he will flunk out of school if he gets another F. The student hopes to persuade the professor by making her feel sorry for him, yet the appeal to pity in this case is fallacious because the student has presumably earned this grade and the others himself and has apparently gotten himself in trouble by getting so many other low grades.

Not all appeals to pity are fallacious, however; some are quite powerful and can be used effectively to support a reasoned argument. (See, for example, Shylock's appeal in Shakespeare's *The Merchant of Venice*, in exercise 2 below.)

Like all powerful persuasion, this passage uses many other appeals as well—the appeal to the people ("If we are like you in the rest, we will resemble you in that"); the appeal to force ("The villainy you teach me I will execute"); and a powerful argument from analogy ("fed with the same food, hurt with the same weapons").

5g.6 Personal Attacks
Quite often, in persuasive writing, the emphasis is switched from the issue to an attack on the person associated with that issue. A

classic example is Thomas Paine's attack on the king of England prior to the American Revolution. (See exercise 4 below.)

Personal attacks often take the "you should talk" form. A preacher's argument against alcohol abuse might be discredited by someone who knows him to be a social drinker, even though his drinking does not make his argument any less valid. In contrast, a person's arguments may be discredited through accusations of self-interest. A biology professor arguing for higher salaries for women might be ignored by her male colleagues on the grounds that "naturally you'd argue for that—you're a woman," even though her interest in the issue does not necessarily keep her from arguing rationally and objectively.

5g.7   Begging the Question

Begging the question is to assume, under the guise of slightly different words, what it is you want to prove. It is similar to a circular argument. But while circular argument is a formal fallacy, begging the question is often a deliberate attempt to avoid addressing an argument. Many highly charged emotional issues end in question-begging ploys because the writer or speaker knows that if the audience reacts readily at an emotional level, it will respond to what sounds like a genuine argument without ever analyzing it. A writer may argue, for example, that abortion is murder because it is taking someone's life without his or her consent. "Taking someone's life without his or her consent" is a definition of "murder," so the writer is really arguing that abortion is murder because it is murder.

5g.8   Red Herring

A red herring is any issue brought in to sidetrack an argument, to stop people from thinking about the real issues and get them instead to concentrate on something else. (The term comes from the old belief that the strong scent of smoked herring could be used to divert the track of a hunting dog.) Someone arguing against gun control legislation, for example, may throw in a red herring by asserting that more people are killed by automobiles than by guns—an assertion that has nothing to do with whether some control should be exercised over the purchase of handguns.

5g.9   Either-Or Thinking

Either-or thinking is a fallacy of oversimplification, of assuming there are only two alternatives when in fact there may be many. An argument like "Either we raise property taxes or we reduce the number of teachers in our schools" is such an oversimplification. Other alternatives are possible: maybe we can get federal aid, introduce a sales tax or local income tax, or fire some administrators. Rarely is anything so simple as to be easily divisible into only two alternatives.

5g.10   Complex Question

A common persuasive technique, especially in legal situations, is to ask a person a complex or "loaded" question, so that no matter how she answers, she incriminates herself. A question like "How long have you been smoking marijuana?" is calculated to trick someone into admitting she has indeed been smoking marijuana. The critical person will realize that there are two questions in one and will respond to them one at a time: "Have you been smoking marijuana?" and "If so, for how long?"

5g.11   False Analogy

Because analogies are one of the most common ways of thinking, they are also one of the most abused. A student who had failed freshman English wrote a letter to his college newspaper complaining that he should get his money back because the professor failed to teach him how to write. The student reasoned that if you called in a plumber to fix your pipes and he failed to do his job, you would not have to pay for his services. This analogy has some persuasive value, but it breaks down at the crucial point. A pipe is an inanimate piece of metal, and if it does not get fixed, it is obviously not the pipe's fault; the plumber is the only one who can be held accountable. On the other hand, a student has a brain, will, emotions, and values, all of which have some bearing on how well he does in a college class. So he can be held accountable as well as the teacher.

5g.12 Doublespeak and the Connotative Value of Words

Many writers, especially ad writers, politicians, and journalists, commonly use *euphemisms*—words with pleasant associations that substitute for words that seem too direct and unpleasant: *sanitary engineer* for *garbage collector*, *pass away* for *die*, *powder room* for *toilet* (see **20b.3**). Similarly, writers and speakers often depend on what S. I. Hayakawa has called *snarl words* (words with strongly negative connotations) and *purr words* (words with strongly positive connotations). In the example from Thomas Paine in exercise 4 below, certain snarl words carry strong negative judgments that reinforce the personal attack in that paragraph—words like *wickedly*, *trampled*, *insolence*, *cruelty*, and *hatred*. Advertisements in magazines, in newspapers, and on radio and television are full of purr words: an ad for scotch, for example, says it is "a rare gift for someone very special"; a cigarette brand gives you "smoother, milder, more satisfying taste." Such words have built-in judgments, whether positive or negative. When writers use euphemisms, snarl words, and purr words to deceive, to make it appear that they are saying the opposite of what they really are saying, we say they are using *doublespeak*.

Every time you use words with intent to deceive or confuse, you run the risk not only of discrediting the argument and alienating critical readers, but also of muddying your own sense of critical judgment.

EXERCISES

Identify the special appeals, fallacies, and doublespeak in each of the following. Do the appeals used seem to enhance the persuasiveness of the piece or detract from it? How do the special appeals, argumentative structure, and highly connotative words reinforce each other to produce the desired effect?

1. But though I was initially disappointed at being categorized as an extremist, as I continued to think about the matter I gradually gained a measure of satisfaction from the label. Was not Jesus an extremist for love: "Love your enemies, bless them that curse you, do good to them that hate you, and pray for them which despitefully use you, and persecute you." Was not Amos an extremist for justice: "Let justice roll down like waters and righteousness like an everflowing stream."

Was not Paul an extremist for the Christian gospel: "I bear in my body the marks of the Lord Jesus." Was not Martin Luther an extremist: "Here I stand: I cannot do otherwise, so help me God." And John Bunyan: "I will stay in jail to the end of my days before I make a butchery of my conscience."

—Martin Luther King, "Letter from Birmingham Jail"

2. He hath disgraced me, and hindered me half a million, laughed at my losses, mocked at my gains, scorned my nation, thwarted my bargains, cooled my friends, heated mine enemies; and what's his reason? I am a Jew. Hath not a Jew eyes? Hath not a Jew hands, organs, dimensions, senses, affections, passions: fed with the same food, hurt with the same weapons, subject to the same diseases, healed by the same means, warmed and cooled by the same winter and summer, as a Christian is? If you prick us, do we not bleed? If you tickle us, do we not laugh? If you poison us, do we not die? And if you wrong us, shall we not revenge? If we are like you in the rest, we will resemble you in that. If a Jew wrong a Christian, what is his humility? Revenge. If a Christian wrong a Jew, what should his sufferance be by Christian example: Why, revenge. The villainy you teach me I will execute, and it shall go bad but I will better the instruction.

—Shakespeare, *The Merchant of Venice*, Act III, scene i, lines 58-78

3. That [unilateral disarmament] is a barren dream, a mythical vision. It flies against all the evidence of the Soviets' unslackened determination, backed by a military buildup of gargantuan dimensions, to exploit every opportunity to extend their military and political influence around the world, wherever and whenever they can. The Soviets' opportunism can be likened to that of a hotel burglar who skulks along the corridors at night, checking doorknobs, ready to enter any room he finds unlocked. The West must keep its doors locked.

—United Technologies ad

4. However, it matters very little now what the King of England either says or does; he hath wickedly broken through every moral and human obligation, trampled nature and conscience beneath his feet, and by a steady and constitutional spirit of insolence and cruelty procured for himself an universal hatred. —Thomas Paine, *Common Sense*

5. In our time, political speech and writing are largely the defense of the indefensible. . . . Thus political language has to consist largely of euphemism, question-begging and sheer cloudy vagueness. Defenseless villages are bombarded from the air, the inhabitants driven out into the countryside, the cattle machine-gunned, the huts set on fire with incendiary bullets; this is called pacification. Millions of peasants are robbed of their farms and sent trudging along the roads with no

5g

more than they can carry; this is called transfer of population or rec-
tification of frontiers. People are imprisoned for years without trial, or
shot in the back of the neck or sent to die of scurvy in Arctic lumber
camps; this is called elimination of unreliable elements.
—George Orwell, "Politics and the English Language"

6

PLANNING AND ARRANGING

6a Ordering Your Writing

It is not always easy to decide on the best order for presenting your main ideas and the supporting details. While there are no absolute rules to follow, there are some common patterns of arrangement that writers use. You must adapt them to your own purposes and the needs of your audience: the dominant method of a piece will often suggest an overall order for your essay, while the supporting methods will often affect the organization of a particular section or paragraph.

6a.1 Spatial Order

Description is usually ordered *spatially* when it is physical. When describing a scene, it is wise to move the way you want your reader to see the scene—from left to right, for instance, or from background to foreground, or in a clockwise movement. In the following example, the author lets the reader see the flight of the butterfly exactly as her own eye followed it:

> I walked out and saw a monarch do a wonderful thing: it climbed a hill without twitching a muscle. I was standing at the bridge over Tinker Creek, at the southern foot of a very steep hill. The monarch beat its way beside me over the bridge at eye level, and then, flailing its wings exhaustedly, ascended straight up in the air. It rose vertically to the enormous height of a bankside sycamore's crown. Then,

fixing its wings at a precise angle, it glided *up* the steep road, losing altitude extremely slowly, climbing by checking its fall, until it came to rest at a puddle in front of the house at the top of the hill.

—Annie Dillard, *Pilgrim at Tinker Creek*

6a.2 Chronological Order

Narration is usually ordered according to some time sequence, as is process analysis—first this happens, then this, then this, and so on: recall Fitzgerald's "Letter to Scottie" in **4b** and Bubel's "How to Make a Terrarium" in **4c**. Of course, it is always possible to jump *in medias res* ("into the middle of things") and use a flash-back technique or to use a series of shifts from past to present to future and back to past—contemporary novels and films often do this effectively. Nevertheless, the reader is left with a domi-nant impression of time. In the following example, the author narrates one phase of the history of medicine:

> Gradually, over the succeeding decades [at the end of the nine-teenth century], the traditional therapeutic ritual of medicine was given up, and what came to be called the "art of medicine" emerged to take its place. In retrospect, this art was really the beginning of the science of medicine. It was based on meticulous, objective, even cool observations of sick people. From this endeavor we learned the details of the natural history of illness, so that, for example, it came to be understood that typhoid and typhus were really two entirely separate, unrelated disorders, with quite different causes. Accurate diagnosis became the central purpose and justification for medicine, and as the methods for diagnosis improved, accurate prognosis also became possible, so that patients and their families could be told not only the name of the illness but also, with some reliability, how it was most likely to turn out. By the time this century had begun, these were becoming generally accepted as the principal responsibil-ities of the physician. —Lewis Thomas, "Medical Lessons from History"

6a.3 Order of Specificity

In contrast to a physical description, a description of something abstract, such as a person's character, often follows an order of increasing specificity, like the description of Wagner in 4a. Many other methods also follow a sequence of general-to-specific or specific-to-general or a combination of both. Cause-effect analy-sis, for example, might begin with a general cause and move to several specific effects. Definition almost always follows a general-to-specific pattern: the definition, which is general because it encompasses all members of the class, is usually followed by specific examples, as in the excerpt from *The Joy of Cooking* in **4d**.

When examples are the dominant method, they may either follow a general statement in a *deductive* or general-to-specific order, as in "That Day at Hiroshima" (**4h**); or they may come first, following an *inductive* or specific-to-general pattern, with the general statement they are meant to illustrate coming last, as in the following example:

> Re-vision—the act of looking back, of seeing with fresh eyes, of entering an old text from a new critical direction—is for us more than a chapter in cultural history: it is an act of survival. Until we can understand the assumptions in which we are drenched we cannot know ourselves. And this drive to self-knowledge, for woman, is more than a search for identity: it is part of her refusal of the destructiveness of male-dominated society. A radical critique of literature, feminist in its impulse, would take the work first of all as a clue to how we live, how we have been living, how we have been led to imagine ourselves, how our language has trapped as well as liberated us; and how we can begin to see—and therefore live—afresh. A change in the concept of sexual identity is essential if we are not going to see the old political order reassert itself in every new revolution. We need to know the writing of the past, and know it differently than we have ever known it; not to pass on a tradition but to break its hold over us.   —Adrienne Rich, "When We Dead Awaken"

6a.4   Alternating Order

When you are discussing two things, people, events, or ideas in order to compare, contrast, or draw an analogy, it will be natural to use an alternating order, going back and forth from one person to the other, as the student does in "Two Viewpoints" (**3e**); or from one time to another, as Fitzgerald does in "Letter to Scottie" (**4b**).

Sometimes writers will organize the two contrasting elements so that they say everything about one first, and then everything about the other; but more often they will alternate frequently back and forth from one to the other. The first, a "block comparison," works best for subjects that are less complex or more familiar. The second, the "point-by-point comparison," works

6a

best for subjects that are complex or unfamiliar to the reader. Whichever form you choose to follow, it is important to keep the details of the two elements you're comparing parallel with each other. In "Two Viewpoints" (3e), for instance, each time the author presents a contrast she talks first about *Modern Times* and second about *Waiting for Godot*. In the excerpt from *America Revised* (4e), the author discusses American society first, then the political system, in both the section on textbooks of the '50s and in the section on new textbooks. The following example illustrates a block comparison:

> Even so, southern whites in the antebellum period never escaped the haunting fear that somewhere, maybe even in their own slave quarters, another Nat Turner was plotting to rise up and slit their throats. They never forgot him. His name became for them a symbol of terror and violent retribution.
>
> But for antebellum blacks—and for their descendants—the name of Nat Turner took on a profoundly different connotation. He became a legendary black hero who broke his chains and murdered white people because slavery had murdered Negroes. Turner, said an elderly black man in Southampton County only a few years ago, was "God's man. He was a man for war, and for legal rights, and for freedom."
>
> —Stephen B. Oates, "Children of Darkness"

6a.5 Order of Climax

We tend to think of narrative writing when we think of climactic order, but much other writing is also organized to save the most emphatic, interesting, or clinching point for the end. This method works particularly well with division and supporting examples. In "Two Viewpoints" (3e), the author saves the action/inaction contrast for last because it is the central difference; in "How We Listen to Music" (4g), the most important point ("the sheerly musical plane") is saved for last. Climactic order also works well in description, as in the Wagner excerpt (4a), where the most telling detail about Wagner is saved for the end to reinforce the dominant impression of his conceit. The following paragraph also illustrates the use of climactic order:

> Most city architectural designers and planners are men. Curiously, they design and plan to exclude men as part of normal, daytime life wherever people live. In planning residential life, they aim at filling the presumed daily needs of impossibly vacuous house-

wives and preschool tots. They plan, in short, strictly for matriarchal societies. —Jane Jacobs, *The Death and Life of Great American Cities*

6a.6   Order of Familiarity

Quite often it is helpful to arrange a series of points according to how familiar they are to the reader. Analogy, for example, often discusses the more familiar, concrete subject first and then moves to the less familiar subject which the analogy is meant to explain. If the analogy is broken up into an alternating pattern, each part within the alternate sections may follow a familiar-to-unfamiliar order. In the excerpt from Freud (**4f**), after stating the analogy in the first sentence, he goes on to explain the familiar (the horse and rider) first, and then to relate the unfamiliar (the id and ego) to it. The following example also illustrates the order of familiarity:

> In this eager, boyish mood, sitting one day in the garden of his widowed mother, he saw an apple fall. . . . What struck the young Newton at the sight was not the thought that the apple must be drawn to the earth by gravity; that conception was older than Newton. What struck him was the conjecture that the same force of gravity, which reaches to the top of the tree, might go on reaching out beyond the earth and its air, endlessly into space. Gravity might reach the moon: this was Newton's new thought; and it might be gravity which holds the moon in her orbit.
>
> —Jacob Bronowski, "The Nature of Scientific Reasoning"

6a.7   General Guidelines for Order

Most methods of writing will follow one or a combination of these six kinds of ordering. Just as methods operate at various levels in a discourse, so does order. For instance, an essay that follows an alternating pattern for its overall structure may have individual sections or paragraphs that follow a chronological or spatial order. A sense of order is something that comes with experience, but here are some guidelines that almost all professional writers follow:

1. Let your thesis suggest an overall order for the whole essay. (Review the sample thesis statements in **3a**.)

2. Consider what order is appropriate for the particular supporting methods as well as dominant methods in your writing. A

chronological order, for example, is more appropriate for narration or process analysis than for definition or examples.

3. Consider the medium in which you are writing; in some kinds of writing (a technical report for instance) you are required to follow a predetermined order.

4. Be aware of your audience and purpose: ask what your readers need to know and when they need to know it. For example,

   • if you want to convince someone of an idea, you may want to use the order of climax, saving your best and strongest argument for the end where your readers will remember it best;

   • if you want to leave someone with a particular impression (whether visual, emotional, or intellectual), consider saving your most telling details for the end, where they will be most memorable;

   • if you want to convey an accurate mental picture of how a scene looks, describe it in some spatial order (left to right, up to down, inside to outside, etc.), so that your readers can reproduce in their minds the picture you are painting for them;

   • if your audience is unfamiliar with the subject, begin with the easiest concepts.

EXERCISES

1. Suppose that you are en route to a friend's apartment when you hear sirens and then, after turning a corner, see an ambulance and firetruck. As you draw closer you see a crowd of people, firefighters and police among them; finally you edge into the circle of bystanders for a closer look. Later you narrate this event to friends. List the number of possibilities for ordering this information for your listeners. Which method would be most informal in its effect? most formal? Which would have the strongest impact on your listeners?

2. The following paragraphs open an essay by Curtis K. Stadtfield. Rewrite them by ordering the information in the following ways, but be careful to maintain the author's general ideas:

   a. specific-to-general (order of specificity)
   b. order of climax

   When you are finished, decide which of the three versions would be most effective for (a) alerting the general public to the danger of toxic chemicals, (b) scaring the general public about the danger of toxic chemicals, (c) informing people in the least biased manner about what happened in Michigan in 1973. The version you prefer will ultimately depend on your purpose and your own relationship to the subject matter.

If Michigan and the Middle West have escaped a disaster of the kind that killed or crippled thousands of people in the Minamata Bay area of Japan, it is no comfort to know that the escape resulted from dumb blind luck. For the fact is that a tremendously toxic chemical was spilled into the Michigan region's food system in 1973. The chemical then spread like a plague through the state's dairy, beef, and swine herds, the poultry flocks, and from there into the groceries and supermarkets. Thousands of cattle and hogs and millions of chickens were killed by the poison, whose toxic quality was known to chemists before the spill; indeed, one company had decided against using it because of what it did to laboratory rats.

The only reason that people, as well as farm animals, have not died from the spill is that humans do not react to the chemical in the same dramatic way that most mammals do. No one knows why, because no one knows exactly why rats, mice, cats, cattle, hogs, and even chickens get sick and die or become sterile after eating it. Yet the long-range effects on humans remain in doubt, so no one can rest easy. Doctors will be watching for signs of sterility, damage to the liver or bone marrow, afflictions of the nervous system, or genetic disturbances.

—Curtis K. Stadtfield, "Cheap Chemicals and Dumb Luck"

6b Beginnings and Endings

Our sense of order demands that we know a writer has begun an essay. A title, of course, is one signal; another is some indication in the first few words that the writer is setting forth the subject or beginning a story. This need for a clear mark of beginning is natural: if you accidentally open a magazine to the middle of an article, you will usually know immediately that you have missed something and will flip back to find the beginning.

We also have a need for *closure*, a sense of finality or completeness. If a writer stops too abruptly, we are left with a feeling of incompleteness, like hearing an unresolved chord at the end of a piece of music.

It is easy, however, to take our human need for order and harden it into some sterile rule that says one must always begin or end in a certain way. An old adage states that you should do three

6b

things when you write an essay: tell your readers what you are going to tell them; tell them; and tell them what you have told them. This formula assumes that the purpose of an introduction is always to declare your intention in the essay, that the purpose of a conclusion is to repeat or summarize what you have done. In a textbook or scholarly article, that may be appropriate to help your reader absorb a great deal of complex material. But in a short essay, a long introduction and a summary conclusion are not only unnecessary; they may also be boring and weaken the effect of your writing.

How, then, do you begin and end a piece of writing? Some kinds of writing, like letters, memos, and technical reports, have a set form that dictates how you should begin and end. When you are writing an essay, there is no formula. Instead, you need to consider your audience and purpose. We can, however, make a few generalizations about the purpose of titles, openings, and closings:

Titles

- usually consist of a brief informative or descriptive phrase (unlike headlines, they do not usually make a statement);
- get the readers' interest and persuade them to read;
- make the readers ponder while reading the essay or article.

Openings

- may be one or more paragraphs, or merely a sentence or two (not all beginnings are formal introductions);
- catch the readers' interest enough to establish momentum and keep them reading;
- usually introduce the subject of an essay and set forth the purpose and thesis (if there is an explicit thesis);
- sometimes predict the structure of an essay, especially when it has an explicit thesis sentence.

Closings

- may be a sentence or two, or a paragraph or more (not all closings draw formal conclusions, and few offer summaries);
- may present the conclusion of an argument or investigation;
- give readers a sense of closure;

• leave readers with something to ponder, often making a rec-ommendation or projecting the subject of the writing into the future or into a larger context.

Following are two examples of the ways in which writers use these three elements to further their purpose in writing. While there are no easy formulas for beginning and ending an essay, these examples give an idea of possibilities. In each of them, the title, opening, and closing are clearly related—picking up the same theme, perhaps with a variation in language, perhaps widening it out to broaden its implications or narrowing it to focus on the reader. The openings establish some kind of connection between the author and reader, and the endings leave the reader with something to think about or something to do.

THE SOCIAL SET

I suppose there are still some intellectuals who denounce tele-vision as the boob tube or idiot box. Perhaps some blinkered critics still believe in "audience flow theory"—that is, viewers sit video-tranquilized in front of the television, tuned to one channel through the evening.

* * *

Television can be a national tongue. At its best, television can provide a common basis for experience, maybe a few laughs, some information and insight, perhaps the chance to engage one's intelli-gence and imagination. In these days of runaway prices, inflated mediocrities, and deflated hopes in our public lives, that's not a bad record. Television has a standing invitation to come to my place.

—Edwin Diamond

The title of this essay is intriguing, because it is ambiguous. Not until after reading the opening paragraph can the reader know that "set" refers to television. The combination of the title (tele-vision as a *social* instrument) and the opening paragraph suggests that Diamond's attitude toward television is positive. When he says, "I suppose there are still . . ." and "Perhaps some blink-ered critics . . . ," we know that he does not agree with those who have negative attitudes toward television. The introduction encourages further reading, if only to discover why Diamond dis-agrees with the "blinkered critics."

6b

The conclusion reinforces Diamond's thesis—that television, far from being damaging, can be a national asset. By calling it a "national tongue," he reinforces the suggestion of the title—that television can serve to bring us together as families, as communities, as a nation.

HOW SHOULD ONE READ A BOOK?

In the first place, I want to emphasize the note of interrogation at the end of my title. Even if I could answer the question for myself, the answer would apply only to me and not to you. The only advice, indeed, that one person can give another about reading is to take no advice, to follow your own instincts, to use your reason, to come to your own conclusions. If this is agreed between us, then I feel at liberty to put forward a few ideas and suggestions because you will not allow them to fetter that independence which is the most important quality that a reader can possess.

*   *   *

. . . I have sometimes dreamt, at least, that when the Day of Judgement dawns and the great conquerors and lawyers and statesmen come to receive their rewards—their crowns, their laurels, their names carved indelibly upon imperishable marble—the Almighty will turn to Peter and will say, not without a certain envy when He sees us coming with our books under our arms, "Look, these need no reward. We have nothing to give them here. They have loved reading."

—Virginia Woolf

Books on writing often tell students that an introduction should be independent and self-contained and should not make reference to the title. In practice, however, professional writers occasionally use the technique Woolf employs here, integrating her title into the essay by making her first sentence refer to it.

Woolf's introduction poses a problem for which the essay will suggest a solution—in this case, the problem of how one reads a book well. This introduction also sets her tone (her attitude toward the reader and subject—here a tone of humility) and establishes a relationship between author and reader.

The ending of Woolf's essay projects into the future, in order to give her subject added significance. Her reference to Peter appearing before the Almighty gives a sense of closure to the essay, since the Almighty, as it were, has the last word. Clearly the reader is left with the feeling that reading books, and being a good reader according to Woolf's definition, is a divine occupation.

EXERCISES

1. Following are the titles, openings, and closings of several student essays. What can you infer about the body of each essay—its method of development, its purpose, and its audience? What function does each of the introductions serve? the conclusions? How are titles, openings, and closings appropriately related to each other? How might they be improved? Write a paragraph on each, or discuss them in class.

a.   THE GOOD OLD DAYS

Many of today's discontented repeatedly yearn for the "good old days." What is so good about the old days? Granted, many hardships and dangers exist in modern life, but no more than existed in the past. Nearly every contemporary peril has a counterpart in "days gone by." Actually, one era is not safer or better to live in than another. The hazards of modern life and those of the American frontier amply evidence this.

*   *   *

These are only a few of the many parallels that can be drawn between the hazards of today and those of yesterday. As can be seen, neither seems any more dreadful than the other, yet some die-hards will continue to dream of the security of the past. And just think, tomorrow today will be one of those good old days.   —Michael Zuravel

b.   MY NEW LIFE

The sun is just beginning to crawl out of the eastern horizon. The air smells clean and fresh as the wind blows through the curtains of my open window. While nature is waking, I lie barely aware of it all under the warm blankets of my bed, still dreaming. Everything is peaceful as I begin to drift back into consciousness. I expect my mother in shortly to make sure that I am awake. Buzz! Ring! Two alarm clocks go off. I struggle to shake myself awake, reach over, and shut off my roommate's clock. I then crawl out of my covers and turn my own off. Another day has dawned in the dorm of my new university.

*   *   *

Life at home was a lot easier and simpler. Everything was done for me, and I took it all for granted. Now that I am away at college,

6b

everything has changed. All of the burden of my actions is on my shoulders. It was hard at first, but I feel better inside knowing that I can handle the responsibilities college life has to offer.

—Debbie McKenna

c. A MATTER OF CULTURE: MEALS, ITALIAN STYLE

It was just after six in the morning, and outside my window I would hear the sounds of the city of Palermo starting a new day. The peddlers had already begun hawking their wares up and down the narrow, winding Sicilian streets.

"Frutta! Frutta fresca!"

"Pane!" Their drawling voices echoed throughout the city, not just this day but every morning, because Italians place great importance on fresh fruits and bread.

I rolled over drowsily, confident that somewhere in the apartment my early-rising aunt and uncle would be preparing for breakfast. Giovanni, I was sure, was already making his way down to purchase bread.

*   *   *

In Italy, food and meals become a part of good manners as they do in the United States. If we didn't finish all the food on our plates, Raimonda would certainly look hurt. However, once the plate is clean, danger of insulting the hostess is still present: look away and then back again, and it will more than likely have been refilled. I finally noticed that the key word was "Troppo! Troppo!" ("Too much!") My aunt always seemed to accept this with a smile; so it wasn't that I didn't like her cooking—I was simply full! Of course, at home I never worried about finishing all the food on my plate; it was always, "If you don't want it, don't eat it." In Italy, however, food is considered part of health; therefore, if you don't eat, you're either sick or don't like the hostess' cooking. Like the *pane* peddlers hawking their goods in the early morning, fresh food and bountiful meals are an important part of each day in Italy.

—Concetta Maida

2. Following are the opening and closing of an essay by Max Beerbohm. Write the middle section of the essay, speculating on what crime it might have been that Beerbohm committed. Be sure that what you write is consistent with the expectations set up by the opening and with the conclusions drawn in the closing.

THE CRIME

On a bleak wet stormy afternoon at the outset of last year's Spring, I was in a cottage, all alone, and knowing that I must be all alone till evening. It was a remote cottage, in a remote county, and had been "let furnished" by its owner. My spirits are easily affected by weather, and I hate solitude. And I dislike to be master of things that are not mine.

*   *   *

. . . I blamed only myself. I had done wrong. The small room became very cold. Whose fault was that but my own? I had done wrong hastily, but had done it and been glad of it. I had not remembered the words a king wrote long ago, that the lamp of the wicked shall be put out, and that the way of transgressors is hard.

—Max Beerbohm

6c   Levels of Abstraction

One problem writers sometimes encounter when organizing essays is keeping parallel ideas parallel in structure. Every piece of writing has various levels of *abstraction*, which are related to each other by *coordination* (on the same level of abstraction) or *subordination* (on a different level). Most of the time, the relationship between coordination and subordination happens "naturally," in the process of planning and arranging. But sometimes understanding these concepts is necessary to arrange your material most effectively.

The word *abstract*, from a Latin word meaning "removed from," generally refers to something removed from concrete reality. Thus the opposite of an abstraction is something very *concrete*, that is, something that can be perceived with the senses (sight, hearing, touch, taste, smell). An individual is quite concrete: Jane Smith is twenty years old, lives at 170 Maple Street in Midtown, Ohio, is 5'9" tall, weighs 130 pounds, has short, curly brown hair, green eyes, a narrow forehead, and straight thick eyebrows. That description of Jane Smith is visually very concrete and is at the lowest level of abstraction (the most concrete) we can perceive, unless we were to see Jane Smith in person (or unless we were to consider her submicroscopically, in terms of the molecules and atoms that make up her person).

As we move up the ladder of abstraction, we *remove* from the description the details that describe Jane Smith herself and concentrate on the characteristics that she shares with other people.

6c

For example, suppose Jane Smith is a junior psychology student at Ohio State University. By putting her in a general class (of junior women psychology majors at o.s.u.), we abstract only those characteristics that apply to everyone in that class. Moving up the ladder, we can say Jane Smith is a woman psychology student at o.s.u. That puts her in a still larger class and omits the distinguishing characteristic that she is a junior. We can move up the ladder in this manner, each time abstracting only those characteristics that belong to the next highest class:

```
      ↗ human beings
      /  students
     /   university students
    /   o.s.u. students
   /   women o.s.u. students
  /   women o.s.u. psychology students
 /  junior women o.s.u. psychology students
/ Jane Smith
```

As our description becomes more *abstract*, it also becomes more *general*; that is, we think of Jane Smith in larger and larger classes. If we move *down* the ladder, the description becomes not only more *concrete*, but also more *specific*;† that is, we think of Jane Smith in smaller and smaller classes, until finally she is in a class by herself.

Now let us describe Jane Smith in an entirely different way, one that is parallel to the description we have just used but which emphasizes a different, and independent, set of characteristics. Suppose she is a marathon runner, enters the Boston Marathon, and sets a new record for twenty-year-old women. If we abstract at each level only those qualities that pertain to her participation in the Boston Marathon, the ladder would look like this:

---

†But not always. It is possible, for instance, that something can be specific without being concrete. For example, *parental love* is more specific than *love* in general, but it is not concrete because we cannot perceive it with the five senses, although we can perceive *evidence* of it.

/ human beings
/ athletes
/ runners
/ marathon runners
/ participants in Boston Marathon
/ participants in Boston Marathon who set records
/ Jane Smith

Suppose Jane Smith is also an avid reader of Dorothy Sayers' murder mysteries. We might abstract her thus:

/ human beings
/ readers
/ readers of mysteries
/ readers of murder mysteries
/ readers of Dorothy Sayers' murder mysteries
/ Jane Smith

Now suppose you were writing a descriptive essay on Jane Smith. You might want to talk about her as a student, an athlete, and a reader. In each case, you would move down the abstraction ladder to offer specific and concrete details about each of those three categories. The dominant impression you want to convey might be that she is an interesting and well-rounded person. You have three *subordinate ideas* or supporting points: she is a student, an athlete, and a reader. These three ideas are all *coordinate* because they are on roughly the same level of abstraction; but they are subordinate to the main point because they are on a different (more specific) level of abstraction. As we move down the abstraction ladder, therefore, we see that each step is subordinate to the one above it and we gather more supporting details, all of which are subordinate to the main idea. Jane's reading of Dorothy Sayers' murder mysteries, the record she set in the Boston Marathon, and her being a junior psychology student at O.S.U. are all on the same level of abstraction and are coordinate to one another but subordinate to the points above them.

To illustrate this relationship of subordination and coordination, let us put the numeral (1) in front of the thesis to indicate it is the first or main idea:

6c

(1) Jane Smith is one of the most interesting and well-rounded women I know.

In front of each of the three ways in which she is well rounded, we will put the numeral (2), to indicate they are all on the second level of abstraction:

(1) Jane Smith is one of the most interesting and well-rounded women I know.
  (2) She is a student,
  (2) an athlete,
  (2) and a reader.

As we develop each of these three characteristics in more detail, we add subordinate points at the next lower level of abstraction, which are designated with the number (3):

(1) Jane Smith is one of the most interesting and well-rounded women I know, because
  (2) She is a student.
    (3) She is majoring in psychology at o.s.u.
    (3) She is planning to attend law school.
  (2) She is an athlete.
    (3) She has set a record in the Boston Marathon.
    (3) She has set records in three other major races.
  (2) She is a reader.
    (3) Among her favorite books are the murder mysteries of Dorothy Sayers.
    (3) Also among her favorites are the plays of Shakespeare.

This structure of coordination and subordination is common to all kinds of writing, whether sentences (in which phrases, clauses, and words may be either coordinate or subordinate to one another; see **18a** and **18b.1**), paragraphs (in which some sentences will be coordinate with one another and subordinate to others; see **11b.3**), or essays and longer pieces of writing (in which some paragraphs or sections will be coordinate with each other and some subordinate to others; see **6d**).

EXERCISES

1. Writers who tend to get stuck at a very general level, high up on the abstraction ladder, often get the advice to "be more concrete and more

specific," in other words, to go *down* the abstraction ladder. It is often difficult, however, to become more concrete when you *start* on an abstract level, unless you have done one of the discovery procedures and generated lots of concrete details that you can go back to. Instead, it is best to practice starting at the bottom, with the most specific and concrete level of your subject. In fact, moving *up* the ladder a number of times, as we did with Jane Smith, is in itself an effective discovery procedure, not only for generating details, but also for arriving at a thesis.

6d

Pick one of the following subjects and use the ladder, moving up at least three times, each time abstracting for a different set of characteristics, as we did with Jane Smith:

a. a person you know well (friend, parent, teacher, employer, etc.);

b. a city or neighborhood that you have lived in or that you like a great deal;

c. a gadget you own or would like to own that has a number of different uses.

2. Devise a thesis that ties together the top levels of each ladder you just generated, as we did with the Jane Smith example.

3. Write an essay based on that thesis, drawing supporting details from low levels of the abstraction ladders.

6d Formal Outlines

In **3e**, we used an example of an *informal* outline—a kind of "blueprint"—with the essay called "Two Viewpoints." In **6c**, we used another kind of informal outline when we labeled each successive level of subordination with a different number. These outlines were made up for the occasion; they do not follow any traditional formula for a "proper" outline. Indeed, rules for "correct" outlining can be more a hindrance than a help if you get too worried about the form. The real purpose behind any kind of outline, whether informal or formal, is to let you see a skeleton of your essay. And that skeleton can be useful for two reasons. It may help you *after* you have written a rough draft to see whether the organization of your essay is clear—whether subordinate ideas are expressed in relationship to main ideas, whether all the supporting evidence is there, whether the order is clear, and so on. For some writers, a formal outline also helps in planning an essay.

6d

The kind of outline you use is not important so long as it is helpful to you, but two methods of outlining are common—one used most often in the humanities and the other in technical and scientific fields.

The first uses a series of letters and numbers to indicate divisions and subdivisions of an essay. Roman numerals are used for the major sections of a paper, capital letters for subdivisions, arabic numerals for sub-subdivisions, and lower case letters for still smaller divisions. There should be at least two subdivisions at any level, since you cannot divide something into only one part. Usually it is not necessary to subdivide more than three or four times; if you need to subdivide further, it may be because you have not sorted out your material into the appropriate classes and subclasses.

Following is an example of this type of outline; it is a conversion of the informal outline in 3e for "Two Viewpoints":

TWO VIEWPOINTS ON THE INDIVIDUAL

I. Introduction
    A. The two films focus on similar themes and should be seen together.
    B. Thesis: Although *Modern Times* and *Waiting for Godot* both center on the dehumanization of an "endangered species"—the individual—*Modern Times* is full of hope, while the characters in *Waiting for Godot* endlessly despair over their situations.

II. Humor as relief from a somber theme
    A. Clown dress in both films (treated together)
    B. Humorous predicaments
        1. Chaplin's arrest
        2. Didi, Gogo, and the fallen traveler

III. Human suffering
    A. Conditions similar to both films
        1. Shabby living conditions
        2. Poor food
        3. Bad working conditions
        4. Treatment by others
    B. Reaction to those conditions
        1. Chaplin maintains an unfaltering hope in all kinds of circumstances
          a. Losing jobs

        b. Strikes
        c. Jail
        d. Losing home
        e. Tight situations
    2. Didi and Gogo are full of despair
        a. Contemplating suicide
        b. Lack of love

IV. Action versus inaction
    A. *Modern Times*
        1. Characters constantly moving
        2. Scenery constantly changing
    B. *Waiting for Godot*
        1. Immobility
        2. No scene changes (desert/nowhere)
    C. Chaplin active mentally as well as physically
    D. Didi and Gogo paralyzed mentally as well as physically

V. Conclusion: Both films depict the socially victimized individual, although *Modern Times* portrays a fighting spirit while *Waiting for Godot* shows dejection and stagnation; they present two different viewpoints on an "endangered species"—the individual.

Notice that this outline is both more detailed than the earlier informal outline and closer to the actual wording of the essay. That is because the author used this second outline to *test* her structure—it was written *after* the first draft, while the informal outline was written as a guide *before* the first draft.

The form of outlining found most often in technical and scientific writing uses numbers only, with a series of decimal points, each decimal point marking a further level of subordination. In this system a single arabic numeral represents the first subdivision; a decimal point followed by another arabic numeral represents the second subdivision; and so on.

The following example could be used in a beginning landscape architecture class for an essay proposing and defending the best ornamentals to plant in a certain part of the country.

THE BEST ORNAMENTALS

1. Introduction
   1.1 A general statement about people's interest in ornamentals
   1.2 Thesis: Red maples make the best ornamentals because they are the most beautiful, they provide excellent shade,

6d

they are easily available and inexpensive, and they grow quickly.

2. Support

2.1 The beauty of red maples

    2.1.1 Their beauty described

    2.1.2 Their beauty contrasted with that of other ornamentals

2.2 The lush shade provided by red maples

    2.2.1 Their lush shade described

    2.2.2 Their lush shade contrasted with the shade of other ornamentals

2.3 The easy availability and inexpensive cost of red maples

    2.3.1 Their availability and cost described

    2.3.2 Their availability and cost contrasted with those of other ornamentals

2.4 The quick growth of red maples

    2.4.1 Their quick growth described

    2.4.2 Their quick growth contrasted with the growth of other ornamentals

3. Conclusion

As you can see, in this kind of outline the indentation is similar to that of the alternating letter and number system.

It is also possible (and quite frequent in technical outlines) to use indentation as the *only* way of showing relationship between main and subordinate ideas, between classes and subclasses. If you are not careful to keep the spacing clear enough, the classes and levels of subordination may become confused; otherwise, this kind of outline is probably the easiest.

One final word about outlines. Use formal outlines if they work for you, or use informal outlines if you prefer. Use outlines that are even more informal than the one in **3e** if you want to. (Often in a pressured writing situation, like an essay exam, you will have time for little more than a sketchy outline with a few major points.) Use them *when* they work best for you—before a rough draft, between drafts, even after a final draft to test structure. But never get hung up on form. An outline is not a medium of public writing; it is meant to be used by the writer only.

Following is a list of questions to ask yourself when you use an outline to help test the structure of your essay:

1. Are parallel ideas treated in parallel fashion? Are items of equal importance given equal weight?

2. Is there a meaningful order to the parts of the essay? (Do they follow one of the methods of organization mentioned in **6a** or some other logical structure?) Is there a clear reason for the order of the subheadings?

3. Does the outline reflect the "abstraction ladder"? That is, are the more concrete and specific items given the greatest subordination?

4. Does the outline reveal places where you need more specific details to support the more general points?

EXERCISES

Analyze the following outline as though you had written it between drafts of an essay assigned in your English class. By asking the questions in **6d** above, as well as the following more specific questions, decide how you might need to revise your essay.

1. Are the two books treated in parallel fashion? Do the structure and order make sense?

2. How useful are the seven levels of subordination in this outline? Compare it with the subordination in the outline for "Two Viewpoints" above.

3. The audience of this essay is an English professor. Can you see things that would need to be changed if it were published as a review in a newspaper's book section?

4. If you had been asked to prepare an outline *before* writing a draft, for your instructor to evaluate, what parts would need to be more explicit? In particular, consider the introduction (especially the thesis) and the conclusion.

COMMON THEMES IN
ALICE IN WONDERLAND AND *A CLOCKWORK ORANGE*

I. Introduction
   A. Themes
      1. Inadequacies of classical education
      2. Difficulty of gaining maturity
   B. Thesis: The development of the common themes and the purpose of using the two themes vary greatly in the two books.
II. Development
   A. Education
      1. In *Alice in Wonderland*
         a. Alice's recitations
            (1) Low value of meaningless memorization
            (2) Low level of child's understanding

6d

    b. Mock Turtle's reminiscences
   2. In *A Clockwork Orange*
    a. Alex's musical taste
    b. Alex's phraseology
  B. Maturity
   1. In *Alice in Wonderland*
    a. Alice's size
    b. Queen of Heart's influence
    c. Creatures' conversations
   2. In *A Clockwork Orange*
    a. Alex's parents
     (1) Dominated by Alex
     (2) Dominated by Joe (lodger)
    b. Alex's friends
     (1) Dominated by Alex
     (2) Revenge on Alex
    c. Alex's actions
     (1) Delinquency
      (a) Missing school
      (b) Committing crime
     (2) Hypocrisy
      (a) Reading Bible
      (b) Attaining honesty
     (3) Consistency
      (a) Using system
       (i) Parole officer
       (ii) Doctor
      (b) Having fantasies
III. Purpose
 A. Ridicule of educational system
  1. In *Alice in Wonderland*
   a. Deficiencies
   b. Improvements
  2. In *A Clockwork Orange*
   a. Failures
   b. Myths
 B. Explanation of maturing process
  1. In *Alice in Wonderland*, identifying with reader
  2. In *A Clockwork Orange*, dismissing myths
   a. Older and wiser
   b. Education improves a person
IV. Conclusion
 A. Dissimilar stories
 B. Similar themes

—Patricia Noyes

7

DRAFTING AND REVISING

7a Writing a First Draft

At some point during the process of discovering ideas, defining a thesis, sorting, selecting, planning, and arranging, you will write a draft of your essay. The most important thing to do when writing a first draft is simply to get your ideas down in the order you want them. You will doubtless change some parts around in the process of revision, but at least you will have a preliminary version of what you want your essay to look like. The first draft is not usually the place to worry about sentence structure, appropriate diction, or troublesome grammatical usage; it is best to concentrate on getting your ideas down, saving fine points for later rewriting and editing.

All writers have rituals that make it easier for them to get started. It is usually a good idea to find yourself a quiet, comfortable place to write, where you will not be easily interrupted. Be sure you have everything you need close at hand: notes, a sharp pencil or working pen or legible typewriter ribbon or computer keyboard, plenty of paper or disk space, and anything—cigarettes, coffee, candy—that makes you comfortable and gets you going. It is best *not* to worry about a dictionary or handbook, since the purpose of the first draft is to get your ideas down, to turn off the internal censors (which dictionaries will turn right back on) in order to let your creativity work for you. If you find you have trouble writing the introduction, or if you get bogged down in a particular place, let it go while you write something else. Usually after you have written the rest of the paper, the introduction will come more easily.

Once you have written a draft, it is a good idea to put it away for a day or two and give your ideas time to incubate. When you come back to the draft, you will see it with fresh eyes.

If you have access to a word processor, or to word processing software on a computer, consider using it to draft your essays. If you are used to writing with paper and pen, try typing your first draft directly on the word processor. It may seem awkward at first, but with practice it will come easily, and there are some definite advantages to working this way:

1. You can see easily what you have already written, and that will help you keep going in the process of drafting. In fact, the very sight of the cursor moving across the screen, always one step ahead of you, pulling you on, as it were, helps your own creative process continue.
2. Many word processors have separate "input" and "edit" modes, which help you separate drafting from revising. While you are entering your initial draft, you are less tempted to stop to rewrite or edit. Once you have your initial draft, on the other hand, you work in "edit" mode, where it is very easy to rewrite.
3. You can let your essay incubate on the computer disk, printing out a clean copy whenever you wish.

7b Revising

The word *revise* comes from a Latin word that means "to see again." Revising, then, is most importantly *seeing* your writing anew and considering two things: how well it achieves your purpose and what you can do to help it achieve that purpose better wherever it falls short. The best way to revise (the easiest on you and the most effective for producing a new version) is in cycles. Go through the first three of the cycles below before recopying or producing a clean draft. You may go through the cycles more than once, skipping the fourth one until the very end. Each time through you will be making marks on the draft—deleting material, adding, substituting, and rearranging.

Cycle 1: Read through the whole piece of writing, looking at the overall organization, the relationship of paragraphs to one another, the order of ideas and examples, and the success with which you have achieved your purpose (considering your audience, of course). Change whatever needs to be changed in the "big picture." Quite often, reading over a draft, you will see a section that fits better somewhere else. Cutting and pasting (whether physically with scissors and paste or electronically on your computer) is a trick of the professional writer that can save you a lot of recopying time and a lot of messy arrows and circles.

Cycle 2: Go through the essay a second time, looking at each paragraph and asking some of the same questions you asked about the piece as a whole: what is the relationship of the parts of the paragraph (sentences or groups of sentences) to the whole?

Cycle 3: The third time through, you can consider the sentences and individual words: how clearly, effectively, and emphatically do your sentences convey your meaning, and how well does your choice of words achieve your purpose?

Cycle 4: The final time through, check grammar, spelling, usage, and mechanics. This fourth cycle is often referred to as *editing*. In this cycle, you check small details—spelling, punctuation, manuscript mechanics, perhaps the choice of a word here and there—rather than make major changes in structure and style. Editing should be followed by proofreading to catch inadvertent errors in the final copy.

But omit this last cycle until you think you are ready for your final draft. There are two important reasons for saving editing until the end. First, if you do major rewriting first, some of the minor problems will have been cut out by the time you get to the editing stage, so you will not have to worry about them. Second, you will have freedom to play with ideas and language without getting hung up on what is "correct" or acceptable to your audience. Preoccupation with little things can have a negative effect on the freedom needed for the creative process to work.

A word processor makes revision, like drafting, much easier:

1. You can move words around, change the order of sentences, even shift whole **paragraphs** by pressing a few keys—no need

to draw arrows and circles or retype each new draft. Nor is it necessary to manually cut and paste when you want to re-arrange parts of a longer paper.

2. If you hate to cut out words you have written, you will find a word processor makes it much easier. First, you will not have all those scratched-out words to mourn, since they will simply disappear from the screen and your sentences will always look neat. Second, if you need to cut a large block of material but are afraid you might want to use it later, you can always copy it into a buffer or into a file of things you want to save—and indeed, you might be able to use it later in another paper. Either way, you will find cutting material much less painful with a word processor.

3. There is something much more objective about a computer screen than a piece of paper; since the electronic equipment comes between you and your writing, you will feel less attached to your work, more able to evaluate it objectively, as though you were editing someone else's writing.

4. It is easy to get a clean copy every time you make extensive changes. And that, too, makes it easier for you to revise.

5. Finally, having a word processor will encourage you to make changes even in small ways. Suppose your essay contains a discussion of the price of peanuts, and you have used the word *peanut* about a dozen times. Suppose also that you decide *walnut* would be a more appropriate example. If you had to type or hand-copy every new draft, you would be reluctant to make a last-minute change from *peanut* to *walnut* because it would take too much time. On a word processor, however, you could use a "global change" command, and every instance of *peanut* would be changed to *walnut* with a key stroke or two.

Here are some other tips to make revising easier:

1. Always leave at least twenty-four hours between drafts to let your ideas incubate. If you get frustrated while revising, you will be surprised how much easier it will go when you have given your subconscious mind time to work on it.

2. Read your draft *aloud* before going through any of the cycles. Much of the potential ambiguity, unnecessary repetition, and awkward phrasing will be immediately obvious.

3. Even better, have someone else read your essay to you. When he trips over words, you will have a quick clue to what needs to be rewritten. When he is finished reading, do not forget to ask him where he was puzzled, what he found particularly good, what he thinks needs revising, and so on.

4. If you have not made an outline earlier, make one before your final draft to test the structure of your essay. If your word processor has an automatic outlining feature, you can create your test outline with no trouble at all.

7c   Revision Checklist

The following checklist provides questions for you to ask yourself in each cycle of the revising process, together with cross-references to the sections of the book that deal with each item.

Cycle 1: The Whole Essay

1. What is my thesis or dominant impression? If a thesis, is it clearly stated in the beginning or somewhere else? If there is a reason not to state it, is the thesis clear to the reader by the end of the essay? If a dominant impression, does it clearly emerge in the essay? (See **3a**.)

2. Is every paragraph and every sentence clearly related to my thesis or dominant impression? Which parts that are not so related can be eliminated? (See **3e**.)

3. What is my purpose in writing? Is everything in the essay clearly aimed at accomplishing that purpose? (See **3b** and **3d**.)

4. Who is my audience? Have I given my reader strong enough arguments or sufficient information to support the thesis or develop the dominant impression? What could I add in the way of evidence, illustrations, or examples to reach my reader more effectively? (See **3b** and **3d**.)

5. Is the essay clearly organized? Have I arranged the arguments, illustrations, or evidence in the most effective order, considering my purpose and the needs of my audience? (See **6a**.) Have I tested the structure of my essay against an outline? (See **6d**.)

6. Is the title sufficiently interesting? Does it sound like a title and

not a headline? Does it reflect the central idea of my essay? (See **6b.**)

7. Is the introduction sufficiently interesting to get my reader involved in the essay? Does it give my reader a clear sense of how and why I am writing on this subject? (See **6b.**)

8. Does the conclusion provide closure? Will my reader feel that I have come to an end and not merely a stopping place? (See **6b.**)

Cycle 2: The Paragraphs

1. Are the paragraphs organized in the most effective manner? Have I consciously pondered whether the order I have followed is the most effective? (See **11b.1**)

2. Is everything in each paragraph clearly related to the topic sentence (or to the topic, if it is not expressed in a single topic sentence)? Do any of the paragraphs need further development? (See **11b.1**)

3. Have I made paragraph divisions in the best places, considering my audience and purpose? Should I have a short paragraph for emphasis or transition? Or do I have too many short paragraphs, which would be more effective if grouped together? (See **11c.**)

4. Are the transitions between paragraphs logical? Are they the most accurate and effective transitions? (See **12b.**)

5. Are the paragraphs coherent? Do they make effective use of structural signals, referential words and phrases, repetition, and ellipsis? (See **12b, 12c, 12d,** and **12e.**)

Cycle 3: Sentence Structure and Word Choice

1. Are the sentences all of similar length and similar structure, or have I varied them in order to emphasize appropriate words or phrases? Have I used passive voice and "it" and "there" patterns sparingly and for special emphasis? (See **19d** and **19e.**)

2. Are links between sentences clear? (See **12b.**)

3. Have I used balance and parallelism in order to emphasize parallel ideas? (See **18d, 18e,** and **18g.**)

4. Have I combined sentences in order to show the relationship

of ideas as clearly as possible, either through coordination or subordination? (See **19a** and **19b**.)

5. Do any sentences sound awkward or confusing when read aloud? (See **19c** through **19g**.)

6. Have I avoided trite expressions that will put the reader to sleep? Can I substitute fresh phrases for clichés or jargon? (See **20b.3** and **20b.7**.)

7. Are all the words consistent with the purpose and audience? Are there intrusive expressions that are too informal in a formal paper or too formal or pedantic in a less formal paper? (See **20b.4**.)

8. Have I used words accurately? If I have chosen a word I do not normally use, have I checked a dictionary to be sure that it means what I think it means and that it is appropriate to my audience? (See **20a.3** and **20b.5**.)

Cycle 4: Editing

1. Are the verb tenses consistent with edited American English? (See **14a**.)

2. Are plural endings consistent with edited American English? (See **15a.1**.)

3. Are comparative and superlative adjective forms consistent with edited American Engish? (See **17b**.)

4. Do the subjects and verbs agree in person and number? (See **16a.1** and **16b**.)

5. Do the pronouns agree with the antecedents? (See **16a.2** and **16b**.)

6. Have I avoided other grammatical problems or inappropriate usage? (See **14, 15, 16, 17**, and the Glossary of Usage.)

7. Have I used commas where I should have used periods or semicolons, producing comma splices? (See **23f.2**)

8. Have I used periods where I should have used commas, producing sentence fragments? (See **23f.1**.)

9. Have I used other punctuation marks effectively? (See **23** and **24**.)

10. Have I documented all secondary sources and included the

necessary footnotes and bibliography in the correct form? (See **8d** and **9c**.)

11. Have I checked the spelling of all words I am unsure of? (See **22**.)

EXERCISES

1. Following are the first and fourth drafts of a student essay. The fifth draft was the final one, but it is not reproduced here; instead, you can practice writing the final draft yourself. The student wrote the kind of article that might be included in a magazine like *Consumer Reports*. Read both drafts carefully. Using the "Revision Checklist" as a guide, examine the kinds of changes made between the first and fourth drafts.
2. Apply the "Revision Checklist" carefully to the fourth draft, assuming this is this last time through the cycles (therefore including Cycle 4). Note the changes you would make in each cycle.
3. Now write the final draft of the essay. If you would like to compare your final draft with that of the original author, ask your instructor to show you the copy in the *Instructor's Guide*.

GM'S NEW FIREBIRDS AND CAMAROS
(Draft 1 of 5)

GMC recently began introducing a lot of new models for the 1980s, that are takeoffs on their old models. Two cars they've changed completely are the Firebird and Camaro, they shortened the bodies of these cars and added on things like hatchbacks and pop up heads. Worst of all, they gave them practically no power.

These cars use to have muscle. Due to the fact that there was a lack of American made sportscars these cars were real popular. But now these cars are just like what happened to the Ford Mustang. At its incepcion the Mustang set American sales records. But then everything that made it great got lost. In more and more body alterations. That's why the early Mustangs still get a good price, but the latter ones are only like regular cars.

GM did the same thing to the Firebird and Camaros. This was because of the gas shortages and switch to unleaded gas. Like Mustangs, people would rather pay big for an old, used Camaro or Firebird than a later, duller model.

GM's new Firebirds and Camaros are all-around disappointing. GM was forced to do it, though. And maybe these cars *will* sell for their good milage on the other hand, the new Firebirds and Camaros may only make some people want the old ones even more.

THE NEW FIREBIRDS AND CAMAROS
(Draft 4 of 5)

General Motors Corporation began introducing many new models for the 1980s. Some models will be completely new designs, but most of the new models are variations of former automobiles. Two cars that have been radically altered are the Pontiac Firebird and the Chevrolet Camaro. The bodies of these cars have been shortened and modified with such things as hatchbacks and pop-up headlights. More importantly, though, there has been a reduction in power.

The Camaro and the Firebird were once known as "muscle" cars because of their power and weight. They were very popular, because there was a lack of American-made sports cars. General Motors began to make changes in the two cars after the gas shortages and the switch to unleaded gas. Smaller engines, which derived less power from unleaded gas, were installed. Used Firebirds and Camaros from the early 70s became popular for their large engines and high performance.

The Firebirds and the Camaros have now lost some more of their muscle. The situation is very similar to the history of the Ford Mustang. At its inception the Mustang set American sales records. By the late 1960s though, the unique style and design of the car had been lost in body alterations. The Mustangs made in the mid-60s are now regarded as classics, but the newer Mustangs never will be.

Car buyers may be disappointed by General Motors' new Firebirds and Camaros. Unfortunately, General Motors was forced into producing smaller, high-mileage cars by the current energy situation. The public, however, can buy whatever they both want and can afford. The new cars may sell very well. On the other hand, the new Firebirds and Camaros will probably promote interest in their more "muscled" predecessors.   —David Lehnus

---

7d Common Editing Symbols

Many writers find it convenient to use symbols, both in the margins and in the text itself, when marking up drafts for revision. Following are some of the most common ones:

adj	adjective needed instead of adverb (**17a**)
adv	adverb needed instead of adjective (**17a**)

d

agr	problem with agreement of subject and verb or pronoun and antecedent (**16**)
cap	capital (upper-case) letter needed; three lines under the letter in the manuscript also indicate the need for a capital letter (**24f**)
case	wrong case of pronoun (**15b**)
cl	cliché; use a fresh expression (**20b.7**)
coh	problem with coherence (**12**)
comp	comparative form of adjective needed (**17b, 17c, 17d**)
concl	problem with conclusion (**6b**)
conj	wrong conjunction used (**13g**)
cs	comma splice (**23g**)
d	problem with diction; check dictionary (**20a.3, 20b.3, 20b.4**)
det	details needed (**2b–2e and 6c**)
dg mod	dangling modifier (**19c.7**)
doc	documentation absent or inaccurate (**9c**)
euph	euphemism; replace with more exact word (**20b.3**)
ex	examples needed (**2b–2e and 6c**)
frag	sentence fragment (**23f.1**)
fus	fused sentence (**23f.3**)
idiom	wrong preposition or other word for idiomatic American English (**20a.3**)
illus	illustrations needed (**2b–2e and 6c**)
intro	problem with introduction (**6b**)
j	jargon; replace with more direct language (**20b.3**)
lc, /	lower-case letter needed; a slash through an upper-case letter also indicates the need for a lower-case letter (**24f**)
m mod	misplaced modifier (**19c.5**)
mod	other problems with modification (**19c**)
ns	*non sequitur*, "does not logically follow" (**5d, 5f, 5g**)
org	problem with organization (**6a**)
p	problem with punctuation (**23, 24**)
pl	plural needed (**15a.1**)
pred	problem with subject-predicate match (**19f**)
red	redundant; omit one of the redundant words or phrases (**20b.2**)
ref	pronoun reference unclear (**12c.2**)
rep	unnecessary or ineffective repetition (**18e**)
shift	shift in person or tense (**12c.1, 14g**)

sp	problem with spelling; check dictionary (**22**)
sub	problem with subordination (**19b**)
sup	superlative form of adjective needed (**17b, 17c, 17d**)
th	thesis absent or unclear (**3a**)
trans	transition absent or unclear (**12b**)
ts	topic sentence absent or unclear (**11b**)
v	problem with voice; change active to passive or vice-versa (**18g.1, 19d**)
vb	problem with verb form (**14**)
tense	problem with verb tense (**14a**)
w	wordy (**20b.2**)
wo	problem with word order (**18g, 19e**)
∧	insert; may be used in margin as well as in the writing
ℓ⌐, [ ]	omit—wordy, unnecessary, or distracting; sometimes brackets are also put around material to be omitted (**20b.2**)
¶	paragraph division needed (**11c**)
//	problem with parallel structure (**19g**)
?	something missing or not clear
#	space(s) needed

EXERCISES _____

1. Here is one paragraph of the first draft of David Lehnus' paper (reproduced in the exercise at the end of **7c**), marked up for editing before the second draft. Considering the advice given in **7c**, Cycle 4, how much of this marking is appropriate at this stage? What rewriting might Lehnus have done if he had not gotten bogged down in some of these details?

sp   These cars use to have muscle. [Due to the fact that]

cap there was a lack of American made sports cars these cars were

adv very popular. [But now these cars are just like what]

The same thing happened to the Ford Mustang. At its inception the Mustang sp

the style and design set American sales records. But then [everything] that made det

frag it great got lost in more and more body alterations.

mid-60s   (they are classics)

dif That's why the [early] Mustangs still get a good price, but

sp the latter ones are [only like regular cars], not in demand at all

2. Which of the editing symbols would be appropriate in marking up draft 4 in preparation for the final draft? (You might reconsider here what you did with exercise 2 at the end of 7c.)

7e   A Style Sheet

Most teachers and employers will ask that whatever you are writing be put in a standard format. The style sheet below is a standard one and should be acceptable if you have not been given a more specific style to follow:

Title and Name: Center the title of your paper near the top of the first page; capitalize the first letter of each important word. (Do *not* enclose your title in quotation marks or underline it.) Put your name, along with the date and any other information requested by your instructor, in the upper right-hand corner. (Use a separate title page only for long works, like research papers; see the sample research paper in chapter 10 for an appropriate format.)

Margins: All papers, whether handwritten, typed, or printed with a word processor, should have ample margins; a good guide is to leave 1 or 1 1/2 inch margins on the sides and bottom of each page, with slightly more room at the top.

Typing: It is usually best to type your papers or print them with a word processor, particularly if they are long; part of the effect of your writing is conveyed by the neatness and clarity of presentation, and typing or printing gives a neater, clearer appearance than handwriting. Another advantage of typing or printing is that more of your writing is visible on a page, so it is easier for your reader to follow your organization. You should carefully proofread papers, correcting minor errors neatly and legibly in ink.

Spacing: Typewritten or printed papers should be double-spaced throughout. Most instructors prefer that you also double-space handwritten papers and write on one side of the paper only.

Paper: For typing, use standard 8 1/2-by-11-inch good quality bond paper. For handwritten papers, use 8 1/2-by-11-inch ruled paper. For papers printed with a word processor, any standard computer paper will do.

Ink and Ribbons: When typing or printing with your word processor, be sure you have a fresh ribbon so that your paper can be easily read; when handwriting, use blue or black ink.

Folders and Binders: Unless your instructor requires a folder, just paper-clip or staple your paper together. Folders and binders are more trouble and expense than they are worth, although occasionally they are useful for very long papers. Do not depend on folding the corners of your paper—the pages may become separated from each other and lost. And have mercy—do not use straight pins or other weapons to hold the pages together. A box of paper clips is cheap and will be one of the best investments you can make.

Copies: It is always a good idea, for your own protection, to keep a copy of any paper you submit. Accidents occasionally happen, and if by some chance your writing is lost, you will have another copy. Xeroxing the finished paper is probably easiest if you type or write by hand. (Keeping a carbon copy is cheaper, but carbon smudges easily.) If you write your papers with a word processor, you can keep a copy on your disk as well as print out an extra "hard" copy for yourself.

Pagination: The first page should not have a number. Beginning with page 2, put the page number (with no punctuation before or after it) in the upper right-hand corner of each page. Including your last name (followed by a comma) before each page number will insure that pages of your paper will not be misplaced. (If you have a title page, do not count it in the pagination.) Most word processors have options for starting pagination on the second page, as well as options for where you want the page number placed on each page and whether you want a running head. (If you use your last name or the title of your essay as a running head, you will be protected should the pages of your paper become separated.)

Documentation: Be sure to cite all sources for quotations, paraphrases, or summary information, using either in-line citations or notes. All quotations of four lines or more should be set off from the main part of your writing by special indentation (see **9b.4**).

7f The Writing Process in Miniature: Writing Essay Exams

When you have to write an answer to an essay exam, you must use all the activities of the writing process but in abbreviated form. You must have a way to get started, some quick discovery technique, a way of selecting what is important and arranging it in the most logical order, a way to draft your answer in a fairly organized and coherent fashion, and time to do some basic revision—at the very least, proofreading.

How can you do all this when you may have as little as ten or fifteen minutes in which to work? Following are a few hints that should make the process easier:

1. First, do not attack the question as though it were a nonstop. While a nonstop is a good discovery technique (see **1b** and **2b.2**), it is not a substitute for an organized, coherent essay.

2. The best starting point is analyzing the question to see what clues your instructor has given. Most exam questions will include a key sentence like one of these:

   a. "Compare and contrast x and y."
   b. "Analyze the reasons for x."
   c. "Classify x into y categories."
   d. "Define x with examples."
   e. "Argue for or against x."

Notice that most of these ways of phrasing questions look very much like the methods we discussed in chapter 4. Since an essay exam is a kind of essay in miniature, one method of development will be clearly dominant. The words in which the question is phrased, then, will be your best clue to several things: how to get started, including what kind of thesis sentence you might want to begin with, what kind of information you will need to include, and how to organize your answer.

3. Even though there is not time in an exam to use a nonstop or more formal discovery techniques, you do not want to avoid the discovery process altogether. Brainstorming is the quickest method. Use the back of your exam sheet or a piece of scratch paper to jot down quickly and briefly some of the main ideas you want to discuss, starting with a simple thesis statement that will directly respond to the question. For example, the exam questions above might yield the following kinds of thesis statements:

a. "X and y are both ———, but x is ——— while y is ———." (Remember that comparison and contrast require a basis of similarity in order to make differences significant.)

b. "There are three reasons for x: ———, ———, and ———."

c. "X can be classified into three groups: ———, ———, and ———."

d. "X is a ——— that . . ." (Remember that a definition involves first placing the thing to be defined into a larger category and then distinguishing it from other members of that category.)

e. "X is . . ." or "X is not . . . ."

4. After jotting down your thesis statement and your main generalizations, continue your brainstorming to come up with some supporting examples. Remember that almost all instructors are looking for evidence of how well you *understand* the issues implied in the question; that will mean not just giving the instructor back the generalizations you have memorized from the textbook or lectures, but coming up with concrete examples to support those generalizations.

5. After you have done the brainstorming, use another few minutes to think about what order you want to put the general points in and which of the supporting examples you will need to use. Jotting down a very brief, informal outline will help you to see whether there are any gaps, either in the main points you need to make or in the supporting details.

6. After you have written a brief outline, write out the answer to

the question, following carefully the outline and not letting yourself get carried away by some point that is not in your outline.

7. Be sure to leave yourself a few minutes at the end to do some minimal revising; at the very least, you want to check to be sure your sentences make sense, that the examples are clearly related to the generalizations they are meant to support, and that you do not have any distracting spelling problems or other obvious grammatical problems.

NOTE: Steps 1 through 4 should altogether take up no more than 20 percent of your time, and step 5 should take no more than 10 percent. As important as planning and revising are, be sure to leave yourself enough time to write a coherent essay.

EXERCISES

Following is an example of an essay question with responses by two students. Which answer would you judge to be the best? Why?

1. What has the study of abnormal language use, as in aphasia, taught us about normal language processes?

The study of individuals who are aphasic has led to many discoveries as to what happens in normal language processes. Broca first substantiated the claim that damage to a specific area of the brain results in a speech deficit. Broca and Wernicke both found that the left hemisphere of the brain is vital to speech and language. Three of the left hemisphere's areas are particularly vital—Broca's area, Wernicke's area, and the supplemental motor area. The left hemisphere is not more important, it is just dominant. The right hemisphere controls visual-spatial relationships, and nonspeech environmental sounds are processed primarily in the right hemisphere.

Studies on people with damage in different areas of the left hemisphere have shown that different linguistic functions are controlled by separate areas of the left hemisphere. In some types of damage, such as that to Broca's area, patients have trouble speaking although they understand what they are saying. Other types of damage, such as Wernicke's aphasia, allow patients to speak fluently although they cannot understand spoken or written language.

Studies on patients who have had their corpora callosa severed revealed that the two hemispheres need to communicate with each other for speech to be normal. These studies revealed that the right hemisphere can understand spoken and written language, but it needs the left hemisphere to be able to articulate what has been heard or seen.

Research has also proven that the right ear has an advantage over the left ear because right ear messages go directly to the left hemisphere. Research also suggests that the left hemisphere controls voluntary movements of the muscles of the speech producers—the larynx, pharynx, tongue, lips, and cheeks.

2. What has the study of abnormal language use, as in aphasia, taught us about normal language processes?

The study of abnormal language use has given us some great insights into normal language use. By studying language impaired individuals and doing autopsies on them, we have discovered that most of the language production and comprehension occurs in the left hemisphere of the brain. However, this research has found that each hemisphere does complement each other. This leads us to infer that although we can pinpoint the area of some deficiencies, the overall language process is very complex and involves a large portion of our cognitive abilities. The study of aphasia has done a great deal in indicating to us the variance and complexity of speech problems. Different aphasiacs have very different problems and degrees of severity. All of these come from a deficiency in a different area. The bottom line is that all linguistic problems are very neurologically complex and further research in the area of language problems is necessary.

Part Two

RESEARCH AND THE WRITING PROCESS

By George F. Hayhoe,
Donald J. Kenney,
and Constance J. Gefvert

8

THE RESEARCH PROCESS

Research is an activity basic to our inquisitive human nature as well as to the writing process. As children, we asked our parents questions, went out to explore nature, read library books on topics that interested us—and when we had explored, we reached some conclusions about our world. As adults, we are continually seeking knowledge about things we want or need to know; we have learned to use research as a systematic way of solving problems, and we have engaged in it many times without calling it research. Choosing a college, fixing a stereo, deciding where to go on vacation—all of these create a need for information that we can meet through research.

Even in academic writing, research is not restricted to the traditional research paper. Whenever you have a paper to write, a report to prepare, or any other writing task to do, research is likely to be an important part of the process. When you are discovering ideas for an essay, for instance, you may find gaps in your knowledge that will require you to consult an outside source.

The important thing about any research you do, whether to meet your own needs or to fulfill the requirements of an instructor or boss, is that you always have a *purpose for seeking information*. Similarly, when you write up any research—a lab report, a marketing analysis, or a history essay—you also have a *purpose for reporting your research*.

8a   The Process

An essential activity in writing a research paper is managing and budgeting the limited time you have to do the research and to prepare and write the paper. You might want to think of planning in terms of the seven-step writing process we described in 1a. Remember that discovery is the most time-consuming part of researched writing; then make a rough plan of how much time you will need to spend on each step. For example, if you have four weeks to complete a research paper, you should not spend more than two or three days choosing and refining a topic; four to six days identifying sources and compiling a working bibliography; eight to ten days reading, analyzing, and taking notes; four to five days writing a first draft; and two to three days completing the paper.

8b   The Starting Point: Your Topic

The care with which you choose a topic (or focus one assigned to you) will go a long way toward insuring the success of your research paper. You should consider the assigned length of your paper, the time you have to work in, and the resources of your library. Many topics, such as "Politics in America," for example, would be too broad for a ten-page paper, and you would end up writing only generalities and abstractions. But "The Effect of the Lowered Voting Age on American Politics" would be a much more focused topic.

Here are some general guidelines to follow if you have been asked to choose your own topic:

1. Select a subject on which information is readily available. Avoid topics that are speculative and not researchable, such as "If the British Had Won the Revolutionary War." Avoid topics so current that information is available only from newspapers and a few popular periodicals.

2. Choose and refine a topic with your audience in mind. Remember that someone else will read your paper and should learn something from it.

3. Write on a subject that is important enough to investigate,

warrants your attention, and will keep your interest over the weeks you devote to it.

4. Avoid subjects that are too narrow. For example, both "Diseases of Fleas" and "Lincoln's Service as a Postmaster" are too specialized for a successful student paper.

5. Select a subject that does not involve technical information beyond your comprehension or that of your audience.

6. Avoid a topic such as "Did John Wilkes Booth Kill Lincoln?" that will not produce any material to write about because the question has long since been answered.

8b

You will learn much more by fully investigating a well-focused topic than by skimming the surface of a much broader one. And you will find that such a topic is much more interesting and easier to work with, as well. Here are some suggestions for limiting a topic, whether assigned or self-chosen:

- *By Time*: "The Advent of Nuclear Energy" is much too broad; limit your research to the early work on the nuclear bomb and write on "The Advent of Nuclear Energy: The Manhattan Project."

- *By Space*: If your instructor requires you to write on some aspect of the American novel, refine the assigned topic by dealing with novelists in one section of the country or in one state.

- *By Historical, Social, or Political Dimensions*: If you are interested in writing on television advertising, consider the effects of television advertising on children.

- *By Comparison*: If you are interested in the "women's movement," compare the efforts of women to gain suffrage to the efforts of Blacks.

- *By Type*: "Violence in Sports" would be too broad, but "Violence in Ice Hockey" would be more manageable for the length of paper you will likely be required to write.

- *By Personality*: If you are working with a literary topic or a historical one like the Civil War, focus on a key personality—Robert E. Lee's and Ulysses S. Grant's military strategies, for instance.

8c Discovery: A Research Strategy

The following process, useful for most kinds of research, moves from general sources to specific ones, thus helping you focus your topic. You will also find that the strategy will be timesaving and will help to generate a working bibliography for your paper. Be sure to ask a librarian whenever you need help.

8c

Step 1: Overview of Topic—Encyclopedias

To make your research easier and to gain a working knowledge of your topic, begin with an overview. A logical place to start is with a general encyclopedia. *Collier's Encyclopedia* and *World Book Encyclopedia* are less scholarly than the *Encyclopaedia Britannica* and the *Encyclopedia Americana*, but they are useful for quick reference to verify a date, to find the exact location of a country, or to learn the population of a state. The *Americana* is particularly strong in the history, culture, and geography of the United States and Canada, while the *Britannica* emphasizes international coverage of subjects. These major encyclopedias are up-to-date on most topics and are revised periodically.

Use the encyclopedia's general index to find information more easily as well as to discover cross-references to the topic you are researching. Longer articles in an encylopedia will be subdivided into various components of the broad topic; these divisions will help you to realize the scope of the topic and focus on a specific aspect of it. Note whether the article you consult is signed, usually with initials keyed to full names in the index volume. While not all articles will be signed, an author's name is often an indication of the authority and accuracy of the article.

The bibliography at the end of the article will reveal further sources and is another indication of the author's knowledge of the topic as well as a test of the currency and relevance of the information presented in the article. Once you have examined several encyclopedia articles, you should have some grasp of the scope of your topic and enough background information to start your research intelligently.

In addition to these general encyclopedias, there are many subject-oriented and specialized encyclopedias. Following are some of the most common, but there are many others as well.

HUMANITIES

The American Political Dictionary. New York: Holt, Rinehart and Winston, 1985.

Dictionary of American History. 7 vols. New York: Charles Scribner's Sons, 1976–78.

Encyclopedia of American History. New York: Harper and Row, 1982.

The Encyclopedia of Philosophy. 8 vols. reprinted in 4 vols. New York: Macmillan and The Free Press, 1972.

Encyclopedia of Religion and Ethics. 12 vols. New York: Charles Scribner's Sons, 1962.

Encyclopedia of World Art. 15 vols. New York: McGraw-Hill, 1959–1968.

An Encyclopedia of World History. Boston: Houghton Mifflin, 1972.

Encyclopedia of World Literature in the 20th Century. 4 vols. New York: Frederick Ungar, 1981–84.

The New Grove Dictionary of Music and Musicians. 20 vols. London: Macmillan, 1980.

SOCIAL SCIENCES

Encyclopedia of Anthropology. New York: Harper and Row, 1976.

The Encyclopedia of Education. 10 vols. New York: Macmillan and The Free Press, 1971.

Encyclopedia of Psychology. 3 vols. Freiburg im Briesgau, West Germany: Herder and Herder, 1972.

The Encyclopedia of Sociology. Guilford, CT: DPG Reference, 1981.

International Encyclopedia of the Social Sciences. 8 vols. New York: The Free Press, 1977.

SCIENCE AND TECHNOLOGY

Encyclopedia and Dictionary of Medicine, Nursing, and Allied Health. Philadelphia: Saunders, 1983.

Encyclopedia of Sport Sciences and Medicine. New York: Macmillan, 1971.

Grzimek's Animal Life Encyclopedia. 13 vols. New York: Van Nostrand-Reinhold, 1972–75.

McGraw-Hill Encyclopedia of Science and Technology. 15 vols. New York: McGraw-Hill, 1982.

Step 2: Finding Books

To find the books and other materials you need for your research, you need to understand both how your library classifies its books and how it files information about its books.

Most libraries use either the Dewey Decimal System or the Library of Congress System for classifying books. These systems give each book either a number or a letter-number combination that indicates which category of knowledge it falls into.

In most libraries you will find information about books in a traditional *card catalog,* in which the same information about each book is listed on a number of file cards: an *author* card, which is filed alphabetically according to the author's name (last name first); a *title* card, which is filed alphabetically according to the first word (other than "a," "an," or "the") of the title; and one or more *subject* cards, which are filed alphabetically according to the subject classification of the book. In the upper left corner of each is the Dewey or Library of Congress classification number.

As you will see from figure 8.1, all three types of cards have the same information about the book. Only the first line varies, according to author, title, or subject heading. The cards contain

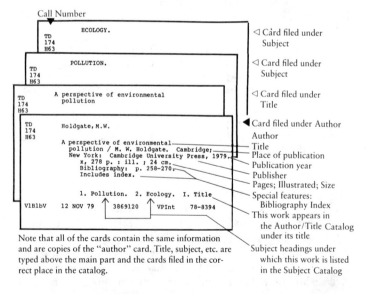

Note that all of the cards contain the same information and are copies of the "author" card. Title, subject, etc. are typed above the main part and the cards filed in the correct place in the catalog.

FIGURE 8.1. Sample Subject, Author, and Title Cards

everything you need for your bibliography, including author, title, place and date of publication, and publisher. If you write this information down in the form required for the bibliography (see **8d**), you will save yourself time later.

Check the card for a preview of how useful the book might be for your research. The date of publication, for instance, will be important in some subjects; the card will show whether the book contains illustrations, bibliographies, and an index; and the information at the bottom of the card (in figure 8.1, "pollution" and "ecology") will indicate subject headings the book is listed under (which might suggest some additional places to look for your topic that you might not have thought about).

8c

A card catalog is usually one of two types: a *dictionary catalog* files all the author, title, and subject cards in one alphabet; in a *divided catalog,* author and title cards are filed in one catalog and subject cards in another. At large academic libraries where some books are housed in branches, the catalog at the main library is usually a *union catalog;* that is, materials in the main library as well as in the branches are listed in a single catalog, whether it is a comprehensive dictionary catalog or a divided catalog. The catalogs in the branch libraries may be either copies of the union catalog, or catalogs of only the materials in that branch.

Many libraries have also begun to use other types of catalogs, including the COM *(Computer Output Microfilm) catalog,* usually on microfilm or microfiche. The newest form is the *on-line computer catalog.* In most cases, however, if a library has adopted a COM or on-line catalog, not all holdings will be included (it takes many years to convert from a traditional catalog to one of the newer forms), so be sure to consult the traditional card catalog as well. Before starting your research, check with a reference librarian to get information on your library's catalog.

Unless you have already found titles of specific books or names of particular authors in your field from the encyclopedia bibliographies, you will want to start your catalog search using a subject approach. But subjects are not always listed in the catalog under the first word or phrase that you think of. Your library probably uses either the *Library of Congress Subject Headings* or *Sear's List of Subject Headings* to assign subject headings to books. A librarian can tell you which to consult to see how your topic is entered in the card catalog. For example, you would find no entries in the catalog under "movies" or "films" if your library uses the *Library of Congress Subject Headings*; instead you would find that the heading is "moving pictures."

In addition to establishing the correct terms to use in looking up material, the headings in the *Sear's* or *Library of Congress* lists (along with the "see" and "see also" cross references) can help you explore related topics and finally focus your topic.

8c

Certain kinds of topics are not found in the *Library of Congress Subject Headings* or *Sear's* but will be in the catalog: names of individuals and families, place-names, and corporate bodies. Writers are treated both as authors and as subjects in the card catalog. Books *by* Herman Melville, for instance, will be on author cards; books *about* him will be on subject cards.

Step 3:   Using Periodical and Newspaper Indexes

For many research topics, you will want to consult periodicals (especially magazines and professional journals) and newspapers for more current information than you can find in books. To locate periodical literature you will need to use an appropriate index or abstract. An *index* is an alphabetical listing of journal articles, reports, and proceedings; material can be found under author, title, or subject. An *abstract* is essentially the same as an index but also provides a brief summary for each entry. You have probably already used some periodical indexes, especially *Readers' Guide to Periodical Literature*, which indexes current, popular periodicals such as *Time*, *Psychology Today*, and *Sports Illustrated*.

For most topics, however, you will want to consult periodicals that are more specialized or focused than those indexed in *Readers' Guide*. You will find information on material in such periodicals by checking the more specialized indexes. Some, such as the *Humanities Index*, cover relatively broad areas, while others, like the *Music Index*, cover more specific areas. (See below for a list of the most common ones.)

When you use indexes and abstracts, write down all the information from the citation to help you find the journal as well as the article itself. To save time later, write it down in the form you will need for your bibliography (see **8d**). Included in index and abstract citations are the author(s), title of the article or work, title of the journal, volume, page numbers, and date of issue.

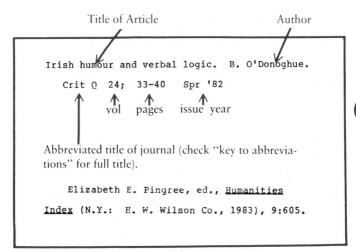

Title of Article   Author

```
Irish humour and verbal logic.  B. O'Donoghue.

    Crit Q  24;  33-40   Spr '82
            vol   pages   issue year
```

Abbreviated title of journal (check "key to abbreviations" for full title).

```
    Elizabeth E. Pingree, ed., Humanities
Index (N.Y.:  H. W. Wilson Co., 1983), 9:605.
```

8c

FIGURE 8.2. Sample Entry from the *Humanities Index*

Figure 8.2, taken from the *Humanities Index*, illustrates a typical citation. Each index is arranged a little differently and uses somewhat different abbreviations; be sure to check the key at the beginning of the volume so you understand the information in each entry.

Depending on your topic, you will probably need to consult more than one volume of an index or abstract. Most, however, have an annual cumulative volume (which combines the separately published issues of an index into a one-volume sequence), although this practice varies somewhat with individual indexes and abstracts.

Below is a selected list of indexes and abstracts, arranged by general and more specific subjects:

HUMANITIES

General Index:	*Humanities Index*
Art:	*Art Index*
Film and Drama:	*Cumulated Dramatic Index*
	Film Literature Index
	A Guide to Critical Reviews

History:	*America: History and Life*
	Historical Abstracts
Literature and Language:	*Abstracts of English Studies*
	MLA International Bibliography
Music:	*Music Index*
Philosophy:	*Philosophy Index*
Religion:	*Religion Index*

8c

SOCIAL SCIENCES

General Index:	*Social Sciences Index*
Anthropology:	*Abstracts in Anthropology*
Business and Economics:	*Business Periodicals Index*
Education:	*Current Index to Journals in Education*
	Education Index
Geography:	GEO *Abstracts*
Government, Law, and Political Science:	*Index to Legal Periodicals*
	International Political Science Abstracts
	Public Affairs Information Service Bulletin
Psychology:	*Psychological Abstracts*
Sociology:	*Sociological Abstracts*
Sports and Physical Education:	*Physical Education/Sports Index*
Statistics:	*American Statistical Index*

SCIENCE AND TECHNOLOGY

General Index:	*General Science Index*
Agriculture and Biology:	*Biological and Agricultural Index*
Chemistry and Physics:	*Chemical Abstracts*
	Physics Abstracts
Computer Science:	*Computer and Control Abstracts*
Energy:	*Energy Index*
Engineering:	*Applied Science and Technology Index*
	Engineering Index
Environmental Science:	*Pollution Abstracts*
Food and Nutrition:	*Food Science and Technology Abstracts*
Mathematics:	*Mathematical Reviews*
Medicine:	*Index Medicus*
Nursing:	*Cumulative Index to Nursing Literature*

Newspaper indexes are similar to periodical indexes except that they index articles for a single newspaper. The major newspapers that publish indexes are the *Christian Science Monitor, Los Angeles Times, New York Times, Times* (London), *Wall Street Journal,* and *Washington Post.*

Many of these indexes can also be used to find information in smaller, local newspapers. For example, if you wanted information about reactions to the oil crisis of 1973 in different parts of the country, you might check the *New York Times Index* until you found the exact date, and then search in other newspapers published on that date.

Step 4: Evaluating Sources

Once you find the books you want to look at, you will need to know how your library physically arranges the books. Signs or charts near the card catalog will tell you where to find books on different topics and will give directions on finding your way around the library.

When you go to the shelves to find the books and periodicals that you have identified from the catalog, take a few minutes to preview them, to see which are most likely to be useful for your research paper. Look at the tables of contents of the books to see if there are chapter headings directly related to your research problem, and check the indexes for key words and phrases related to your topic. Books that do not include major chapters or sections dealing directly with your research problem will probably not be useful.

Check to see whether the authors document their sources (in footnotes or endnotes) and whether they include bibliographies or lists of suggested reading. Note the publication dates of the works the author has drawn upon; if your topic requires current information, a book or journal article that relies heavily on outdated material will be of little value. A bibliography and thorough documentation indicate the author's knowledge of other scholars' work in the field.

Another helpful way to evaluate materials is to check the authors' credentials. Two excellent sources, particularly for authors with an academic background, are the *Directory of American Scholars* and *American Men and Women of Science.* The book's publisher is another gauge of its reliability. University presses generally publish scholarly works and are usually highly respected in the academic community.

If a book or periodical article has tables, graphs, and statistics, check to see whether sources for the statistics are included, and note whether the graphs give an accurate representation of the data being presented. Statistics should be based on actual surveys, field studies, or findings of other scholars in the field; the United States government is also a major source of reliable statistics.

Develop these habits of critically examining the sources you use. Do not be deceived into thinking that the facts and theories advanced by an author are based on sound research and scholarship just because a book is in the library.

8d Discovery: The Preliminary Bibliography

As you examine the books and articles you find, you should immediately record some important data about each potential source. This information has two purposes: you will be able to find the book or article if you need to return to it later in your research or writing, and you will be able to construct the notes and bibliography which will form a part of the completed research paper.

The basic information you should record for books includes the name of the author(s) and/or editor(s), the book's title, and the publication data (city, publisher, and date). For periodical articles, you should record the name of the author(s), article title, periodical title, publication information (volume and issue number, and/or date of issue), and inclusive page numbers of the article.

Most humanities instructors will require that research papers for their courses be prepared according to the style described in the MLA *Handbook for Writers of Research Papers, Theses, and Dissertations*, 2nd ed. (New York: Modern Language Association, 1984). For papers in the social sciences, the *Publication Manual of the American Psychological Association*, 3rd ed. (Washington: APA, 1983) is the style manual most frequently used. Moreover, many scientific and technical disciplines use variations of the APA format.

Examples of the most frequently used types of bibliography entries are provided below in both MLA and APA style. If you are unable to locate the proper format for a book, article, or other source among the examples on this list, consult either the MLA *Handbook* or the APA *Publication Manual* for its more comprehensive guide to citations. If your instructor has requested that you observe the conventions of another style manual (see **8d.2**), consult its section on constructing bibliographies or lists of sources. Most college and university libraries, as well as large public libraries, keep copies of the major style manuals available for reference.

8d.1 MLA and APA Bibliography Styles
Each of the most common forms of citations is given first in the MLA form and then in the APA form.

a. Books

BOOKS BY A SINGLE AUTHOR

MLA: Lakoff, Robin. <u>Language and Woman's Place</u>. New York: Harper, 1975.

APA: Lakoff, R. (1975). <u>Language and woman's place</u>. New York: Harper and Row.

BOOKS BY TWO OR THREE AUTHORS

MLA: Miller, Casey, and Kate Swift. <u>Words and Women</u>. Garden City: Anchor, 1977.

APA: Miller, C., & Swift, K. (1977). <u>Words and women</u>. Garden City, NY: Anchor.

MLA: Crane, L. Ben, Edward Yeager, and Randal Whitman. <u>An Introduction to Linguistics</u>. Boston: Little, 1981.

APA: Crane, L. B., Yeager, E., & Whitman, R. L. (1981). <u>An introduction to linguistics</u>. Boston: Little, Brown.

BOOKS BY MORE THAN THREE AUTHORS

MLA: Nilsen, Alleen Pace, et al. <u>Sexism and Language</u>. Urbana: NCTE, 1977.

APA: Nilsen, A. P., Bosmajian, H., Gershuny, H. L., & Stanley, J. P. (1977). <u>Sexism and language</u>. Urbana, IL: National Council of Teachers of English.

NOTE: For books by three or more authors, provide the name of the first author given on the title page followed by the Latin abbreviation *et al.* ("and others") when using MLA style. Provide names of all authors when observing APA format.

BOOKS BY CORPORATE AUTHORS

MLA: Modern Language Association. <u>MLA Handbook for Writers of
Research Papers, Theses and Dissertations</u>. 2nd ed.
New York: MLA, 1984.

APA: Modern Language Association. (1984). <u>MLA handbook for
writers of research papers, theses and dissertations</u>
(2nd ed.). New York: Author.

NOTE: APA format substitutes *Author* for publisher's name when a
book is published by its author.

ANONYMOUS BOOKS

MLA: <u>The New Copyright Law</u>. Glenview: Scott,
1979.

APA: <u>The new copyright law</u>. (1979). Glenview, IL: Scott,
Foresman.

LATER EDITIONS OF BOOKS

MLA: Modern Language Association. <u>MLA Handbook for Writers of
Research Papers, Theses and Dissertations</u>. 2nd ed.
New York: MLA, 1984.

APA: Modern Language Association. (1984). <u>MLA handbook for
writers of research papers, theses and dissertations</u>
(2nd ed.). New York: Author.

EDITED BOOKS

MLA: Pickens, Judy Lee, ed. <u>Without Bias: A Guidebook for
Nondiscriminatory Communication</u>. 2nd ed. New York:
Wiley, 1982.

APA: Pickens, J. L. (Ed.). (1982). <u>Without bias: A
guidebook for nondiscriminatory communication</u> (2nd
ed.). New York: Wiley.

NOTE: Cite books with two, three, or more editors in the same way
as books with two, three, or more authors according to MLA or APA
style.

BOOKS IN A SERIES

MLA: Stanford, Gene, ed. <u>Dealing with Differences</u>. Classroom
Practices in Teaching English, 1980-1981. Urbana:
NCTE, 1980.

APA: Stanford, G. (Ed.). (1980). <u>Dealing with differences:
Classroom practices in teaching English, 1980-1981</u>.
Urbana, IL: National Council of Teachers of English.

MULTIVOLUME BOOKS WITH A SINGLE TITLE BY A SINGLE AUTHOR

MLA: Blotner, Joseph.   <u>Faulkner: A Biography</u>.   2 vols.   New
York: Random, 1974.

NOTE: To cite only one volume of a multivolume book by a single
author according to MLA style, the first part of the citation may be
given as follows:

MLA: Blotner, Joseph. . . . 1974. Vol. 2.

APA: Blotner, J. (1974). <u>Faulkner: A biography</u> (Vols. 1-2).
New York: Random House.

NOTE: If you want to cite only one volume of a multivolume book
by one author using APA format, give the first part of the entry as
follows:

Blotner, J. (1974). <u>Faulkner: A biography</u> (Vol. 2)....

MULTIVOLUME BOOKS BY A SINGLE AUTHOR WITH A
SEPARATE TITLE FOR EACH VOLUME

MLA: Brooks, Van Wyck. <u>The Flowering of New England</u>. Vol. 2
of <u>Makers and Finders: A History of the Writer in
America, 1800-1915</u>. 5 vols. New York: Dutton,
1936.

APA: Brooks, V. W. (1936). <u>The flowering of New England:
Vol. 2. Makers and finders: A history of the writer
in America, 1800-1915</u>. New York: Dutton.

MULTIVOLUME BOOKS WITH A DIFFERENT AUTHOR AND
TITLE FOR EACH VOLUME

MLA: Woodward, C. Vann. <u>Origins of the New South, 1877-1913</u>.
Vol. 9 of <u>A History of the South</u>. 10 vols. Baton
Rouge: Louisiana State UP, 1951.

APA: Woodward, C. V. (1951). <u>Origins of the New South, 1877-
1913: Vol. 9. A history of the South</u>. Baton Rouge:
Louisiana State University Press.

EDITED BOOKS WITH SELECTIONS BY DIFFERENT AUTHORS

MLA: Morahan, Shirley, ed. <u>A Woman's Place: Rhetoric and
Readings for Composing Yourself and Your Prose</u>.
Albany: State U of New York P, 1981.

APA: Morahan, S. (Ed.). (1981). <u>A woman's place: Rhetoric
and readings for composing yourself and your prose</u>.
Albany: State University of New York Press.

PARTS OF BOOKS BY A SINGLE AUTHOR

MLA: Wilson, Edward O. "Heredity." <u>On Human Nature</u>.
     Cambridge: Harvard UP, 1978. 15-53.

APA: Wilson, E. O. (1978). Heredity. In <u>On human nature</u>
     (pp. 15-53). Cambridge, MA: Harvard University Press.

PARTS OF COLLECTIONS OF WRITINGS BY DIFFERENT
AUTHORS

MLA: Foerster, Loisanne. "Regardless of Sex: Toward
     Communication Free of Bias." <u>Without Bias: A
     Guidebook for Nondiscriminatory Communication</u>.
     2nd ed. Ed. Judy E. Pickens. New York: Wiley,
     1982. 23-44.

APA: Foerster, L. (1982). Regardless of sex: Toward
     communication free of bias. In J. E. Pickens (Ed.),
     <u>Without bias: A guidebook for nondiscriminatory
     communication</u> (2nd ed.) (pp. 23-44). New York:
     Wiley.

ARTICLES IN ENCYCLOPEDIAS OR OTHER REFERENCE WORKS

MLA: Olmstead, David L. "Language, Science of." <u>Encyclopedia
     Americana</u>. 1982 ed.

APA: Olmstead, D. L. 1982). Language, science of. In
     <u>Encyclopedia Americana</u> (Vol. 16, pp. 718-724).
     Danbury, CT: Grolier.

TRANSLATED BOOKS

MLA: Camus, Albert. <u>The Stranger</u>. Trans. Stuart Gilbert.
     New York: Knopf, 1946.

APA: Camus, A. (1946). <u>The stranger</u> (S. Gilbert, Trans.).
     New York: Knopf. (Original work published 1942)

b. Periodical Articles

ARTICLES IN JOURNALS WITH CONTINUOUS PAGINATION
THROUGHOUT ANNUAL VOLUMES

MLA: Sklar, Elizabeth S. "Sexist Grammar Revisited." <u>College
     English</u> 45 (1983): 348-58.

APA: Sklar, E. S. (1983). Sexist grammar revisited. College
    English, 45, 348-358.

ARTICLES IN JOURNALS WITH SEPARATE PAGINATION FOR EACH ISSUE

MLA: Kamin, June. "Writing: Painting with Words." Journal
    of Basic Writing 2.3 (1979): 91-5.

APA: Kamin, J. (1979). Writing: Painting with words.
    Journal of Basic Writing, 2(3), 91-95.

NOTE: "2.3" (MLA) and "2(3)" (APA) indicate the volume and issue numbers of the journal in which the article is found.

SIGNED ARTICLES IN MONTHLY OR WEEKLY MAGAZINES OR NEWSPAPERS

MLA: Hofstadter, Douglas R. "Metamagical Themas: 'Default
    Assumptions' and Their Effects on Writing and
    Thinking." Scientific American Nov. 1982: 18+.

APA: Hofstadter, D. R. (1982, November). Metamagical themas:
    "Default assumptions" and their effects on writing and
    thinking. Scientific American, pp. 18, 22, 26, 30,
    36.

UNSIGNED ARTICLES IN MONTHLY OR WEEKLY MAGAZINES MAGAZINES AND NEWSPAPERS

MLA: "Chairman's Lib: The British Draw the Line." Time 2
    Apr. 1979: 87.

APA: Chairman's lib: The British draw the line. (1979, April
    2). Time, p. 87.

SIGNED ARTICLES IN DAILY NEWSPAPERS

MLA: Kifner, John. "Thousands March in Polish Cities on the
    Founding Day of Solidarity." New York Times 1 Sept.
    1983, late ed.: A1+.

APA: Kifner, J. (1983, September 1). Thousands march in
    Polish cities on the founding day of Solidarity. New
    York Times, sec. A, pp. 1, 10.

NOTE: MLA style requires that the edition, if specified in the newspaper's masthead, should be cited. If the paper's sections are numbered rather than lettered, the number, preceded by *sec*, is indicated before the colon.

UNSIGNED ARTICLES IN DAILY NEWSPAPERS

MLA: "Chinese Musician Seeks Asylum in U.S." <u>Washington Post</u>
3 Sept. 1983: C3.

APA: Chinese musician seeks asylum in U.S. (1983, September
3). <u>Washington Post</u>, sec. C, p. 3.

EDITORIALS AND LETTERS TO THE EDITOR IN DAILY NEWSPAPERS

MLA: Stenholm, Charles W. "Organ Transplants: Personal Pleas
Work." Letter. <u>Washington Post</u> 3 Sept. 1983: A13.

APA: Stenholm, C. W. (1983, September 3). Organ transplants:
Personal pleas work [Letter to the editor].
<u>Washington Post</u>, sec. A, p. 13.

ARTICLE FROM DISSERTATION ABSTRACTS OR DISSERTATION ABSTRACTS INTERNATIONAL

MLA: Moriarty, Deirdre Morgan. "The Relationship of Risk-
Taking and Self-Esteem in Working Women." <u>DAI</u> 44
(1983): 594B (United States International U).

APA: Moriarty, D. M. (1983). The relationship of risk-taking
and self-esteem in working women. <u>Dissertation
Abstracts International</u>, <u>44</u>, 594B.

c. Non-Print Sources

INTERVIEWS CONDUCTED BY THE AUTHOR OF THE RESEARCH PAPER

MLA: Updike, John. Personal interview. 17 May 1983.

NOTE: In the case of interviews conducted by telephone, substitute *Telephone* for *Personal* above. When citing an interview with a person who is not widely known, follow the first name with a comma and the person's title or a brief identification.

APA: Updike, J. (1983, May 17). Personal communication.

NOTE: Interviews are ordinarily not included in an APA-style bibliography.

LECTURES, ADDRESSES, AND PUBLICLY DELIVERED PAPERS

MLA: Stewart, Donald C. "Some History Lessons for Composition
     Teachers." 1st General Session, Conference on
     College Composition and Communication. Detroit, 17
     March 1983.

APA: Stewart, D. C. (1983, March). Some history lessons for
      composition teachers. Paper presented at the meeting
      of the Conference on College Composition and
      Communication, Detroit.

FILMS

MLA: The Big Sleep. Dir. Howard Hawks. Warner Brothers,
     1946.

APA: Hawks, H. (Director). (1946). The big sleep [Film].
      Los Angeles: Warner Brothers.

TELEVISION AND RADIO PROGRAMS

MLA: On the Road. Narr. Charles Kuralt. CBS. WDVM,
     Washington. 19 July 1983.

APA: Kuralt, C. (Producer and Narrator). (1983, July 19).
      On the road. Washington: CBS.

NOTE: Individual episode titles, where applicable, should be
followed by a period and placed before the series title. (In MLA
style, the episode title is also placed within quotation marks.)

RECORDINGS

MLA: Brooks, Gwendolyn. Gwendolyn Brooks Reading Her Poetry,
     with an Introductory Poem by Don L. Lee. Caedmon,
     TC 1244, 1977.

APA: Brooks, G. (1977). Gwendolyn Brooks reading her poetry,
      with an introductory poem by Don L. Lee. New York:
      Caedmon.

d. Summary of Differences

You have probably noticed that bibliography entries prepared according to APA style are very similar to MLA citations. The major differences are listed below:

8d

1. MLA citations provide authors' or editors' first names in full, while APA entries substitute initials.

2. In lists of multiple authors' or editors' names before book and article titles, MLA form requires that only the first author's name be reversed (Jones, John, and Ann Smith), whereas APA style reverses the order of all names (Jones, J., & Smith, A.). Note also that APA form uses an ampersand (&) in place of *and*.

3. For MLA entries, all significant words in book and article titles are capitalized, and article titles are enclosed in quotation marks. According to APA form, only the first word of a book or article title or subtitle is capitalized, as are proper nouns; article titles are not placed within quotation marks. Journal titles in APA citations are capitalized as in MLA-style entries.

4. APA style requires that labels such as *ed.*, edition and volume numbers of books, and issue numbers of periodicals not paginated continuously throughout annual volumes be enclosed in parentheses, but MLA does not.

5. In publication information, APA style provides the state abbreviation following names of cities that are not well known or might be confused with other cities of the same name; in both APA and MLA form, publishers' names are given in the briefest intelligible form.

6. MLA repeats only the final two digits when indicating pagination of more than one page—e.g., 352-53—while APA form requires that page numbers be given in full—e.g., 352-353. MLA style also omits the abbreviation *p.* or *pp.*, whereas APA style calls for the abbreviation to be used for parts of books and monthly or weekly magazine or newspaper articles as well.

7. APA style does not abbreviate names of months, as MLA does. It further differs from MLA form by placing the year first, followed by the month and day of the month and by separating

year and month with a comma. Dates in APA entries follow the authors' names, while in MLA citations, dates are included with publication information.

8. APA format for lectures, addresses, and publicly presented papers does not provide the day of the month as MLA style does.

9. MLA indents second and subsequent lines of bibliography entries five spaces; APA style indents only three.

8d

8d.2   Other Bibliographical Styles

While the MLA and APA styles are the most frequently used in college research, many other style manuals are used in specific disciplines. If neither your instructor nor your major department specifies a particular style manual, you should probably select one used in the field of study for which you are writing the paper. Listed below are some of the other style manuals in common use:

GENERAL

Campbell, William Giles, et al. *Form and Style: Theses, Reports, Term Papers*. 6th ed. Boston: Houghton Mifflin, 1981.

University of Chicago Press. *The Chicago Manual of Style*. 13th ed. Chicago: University of Chicago Press, 1982.

SUBJECT-ORIENTED

American Chemical Society. *American Chemical Society Style Guide*. Washington: American Chemical Society, 1986.

American Institute of Physics. *Style Manual*. 3rd ed. New York: American Institute of Physics, 1978.

American Mathematical Society. *Manual for Authors of Mathematical Papers*. 8th ed. Providence: American Mathematical Society, 1984.

Barclay, William R. *Manual for Authors and Editors: Editorial Style and Manuscript Preparation*. 7th ed. Los Altos: Lange Medical Publications, 1981.

Council of Biology Editors, Committee on Form and Style. *CBE Style Manual*. 5th ed. Washington: The Council, 1983.

Dawe, Jessamon. *Writing Business and Economics Papers, Theses and Dissertations*. Totowa, NJ: Littlefield, Adams, 1975.

Engineers' Joint Council, Committee of Engineering Society Editors. *Recommended Practice for Style of References in Engineering Publications*. New York: Engineers' Joint Council, 1966.

Gray, Wood, et al. *Historian's Handbook: A Key to the Study and Writing of History.* 2nd ed. Boston: Houghton Mifflin, 1964.

Irvine, Demar, ed. *Writing About Music: A Style Book for Reports and Theses.* 2nd ed. Seattle: University of Washington Press, 1968.

8d.3   Compiling the Preliminary Bibliography

8d

As you find potential materials for your research paper, write them down on index cards or on one or more pages of a notebook. (Index cards are better because they will be easier to sort through and alphabetize when the time comes to prepare the final bibliography.)

If you are working with a word processor, record each bibliographical entry in a computer file. You can add and subtract entries as you find new material or find that something is not useful; you can keep entries in alphabetical order for easy reference; and when it is time to prepare the final draft of your research paper, you can easily append the bibliography to the end of your paper before printing out the final copy.

In addition to the information required for the bibliographical citation, your preliminary bibliography should include a note of the call number, so you will not have to go back to the card catalog if you want to find the book again. (This information is especially important for reference books that you have to use in the library.) You may also want to record the floor of the library where the volume is shelved or provide some more detailed information about its location.

EXERCISES

Follow the steps outlined below to prepare a preliminary bibliography for a research paper topic. Use MLA or APA style or the format designated by your instructor. If you follow this procedure step by step, you will not only get practice in a useful research process; you will also produce a useful bibliography should you need to write a research paper, you will have a good overview of your general topic, and will be able to narrow and focus your topic.

1. *Overview of the Topic*: Find one general encyclopedia and one specific one in your general topic area, and list one article that contains material on your topic from each, in appropriate bibliographical form. Read the articles to get an overview of your general topic and to begin to

narrow it. Check the end of each article for a bibliography of books in the area.

2. *Author-Title Catalog*: Look up the titles of at least two of the books mentioned in the encyclopedia bibliographies, and write a bibliographical citation for each. Then browse through the books to see how useful they might be to you. Check the tables of contents, the prefaces, and any introductory material, and note how the books are organized, so that you begin to think about how you might narrow your topic.

3. *Subject Headings*: Before checking the subject catalog, find the correct subject headings in *Sear's List of Subject Headings* or the *Library of Congress Subject Headings*. List the most appropriate subject heading(s) for your topic, as well as the *sa* ("see also") and *xx* (related) headings.

4. *Subject Catalog*: In order to find books on your topic, look up the appropriate subject heading(s) in the subject catalog (or in the general card catalog or on-line catalog if your library does not have a subject catalog). Using the bibliographic form indicated by your instructor, list at least five books on your topic. Check these books in the same way you did the books you found in the encyclopedia bibliography.

5. *Finding Periodical and Newspaper Articles*: First, list at least three different periodical indexes you can use to find articles on your topic, including a newspaper index if appropriate. Then use each of the indexes to find at least six articles containing information on your topic. List them in the bibliographic form requested by your instructor, and read them to see how you might focus your topic further.

6. *Further Searching*: By this time, you should have a good working bibliography, an overview of your topic, a clearer focus for your topic, and an idea of what information you still need. Find the material you need to fill in the gaps.

8e

8e   Discovery: Taking Notes

8e.1   Summarizing, Paraphrasing, and Quoting

When you take notes from your reading, you will sometimes need to jot down just a few words or phrases—names, dates, places, and other basic factual data. But most of the time your notes will be more extensive. They can take the form of a summary, a paraphrase, or a quotation.

A *summary* outlines the major points of a part of the book or article you are reading and is much briefer than the original source.

It can be in outline or sentence form. A *paraphrase* is a restatement of an author's ideas in your own words and sentence structure, and is usually about the same length as the original. A direct *quotation* is an exact reproduction of the author's words, and it is always enclosed in quotation marks or set off from the main text of your paper (see **9b.4**).

8e

Most of your notes should be summaries or paraphrases; they require you to express an idea in your own words, and therefore to understand and assimilate it into your own thinking on the subject. If you quote too much and do not really master your sources, your paper will be a patchwork quilt of undigested quotations rather than a creative product of your own thinking.

If most of your notes are summaries, with some use of paraphrase and occasional instances of quotation, it should be easy to use them in the first draft of your research paper almost exactly as you have taken them. You will simply incorporate them into the sentences and paragraphs you write.

All of your notes—brief jottings, summaries, paraphrases, and quotations—should be written down accurately and legibly, and their sources carefully noted. (See **8e.2** for suggestions of how to do this.) You will then find it is easy to produce the necessary documentation when you use the notes in your research paper.

a. Quotations
When you begin your research you often will be unable to distinguish between the routine information which should be summarized or paraphrased and the sort of data or insight that deserves to be quoted. Such difficulty is not surprising, for like most researchers, you are beginning your task with a very general idea about your topic. It is therefore a good idea to skim through several sources before taking any notes to give yourself a better idea of the relative value of the information you find there.

The following questions may be helpful in identifying quotations for use in your paper:

1. Would the impact be significantly lessened if the quotation were summarized or paraphrased?
2. Is this author one of the experts in the field about which I am writing?

3. Will I be using only a few direct quotations from this source in my paper?

4. Is the quotation less than one hundred words long?

If the answer to all these questions is yes, take the note as a direct quotation. If your response to the first question is negative or if you have answered no to two or more of the other questions, you should record the note as a summary or paraphrase.

8e

You should always enclose direct quotations in quotation marks when you take notes so that you will not mistake the words of the source for your own. Also, compare your transcriptions of quotations with the original from which you copied. The omission of even the smallest words can change the meaning of a passage quite drastically. Meaning can also be changed or obscured altogether when your eye skips and you omit lines or parts of lines because words or sentence structures are similar.

b. Summaries and Paraphrases

Summaries are useful when the passage you are taking notes from is relatively long (100 words or more) and when it is composed primarily of material that can be easily reduced to facts and statistical data. Paraphrases are more useful when you want to record the essence of a short passage, particularly when it expresses opinions and interpretations that could be distorted if reduced to summary form.

If the material requires summarizing, look for topic sentences, conclusions or solutions to problems, and vital details which need to be included. Consider the following selection:

By the end of the 1970s, a few people were beginning to talk about *an organized effort to introduce a new generic singular pronoun into English as it is spoken in the United States.* The impetus for this move did not come from linguists or communication specialists. It came *from psychologists whose studies had confirmed that for most native speakers of English "he,"* in a generic context, *does not mean "he or she."* As part of this effort experimenters have been running *tests with college students to assess the effectiveness of various coined words,* including some of those mentioned above, as sex-inclusive pronouns. The one that proves *the most accessible to large numbers of test subjects*—that is, the term most understandable and easy to use in a variety of sex-inclusive contexts—*will be proposed for adoption* (Casey Miller and Kate Swift, *The Handbook of Nonsexist*

Writing for Writers, Editors and Speakers [New York: Barnes and Noble, 1980] 46-47).

The italicized portions of this paragraph contain the most important information. The passage might be summarized as follows, transforming a paragraph of more than 130 words into a sentence:

> Psychologists whose surveys demonstrate that the generic *he* is not sexually inclusive are testing the effectiveness of coined words proposed as alternatives; the substitute which is best understood by the sample population of college students may eventually be adopted by native speakers of the language.

Similarly, sentences to be paraphrased can be easily converted from the author's language to your own, but in these cases the imitation should be much closer to the original. In paraphrasing, attempt to retain the structure and approximate length of the original, as well as its emphasis. Look for synonyms to reword the original without changing the meaning. Consider the following passage:

> Present-day linguists, tracing the history of the so-called generic *he*, have found that it was invented and prescribed by the grammarians themselves in an attempt to change long-established English usage (Miller and Swift, 36).

Here is an effective paraphrase:

> Language experts who have attempted to discover the origin of the generic singular pronoun have discovered that it originated with grammarians who were trying to change a common usage they considered incorrect.

Note that in the above example, some information (the grammarians' opinion of what they wished to change) has been added to the original sentence. It has been drawn from the context of the source's sentence and is a perfectly legitimate transformation, in effect combining summary with paraphrase.

When you summarize or paraphrase the bulk of a passage, you may still retain phrases or even whole sentences of the original, as long as you enclose the author's exact words in quotation marks whenever you use them. Thus, parts of your paraphrases and summaries might include direct quotations as a means of retaining some of the "flavor"—style, aptness, or tone—of the original without losing the proper balance of paraphrase and summary to quotation that is desirable in a research paper.

8e.2 Managing Your Notes

No matter what kind of notes you take, you should have some system for recording and organizing them, so that your research does not become unmanageable and so that you have easy access to it when it comes time to draft your paper. Four methods for managing your notes are suggested below. You might want to choose one, combine several, or learn from them to devise your own approach. Whatever system you use, it should:

1. record information accurately, discriminating clearly between an author's exact words and your summary or paraphrase of them;

2. indicate the precise source of each piece of information so you can document the research paper easily;

3. be capable of easy organization.

Be sure that each note bears the appropriate page number(s) of the source from which you take the information and that each card or page of notes also contains the author's name, as well as an abbreviated title if you are using more than one work by the same author or if you are using works by two or more authors with the same last name.

Keep all of your notes together so you can easily find and use them whenever you go to the library or do any other work on your research paper. Consider keeping all your research materials in a large envelope or box so they will not be misplaced.

a. Note Cards

Note cards can be efficient and simple research tools. Record items of information from books and articles on three-by-five- or five-by-eight-inch index cards (or make your own by cutting sheets of plain notebook or typing paper into quarters). Record just one piece of information on each, and label each card with a descriptive heading and the source of its information. See figure 8.3 for a sample note card.

The great advantage of this form of note-taking is its limited

Alternative Pronouns

[Psychologist are testing the effectiveness of coined alternatives to _he_ among college students. They will propose the adoption of the pronoun "that proves most accessible to large numbers of test subjects — that is, the term most understandable and easy to use in a variety of sex inclusive contexts . . . ."]

Miller and Swift, _Handbook_ 47

FIGURE 8.3. Sample Note Card

space, which forces you to restrict each card to a single piece of information and therefore makes organizing information later much easier. Furthermore, that bit of data can be readily classified by subject and the card headed with a brief subject label, such as "Alternative Pronouns" in figure 8.3, thus making the task of organizing notes quite easy. Or you can key note cards to works in the preliminary bibliography by assigning each work a separate letter of the alphabet and writing only the letter and page numbers on the note card, e.g., "F 97-98."

Those who work methodically can appreciate that the built-in discipline of the note-card system will make filing notes and planning the first draft less painful because cards can be arranged and rearranged in whatever order the writer wishes, quickly and easily. Those who prefer a less structured technique will find themselves performing similar chores at a later stage of the prewriting process.

b. Research Notebook
Often, students who have been required to use note cards object that similar results can be obtained by writing notes on ordinary

paper. But using a variety of paper types and sizes can make notes difficult to work with in planning the initial draft. The research notebook is the perfect solution to this problem.

In this approach, notes are recorded on the pages of a spiral-bound notebook in much the same way they would be written on cards. The author and title of a work are recorded at the top of a page, with all notes taken from that source written below and on subsequent pages. Page references for each note can be placed in the margin. See figure 8.4 for an example.

8e

When using the notebook technique, write on only one side of each notebook page. Otherwise, you will need to photocopy the reverse sides if you have to cut the pages up later, resulting in added time and expense. It is also possible to miss notes on the reverse sides when you are classifying the results of your research.

The great advantage of this system is that all notes for the project are in one place. Any time you go to the library to read sources for your paper, all you need to take along is the notebook and a pen or pencil. Similarly, you need not write the author and title of each source every time you take a note from it, since that information will be recorded at the top of the page on which you begin your notes from that source. You must, however, be sure notes from each book or article are written successively on the same page(s) of the notebook or are otherwise carefully labeled, so you will not confuse their sources.

After you have completed your research, the easiest method for sorting and organizing the information will be to cut individual notes from the notebook pages. The varying sizes of these parts of pages will make them awkward to use, however, so you may want to paste them up individually on cards or (after classifying and ordering) in groups arranged by subject on new sheets. Before you do any cutting, though, write the author's name (and a short title of the source if necessary) in the margin opposite each note. The page fragments or the sheets or cards on which you paste the notes can be labeled with subject headings in the same way as note cards. Portions of pages which are loose or pasted on cards can be arranged in the order that you expect to use the information.

Miller, Casey, and Kate Swift. *The Handbook of Nonsexist Writing for Writers, Editors and Speakers*. New York: Barnes and Noble, 1980.

3   "Since English, through most of its history, evolved in a white, Anglo-Saxon, patri-archal society, no one should be surprised that its vocabulary and grammar frequently reflect attitudes that exclude or demean minorities and women."

[Getting rid of linguistic bias is difficult because people resist changes in language which "signal widespread changes in social mores."]

35   [The generic *he* was invented by 18th cen. grammarians who objected to "the widespread acceptance of *they* as a singular pronoun.]

35-36   [British Parliament adopted the generic *he* in 1850, declaring that "words importing the masculine gender shall be deemed and taken to include females."]

FIGURE 8.4. Sample Page from a Research Notebook

c. Annotated Photocopies

While books can be borrowed and used at home, having to carry away ten volumes, each of which contains only a few pages on your topic, is inconvenient, and frustrating as well. Moreover, periodicals at most libraries do not circulate. Making and annotating photocopies judiciously can be a valuable supplement to other methods of taking notes.

8e

Instead of writing notes out, photocopy the pages, clearly marking each copy with the author's name and, if necessary, a short title of the source. Be sure page numbers are not cut off during the copying process. You can annotate the copies while reading the pages more carefully at home; highlighting, underlining, commenting, labeling in the margins, and making cross-references to other pages can all be helpful means of recalling the importance of various passages when preparing a draft of your paper. If a photocopy contains more than a single item of information, you can cut out the several usable parts of the photocopy, perhaps pasting them on separate sheets of paper or cards, making sure each contains the necessary identifications of the source and page number. Or you can return to the photocopying machine and make as many copies per page as there are bits of data on the page.

Two disadvantages of this method are the expense and the temptation it offers to do indiscriminate photocopying if you find yourself with a fast-approaching deadline. Be sure to skim what you want to copy to be certain it is significant enough to reproduce for later, more careful reading.

While this technique does not significantly decrease the amount of time spent taking notes, it can add to the convenience of scheduling your research time. Moreover, it is the best means of assuring the accuracy of quotations because you copy them directly from the photographic reproduction of the source when you draft the paper, and you can easily consult the text again at subsequent stages of the writing process if you are uncertain of a quotation's correctness. But this advantage is balanced by the need to spend time when you draft your paper re-reading sections of photocopied pages and summarizing or paraphrasing their contents to avoid overusing quotations or accidentally plagiarizing (see **9c.3**).

d. Computer Files

If you have a computer, consider using it to record your notes as well as to write the paper. Many word-processing programs have special note functions, and all of them enable you to copy information from one file into another, so your notes in one file could be easily copied into a draft of your paper in another file.

Using a computer to manage your notes will obviously work well with books you can check out of the library. For periodical articles and reference books which do not circulate, make photocopies or transcribe handwritten notes into a computer file.

8e

9

RESEARCHED WRITING

9a Incubation and Preliminary Choices

Once you have completed your reading and note-taking, allot a few days, if possible, for relaxation. During this time, your topic and the work done so far will still be engaging your subconscious mind, but you can devote your conscious energies to recreation or assignments for other courses. This incubation period will allow you to return refreshed, stimulated perhaps by new insights.

After a few days, review the notes you have taken and then do some careful thinking about your thesis, your purpose for writing, the medium in which you will write, and your audience. Review the discovery procedure for rhetorical choices outlined in **3d**. This device is especially helpful for a research paper because it forces you to think systematically about real choices which you might otherwise overlook.

9a.1 Purpose and Thesis

Of the four purposes for writing (see **3b**), two can usually be eliminated where researched writing is concerned. By its very nature, the research paper is not expressive; its focus is not the writer but some external topic. Similarly, researched writing is almost never exclusively literary in purpose, although a creative writer may use a great deal of background research.

The primary purpose of researched writing is usually to *inform* the reader (about types of energy-efficient automobiles, for instance, or methods of food preservation) or to *persuade* the reader (for instance, about the superiority of cars with front-wheel drive or the advantages of dehydration over canning). Frequently the two purposes work together. For example, while your purpose may be mainly persuasive, you could also present your reader with a variety of views or approaches to the topic while arguing for the preeminence of one.

9a

When you have determined the purpose of your paper, write out a preliminary statement of your thesis. While you will almost certainly change or at least refine your thesis as you work, it is helpful to have a single sentence to refer to whenever you are confused about the direction you intend to take.

9a.2 Medium and Levels of Formality

A research report or research paper usually has a format clearly specified by your instructor; often it is meant to imitate the scholarly article or technical report, and so it will be written in a more formal style than some other writing (see **3c**). The sample research paper in chapter 10 will give you a student model of this kind of writing.

Notice both the external characteristics of the medium (the way the paper looks on the page, including the format for citations) and also the tone, word choice, and level of formality (see **3c**). If your instructor has prescribed another medium for the research paper—a documented script for an investigative news program, for instance—you should, of course, familiarize yourself with that.

9a.3 Audience and Selection of Details

You may be expected to write for your instructor alone, in which case you should keep in mind your knowledge of the instructor's background, interests, and preferences in matters of style. You may discover your instructor is the easiest audience to write for: you already know so much of what he or she expects.

You may be asked to write for an audience consisting of classmates. You should recognize that composing for these readers is different from writing for yourself because your peers will often have varied interests and backgrounds. Classmates may be less likely than your instructor to have extensive knowledge of your subject, particularly when your topic is specialized. Moreover, they too have certain expectations which you need to be aware of before you begin to write.

You may be asked to write for a general audience of people who are interested in but not experts on your subject. This is the most difficult kind of readership because, while your audience is potentially everyone, determining the backgrounds, interests, and expectations of such a large but nonspecified group of readers is not easy.

9b   Preparing Your Paper

Read through your research notes while you keep in mind both your thesis and the choices you have made about purpose, medium, and audience. As you read, jot down some informal reminders to yourself about which notes are most relevant to your thesis and audience and how you might best arrange the categories of information to convey your purpose in the required format. Then you can begin to think more systematically about ways of developing your thesis.

9b.1   Methods of Development

You will recall from chapter 4 that all effective writing has a dominant method as well as supporting methods of development. Your thesis and purpose in writing will suggest the most effective methods, and you will find that various sections or paragraphs of your paper will call on various methods.

Following are examples of how two different research papers on the general subject of audiocassettes and compact discs might use dominant and supporting methods (many supporting methods other than those shown here would be used as well). The medium of both is a typical college research paper, and the audience is the middle-class consumer who is a potential purchaser of the equipment.

PURPOSE: To *inform* readers about the uses of audiocassettes and compact discs.

THESIS: As audiocassette and compact disc players become less expensive and therefore more accessible to people of moderate income, it is important for consumers to know something about the increasingly sophisticated technology behind them.

DOMINANT METHOD:

Comparison: Cassettes and discs use different technology but for most purposes produce similar results for comparable costs.

SUPPORTING METHODS:

Description: Audiocassettes use magnetized plastic to record sound.

Process Analysis: The disc player uses a laser to decode signals recorded on an object resembling a metallic phonograph record.

Contrast: While audiocassette machines can record as well as play back tapes, disc players have no recording capacity.

PURPOSE: To *persuade* readers that compact disc players are superior to audiocassette recorder / players.

THESIS: Even though compact disc players cannot record, they are superior to audiocassette machines in so many ways that consumers should consider buying one instead of an audiocassette machine.

DOMINANT METHOD:

Contrast: The lack of recording capacity of disc players is more than compensated for by their superior sound and the durability of the discs.

SUPPORTING METHODS:

Description: The technology of cassette recording and playback produces inferior quality of sound.

Analogy: While the compact disc player uses the most current technology, it operates much like the early phonograph.

9b.2 Planning and Arranging

While many writers prefer to do their planning and arranging while they draft, rather than using an outline, a research paper that is longer than a couple of pages usually requires a more formal method of planning.

No matter what method you have used to take notes (see **8e**), you must organize them in a usable way. Whether you do this by rearranging note cards or cutting up and ordering parts of research notebook pages, the result is the same: you classify each item of information by subject (usually one of a relatively small number of subtopics of your research subject area) and arrange the material within each classification in the order you expect to use it.

When you think you have completed your research and have classified, labeled, and filed your notes, check to be sure you have gathered enough information on each point you want to include in your paper. If there are gaps in your coverage of subtopics, return to the sources you have already used to be certain you have not missed anything significant and, if you are unable to find additional material, try to locate other sources of information on these aspects of the subject.

9b

After you have sorted and classified your notes, review them once again and decide, on the basis of your thesis, which of three categories each piece of data belongs in: must use, may use, or won't use. The notes you must use are those containing material vital to an understanding of your subject or presenting important evidence to help persuade your audience of the validity of your argument. In the won't-use category are notes whose contents are not closely related to your thesis statement or which offer weak or unconvincing evidence. The research notes about which you are uncertain go in the may-use stack. Be sure to retain the order of your notes within each stack to make it easy to combine the cards in the must-use stack with those you eventually select from the may-use category.

Having completed the preliminary sorting of your research material, compare the notes in the may-use category with those you have definitely decided to include in your paper. Which of the may-use notes contribute to the development of the thesis and therefore should be included in the paper? Put aside any notes you will not include in your paper, and consolidate the two stacks into one.

Review the notes once again, this time separating them by subtopics. Make sure all notes within each subtopic stack are arranged in the order in which they will most likely be used, and then combine the stacks in the proper order. Next, make a formal or informal outline (see 6c and 6d) that reflects the order of your notes.

Some people can *mentally* organize vast amounts of material before beginning the first draft. If you possess this ability, use it—but before taking the gamble be certain you can apply it to a lengthy assignment. Writing an essay of a few hundred words on the basis of a mental outline may be easy; attempting a ten-page research paper the same way may lead to disaster.

When you have completed your outline, it may require revision before you are ready to write, so set it aside for a day or two if possible. Read through your notes once again, this time following your outline as you go. Some adjustments may be relatively minor, changing the order of a point or two. In other cases, more elaborate rearranging will be necessary. You may decide to reorder large blocks of material or to present some information in an entirely different way. You may even decide that a different primary method of development will result in a more effective research paper.

Usually, it is easier to make structural changes in your paper at the outline stage, although some writers do not see the problems in their papers until they actually begin to write. Try to work out the major structural problems in outline form, but make further changes if necessary as you write your first draft.

If you use a word processor, it will be easy to rearrange parts either in outline or after you have drafted the paper.

9b.3 Writing the First Draft

After you have made some sort of plan or outline, whether informal or formal, you are ready to write the first draft of your paper. To manage your notes efficiently, you need a way of identifying which notes will be used in which part of your paper. If you have an outline that uses numbers and / or letters, on each note card you can write the numbers and letters of the outline section in which you will use that note. If you do not have a formal outline, try numbering your notes and putting the corresponding numbers on your informal outline or plan of your paper.

Writing the draft is really just a matter of filling in your outline with the details, summaries, paraphrases, and quotations from your notes. If you use a word processor, make a copy of your outline and simply expand it as you draft your paper, keeping the original outline in a separate file for reference (or better yet, keeping a printout of the outline next to you while you fill in the outline on the screen).

While you write the first draft, do not worry too much about grammar and usage. As with any kind of writing, it is easiest for most people to get their thoughts down in preliminary, rough form without stopping the flow of ideas to worry about surface details. Later, you can revise and produce drafts that will become progressively more polished (see **9d**).

9b.4 Quotations

When you use quotations in your draft, follow two simple rules regarding their format. Short quotations—those which are less than four lines long—are written or typed "in line," just like other sentences within a paragraph. However, with quotations of four lines or more, you should indent the entire quotation (ten spaces in MLA style or five in APA style), with no extra space before or after.

You should also be sure to integrate quotations adequately into your text by providing necessary introductions and transitions and by incorporating quotations into your own sentences in ways that observe the rules of American English sentence structure. Whenever you omit words, phrases, or sentences from a quotation, indicate the omission with an ellipsis (three *spaced* periods). If you change words in any way (the person of pronouns or verb tense, for example) to make a quotation fit more smoothly into your own sentence or the context of your paragraph, or if you insert words like pronoun antecedents to clarify a quotation, enclose the changed or inserted words in *brackets*, not parentheses. For further information on correct use of brackets and ellipses with quotations, see **24e**.

Note how the quotation below has been incorporated into the writer's sentence which follows it; notice too how alterations to and omissions from the quotation are indicated with ellipses and brackets:

> Since English, through most of its history, evolved in a white, Anglo-Saxon, patriarchal society, no one should be surprised that its vocabulary and grammar frequently reflect attitudes that exclude or demean minorities and women (Casey Miller and Kate Swift, *The Handbook of Nonsexist Writing for Writers, Editors and Speakers* [New York: Barnes and Noble, 1980] 3).

Regarding the history of our language, Miller and Swift note that "Since [it] . . . evolved in a white, Anglo-Saxon, patriarchal society, no one should be surprised that its vocabulary and grammar frequently reflect attitudes that exclude or demean minorities and women" (3).

9b.5 Title, Opening, and Closing

Sometimes the most difficult part of drafting any piece of writing—particularly a research paper—is beginning it. You may find the opening and even your title easier to write after you have written the first draft. Finding a satisfactory conclusion can also be difficult. Review the suggestions about beginnings and endings in **6b**, and then consider the following points that apply more specifically to research papers.

1. Make your title as direct and unambiguous as possible. While clever, imaginative titles are appropriate for less formal essays, the research paper is a different medium with different formal requirements. When you cannot resist the urge to demonstrate your creativity in a title, make sure you include a more descriptive subtitle. For example, without the subtitle *A Study in the Imaginative Literature of 1870-1930*, Edmund Wilson's famous book *Axel's Castle* might easily be mistaken for an architectural treatise or a Gothic romance.

2. A research paper needs a more extensive and explicit introduction than shorter, more informal writing does. You want to capture your reader's interest, announce your subject, perhaps provide some background, and usually include an explicit statement of your thesis and purpose.

3. The concluding section of your paper should summarize your main points and, if your purpose is primarily persuasive, it should present the conclusion of your argument. Your closing might also speculate on future developments in the field you are writing about or give your readers a way of thinking further about the subject.

9c Documenting Your Paper

Documentation of your research paper gives credit for direct quotations, paraphrases, and summaries of facts, ideas, and opinions. This may be done in the form of parenthetical notes, footnotes, or endnotes.

9c.1   Parenthetical Notes

MLA parenthetical documentation includes the last name(s) of the author(s) and page number(s) of the source from which the quotation, paraphrase, or summary is taken. The title of the work, or a shortened version of it, should be provided if you are using more than one work by the author in your paper. Author and title may be given in the sentence(s) introducing the cited material or within parentheses. Page numbers are always provided parenthetically.

9c

If you use APA style, your parenthetical notes should include the last name(s) of the author(s) and the date of publication. On first mention in the text, specify all authors' names unless there are more than five authors; for a work by six or more authors, give the first author's name and *et al.* For second and subsequent mentions in the text, use the first author's name and *et al.* for all works by three or more authors. Whenever any of these data are included within the text itself, however, they are omitted from the parenthetical note. Page numbers are usually omitted from APA citations because documentation in scientific and technical fields generally refers to an entire experiment or theory, not usually to a specific brief passage within the source. If you quote or refer to a specific page or pages, specify them in your parenthetical citation.

Compare the following parenthetical notes to see exactly how MLA and APA styles differ.

MLA: Research indicates that men and women select different generic pronouns in different situations, and that women use *he* less often than men (Martyna, "What Does 'He' Mean?" 133-35).

APA: Research has shown that men and women use generic pronouns in different ways (Martyna, 1978b).

MLA: Stanford describes numerous differences . . . (82-84).

APA: According to Stanford (1981), numerous differences . . .

MLA: Kwitzel did not believe the teaching of philosophi-
cal humanism violated the principle of separation
of church and state. "Humanistic values in literature, science, ethics, and society cut across religious
commitments and are common possessions of the
culture" (5).

9c

APA: Kwitzel (1976) did not believe the teaching of phil-
osophical humanism violated the principle of separation of church and state. He notes that
"Humanistic values in literature, science, ethics, and
society cut across religious commitments and are
common possessions of the culture" (p. 5).

Notice that APA uses "b" following the date in the first example to identify the work as the second by the author listed in the
bibliography and published in 1978; MLA includes the title to
identify the exact work by Martyna. Note also that APA gives
specific page numbers to document direct quotations but not to
document summaries or paraphrases.

9c.2   Footnotes and Endnotes

If your instructor requires notes instead of parenthetical documentation, you may use footnotes (placed at the bottoms of pages
on which cited material appears) or endnotes (grouped together
at the end of the paper). Every time you need to cite a source,
you should place a *superscript* number (raised slightly above the
line) at the end of the material you are quoting, paraphrasing, or
summarizing, after all punctuation except a dash. These numbers
will refer the reader to the note with the corresponding number
at the bottom of the page or the end of the paper. (APA style
ordinarily uses parenthetical documentation to cite sources, while
it uses footnotes or endnotes only to amplify information in the
text of the paper.)

The first lines of the footnotes or endnotes themselves should
be indented and the notes numbered consecutively, using superscript arabic numbers corresponding to the numbers in your paper,
without periods or any other punctuation marks after the note
number.

The basic information you need to cite from books includes

the author(s) and/or editor(s), the book's full title (including sub-title), publication data (city, publisher, date), and page number(s) of material used. For periodical articles, cite the name of the author(s), article title, periodical title, publication information (volume and sometimes issue number, and/or date of issue), and number(s) of pages used.

Although the information needed for notes is much the same as that used for the bibliography (see **8d**), there are several differences in format. Because the notes are intended to supplement the text and are punctuated like sentences, the publication data are enclosed within parentheses. Unlike bibliography entries, the author's or editor's name is given in standard order (first name, middle name or initial, and last name). The first letter of each word in the title is capitalized, except articles, short prepositions, and conjunctions (unless one is the first or last word of the title or subtitle). Each word of the title of a book or periodical is underlined. A colon follows the name of the city, and a comma follows the publisher's name. Subsequent references to the same work are cited in shortened form.

The following examples provide models for you to use in documenting your research paper.

a. First Note References for Published Books

BOOKS BY A SINGLE AUTHOR

[1] Robin Lakoff, <u>Language and Woman's Place</u> (New York: Harper, 1975) 126.

BOOKS BY TWO OR THREE AUTHORS

[2] Casey Miller and Kate Swift, <u>Words and Women</u> (Garden City: Anchor, 1977) 25.

[3] Ben L. Crane, Edward Yeager, and Randal L. Whitman, <u>An Introduction to Linguistics</u> (Boston: Little, 1981) 79.

BOOKS BY MORE THAN THREE AUTHORS

[4] Alleen Pace Nilsen et al., <u>Sexism and Language</u> (Urbana: NCTE, 1977) 13.

BOOKS BY CORPORATE AUTHORS

[5] Modern Language Association, <u>MLA Handbook for Writers of Research Papers, Theses, and Dissertations</u>, 2nd ed. (New York: MLA, 1984) 62.

ANONYMOUS BOOKS

[6] <u>The New Copyright Law</u> (Glenview: Scott, 1979) 27.

LATER EDITIONS OF BOOKS

[7] Modern Language Association, <u>MLA Handbook for Writers of Research Papers, Theses, and Dissertations</u>, 2nd ed. (New York: MLA, 1984) 62.

EDITED BOOKS

[8] Theodore Dreiser, <u>Sister Carrie</u>, ed. Donald Pizer, Norton Critical Editions (New York: Norton, 1970) 99.

BOOKS IN SERIES

[9] Gene Stanford, ed., <u>Dealing with Differences, Classroom Practices in Teaching English, 1980-1981</u> (Urbana: NCTE, 1980) 43.

MULTIVOLUME BOOKS WITH A SINGLE TITLE BY A SINGLE AUTHOR

[10] Joseph Blotner, <u>Faulkner: A Biography</u>, 2 vols. (New York: Random House, 1974) 1: 259.

EDITED BOOKS WHICH CONTAIN SELECTIONS BY DIFFERENT AUTHORS

[11] Shirley Morahan, ed., <u>A Woman's Place: Rhetoric and Readings for Composing Yourself and Your Prose</u> (Albany: State U of New York P, 1981) 92.

PARTS OF BOOKS BY A SINGLE AUTHOR

[12] Edward O. Wilson, "Heredity," in <u>On Human Nature</u> (Cambridge: Harvard UP, 1978) 35.

PARTS OF COLLECTIONS OF WRITINGS BY DIFFERENT AUTHORS

[13] Loisanne Foerster, "Regardless of Sex: Toward Communication Free of Bias," <u>Without Bias: A Guidebook for Nondiscriminatory Communication</u>, ed. Judy E. Pickens, 2nd ed. (New York: Wiley, 1982) 37.

ARTICLES IN ENCYCLOPEDIAS AND OTHER REFERENCE WORKS

[14] David L. Olmstead, "Language, Science of," <u>Encyclopedia Americana</u>, 1982 ed.

TRANSLATED BOOKS

[15] Albert Camus, <u>The Stranger</u>, trans. Stuart Gilbert (New York: Knopf, 1946) 121.

b. First Note References for Periodical Articles

ARTICLES IN JOURNALS WITH CONTINUOUS PAGINATION
THROUGHOUT ANNUAL VOLUMES

[16] Elizabeth S. Sklar, "Sexist Grammar Revisited," <u>College English</u> 45 (1983): 348-58.

ARTICLES IN JOURNALS WITH SEPARATE PAGINATION FOR EACH
ISSUE

[17] June Kamin, "Writing: Painting with Words," <u>Journal of Basic Writing</u> 2.3 (1979): 91-93.

SIGNED ARTICLES IN MONTHLY OR WEEKLY MAGAZINES
AND NEWSPAPERS

[18] Douglas R. Hofstadter, "Metamagical Themas: 'Default Assumptions' and Their Effects on Writing and Thinking," <u>Scientific American</u> Nov. 1982: 35.

UNSIGNED ARTICLES IN MONTHLY OR WEEKLY MAGAZINES OR
NEWSPAPERS

[19] "Chairman's Lib: The British Draw the Line,"
Time 2 April 1979: 87.

SIGNED ARTICLES IN DAILY NEWSPAPERS

[20] John Kifner, "Thousands March in Polish
Cities on the Founding Day of Solidarity," New York
Times 1 Sept. 1983, late ed.: A1.

UNSIGNED ARTICLES IN DAILY NEWSPAPERS

[21] "Chinese Musician Seeks Asylum in U.S.,"
Washington Post 3 Sept. 1983: C3.

ARTICLES FROM DISSERTATION ABSTRACTS OR DISSERTATION
ABSTRACTS INTERNATIONAL

[22] Deirdre Morgan Moriarty, "The Relationship of
Risk-Taking and Self-Esteem in Working Women," DAI
44 (1983): 594B (United States International U).

c. Non-Print Sources

INTERVIEWS CONDUCTED BY THE AUTHOR OF THE RESEARCH PAPER

[23] Personal interview with John Updike, 17 May
1983.

LECTURES, ADDRESSES, AND PUBLICLY DELIVERED PAPERS

[24] Donald C. Stewart, "Some History Lessons for
Composition Teachers," 1st General Session, Con-
ference on College Composition and Communication,
Detroit, 17 March 1983.

FILMS

[25] The Big Sleep, dir. Howard Hawks, Warner
Brothers, 1946.

TELEVISION AND RADIO PROGRAMS

[26] On the Road, narr. Charles Kuralt, CBS, WDVM,
Washington, 19 July 1983.

RECORDINGS

[27] Gwendolyn Brooks, Gwendolyn Brooks Reading
Her Poetry, with an Introductory Poem by Don L.
Lee, Caedmon, TC 1244, 1977.

d. Subsequent Reference Notes

You may use an abbreviated form of a citation after the first full
reference note. This abbreviated form consists of the author(s)
and page(s) being cited. If you use more than one work by an
author in your paper, or if two or more authors whose works
you use have the same last name, include a shortened title of the
book or article in subsequent reference notes. In the case of a
book or article that does not have an author, the subsequent reference includes the title of the book or article (without subtitle),
and the page(s) cited.

BOOKS BY A SINGLE AUTHOR

[28] Lakoff 35-37.

BOOKS BY TWO OR THREE AUTHORS

[29] Miller and Swift, Handbook 10.

[30] Crane, Yeager, and Whitman 57.

BOOKS BY MORE THAN THREE AUTHORS

[31] Nilsen et al. 26.

BOOKS BY CORPORATE AUTHORS

[32] Modern Language Association 23.

SIGNED ARTICLES

[33] Sklar 351.

UNSIGNED ARTICLES

[34] "Chairman's Lib" 87.

9c.3   Avoiding Plagiarism

Remember that any material drawn from your sources that is not common knowledge (nonspecialized information that the typical educated person might be expected to know) must be documented by using one of the forms described in the previous sections or another method prescribed by your instructor. Regardless of whether you quote, paraphrase, or summarize, any time you use specialized data from your sources, you must provide a citation which explains the origin of the information. If you have taken notes and recorded them carefully throughout the processes of research and writing, you will have no difficulty documenting your paper clearly and accurately. Thus, you will avoid the problem of plagiarism—the unacknowledged use of the words, ideas, information, or illustrative materials taken from a source.

Some people mistakenly believe that if they find the same information in several sources, it must be common knowledge. This conclusion is not necessarily true. In fact, several writers may have used the same sources. If you are uncertain whether an item of data is common knowledge or not, ask your instructor or a librarian for guidance. When in doubt, document; if you regularly provide citations for questionable bits of information, you may save yourself the unpleasant consequence of being accused of plagiarism.

Similarly, you should assemble the necessary documentation for your paper—at least in preliminary form—no later than when you complete your first draft. Then, if you are unable to determine the precise location of information included in your paper because of incomplete or illegible notes, you can return to your research sources to obtain the data needed to provide a complete citation.

9d Revising Your Paper

Revision is particularly important in researched writing, because the length and the complexity of working with sometimes unfamiliar material may lead to problems of coherence. You will find that a number of cycles of revision (see **6c**) will be necessary before you have a next-to-final version that can be typed or copied over neatly. Allow plenty of time for revising as well as for breaks from the tedious job of looking critically at your own writing: you may find that you become easily tired when examining work you have already invested many hours in.

In addition to the suggestions in **6c,** keep in mind the following points that apply specifically to the research paper:

1. Read carefully through your outline, checking to see where your draft departs from it. Where the differences are justifiable, make the necessary changes in the outline; where not, target that section of the paper for rewriting. Then analyze the revised outline. If there are any problems with structure and logic within the outline, similar difficulties will need to be eliminated from the draft as well.

2. Read your draft aloud, listening to how it sounds, being especially sensitive to your choice of words. While a certain amount of technical jargon is necessary when you write for other experts, it can make a research paper nearly incomprehensible to a nonspecialist. If your audience includes nonexperts, be sure to define specialized terminology.

    Another potential trouble spot is tone. Choose words with sensitivity toward the message they indirectly send your readers. Avoid the pomposity and dryness sometimes mistaken for expertise. Just because you are an expert on the subject, there is no need to put on linguistic airs. Familiar words are preferable to pretentious ones in a research paper as well as in other types of writing. Try to avoid sounding overly academic.

    On the other hand, your research paper should aim for a scholarly or technical level of formality (see **3c**). It should not be chatty or intimate, but neither should it be stilted or artificial. If a research paper wore clothes, it would wear a conservative business suit, not a tuxedo or evening gown.

3. Because a research paper draws on a variety of sources, you must be careful to join its parts into a coherent whole. Read your draft looking especially for places within the paper where relationships between the parts are not clearly established or maintained. Clear and adequate transition is especially important in the research paper because of its length and complexity. Assist your reader in understanding relationships of time, space, similarity or difference, and cause or effect by providing the necessary transitional signals. (A list of examples of transitional words and phrases can be found in **12b.**)

4. When you reach the next-to-final draft stage, some last-minute details special to the research paper will require your attention. Check the quotations in the paper against your notes to ensure their accuracy. Similarly, double-check all citations of sources in the paper to be certain they are correct. (It is good to repeat this step after the final version of the paper is prepared to catch typing or copying errors.) Also check the spellings of proper names and specialized terminology.

10

SAMPLE
RESEARCH PAPER

Third-Person Unbiased:

The Generic Pronoun in English

John Fredericks

English 102

24 February 1988

Third-Person Unbiased:

The Generic Pronoun in English

We usually think of language as a tool, the means of communicating. But unlike other tools shaped by humans, it is likely that language also shapes us. Benjamin Whorf, an important twentieth-century linguist, believed that language patterns influence users to see the world in certain ways and that these conventions of perception differ from one language to another (Morahan 32-33). Although linguists have debated the extent of the application of Whorf's hypothesis, there is no doubt that language has some definite effects on perception, and vice versa (Miller and Swift, <u>Words</u> 125). There can be no doubt, in the words of Sol Steinmetz, that Whorf's beliefs about the influence of language make "profound psychological sense" (8).

In recent years, the feminist movement has sparked questions about how the subordinate role of women in our culture has been reflected in our language and how our linguistic habits have reinforced that social bias. Casey Miller and Kate

Swift, authors of several books on sexism in language, have observed that "Since English . . . evolved in a white, Anglo-Saxon, patriarchal society, no one should be surprised that its vocabulary and grammar frequently reflect attitudes that exclude or demean minorities and women" (Handbook 3). If there really is a problem of sexism in English, what are its effects and how can both the problem and its effects be prevented?

The question of sexist language is too complicated to consider here, so this paper will examine only a limited aspect of it: the fact that, like most languages, English uses the third-person singular masculine pronoun to refer to individuals in a sexually mixed group (Lakoff 43). Douglas Hofstadter calls this generic use of he the "default assumption" of masculinity in language, because we implicitly assign male characteristics to human beings when sex is not specified. While default assumptions of all kinds make everyday life easier by preventing our brains from becoming overloaded with details, they certainly also reflect prejudices (18). The extent of this phenomenon and its effects make a good case for the validity of Whorf's views about language and argue cogently for changes in the way we refer to human beings generically.

The use of he as a generic pronoun is a relatively recent aspect of English grammar. Not until the eighteenth century was there an attempt to counter the use of they to refer to singular antecedents of unspecified gender, although it had been so used for centuries by common people as well as eminent writers. To grammarians trained in the classics, however, this practice was illogical and vulgar, so they substituted he for the generic they (Miller and Swift, Handbook 35-37).

The British Parliament gave unofficial government approval to this arbitrary rule by adopting the generic he in laws and documents: "words importing the masculine gender shall be deemed and taken to include females" (Miller and Swift, Handbook 37). That attitude has been accepted in U. S. law as well, but only for the convenience of government; it could be forgotten when convenience dictated. In an 1893 case involving the admission of a woman to the Virginia bar, for example, the U.S.Supreme Court held that a woman was not a "person," this indefinite pronoun and the generic use of he being crucial points in interpreting the state law governing bar membership.

In their opinion, the "brethren" of the Court appealed not to the precedent of British parliamentary usage but to the earlier jurist Blackstone, who observed that "the very being or legal existence of woman is suspended during . . . marriage" (Bosmajian 100-1).

While the feminist movement has come a long way in challenging the long-held view that women are chattels, laws have frequently proved easier to change than the language habits of most speakers and writers of English. Several important arguments for and against the generic <u>he</u> have been advanced.

In her essay "The Myth of the Neutral 'Man,'" Janice Moulton explains two of the many claims that have arisen in recent years about supposedly gender-neutral terms like <u>he</u>. Some people, according to Moulton, claim that these words are indeed neutral but are still unfair because they make women feel inferior and thus should be eliminated as a sign of goodwill. Others charge that these terms are not neutral and thus cause unfair treatment of women. While Moulton herself feels that the first claim has greater validity, she makes a case for the second (101-2).

The intention of neutrality alone is not

sufficient to make language truly sex-neutral,
Moulton says. In fact, she claims, attempted uses
of purportedly gender-neutral words (like _he_) often
fail to communicate accurately because they often
imply "male" to the listener or reader (113).

Disagreeing with Moulton, Jane Duran advises
that audiences have "a keen awareness of context and
a reservoir of good faith" to insure the gender-
neutrality of generics such as _he_ (154). Duran's
approach to the problem, however, is naive. Is
awareness of context a sure method of countering the
possibility of ambiguity these words raise? Why
should those who are offended or feel excluded by
these terms assume that those who use them do not
mean to exclude or offend?

Miller and Swift point out that the generic _he_
is probably easier for male children to internalize
as a rule of grammar than for female children.
Moreover, the sense of exclusion that it can
engender in females can cause a severe ego-blow
(_Words_ 26-27). And one of the most active
researchers in this field, Wendy Martyna, claims
that in addition to ambiguity and exclusion, the
generic use of _he_ raises the problem of inequity,
since there is no female pronoun which can always be

Fredericks 6

used generically ("What Does 'He' Mean?" 131-32).

Recent studies show that the objections to the
use of <u>he</u> and other generic pronouns have a real
basis and are not motivated solely by theoretical or
political disagreements. This research makes it
clear that by no means do all people intend or
understand such words to include females as well as
males (Miller and Swift, <u>Handbook</u> 37) and that women
perceive these terms differently than men do and
react to their use in different ways.

In the early 1970s, three experiments conducted
by researchers at Drake University, the University
of Iowa, and Western Michigan University
demonstrated the inadequacy of <u>man</u> as a generic
pronoun. The subjects, who ranged in age from
nursery-school pupils to college students, indicated
that they understood this pronoun to refer to males
more often that to both men and women, even when the
context seemed to call for a generic interpretation
(Miller and Swift, <u>Words</u> 1922).

Later in the 1970s, Wendy Martyna conducted
extensive studies of the use of the generic <u>he</u>. The
most comprehensive of her investigations, a series
of six experiments reported in her 1978 Stanford
University doctoral dissertation, analyzed the use

and perception of he by a variety of subjects.
Experiments 1 and 2 required 435 students between
the ages of five and twenty-five to complete
sentence fragments about male, female, and sex-
neutral roles. They used he for male, she for
female, and he or she or they for neutral roles most
often ("Using" 3050B).

Martyna's experiments 3 and 4 involved 120
college students. Shown sentences about sex-
unspecified persons referred to as he, they, or he
or she, they were asked whether pictures
corresponded to the sentences. Nineteen percent of
the participants in experiment 3 said female
pictures did not correspond to sentences using the
generic he. In experiment 4, when the sentences
were changed to emphasize he, 34 percent said that
female pictures were inappropriate as illustrations
("Using" 3050B).

In experiments 5 and 6, Martyna asked 390
college students to suggest typical names for sex-
unspecified persons referred to as he, they, or he
or she, all used generically. Male names were most
often given in response to he, least often in
response to he or she ("Using" 3050B).

An experiment with a slightly different

emphasis allowed Martyna to examine the differences
in pronoun selection between males and females in a
variety of situations. In her article "What Does
'He' Mean?" she details a study of twenty male and
twenty female Stanford students who were asked to
complete sentence fragments involving male, female,
and sex-neutral roles. She found that women used <u>he</u>
significantly less often than men did and that a
generic use of <u>she</u> appeared only in female-role
sentences. She also discovered that <u>they</u> was used
as a singular generic pronoun more often in spoken
responses, while <u>he or she</u> appeared more frequently
in written answers (133-35).

    In summarizing her research, Martyna has noted
that <u>he</u> is ambiguous

> even in a clearly generic context . . .
> allowing both specific and generic
> interpretations to be drawn. My research
> does not argue that [<u>he</u>] <u>cannot</u> function
> generically, but that it allows for both
> specific and generic interpretation, even
> in a context which should force a generic
> inference.

More important are her observations that women use
<u>he</u> less often and alternative generics more often

than men do, and that men are able to envision

themselves more readily as members of a group

described using the generic he ("Beyond the 'He/Man'

Approach" 488-89).

Because the research shows the inadequacy of he

as a generic pronoun, why not change the language to

rid it of such problems? Moreover, although it does

not indicate to women how society expects them to

behave, the generic he does cause a sizable number

of women to feel left out, thus providing even more

reason for seeking a different solution to the

problem (Lakoff 44-45). The difficulty is that many

speakers of the language resist such changes. These

people find linguistic change threatening because it

usually reflects intimidating social changes;

others simply find any opposition to the linguistic

status quo exasperating (Miller and Swift, Handbook

3). Moreover, linguistic change usually occurs

slowly, typically over several generations, because

meaning is dependent on conventional usage and is

largely independent of dictionaries and even of

formal schooling (Miller and Swift, Words 21).

Given the difficulty associated with such

changes, some theorists feel that there are problems

of linguistic sexism more worth their attention than

the generic <u>he</u>. Robin Lakoff, for example, notes
that "this area of pronomial neutralization is both
less in need of changing and less open to change"
than other linguistic disparities between the sexes
(45). Others, like Janice Moulton, acknowledge the
difficulties involved but insist that truly gender-
neutral terms should not foster assumptions about
the gender of persons to which they refer (103-04).
Still others feel the need to protect the language
from those they call "the enemy," who threaten the
purity of English (Stanley 51). Despite resistance,
though, English continues to change, just as it has
for more than a thousand years. As Miller and Swift
observe, "The point is not that we should recognize
semantic change, but that in order to be precise, in
order to be understood, we must" (<u>Handbook</u> 4-8).

The fact is that the women's movement of the
past fifteen years has already had a considerable
effect in removing sex bias from English. Much
progress has been made, especially over the past
decade, in eliminating sexist language in schools,
the media, churches, business, and government
(Foerster 23-25). Writers, editors, and teachers
have been particularly responsive in altering their
use of words and expressions which are biased

(Steinmetz 6). For example, doctors Benjamin Spock
and Lee Salk have both eliminated the generic <u>he</u>
from recent editions of their books on child
development (Miller and Swift, <u>Words</u> 28-29).

Perhaps most notable, however, is the fact that
some of the language changes in this area have been
inspired not only by the influence of feminism but
by other pragmatic and theoretical concerns as well.
For instance, "Changing business practices and
social patterns (which include women in increasing
numbers in areas previously off limits to them) make
certain language habits obsolete" (Foerster 26).
Others find themselves personally involved in
linguistic change in other ways. "I am hardly one
to believe that language 'pushes us around,' that we
are its slaves," Douglas Hofstadter maintains, but
he adds, "I think we must do our best to rid
language of usages that may induce or reinforce
default assumptions in our minds" (22).

There are other more truly neutral terms
available as replacements for the generic use of <u>he</u>,
and though they may be awkward at first, their use
will remind us of past injustices committed against
women (Moulton 102-03). Indeed, we have a choice
between alternatives which have been coined over

more than a century as substitutes for the generic
<u>he</u> and words and phrases which have been elements of
the language since its beginnings and which can also
be used in place of <u>he</u>.

Some of the artificial generic pronoun
substitutes were invented in the nineteenth century.
For example, Charles Converse proposed <u>thon</u>, a
contraction of <u>that one</u>, as a replacement for <u>he</u> in
1859. More than fifty years later, <u>Funk and
Wagnall's New Standard Dictionary</u> (1913) listed not
only Converse's pronoun but also <u>he'er</u>, <u>his'er</u>, and
<u>him'er</u> as sex-unspecific pronouns. In the more
recent past, June Arnold's <u>The Cook and the
Carpenter</u> (1973) employed <u>na</u>; Marge Piercy's <u>Woman
on the Edge of Time</u> (1976) used <u>per</u>, derived from
<u>person</u>; and Mary Orovan of the Twin Oaks Community
suggested <u>co</u>, based on an Indo-European root, as a
generic pronoun in 1970. Among other choices are
<u>hir</u>, <u>E</u>, <u>tey</u>, <u>hesh</u>, <u>po</u>, <u>ve</u>, <u>xe</u>, and <u>jhe</u> (Miller and
Swift, <u>Handbook</u> 46, and <u>Words</u> 116-17; Eade 231).

Alleen Pace Nilsen does not think that a coined
pronoun is the best solution to the problem,
however.

> Rather than inventing a new pronoun I
> think we are gradually increasing the role

of an old one: they, their, and them.
This pronoun is changing from being
strictly plural to being plural and
singular, just as you is both plural and
singular. (368)

Julia P. Stanley agrees with Nilsen, noting that "I
suspect that we still use they" more than two
centuries after grammarians consigned it to oblivion
as a singular generic "because we know more about
our language than those who would protect us from
error" (52).   Indeed, this conclusion is borne out
by Martyna's observation that they is commonly used
in speech as a substitute for the generic he ("What
Does 'He' Mean?" 134).

The colloquial use of they as a singular
generic pronoun is not yet acceptable in more formal
conversation or writing, but there are several other
methods of eliminating he.   One of the best is to
pluralize the antecedent and use they with the
grammarians' seal of approval.   Similarly, sentences
can be reworded to avoid the necessity of a generic
pronoun ("Each employee must submit a time sheet
initialled by the appropriate supervisor" in place
of "Each employee must submit a time sheet
initialled by his supervisor").   Second-person

pronouns may be substituted for thirdperson singular
generics, and the use of <u>one</u> is yet another
alternative. Finally, writers and speakers may
employ <u>he or she</u>, though that compound tends to be
clumsy when repeated, or they may alternate male and
female gender-specific pronouns (Foerster 27-35;
Miller and Swift, <u>Handbook</u> 38-44; "Appendix" 183-
84).

Although some opponents of nonsexist language
have claimed it is clumsy or ineffective, they have
been proved wrong. While most people are unlikely
to adopt constructs such as <u>thon</u> and <u>na</u>,
psychologists have been studying the effectiveness
of a variety of these alternative generics since the
late 1970s. When their research is completed, they
will propose the general adoption of the most
accessible (Miller and Swift, <u>Handbook</u> 46-47). It
is more likely that one of the natural alternatives
of the language will receive popular acceptance,
however, particularly given the persistent and
common use of <u>they</u> as a singular generic pronoun
(Foerster 25). Therefore, while we cannot predict
the future with certainty, it is quite possible that
the generic use of <u>he</u> will be labeled "archaic" in
the dictionaries of future generations and the use

of _they_ with singular antecedents will again be

considered the standard.

Works Cited

"Appendix: Guidelines for Nonsexist Use of
     Language in NCTE Publications." <u>Sexism and
     Language</u>. By Alleen Pace Nilsen et al.
     Urbana: NCTE, 1977. 181-91.

Bosmajian, Haig. "Sexism in the Language of
     Legislatures and Courts." <u>Sexism and
     Language</u>. By Alleen Pace Nilsen et al.
     Urbana: NCTE, 1977. 77-104.

Duran, Jane. "Gender-Neutral Terms." <u>Sexist
     Language: A Modern Philosophical Analysis</u>.
     Ed. Mary Vetterling-Braggin. n.p.:
     Littlefield, 1981. 147-54.

Eade, Alan J. "Words and Politics: To Each Their
     (?) Own." <u>Etc</u>. 36 (1979): 230-33.

Foerster, Loisanne. "Regardless of Sex: Toward
     Communication Free of Sexual Bias." <u>Without
     Bias: A Guidebook for Nondiscriminatory
     Communication</u>. Ed. Judy E. Pickens. 2nd ed.
     New York: Wiley, 1982. 23-44.

Hofstadter, Douglas R. "Metamagical Themas: 'Default Assumptions' and Their Effects on Writing and Thinking." Scientific American November 1982: 18 +.

Lakoff, Robin. Language and Woman's Place. New York: Harper, 1975.

Martyna, Wendy. "Beyond the 'He/Man' Approach: The Case for Nonsexist Language." Signs 5 (1980): 482-493.

---. "Using and Understanding the Generic Masculine: A Social-Psychological Approach to Language and the Sexes." DAI 39 (1978): 3050B (Stanford U).

---. "What Does 'He' Mean?" Journal of Communication 28.1 (1978): 131-138.

Miller, Casey, and Kate Swift. The Handbook of Nonsexist Writing for Writers, Editors and Speakers. New York: Barnes, 1980.

---. Words and Women: New Language in New Times. Garden City: Anchor, 1977.

Morahan, Shirley, ed. A Woman's Place: Rhetoric and Readings for Composing Yourself and Your Prose. Albany: State U of New York P, 1981.

Moulton, Janice. "The Myth of the Neutral 'Man'"

    <u>Sexist Language: A Modern Philosophical</u>

    <u>Analysis</u>. Ed. Mary Vetterling-Braggin. n.p.:

    Littlefield, 1981. 100-15.

Nilsen, Alleen Pace. "You'll Never Be the Man Your

    Mother Was, and Other Truisms." <u>Etc.</u> 36

    (1979): 365-70.

Stanley, Julia P. "Gender-Marking in American

    English: Usage and Reference." <u>Sexism and</u>

    <u>Language</u>. By Alleen Pace Nilsen et al.

    Urbana: NCTE, 1977. 43-74.

Steinmetz, Sol. "The Desexing of English." <u>New</u>

    <u>York Times</u>, 1 Aug. 1982, late ed., sec.6: 6,+.

10a   The Commentary

Title: Note that although his title is imaginative, Fredericks has also provided a specific subtitle to specify the paper's purpose more fully to his audience.

Paragraphs 1-3: Because his paper is lengthy, Fredericks' introduction is longer than would be necessary for a shorter assignment. In paragraph 1 he briefly describes the linguistic theory which underpins the argument he will present in the body of the paper, while paragraphs 2 and 3 present the specific thesis: If the pronoun *he* is sexist, what are the effects of the problem, and how can both problem and effects be prevented? Readers will thus be able to see from the beginning the paper's persuasive purpose and its primary method of development—cause-effect analysis.

Although these three paragraphs contain six parenthetical notes, most of the secondary material is presented as summary (e.g., Whorf's hypothesis in paragraph 1) or paraphrase (the first reference to Miller and Swift, for example). Also notice that the only long quotation here (in paragraph 2), as well as the earlier reference to Whorf, is preceded by a brief comment about the credentials of the authority. Note too the use of the ellipsis in the quotation in paragraph 2 to indicate the omission of part of the source's sentence.

Because he refers to more than one work by Miller and Swift, Fredericks has included in his parenthetical notes a shortened title of each source he cites by these writers.

Paragraphs 4-5: The first developing paragraphs present a brief narrative of the history of *he* as a generic pronoun and the problems women have encountered as a result of its use. Since his audience consists of a general readership, this section provides background necessary to convince readers unfamiliar with his subject.

Paragraph 6: While not ordinarily found in shorter pieces of writing, a transition paragraph like this is valuable in a longer paper as a means of moving from one major section (historical background of the problem) to another (the case for and against *he* as a generic).

Paragraphs 7-12: In this second developing section, Fredericks presents some of the major arguments for retaining and for replacing *he* as a generic in terms of the problems it is believed to effect. Because the question is complicated, he does not attempt to survey all positions comprehensively (such an approach would not be possible within the scope and focus of his paper); he does, however, address two different sides of the issue to provide the audience with an understanding of the issue's complexity.

10a

Fredericks begins building a convincing case for his point of view here by posing a series of compelling rhetorical questions challenging the opposing view in paragraph 10 and pointing to several problems resulting from the use of sexist generic pronouns in paragraphs 8 and 12. The last of these examples also provides transition into the next section, a review of linguistic studies of the problem. This section is effective, then, because it demonstrates to the reader the existence of opposing points of view and leads to a consideration of evidence for Fredericks' side of the question.

Paragraphs 13-19: This section provides details of several experiments which studied users' perceptions of *he* and other generic pronouns. Fredericks presents his most important evidence here, and thus he devotes considerable space to discussing its significance.

Note that the first of two indented quotations included in this paper does not appear until paragraph 19. Fredericks has continued to use quotations sparingly and has avoided using frequent, lengthy ones. Also, as with Miller and Swift's works, Fredericks has included short titles in references to sources by Martyna, either within his sentences introducing the material or in parenthetical references.

Paragraphs 20-27: The final major section discusses possible solutions to the problem caused by the sexist generic *he*. Paragraphs 20 and 21 provide transition from the preceding section by examining the need for replacing discriminatory pronouns with more neutral ones, while paragraphs 22 and 23 survey progress already made in this area. Paragraphs 24-27 discuss several coined and natural alternatives to the generic *he*.

Note that while analyzing substitutes for *he*, Fredericks continues to use examples frequently to inform an unfamiliar audience.

The extensive list of artificial generic pronouns in paragraph 25 is especially effective in demonstrating the unfeasibility of this approach, a point which would have been more difficult to show if only a few had been included.

Paragraph 28: The final paragraph presents the conclusion of Fredericks' argument very concisely. He cogently summarizes several of the important points which have led to the solution he endorses, and he ends his paper by speculating about the future, a good way to finish an argumentative essay which presents the causes and effects of a problem and evaluates various solutions. It is possible that not every reader will agree with the positions presented here, but most will acknowledge that he has accomplished his purpose quite effectively.

10a

Bibliography: Fredericks has utilized examples of many types of research sources in preparing his paper, including books, articles in scholarly journals, selections by individual authors contained in edited books, a dissertation abstract, and a newspaper article.

Notice that Fredericks has arranged the first item in the bibliography, an anonymous work, alphabetically by the first word of the title. He has also used three hyphens to replace the author's name in second and subsequent entries by Martyna and by Miller and Swift and has ordered entries by these writers alphabetically by title.

In the titles of Hofstadter's article, the first and last articles by Martyna, and Moulton's essay, which contain words enclosed in quotation marks, Fredericks has changed these marks to single quotes and enclosed the titles with double quotes.

Part Three

PARAGRAPHS AND THE WRITING PROCESS

11

PARAGRAPHING

The title of this chapter is *paragraphing* rather than *paragraphs* for an important reason: too often people think of paragraphs as if they were static blocks of prose used to build an essay—much as a mason piles bricks on top of one another to form a building. Paragraphing, however, more often resembles a sculptor's carving a figure out of stone. Paragraphing is an active process, whether you write paragraph by paragraph, developing one at a time the various sections of an outline, or whether you write your essay all at once, perhaps indenting when it seems logical to do so and then returning to your essay later to see if the paragraph divisions make sense.

Whichever way you paragraph, at the beginning of the writing process, in the middle, or only in a revision stage near the end, you need to be aware of how paragraphs function in different kinds of writing. There are at least four points of view from which to consider paragraphing:

1. Paragraphs can be seen as extended sentences.
2. Paragraphs can be seen as miniature essays.
3. Paragraphs can be seen as a kind of punctuation.
4. Paragraphs can be seen as parts of an essay.

11a Paragraphs as Extended Sentences

When writing a first draft, some writers sketch out sentences that later can be developed into full paragraphs. A paragraph, then, often develops from an extended sentence. It should have the equivalent of a subject and verb (topic sentence and supporting sentences), and it should be as unified as a sentence is, with no material that does not support the topic sentence. Take for example the following sentence:

> The Civil War nearly devastated the South because it left many of the plantations burned and stripped, it left many plantation owners without anyone to do the manual labor required to raise and harvest crops, and it left both blacks and whites at the mercy of carpetbaggers and other exploiters of Reconstruction.

If we turned just that one sentence into a paragraph, the main clause of the sentence would become the *topic sentence* (the sentence that expresses the main idea of the paragraph), and the three subordinate clauses following *because* would become *supporting sentences*:

11a

> The Civil War nearly devastated the South. It left many of the plantations burned and stripped. It left many plantation owners without anyone to do the manual labor required to raise and harvest crops. It left both blacks and whites at the mercy of carpetbaggers and other exploiters of Reconstruction.

This short paragraph is choppy—too brief really to function as a whole paragraph in a formal essay. But it could be expanded into a longer one by adding supporting details for each of the three points, and of course it could also be expanded into an essay in which each of the three supporting sentences would become the topic sentence for a full paragraph, with sufficient supporting detail at a low level of abstraction.

EXERCISES

1. Turn each of the following sentences into a paragraph, first by simply breaking up the phrases and clauses to produce a series of sentences; second, by filling in details, at a low level of abstraction, that will support the topic sentence:

   a. Modern college students have three characteristics not shared by earlier generations: awareness of how technology governs American culture; a desire to get the most practical education as quickly as possible, in order to move into a career; and a consequent lack of concern for "impractical" subjects, like music, art, and literature.

   b. Nature is like the cycles of human growth: a season of new life is followed by a season of growth and fruition, which is followed by a season of death and decay, and finally by a season of dormancy.

c. The process is a simple one that includes cleaning the sink, then filling it with warm, soapy water, then scrubbing and rinsing, and finally drying.

d. The majority of all headaches result from three causes: muscle tension, which is generally the result of stress; dietary irregularities, especially for hypoglycemics and diabetics; and hereditary predisposition, as in the case of migraine sufferers.

e. The best way to become a better writer is to write often, to give yourself lots of time to discover material when you have a formal writing project, and to take time to revise and not merely edit.

2. Choose one of the paragraphs you have written and expand it into an essay. The topic sentence will become the thesis in the introductory paragraph of the essay, and each of the supporting sentences will become the topic sentence of a paragraph.

11b

11b   Paragraphs as Miniature Essays

11b.1   Unity, Completeness, Order, and Relationship

A paragraph can also be viewed as a miniature essay that follows certain principles which apply to writing of any length:

1. A paragraph should have *unity*: like an essay, nothing should be in it that does not support the main point (which is often expressed in the topic sentence). You must choose carefully which of the many potential supporting details are relevant to your purpose and audience. If you are arguing that students should be able to design their own majors, then a statement about life in dormitories or length of vacations will not be relevant and will distract readers from your central point.

2. A paragraph should be *complete*: as in an essay, there should be enough material to develop and support the main point, according to the needs of the audience. If, for example, you were describing a fishing trip you took to Alaska in order to convince someone else to go, you would need to describe the surroundings, the fish, and the atmosphere in as much detail as possible. If you were to describe the same fishing trip to provide a humorous account of your companion's fight with a giant fish, then many of the details of the first version would

be irrelevant and you would want to add details about your friend's struggle with the fish.

3. A paragraph, like an essay, should have a clear *order*, with a logical structure suitable to the audience and subject, and with subordinate and coordinate ideas clearly distinguished. It will usually follow one of the patterns discussed in **6a**.

4. A paragraph, like an essay, should have clear marks of *relationship* between parts, including accurate transitional phrases and clear pronoun reference. (Chapter 12 will discuss these marks of relationship in detail.)

The following student-written paragraph illustrates all four of these points. Some of the key words indicating relationships are in italic type.

11b

> The magnetic field of tapes is *less* susceptible to damage *than* records. *Unlike* records, tapes cannot be scratched easily and do not lose quality after being played. *When* a record is played, the needle tracing the groove actually scrapes off a microscopic amount of the surface. *After* several playings of the record, this damage can be heard in the form of a hiss or crackle in the background. *Although* there have been several attempts to eliminate this damage, *even* the finest needle and cartridge played on a specially treated record will have this effect. Tapes run across a tape "head," which detects the variations in the magnetic field. The only possible damaging effect from this process occurs if a build-up of an oxide from the tape forms on the head. *Usually*, this would require cleaning at periodic intervals to prevent damage to the tape, *but* a new feature on almost all new tapes eliminates the need for this. The new feature is a five second "leader" which cleans the heads before each playing. *Since* there is virtually no damaging contact between tape and the tape head, tapes maintain their sound quality for a very long time.
>
> —Cassian Pallansch

Notice how the first sentence states the "thesis" or topic sentence of the paragraph. Everything in the paragraph works to support the claim it makes, so it is *unified*. The paragraph is also *complete*—the author gives us enough information to make his claim convincing. The paragraph has a clear *order*: after the first two sentences, he discusses first records, then tapes, and in each category he discusses first what happens when records and tapes are played and then what attempts have been made to improve the quality of tapes. Finally, he uses signals of *relationship*, especially pronouns and transitional words and phrases, very effectively.

11b.2   Paragraph Structure: Topics, Problems, and Questions

If you think of a paragraph as an essay in miniature, you will find that it follows one of several common structures:†

Problem	+	Solution			(PS)
Question	+	Answer			(QA)
Topic	+	Restriction	+	Illustration	(TRI)

11b

You can see these patterns in most of the methods of development we discussed in chapter 4. A Problem + Solution structure, for example, is often found in a paragraph whose dominant method is cause-effect. The topic sentence might pose the *problem*—how to avoid the negative effects of the shortage of foreign oil—while the rest of the essay would develop a suggested *solution*—to find more domestic sources of oil and to develop alternative forms of energy.

A variation on the PS structure is the Question + Answer pattern. For instance, a cause-effect paragraph might pose a problem in the form of a *question*: "What were the major causes of the Civil War?" Then the rest of the paragraph would provide *answers*—in this case, the causes.

Like the QA structure, the Topic + Restriction + Illustration pattern is found in many different types of paragraphs. The first sentence of such paragraphs states the *topic*, as in the essay in **11b.1**: "The magnetic field of tapes is less susceptible to damage than records." The next sentence *restricts* the topic, stating *why* magnetic tapes are less susceptible to damage: "Unlike records, tapes cannot be scratched easily and do not lose quality after being played." And the rest of the paragraph provides illustrations to support the topic. The following examples will illustrate some of these patterns:

†This scheme was developed by the contemporary rhetorician Alton Becker.

TRI *structure with example as dominant method*:

Everywhere there is destruction, and everywhere there is hope. Faith in the new government ranges from outright enthusiasm among the poor to cautious optimism in the middle and upper classes. The unifying sentiment is a tremendous joy that Somoza and the Guard are finally gone.   —Edward Holland

TOPIC
RESTRICTION

ILLUSTRATION

PS *structure with cause-effect analysis as dominant method*:

A photograph or a painting is flat—we can lay it on a table, we can look behind it, we can even bend it or roll it up. Yet a picture of a scene also looks like the scene: when the picture is hung on a wall, it is like a window through which we can see the actual three-dimensional scene. Is it a trick or some power of suggestion that allows marks on a flat surface to fool us into perceiving a scene in depth? Clearly not. Rather, we perceive scenes in depth from flat pictures, paintings, or photographs because the same kind of information reaches our eyes from pictures of scenes as from the scenes themselves.   —Ralph Haber

PROBLEM

SOLUTION

The *problem* or *question* in a PS or QA paragraph may also be followed by a restricting sentence, and the solution or answer is often supported by an illustration:

PRSI *structure with cause-effect analysis as dominant method*:

To write English perfectly is impossible in practice; occasional ambiguities or slight improprieties of phrase are discoverable in every book—there has never been a writer who did not have some blind spot in his reading eye. Even to write it well is difficult. The alternative chosen by those who cannot carry on their daily business without constantly writing reports, demands and orders is a dialect of limited vocabulary with no pretense to the literary graces designed as a vehicle of restricted meaning. "Officialese," "legal English" and "business English" merge into one another as the general service dialect of impersonality, for use in every case where people are not private individuals but merely (according to the contest) the public, the electorate,

PROBLEM

RESTRICTION
SOLUTION

ILLUSTRATION

the parties concerned, age groups, man power, personnel, consumers.   —Robert Graves and Alan Hodges,
                              The Reader over your Shoulder

QAI *structure with definition as dominant method*:

Is war a biological necessity? As regards the earliest   QUESTION
cultures the answer is emphatically negative. The blow   ANSWER
of the poisonous dart from behind a bush, to murder   ILLUSTRATION
a woman or child in their sleep, is not pugnacity. Nor
is head-hunting, body-snatching, or killing for food
instinctive or natural.   —Bronislaw Malinowski

11b.3   Levels of Subordination

11b

When looking on a paragraph as a miniature essay, you will find
that it is constructed according to various levels of abstraction or
subordination, depending on whether the relationship of one sentence to the next is *coordinate* or *subordinate*. It is often useful
to analyze your own paragraphs in this way, in order to see whether
ideas that are *coordinate* with each other (on the same level of
abstraction) and those that are *subordinate* to another (on lower
levels of abstraction) are clearly defined in your writing. Consider
the following paragraph:

From the very beginning of school we make books and reading a
constant source of possible failure and public humiliation. When
children are little we make them read aloud, before the teacher and
other children, so that we can be sure they "know" all the words
they are reading. This means that when they don't know a word,
they are going to make a mistake, right in front of everyone. Instantly
they are made to realize that they have done something wrong. Perhaps some of the other children will begin to wave their hands and
say, "Ooooh! O-o-o-oh!" Perhaps they will just giggle, or nudge
each other, or make a face. Perhaps the teacher will say, "Are you
sure?" or ask someone else what he thinks. Or perhaps, if the teacher
is kindly, she will just smile a sweet, sad smile—often one of the
most painful punishments a child can suffer in school. In any case,
the child who has made the mistake knows he has made it, and feels
foolish, stupid, and ashamed, just as any of us would in his shoes.
          —John Holt, "How Teachers Make Children Hate Reading"

Assuming a paragraph has an explicit topic sentence, it will
often be the sentence of greatest generality. Begin, as we did in

6c, by giving that sentence a number (1); in this case it is the first sentence of the paragraph. Then give each subsequent sentence either the same number (if it is coordinate with the previous sentence) or a higher number (if it is subordinate to the previous sentence).†

(1) From the very beginning of school we make books and reading a constant source of possible failure and public humiliation.

  (2) When children are little we make them read aloud, before the teacher and other children, so that we can be sure they "know" all the words they are reading.

    (3) This means that when they don't know a word, they are going to make a mistake, right in front of everyone.

    (3) Instantly they are made to realize that they have done something wrong.

      (4) Perhaps some of the other children will begin to wave their hands and say, "Ooooh! O-o-o-oh!"

      (4) Perhaps they will just giggle, or nudge each other, or make a face.

      (4) Perhaps the teacher will say, "Are you sure?" or ask someone else what he thinks.

      (4) Or perhaps, if the teacher is kindly, she will just smile a sweet, sad smile—often one of the most painful punishments a child can suffer in school.

  (2) In any case, the child who has made the mistake knows he has made it, and feels foolish, stupid, and ashamed, just as any of us would in his shoes.

The second sentence is put on the second level because it is an example of the first and therefore subordinate to it: the first states that we do a poor job of teaching children to read "from the very beginning"; the second gives a concrete example of how we do that. The next two sentences are placed on level three because they state more specifically what happens when children are made to read aloud. The next four sentences are placed on level (4) because they are all examples of how the children might react, given the situation in the two level (3) sentences. And the last sentence in the paragraph is put on level (2) because it restates

---

†Francis Christensen was the first to suggest this method of analyzing paragraph structure.

the point of the second sentence—that our methods of teaching reading humiliate students.

EXERCISES _____

1. Analyze and evaluate the following paragraphs for completeness, unity, order, and signals of relationship.

   a. People used to be attracted to the sea for many reasons, one of which was to travel. There are a multitude of cultures that I have never seen and would like very much to see. Every time I see something new it reminds me how much I have yet to discover. Although I have traveled a great deal, there is more that I have not seen. I wish to visit the Far East, the South Pacific, Brazil . . . "the road goes ever ever on." Life as a sailor would allow me to travel and see the variety that exists in life.   —John Davis

   b. The area of downtown in which we reside is called "Old Louisville." Old Louisville has been in existence for nearly one hundred years, and the renovation of the area is just now being started. The house in which we live is an eighty-one-year-old, one-story house with a loft that was converted from an attic to a bedroom. The cellar is completely dirt and can only be reached from the outside. Because it is so old, the house creaks and settles frequently, making sleep a chore. Every time we hear a noise it has to be checked out to make sure that no one is trying to enter the house.   —Randy Seligman

   c. From my position on top of the dugout, I watched my family lumber out of the LTD. I jumped fifteen feet to the ground, letting my spikes sink into the tobacco juice-soaked clay behind the backstop. My mother flinched as I spilled more tobacco juice into my beard and onto the ground. My father asked the usual pre-game questions about the lineup; I gave him the answers that I gave him before every game. After pointlessly discussing the fact that I should be batting higher than seventh, he told me that I had gotten a call for work the next day at a warehouse in Norfolk. I told him I didn't want to talk about work while I was playing baseball. Nothing depressed me more than the thought of working in a Norfolk warehouse.   —Mark Slupek

2. Rewrite each of the above paragraphs to correct any problems you discover in completeness, unity, order, and signals of relationship.

3. Analyze the patterns of subordination in the paragraphs in exercise 1 or in the sample paragraphs in **9b.2,** by diagramming them as we did in the John Holt example above. Do you notice any connection between the amount of subordination and the subject matter of the paragraphs?

4. Choose a subject that interests you (perhaps one you chose for exercise 1 in **3a**). Write the *beginnings* of three paragraphs, as follows:

11b

a. a *topic* sentence and a *restriction* sentence for a TRI paragraph;
b. a *problem* sentence for a PS paragraph;
c. a *question* for a QA paragraph.
5. Complete the paragraphs you started above:

a. provide the *illustrations* for the TRI paragraph;
b. provide the *solutions* for the PS paragraph;
c. provide the *answers* for the QA paragraph.

11c   Paragraphing as Punctuation

Paragraphing can also be viewed as a method of punctuating, of signaling to the reader the beginnings and endings of units that you wish to be independent yet linked to other units. The word *paragraph* comes from two Greek roots: *para*, meaning "beside," and *graph*, meaning "write"; long before paragraphs were indented, they were indicated by a ¶ sign that was placed in the margin opposite the first sentence in the new paragraph. Indenting a paragraph is parallel to starting a new sentence with a capital letter: a paragraph indentation signals the beginning of a new section of your writing, just as a capital letter signals the beginning of a new sentence.

11c.1   Readability and Space

Writers sometimes need to consider the reading level of their audience and the space that is available. Newspaper articles, for instance, are printed in narrow columns and therefore read more easily if paragraphing is frequent. And advertising copy writers often use even shorter paragraphs, aiming their ads at a relatively low reading level and using graphic devices to achieve the emphasis that different paragraphing might otherwise provide. In other cases, readability is not so important as space. In dictionaries and encyclopedias for instance, because space is at a premium and readers are not being coaxed, articles are often paragraphed with few if any divisions.

While popular ads and encyclopedia articles represent two extremes, they illustrate how important it is to take your audience into account when you paragraph your own writing. If you are explaining a difficult concept or developing a closely structured argument, you might consider breaking your paragraphs more frequently than in a narrative or descriptive essay that requires less concentration on the part of the reader.

11c.2   Logical Relationships

In the article entitled "Two Viewpoints" (3e), the author paragraphed each time she started one of the three main points in her thesis. She could have broken each paragraph into two smaller paragraphs (one on each film), but that might have de-emphasized their close relationship. Similarly, in an essay whose dominant method is comparison and contrast, it will help your reader if you make the paragraph divisions correspond to the alternation of the items you are comparing. The more complex your writing becomes, the more closely reasoned the argument or the more difficult the ideas you are discussing, the more important it is to use paragraphing to help your readers follow the structure of your essay.

11c.3   Transitions

You can make a single sentence (or two) act as a *transition* between two sections of an essay by paragraphing it separately. Or you may place a transitional sentence at the end of one paragraph or the beginning of the other. Whatever your choice, your placement of the sentence will affect the emphasis the reader gives to the transition. Notice in "Two Viewpoints" (3e) how the first two sentences of paragraph three serve as a transition from the first supporting point (humor) to the second (suffering). Consider the different effect we would create if we put those two sentences at the end of the previous paragraph (the transitional sentences are italicized):

Didi and Gogo strike a note of humor and pain, also, as they attempt to help a fallen traveler; both of them, being rather old and helpless themselves, fall down on the traveler and none of them is able to get up. This all seemed hilariously funny until I stopped to think about the condition the actors were in and the hopelessness of the whole situation. *Humor is not, however, one of the dominant characteristics of either film. It exists to relieve the viewers of the constant suffering that is evident throughout.*

The transitional sentences create a kind of letdown here while in the original, where they are placed at the beginning of the next paragraph, they create momentum.

In other cases, the opposite technique may be more effective. If a climactic sentence is placed at the end of a paragraph, it can create a feeling of suspense about what might follow, thus preparing the reader for the next paragraph.

It is also possible to paragraph transitional sentences separately. Consider the effect when the following sentence stands alone:

> Humor is not, however, one of the dominant characteristics of either film. It only exists to relieve the viewers of the constant suffering that is evident throughout.

In "Two Viewpoints," the effect would be to slow down the pace of our reading, to give us time to catch a breath and to ponder. At the same time, the beginning of the following paragraph (where the transitional sentences were originally placed) would lose a little of its natural progression.

There are, then, no absolute rules to follow when paragraphing transitional sentences—you need to consider each one in the context of the whole essay and the effect you want to create (See also **12b** and **12f.**)

EXERCISES

1. Pick examples of these four types of writing: an advertisement with very brief paragraphs; a news story with only slightly longer paragraphs; an essay from *Time*, *Newsweek*, or another magazine, with medium-length paragraphs; and an encyclopedia article with one very long paragraph. Read each one and then answer the following questions:

   a. How is the paragraphing appropriate to the audience and purpose of each selection?

   b. How is the paragraphing appropriate to the medium in which each is written?

   c. What do you notice about sentence length in each? Does it bear any relationship to the paragraphing?

   d. How is the paragraphing related to the intellectual depth, detail, or difficulty of the pieces?

   e. How is the paragraphing related to the level of formality (formal, informal, or casual)?

f. Do you see ways of altering the paragraphing to make the writing more effective?

2. Use the content from one of the selections and rewrite it for another medium. For instance, rewrite the ad as a newspaper article or an essay. Rewrite the essay as an ad or an encyclopedia article. In short, try any combination you think would be interesting, and be guided by what you learned from answering the six questions in exercise 1.

11c

12

COHERENCE

12a Paragraphs as Parts of Essays

When we consider paragraphs as parts of larger pieces of writing, we are concerned primarily with the question of *coherence*: how the paragraphs fit in the whole, as well as how the whole piece hangs together. *Coherence* (which comes from a Latin word that means "to stick together") makes the difference between a piece of writing that is clear and easy to follow and one that seems disjointed or hard to follow. If an essay coheres, all words will work together to achieve the writer's aim. A coherent piece of writing is like a symphony orchestra in perfect tune and perfect synchronization. An incoherent piece of writing is as displeasing (and often as confusing) as an orchestra's playing out of tune.

Coherence depends on four basic principles (see **11b.1**):

1. *Unity*: Just as every sentence in a paragraph should relate to the topic sentence, so every paragraph in an essay should relate to the thesis.

2. *Completeness*: Just as paragraphs should say whatever is necessary for the audience to completely understand the topic sentence, essays should be developed with enough supporting paragraphs to make the thesis convincing.

3. *Order*: In a paragraph, the most general idea is ordinarily in the topic sentence with subordinate ideas in supporting sentences. Likewise, in an essay the main or most important idea is expressed as a thesis, often (but not always) in the introductory paragraph, with subordinate ideas expressed in support-

ing paragraphs. In both cases, the structure will depend on a logical order—of sentences in a paragraph, of paragraphs in an essay.

4. *Relationships*: Coherence involves clear relationships between the parts of a piece of writing—between sentences and between paragraphs.

It is this latter form of coherence that we will discuss in more detail in the rest of this chapter, since this is where most writers have the greatest difficulty. Relationships in a piece of writing are established through several devices that our language naturally provides. We often use these devices unconsciously, but in writing, it is easy just to think them and forget to write them; in such cases, the reader cannot see the connections in the writer's mind.

12b   **Transitional Words and Phrases**

12b

Transitional words and phrases signal how one part of an essay is related to another part by providing transitions from one sentence to another, from one paragraph to another, and from one section to another. They also function as structural signals, indicating when the writer has moved from one part of a structure to another. Since various methods of development provide structure in an essay, you will find that many of the methods have certain characteristic transitions, most of which are prepositions, adverbs, and conjunctions. Here are some examples of the most common:

- IN NARRATION AND PROCESS ANALYSIS, words that express time relationships: *after, again, during, every time, first, next, second, the next day, then, while.*
- IN DESCRIPTION, words that express spatial relationships: *behind, in back of, inside, on the left side, on top, over, under.*
- IN COMPARISON, words that express relationships of likeness or similarity: *also, comparable, either . . . or, likewise, neither . . . nor, similarly.*
- IN CONTRAST, words that express relationships of dissimilarity: *but, however, in comparison,† in contrast, more, on the other hand, rather, unlike, less.*

---

†But see Glossary of Usage.

- IN CAUSE-EFFECT ANALYSIS, words that express causal relationships: *as a result, because, consequently, hence, therefore, thus.*†
- IN DIVISION, words that signal the order of division: *after, before, finally, first, next, second, then.*
- IN EXAMPLES, words that signal an example or illustration is to follow: *as, for example, for instance, like, such as, thus, to illustrate, with respect to.*

The most frequent problem many writers have with transitional words is not using them frequently enough. Consider the following paragraph:

> I have seen many bears in zoos. This one near my dinner, my cooler, and my tent etched a clearer picture in my mind. He appeared disarmingly cute as he ambled toward our site. Larry removed a few things from the site and went quickly to get the ranger. I grabbed my camera.

Now consider a revision of that paragraph, with transitional words and phrases added:

> *Although* I have seen many bears in zoos, *somehow seeing* this one near my dinner, my cooler, and my tent etched a clearer picture in my mind *than any previous glimpse at that safe zoo distance. Here at the campground,* the bear appeared disarmingly cute as he ambled toward our site. *But Larry was not fooled. First he* removed a few things from the site, and *then he* went quickly to get the ranger. *Meanwhile,* I grabbed my camera.

Not only do the transitions in this paragraph make it internally more cohesive, but they also help to provide effective connections with the previous paragraph in the essay from which this paragraph comes, an essay narrating a camping trip. The previous paragraph ends like this:

> Everything seemed to be going well our first night in Yosemite. But then, as we sat down to supper in front of our campfire, an unwelcome visitor approached us.

Phrases in the revised paragraph like *Although* and *here at the campground* provide necessary links with the warning at the end of the previous paragraph about the unwelcome visitor. And the phrase *seeing this one* makes sense only because the previous paragraph has set us up to expect the bear.

12c Referential Words and Phrases

These include pronouns and determiners (see **13c**), which point to something referred to earlier (called the *antecedent*) or, occasionally, to something that is to follow. Adjectives and nouns that are substitutes or synonyms for previously stated words function in this referential manner. Here are some examples:

> Mr. Connor . . . *he* . . . *the man* . . . Connor . . . *him*
> Moby-Dick . . . *this book* . . . *it* . . . *Melville's novel*
> The riots . . . *they* . . . *the disturbance*
> London . . . *the city* . . . *England's capital* [*city*]
> [A paragraph of information] . . . *the above information*
> . . . *this information* . . . *the data*

Two common problems with referential words and phrases are shift in point of view and unclear pronoun reference.

12c

12c.1 Shift in Point of View

Point of view refers to the angle from which the essay is written—through whose eyes (or whose pen) we see the writing. Quite frequently, writers will shift between second person (*you*) and third person (*she, he, the student*). When this happens, coherence is weakened because we are shifting back and forth from one point of view to the next, as the following paragraph shows:

> Had I had a movie camera, the thing to film would not have been the bear but the other campers, myself included. You should have seen how it was placing an exclamation point at the end of their camping sentence. They all wanted to be sure to have a story to tell, a picture to prove we had all been there.

Consider how much clearer the revision is:

> Had I had a movie camera, I would have filmed not the bear but the other campers. I noticed how the sight of the bear seemed to place an exclamation mark at the end of their camping sentence. They all wanted to be sure to have a story to tell, a picture to prove they had been there, and I wished my camera could have captured their scurrying around to get their own cameras.

12c.2 Unclear Pronoun Reference

If the antecedent (the person or thing to which a pronoun refers) is unclear, the coherence of the sentence or paragraph is disturbed because we have to stop to figure out how to interpret the sentence. Following are some guidelines to help you keep your writing clear and unambiguous:

1. Be sure the pronoun has an exact reference:

AMBIGUOUS: The university's enrollment is decreasing each year because *they don't* have a very good recruiting program.

(Does *they* refer to the university? Since the university is both singular and an abstraction, *they* might refer to a particular group of people, like the staff of the admissions office.)

CLEAR: The university's enrollment is decreasing each year because *the admissions staff doesn't* have a very good recruiting program.

2. The pronoun should refer to only one antecedent (whether the antecedent is singular, plural, or a compound):

AMBIGUOUS: When the boss gave John a raise, *he* was unhappy.

(Does *he* refer to the boss or to John?)

CLEAR: The boss was unhappy when *he* gave John a raise. (or) John was unhappy with the raise his boss gave *him*.

3. Do not use a demonstrative or relative pronoun to refer to an entire clause or sentence unless the antecedent is perfectly clear:

AMBIGUOUS: The murder of the mayor was reported by the newspaper, *which* was a pity.

(Does *which* refer to the murder or to its being reported by the newspaper?)

CLEAR: The murder of the mayor, reported by the newspaper, was a pity. (or)
The reporting of the murder was a pity.

4. Be careful that the antecedent of a pronoun is not so remote that the reader forgets what the original reference was.

AMBIGUOUS: The prospect of running off to sea strikes me as an unusually inviting idea. We have all heard of how young men used to run off to sea, but this alternative to life ashore seems to have all but disappeared. The development of the airplane and the mechanically powered cargo vessel have destroyed the usefulness of the large sailing ship, and with its passing, life on the ocean has lost much of its romance. I find myself dreaming of *it* and wishing that I could sail on a clipper ship just like one of those men two hundred years ago.

(What does *it* in the last sentence refer to? The large sailing ship? The passing of the large sailing ship? The prospect of running off to sea?)

12c

CLEAR: I find myself dreaming of *running off to sea* and wishing that I could sail on a clipper ship just like one of those men two hundred years ago.

EXERCISES

1. Provide transitional words and phrases to make the following paragraph as clear and graceful as possible. You may also change the sentences or order of information as necessary.

   The Dalai Lama is the temporal and religious head of Tibet. More than two decades ago the Communist Chinese took over. The Dalai Lama and his followers fled to India. He continues to lead a small group of faithful followers. The Communist government acknowledges no such group in exile.

2. Rewrite the following passage to maintain a single point of view and to insure that all pronoun references are clear. You may change the sentences or order of information as necessary.

   Their eyes were dazzled. No one had ever seen such treasures as everyone there saw when the tomb of King Tut was first opened by Lord Carnarvon's archaeological team. We all knew that he was lying there, preserved, in close to his original state. And even more than by that almost living presence, they were overwhelmed by the surrounding wealth.

3. Rewrite each of the following sentences to eliminate any ambiguity caused by unclear pronoun reference. In some cases, there will be a number of possible interpretations.

a. The hijacking of the plane was reported to be a rumor, which was a pity.
b. Louise informed her assistant she had been fired.
c. The attorney missed her plane because the airline overbooked the flight. This caused a lawsuit.
d. Both teams were nervous and tense before the reporters. They were told this was an important game.
e. The election of the mayor was rumored to have been fixed. This caused the need for a re-election.

12d Repetition of Words and Parallel Word Patterns

12d

Another significant source of coherence in a piece of writing is the repetition of parallel or similar grammatical structures to express parallel ideas (see also **16e**) and the repetition of words and phrases in order to clarify who or what is being referred to. Consider the following paragraph:

> In our country the masses may turn to organized, conventional types of Christianity such as the Anglican, Baptist, Catholic, Lutheran, or Methodist religions. Or they may seek out splinter groups and cults. Others reject these and rely on philosophy, the evidence of nature, and their own reason to prove to them the existence of God. We have a popular and traditional culture in which high holy days are also secular holidays, and in which merchants may flourish who are aware of the Christian calendar. Some don't need cultural reminders and cues; they draw their consolations from their thinking minds, which create order out of the play of the senses and the patterns of the universe.

It is hard to tell exactly what the point of this paragraph is, what the writer wants to emphasize, because ideas the writer intended to be parallel and contrasting are not presented that way. Consider how much clearer this revised version is; the key words that signal parallel relationships are italicized:

> In the eighteenth century, *Voltaire* announced that Christianity was fine *for the masses*, but *for the elite* a simple deism would do. In the twentieth century, *many with Voltaire's inclination* maintain a similar distinction. These *latter-day Voltairians* find that *for the masses* in the west, there are the organized, mainline Christian churches: Anglican, Baptist, Lutheran, Methodist, Roman Catholic, etc. Or

the masses may seek out splinter groups and cults. *For the elite* (who are *the Voltairians* themselves), there are the consolations of the mind; reason, philosophy, and the evidence of nature all suggest to them the existence of God. *While the masses* may take refuge in the popular and traditional culture, in which high, holy days are also secular holidays, and in which merchants may flourish who are aware of the Christian calendar, *the Voltairian elite* find they need no such refuge of cultural reminders and cues. Their minds alone will create God's great order out of the play of the senses and the patterns of the universe.

Another frequent problem with repetition and parallelism is *unnecessary* repetition that becomes tedious and detracts from the writing rather than adding coherence, as in the following paragraph:

12d

American culture is *no more than* a naked newborn. *No other thing* makes this so clear as the historical sites along the highway in Idaho and Wyoming, which are *no more than* places to drive off the road and read a historical marker. There are *no* requirements for such enlightenment except a car and a simple sign. *No* building remains; there is *no* art; there is only a pole stuck in the dust with *no more than* an explanatory note. There is also *no* apology for the failure to preserve what is commemorated, be it a pony express station or a fort or a pioneer outpost. As we drive off, *no more than* meaningless words on a sign float back into the dust, like exhaust from a tired engine.

The repetition of *no* and its variations is so evident that it calls attention to itself, and instead of emphasizing the idea that American culture is a "naked newborn," the passage seems to focus on the nothingness of the highway scene. Consider how much clearer and more effective the revision is, where the words in italics demonstrate a use of repeated words and referential words (see **12c**) that reinforce rather than distract from the main point of the paragraph:

American culture is a naked newborn. In Idaho and Wyoming, historical sites consist of places to drive off the highway and read a *historical marker*. The requirements for such enlightenment are a car and a *simple sign*, nothing more—no remaining building, certainly no art, *just a pole stuck in the dust with an explanatory note*. There isn't even a note of apology for the failure to preserve *what is here commemorated*, be it a pony express station or a fort or a pioneer outpost. As we drive off, *the meaningless words on the sign* float back into the dust, like exhaust from our tired engine.

Repetition of words and parallel word patterns is important in creating coherence and clarity in your writing (as in the example about Voltaire). But unnecessary repetition, or repetition of insignificant words, can be distracting and misleading (as in the example about American culture). There is no easy rule for knowing when repetition is effective and when it is distracting. As a general guideline, try to express parallel ideas in parallel and related words, and avoid repeating words and ideas that are not central to the main point of the paragraph.

12e Ellipsis

Coherence is also achieved through *ellipsis*, the omission of a part of a parallel clause or phrase that the reader can supply, as in this illustration:

John was majoring in music and Steve was too. (John was majoring in music and Steve was *majoring in music* too.)

As with repetition, writers frequently have problems with knowing when omitting something would be effective and when leaving it in is needed for clarity. Some of the most difficult decisions concern prepositions. Consider the following:

The provost discovered the students *before* the security officer.

Because we do not know what has been left out, this sentence would have to be rewritten to clarify the meaning:

The provost discovered the students before the security officer did. (or)

The provost discovered the students before she discovered the security officer.

On the other hand, the second sentence below is *too* explicit:

The Republicans applauded the speech. Surprisingly, the Democrats applauded the speech too.

In this case ellipsis would improve the directness and clarity of the sentences:

> The Republicans applauded the speech. Surprisingly, the Democrats did too.

12f   Summary

All these ways of achieving coherence in your writing (transitions, referential words and phrases, repetition, parallelism, and ellipsis) work together to help your reader grasp the purpose of your writing, and they are important ways of linking ideas both within and between paragraphs.

The following short essay illustrates the use of many of these techniques. Some of the most effective transitions between paragraphs and sections of paragraphs are in italic type, as are many referential words and phrases. Try to imagine what the essay would be like without those key words and phrases.

THE TOWER PROJECT

Many of our personnel, conscious of the uncertainties of the construction business, have voiced concern relative to their future employment with *the Company*. What lies ahead on our horizon, they wonder, of the magnitude of the Fred M. and Ida S. Freebold Performing Arts Center, the Tannersfield Freeway Overpass, and other works that have put us in the construction forefront? They recall the cancellation in mid-contract of the Vietnam Parking Lot project, and they ask, "Will the Super-Tall Tower project, too, go down the drain, with a resultant loss of jobs and *Company* postion in the building field?"

The Company believes *such will not be the case*. While *we* aren't putting all our "eggs" on one tower and are keeping an eye on the Los Angeles-Honolulu Bridge option and the proposed Lake Michigan Floating Airport, we feel that the Super-Tall Tower has achieved priority status in Washington, and all phases of research and development, land clearance, and counter-resistance are moving forward in expectation of final approval.

As for the Tower critics, *they* are few in number, and there isn't one of their objections that we haven't answered. Let's look at the record. Their favorite line is "Why build a Super-Tall Tower when money is so urgently needed for cancer and poverty?" With all due respect to the unwell or impoverished person and his or her family, we state our case *as follows*:

First, Tower construction will create a hundred thousand new jobs, not only in the Babel area and the Greater Southwest but also in other places where the bricks and slime will be made by subcontractors.

Second, because it will be the world's tallest tower, we will be able to see more from it than from any existing tower.

Third, we have reason to believe the *Chinese* are well along in the development of *their* tower. If we don't wish to abdicate tower leadership to *Communist nations*, however friendly at the moment, we can't afford to slow down now. To do so would mean the waste of all the money spent on tower research so far and would set back American tower technology for decades to come. *Thus, our national prestige is at stake*—not merely national pride but the confidence in our ability to rise toward the heavens. When a nation turns away from the sky and looks at its feet, it begins to die as a civilization. Man has long dreamed of building a tall tower from which he could look out and see many interesting and unusual things. Most Americans, we believe, share *this dream*.

Fourth, environmentalist groups have predicted various disastrous effects from the Tower—that the humming noise of its high-speed elevator will be "unbearable" to the passengers and to nearby residents, that its height will confuse migrating birds, that its long shadow will anger the sun, and so forth. The Company's research laboratory has engaged in a crash program that has already achieved a significant degree of hum reduction; at the same time, our engineers are quick to point out that since no elevator now in service can approach the speed and accompanying hum projected for the Tower elevator, there is no viable data on which to base the *entire concept* of an "unbearable" hum. *Such a determination* must wait until the completion of the Tower. *In any event*, the hum may serve to warn off approaching birds. *As for the sun*, we feel that, with certain sacrifices, *this problem* can be taken care of.

—Garrison Keillor

EXERCISES

1. Reread "The Tower Project" in **12f** and look for other ways in which Keillor achieves coherence: where does he use referential words and phrases? repetition of words? repetition of sentence patterns? ellipsis?
2. The following three paragraphs were taken from different places in an essay by Anthony Burgess. Examine each paragraph individually to determine how, and to what degree, they achieve coherence. Underline

transitional words and phrases, and circle referential words and phrases along with their antecedents. Finally, draw arrows to references and bracket the ellipses.

Let me stay for a while on this subject of consumption. American individualism, on the face of it an admirable philosophy, wishes to manifest itself in independence of the community. You don't share things in common; you have your own things. A family's strength is signalized by its possessions. Herein lies a paradox. For the desire for possessions must eventually mean dependence on possessions. Freedom is slavery. Once let the acquisitive instinct burgeon (enough flour for the winter, not just for the week), and there are ruggedly individual forces only too ready to make it come to full and monstrous blossom. New appetites are invented; what to the European are bizarre luxuries become, to the American, plain necessities.

12f

But if the car owner can ignore the lack of public transport, he can hardly ignore the decay of services in general. His car needs mechanics, and mechanics grow more expensive and less efficient. The gadgets in the home are cheaper to replace than repair. The more efficiently self-contained the home, primary fortress of independence, seems to be, the more dependent it is on the great impersonal corporations, as well as a diminishing army of servitors. Skills at the lowest level have to be wooed slavishly and exorbitantly rewarded. Plumbers will not come. Nor, at the higher level, will doctors. And doctors and dentists, in a nation committed to maiming itself with sugar and cholesterol, know their scarcity value and behave accordingly.

When Europe, after millennia of war, rapine, slavery, famine, intolerance, had sunk to the level of a sewer, America became the golden dream, the Eden where innocence could be recovered. Original sin was the monopoly of the dirty continent over there; in America man could glow in an aura of natural goodness, driven along his shining path by divine reason. The Declaration of Independence itself is a monument to reason. Progress was possible, and the wrongs committed against the Indians, the wildlife, the land itself, could be explained away in terms of the rational control of environment necessary for the building of a New Jerusalem. Right and wrong made up the moral dichotomy; evil—that great eternal inextirpable entity—had no place in America.

—Anthony Burgess, "Is America Falling Apart?"

3. All three of these paragraphs are drawn from the same source. Which is the most coherent? Which is the least? Why? How might the lapses in coherence be justified by looking at these paragraphs in the context of the entire essay? Where do you think these paragraphs might appear in the essay as a whole? What are the transitions at the beginning or end of the paragraphs that give you a clue as to their context?

Part Four

GRAMMATICAL
SENTENCES

13

BASIC SENTENCE GRAMMAR

Grammar may seem mysterious, even frightening, to you, but in fact you know a great deal more about the grammar of English than you may think you do. Consider the following sentences:

The minters dagged a toon.
*Dagged toon a minters the

Even though you do not know the meanings of these sentences, because the words are nonsense words, you somehow recognize the first sentence as "grammatical," while the second is certainly not.

How can we tell that a sentence is "grammatical" when we do not even know what the words mean? One way is through the *form* of the words (their endings, for instance). The *-ed* on *dagged* is a clue that the word is a verb (like *jumped* and *walked*). The *-er* on *minters* is like the *-er* on other words called nouns: *painter*, *reader*, *singer*. The *-s* is also common on nouns: *painters*, *readers*, *singers*.

But some verbs also have *-s* endings (the minter dags a toon), so we also have to look at the *positions* of words in the sentence. The fact that *minters* comes after *the* and before the verb (*dagged*) is a further clue that it is a noun; *toon* also comes after a noun

---

*An asterisk at the beginning of a sentence indicates that the sentence is ungrammatical or simply impossible in English.

signal (*a*). And since *dagged* comes between two nouns, we have further evidence it is a verb.

Finally, we can distinguish the grammatical from the ungrammatical version because of the *function* of the words. The minters, for instance, have done something to a toon ("dagged" it). In the second sentence, nobody has done anything, at least that we can figure out—and who or what is the sentence about?

Thus the *forms* of words, their *positions*, and their *function* in relation to one another all let us know that "The minters dagged a toon" follows the grammatical rules of English even though it is nonsense.

To verify this knowledge, we can substitute real words that are similar in form, position, and function to the ones in the nonsense sentence:

> The singers planned a concert.
> The winners picked a prize.

Any major reversal of word order would signal an ungrammatical sentence:

> *Concert the planned a singers
> *Winners prize a picked the

Even though you are confronted with nonsense words, you know when a sentence is grammatical and when it is ungrammatical; and though you might not know grammatical labels or be able to define "parts of speech," you know a noun, a verb, a subject, and an object when you see them. Knowing that you already have this much knowledge about grammar, you should be able to face the rest of the grammar in these chapters with confidence.

13a Verbs

Verbs express an action, an occurrence, or a state of being; but different kinds of verbs work differently, depending on their relationship to the subject. Some verbs make a statement about the subject; others link the subject with words that describe or complete it.

13a.1 Transitive Verbs

As the Latin root *trans*, "across," suggests, *transitive* verbs (abbreviated TV) "carry across" or transfer the action from an actor to a receiver of the action.

Joseph *kicked* the bucket.
^{TV}

The dog's owner *had forgotten* the leash.
^{TV}

13a.2 Intransitive Verbs

Intransitive verbs (abbreviated IV) simply make an assertion about the subject, without extending the action to an object or receiver:

The dog *barked*.
^{IV}

The dog *howled* at night.
^{IV}

Some verbs can be either transitive or intransitive, depending on the context:

Joseph *kicked* furiously.
^{IV}

The dog's owner *had forgotten* again.
^{IV}

13a.3 Linking Verbs

Linking verbs (abbreviated LV) include forms of the verb *be* (*am, is, was, were*), as well as *seem, appear, become*, and the verbs of sense (*taste, look, feel, sound, smell*). They are called linking verbs because they convey no action but rather serve as a sign of identification, connecting the subject with a *complement* (a word or phrase that comes after it and completes its meaning):

Mary *is* a pianist.
^{LV   C}

She *appears* frazzled.
^{LV}

Certain linking verbs that relate to the senses (*look, appear*, and *smell*, for example) can also function as transitive or intransitive verbs. It is important to know which is which, since transitive or intransitive verbs are followed by *adverbs*, while linking verbs are followed by *adjectives* (see **15a.2**):

13a

LV   ADJ
Pat *looked serious*; she must have had bad news.

IV   ADV
Pat *looked seriously*; she had to find the money he had lost.

TV   DO   ADV
Ray *tasted* the *cookies gratefully*.

IV   ADJ
The cookies *tasted delicious*.

If you are in doubt as to whether a verb is linking or not, try substituting a form of the verb *be*. For instance, "The cookies tasted delicious" can be rewritten "The cookies *were* delicious," but "Ray tasted the cookies gratefully" cannot be rewritten with *was* without producing a nonsense sentence.

EXERCISES

Underline the verbs in the following sentences, and indicate whether they are transitive, intransitive, or linking by putting a TV, IV, or LV above each verb.

13b

1. Peter had a spectacular garden.
2. Japanese beetles ate holes in his cabbage.
3. He was extremely frustrated.
4. He used a foul-smelling bug killer.
5. His dinner guests fainted.
6. He seems happier now.
7. The cuckoo clock stopped suddenly.
8. My father shot the clock off the wall.
9. The cuckoo yelled.
10. It appears dead.

13b Nouns and Verbal Nouns

Nouns are words that name or identify people, places, things, ideas, or even actions (*Chris, the farmer, Cincinnati, a book, love, tennis*). They often come immediately after *articles* (*a, an, the*) or certain kinds of pronouns (*my, your, this*). Many nouns change form, usually to show plural number (*child, children*).

Verbal nouns are made from verbs. They often look like verbs in form (*to swim*, *swimming*), but they function in the sentence to *name* an action, and they occupy the space in a sentence that other nouns do. Verbal nouns that end in *-ing* are called *gerunds* (abbreviated GER), while verbal nouns preceded by *to* are called *infinitives* (abbreviated INF):

GER
Swimming is the best sport for physical fitness.

INF
One thing I always wanted was *to play* the piano.

13b.1   Subjects

A noun may function as the *subject* (abbreviated S), that is, the topic of the sentence, the word which the verb makes a statement or asks a question about:

S
The *dog* barked.

S
The *visitors* fled.

13b

13b.2   Subject Complements

A *subject complement* (abbreviated SC) names or identifies the subject, which is connected to it through a linking verb:

S   SC
The dog's name is *Norma*.

S   SC
Henry was a *visitor*.

13b.3   Direct Objects

A *direct object* (abbreviated DO) is acted upon by the subject through a transitive verb:

S   DO
The visitors saw the dog's *owner*.

S   DO
The dog's owner had forgotten her *leash*.

13b.4   Indirect Objects

An *indirect object* (abbreviated IO) is used with certain transitive verbs that require two objects: the subject gives, offers, or provides something or someone (the direct object) to something or someone else (the indirect object). Notice that indirect objects can come before or after the direct object; when they come after, they are usually preceded by *to* or *for*.

$$\overset{\text{S}}{\text{The visitors brought the}} \overset{\text{IO}}{\textit{dog}} \overset{\text{DO}}{\text{a bone.}}$$

The visitors brought the *dog* a bone.

The visitors brought a bone for *the dog*.

When indirect objects follow *to* or *for* they can also be classified as the object of a preposition (see **13b.5**). Indirect objects following prepositions are simply a specific kind of prepositional object.

13b.5 Objects of Prepositions

Objects of prepositions (abbreviated OP) follow prepositions (words that indicate direction or relation, like *at*, *in*, and *toward*; see **13f**). In the following examples, the prepositional phrases (which include the prepositions and their objects) are enclosed in brackets:

The dog barked [at the *visitors*].

[In the *evening*], the visitors left.

13b.6 Object Complements

Just as a subject complement completes the meaning of the subject, so an *object complement* (abbreviated OC) completes the meaning of the object, which it always follows.

The president appointed John assistant *manager*.

The American people elected John F. Kennedy *president*.

13b.7 Infinitive and Gerund Objects

Because infinitives and gerunds are derived from verbs, they express a sense of action even though they function like nouns. When an infinitive or gerund is the direct object, therefore, it can have its own object. Thus an infinitive as direct object may be followed by an *infinitive object* (INF O), and a gerund as direct object may be followed by a *gerund object* (GER O):

13b

S   DO (INF)   INF O
Pattie wanted to be a *firefighter*.

S   DO (GER)   GER O
John tried acting the *part*.

13b.8 Infinitive Subjects

Some infinitives have an *infinitive subject* (INF S) as well as object:

S   INF S INF (DO)   INF O
Pattie wanted *Jim* to find a roommate.

13b.9 Appositives

An *appositive* refers to the same thing as the preceding noun or defines the preceding noun. Either could stand alone in the sentence, but together they give sharper definition to the point the writer is making. The appositives in the following sentence are abbreviated A:

S   A   DO   A
Jane, an *attorney*, helped the old man, her *father*, with an

OP   A
important document, *his will*.

Most appositives are set off with a comma before and after, but when they serve a defining or restrictive function (see **23b.4**), the commas are omitted and the noun and its appositive are treated as a single phrase (her brother Pete, my friend the plumber, Eliot's novel *Middlemarch*).

EXERCISES

1. Underline the subjects and subject complements in the following sentences. If they are part of a noun phrase, bracket the phrase. Put an S above each subject and an SC above each subject complement.
   a. Victoria's auburn hair was the cause of her nickname, "Big Red."
   b. My favorite teacher is also our track coach.
   c. Performing in stock company productions seems a difficult job.
   d. To witness a crime is to feel helpless.
   e. That house is a remodeled barn.
2. Underline the direct and indirect objects in the following sentences.

Put a DO above each direct object and an IO above each indirect object. Then rewrite each sentence, reversing the position of the direct and indirect objects. (Remember that when the indirect comes *after* the direct object, it follows a preposition like *to* or *for*.)

a. Mr. Capote gave my husband a zucchini squash.
b. My husband offered a dish of lasagna to Mr. Capote.
c. Her riding skills earned Anne a blue ribbon.
d. She gave three lumps of sugar to her horse.
e. Finding a summer job gives Ralph a headache.

3. In the following sentences, underline the nouns that serve as objects of prepositions, and mark OP over each.

a. The owl screeched at midnight.
b. Cars skidded into the ditch during the snowstorm.
c. Alice barked her shin on the coffee table in the dark.
d. After the matinee, we jumped into a cab and sped to the airport.
e. Aaron pulled the covers over his head.

4. Underline the object complements (OC), infinitive objects (INF O), gerund objects (GER O), and infinitive subjects (INF S) in the following sentences. Identify them by putting the appropriate initials above each.

a. The Student Senate voted Virginia president.
b. Harold wanted to be an engineer.
c. The pesky children called her names.
d. The injured football player tried being stoic.
e. Wilma Rudolph wanted her daughter to be an Olympic runner.

5. Underline the nouns that function as appositives in the following sentences, and draw an arrow to the noun each is appositive to.

a. Erin has features of both her mother, an Italian, and her father, an Irishman.
b. My cat, a calico, likes to live outdoors.
c. Bill asked his father, an attorney, to defend him.
d. The 1973 Triple Crown winner, Secretariat, is sire to General Assembly, a Kentucky Derby contender.
e. The car, a vintage Rolls Royce, was stolen in broad daylight.

13c Pronouns

Pronouns function in the same way nouns do—as subjects, objects, complements, and objects of prepositions. They can appear in most of the same places in sentences that nouns can, as well as directly in front of nouns (*her* book). Often a pronoun refers to a noun previously named (Give Josephine *her* book), but not always (*It* was raining). Pronouns change form, like nouns, to show plural (*I*, *we*) and possession (*my*), but also to show gender (*he*, *she*) and person—that is, who the speaker is in relation to the audience (*I*, *you*, *she*). Here are some examples of pronouns used in noun slots; subjects are marked s, complements c, direct objects DO, and objects of prepositions OP:

$\overset{\text{S}}{He}$ growled at $\overset{\text{OP}}{them}$.

$\overset{\text{S}}{She}$ frightened $\overset{\text{DO}}{us}$.

$\overset{\text{S}}{It}$ was $\overset{\text{C}}{he}$.

$\overset{\text{S}}{He}$ was expecting $\overset{\text{DO}}{them}$.

Pronouns can be divided into several groups, according to their forms and the kinds of words they refer to:

Personal pronouns refer to specific persons (or animals or objects):

> I, me, my, mine
> we, us, our, ours
> you, your, yours
> he, him, his, she, her, hers, it, its
> they, them, their, theirs

Reflexive pronouns refer to the person or thing already mentioned in a clause:

> myself, ourselves
> yourself, yourselves
> herself, himself
> itself, themselves

Demonstrative pronouns point to something:

> this, that
> these, those

Relative pronouns link a relative clause to a main clause (see **13g.5**):

> who, whom, whose, whoever, whomever
> that, which

Interrogative pronouns are used to ask questions:

13c

who, whom, whose
which, what, whatever

Indefinite pronouns refer to an unidentified person or thing:

anyone, everybody, someone, nobody, etc.

EXERCISES

Identify the pronouns in each of the following sentences, and indicate what functions they serve (subject, object, etc.).

1. Bertie appointed herself to the committee, which had been formed by the college senate.
2. John's final wish was to be remembered fondly by his relatives, who never seemed to notice him.
3. The president gave her students permission to drink beer on campus but not to sell it.
4. "Rip off" is a slang term for stealing; it's used all the time in this part of the country.
5. Fleetwood Mac performed before an enthusiastic audience of fans.
6. Because of a flare-up of bursitis in his shoulder, he lost the match in straight sets.
7. When the ball was fouled away, hopeful fans leaped from their seats, positioning their baseball gloves.
8. Their persistent efforts yielded this solution, which brought them much favorable publicity.
9. Sociobiology is a relatively new discipline that studies the relationship between biology and behavior.
10. The customs official asked Steven to hand over his passport and step into the office by himself.

REVIEW EXERCISES

In the following sentences, underline each noun and pronoun and identify its function (subject, object, etc.). Be prepared to discuss the clues you use to identify each (form, function, or position in sentence).

1. Aaron had his picture taken at the airport.
2. When I saw the bloody fight, which seemed to go on forever, I almost became nauseous.
3. Adrienne wants to play in the tennis tournament, but her doctor advises against her doing that.
4. If you want to go to that graduate school, I'll talk to Dr. Smith and

13c

ask him to write a letter of recommendation for you, and I'll write one myself.

5. Running two miles is exhausting if you are out of shape.

6. When I saw Bob and Barb, he was mowing the yard, and she was killing rattlesnakes.

7. After the movie, someone came by to get him, and they took a train into the city.

8. Because he didn't see the step that was broken, he tripped and fell, landing with a thud.

9. She talked to the audience for about an hour concerning the possibility of life on Mars.

10. Until we receive some news, we will not know when to leave.

13d   Adjectives and Verbal Adjectives

Adjectives function as modifiers of nouns and pronouns. That is, they change (modify) our perception of nouns and pronouns by describing, defining, specifying, or qualifying. Adjectives usually come between articles and nouns (the *red* pajamas) or after linking verbs (his pajamas are *red*). Adjectives can change form to show comparison (*red, redder, reddest; good, better, best*). In the following examples, the arrows point from the adjectives to the words they modify:

13c

The *tiny* dog barked at the *fearful* visitors.

She was the *tiniest* dog on the block.

[Henry and Josephine] became *friendlier*.

Adjectives that follow linking verbs, like the one in the last example, are a kind of complement called *predicate* adjectives.

Adjectives include a special group called *articles* (*a, an, the*), which always come before nouns or other adjectives (*the* book, *the* red book).

Verbal adjectives are adjectives made from verbs and are usually called *participles*. Although they look like verbs (*frustrated, winning*), they modify nouns or pronouns; sometimes they are in adjective slots (before a noun or after a linking verb) and some-

times they come at the beginning of the sentence and are set off
with a comma:

Georgia played on the *losing* team.

Frustrated, she decided to give up.

13e   Adverbs

Adverbs modify verbs, adjectives, other adverbs, or whole sentences. They can appear almost anywhere in the sentence as long
as it is clear which words they modify. Often, however, they come
just before or after the words they modify. They often but not
always end in *-ly* (*quickly, neatly*), and they can change form as
adjectives do to indicate comparison (*well, better, best; fast, faster,
fastest*). In the following examples, the arrows point from the
adverbs to the words they modify, which are marked v for verbs,
ADJ for adjectives, ADV for adverbs, and SEN for the entire sentence:

Henry and Josephine ran *quickly* from the fierce dog.

The dog was *extremely* small.

The dog's owner handled the situation [*very well*].

Fortunately, [they had nothing to worry about].

Adverbs are often classified according to the specific kind of
modifying function they have. The most common types are the
following:

ADVERBS OF PLACE:	*here, away, upstairs, outside, underneath*
ADVERBS OF TIME:	*yesterday, tomorrow, now, soon, monthly*
ADVERBS OF MANNER:	*nicely, fondly, kindly, quickly, reluctantly*

| INTENSIFIERS: | *very, truly, definitely, extremely, rarely* |
| CONJUNCTIVE ADVERBS: | *however, nevertheless, therefore* |

EXERCISES

In the following sentences, underline the adjectives and adverbs. Draw an arrow from each adjective and adverb to the word it modifies; if an adverb is a sentence modifier, write an s above it.

1. Luckily, I finished the last race first.

2. The marketing campaign immediately resulted in exceedingly high profits for the company.

3. She was very pleased that her grateful guests liked the dinner so well.

4. Good gymnasts train themselves to perform gracefully.

5. My boss always wants today's work finished yesterday.

6. He generously gave the university a large donation so that future students would receive a better education.

7. Editors, writers, and layout artists generally have to work feverishly to meet deadlines.

8. Her carefully documented findings were truly revealing.

9. The mighty defense forced the new quarterback to run backwards and lose thirty yards.

10. Falling leaves and chilly winds are signs that winter will be upon us soon.

13f   Prepositions

Prepositions show relationships between a noun or pronoun and something else in the sentence (usually a relationship of space or time). They almost always come just before a noun or pronoun, or just before an article; they never vary in form. The preposition together with its noun or pronoun object is called a *prepositional phrase*, and the whole phrase functions as an adjective or adverb.

In the following examples, N stands for nouns, V for verbs, ADJ for adjectives, and ADV for adverbs:

N   ADJ   V   ADV
The dog was [*off* the leash], barking [*at* the visitors].

V   ADV
The visitors started to run [*from* her].

V   ADV
She chased them [*up* the street].

13g Conjunctions

Conjunctions are used to connect words, parts of a sentence, or sentences. (When two sentences are joined to one another, they are called *clauses*; see **13i**.) The word *conjunction* comes from two Latin roots: *con* means "together" and *junction* means "joined." There are several kinds of conjunctions, each of which performs the connecting or joining in a slightly different way.

13g.1 Coordinating Conjunctions

Coordinating conjunctions join parts of equal status. There are just seven of them: *and, but, for, nor, or, so, yet.* Here are some examples:

NOUN   NOUN
My favorite sandwich is [peanut butter] *and* [jelly].

VERB   VERB
The children [ran] *and* [played] in the street.

PARTICIPLE
The loser of the tennis match was [beaten] *but* not
PARTICIPLE
[discouraged].

PREPOSITIONAL   PREPOSITIONAL
PHRASE   PHRASE
You'll find the book [on the table] *or* [under the bed].

CLAUSE   CLAUSE
[Jamie cried when her parents left], *yet* [she loved her baby-sitter].

13g.2 Correlative Conjunctions

Correlative conjunctions work in pairs, to form a correlation between two parts of a sentence. The most common are *either*

. . . or, neither . . . nor, both . . . and, not only . . . but also.
Like coordinating conjunctions, correlative conjunctions join parts
of equal status, but with more emphasis, since a word comes not
only *between* the two parts but also *before* them, signaling that
a coordinate structure will follow:

I like *both* [peanut butter] *and* [jelly].

Either [you'll find the book at home], *or* [you'll find it at
school].

13g.3 Subordinating Conjunctions

A *subordinating* conjunction introduces a clause that depends on
another clause for its meaning. The most common subordinating
conjunctions are *after, although, as, as if, as though, because,
before, except that, even though, if, since, so that, than, that, till,
unless, when, whenever, where, whereas, wherever.*

While coordinating conjunctions come *between* the parts joined,
subordinating conjunctions come at the *beginning* of the clauses
they introduce; and while coordinating conjunctions can join
words, phrases, or clauses, subordinating conjunctions join clauses
only. The clause introduced by the subordinating conjunction
functions in the sentence as an adverb (ADV), a subject (S), or a
direct object (DO). In the following examples, the subordinating
conjunctions are in italics, and arrows point to the words the
adverb clauses modify:

ADV CLAUSE

[They went to the football game] [*although* it was raining].

ADV CLAUSE

[*Since* it was the end of the month], [I had to pay my bills].

ADV CLAUSE   DO

[*After* an hour had gone], [I decided [*that* he would not
come]].

S

[[*That* she was ill] was obvious].

Occasionally, subordinating conjunctions are used to introduce
elliptical clauses, in which the subject and verb may be understood rather than stated:

[*While* riding down the highway], [Susan fell off her bike].
(Compare "While Susan was riding down the highway . . .")

13g.4   Conjunctive Adverbs

Conjunctive adverbs are a special class of adverbs that can be used, like conjunctions, to introduce clauses. The most common are *besides, consequently, finally, first, furthermore, hence, however, likewise, moreover, next, nevertheless, therefore, thus.* In addition to these, some common adverb phrases function in the same way, such as *for example, for instance, in conclusion, in fact, on the contrary,* and *on the other hand.* Like conjunctions, conjunctive adverbs join closely related clauses, but notice that some of them can occur in the middle or at the end of the clause:

[This weekend is Homecoming]; [*consequently*, the motels are filled].

[I don't feel well today]; [I'll try to go to all my classes, *however*].

[Peterson is staging a vigorous campaign for the presidency]; [he will, *moreover*, win with a landslide victory].

13g.5   Relative Pronouns

Relative pronouns, which include *who, whom, whose, which,* and *that,* are a special class of pronouns that function as conjunctions. Like subordinating conjunctions, they introduce a clause that is dependent for its meaning on the other clause (the "main clause") in a sentence. In the following examples, the relative pronouns are in italics, and arrows point to the words the clauses modify:

N   ADJ CLAUSE
[Patricia is the girl [*who* would not tell a lie]].

Notice, however, an important difference between relative pronouns and subordinating conjunctions: while subordinating conjunctions serve merely to join two clauses and are not part of either clause, relative pronouns are a part of the clause they introduce and usually serve a noun function in those clauses:

V ⟵——————— ADV CLAUSE

[I like that professor], [*although* she is a hard grader].
    (The subordinating conjunction introduces the subordinate clause.)

N ⟵——— ADJ CLAUSE

[I like that professor, [*who* is a hard grader]].
    (The relative pronoun does not merely join the two clauses but also serves as the subject of the second clause.)

13g.6   Interrogative Pronouns

Interrogative pronouns also function as conjunctions. They include *who*, *whom*, *whose*, *what*, *where*, *when*, *why*, and *how*. Interrogative pronouns serve to introduce a clause that is a direct question or an indirect question (see **23a.2**); in either case, the question serves as direct object of the main verb:

[He asked me, [*"Why* do you like the ballet?"]]   DIRECT QUESTION

[He asked me [*why* I like the ballet]].   INDIRECT QUESTION

EXERCISES ———————————

Identify the prepositions and conjunctions in the following sentences.

1. Not only did the Civil War help to destroy an existing social and economic order, but it also helped to create a new one.
2. Black Americans may have been freed, but they rapidly became enslaved to finance capitalism and to an increasingly industrialized world, where many workers were needed to do menial jobs, under bad conditions, for extremely low pay.
3. The robber barons, who made large fortunes by ruthless means, became synonymous with the changing character of our nation; nonetheless, many of them who are associated with the rise of big business and the bloody history of labor were also, curiously, philanthropists.
4. Andrew Carnegie, for example, helped create the institution of the free public library in towns all over America.
5. Neither the president nor Congress was able to stem the tide of change— if, indeed, either wanted to—because laissez-faire capitalism grew quite naturally out of the characteristic postwar exhaustion of moral energy.

REVIEW EXERCISES ————————————————

Identify the word class (part of speech) of as many words as possible in the following sentences.

1. The summit was only one hundred feet away, yet it seemed far to the exhausted climber.
2. The burglars moved through the bank quickly but quietly.
3. Because they had not been adequately trained, the guides were both unable to give clear directions and unable to answer simple questions about the museum.
4. American teenagers worry about their appearance; therefore, they spend millions of dollars on clothes, cosmetics, and hair styling.
5. Winston Churchill was a popular British leader who was also a gifted writer.

————————————————————————

13h Phrases

A *phrase* is a group of related words without a subject and a predicate. (A group of related words *with* a subject and a predicate is a clause or a sentence.)

13h.1 Verb Phrases

Verb phrases consist of a main verb with its auxiliaries (see **14d**) and modifiers:

She [sang].	SINGLE VERB
She [didn't sing].	VERB PHRASE
She [didn't sing very well].	VERB PHRASE

13h.2 Noun Phrases

Noun phrases consist of a noun or pronoun or both, along with their modifiers. In the following examples, subjects are marked s, direct objects DO, indirect objects IO, and complements c:

    s
[Fritz] sang beautifully.   SINGLE NOUN

      s   DO
[The old tenor] sang [the aria]

      IO
for [his friend].   NOUN PHRASES

[My favorite aria] is [that one].   NOUN PHRASES

Infinitive phrases, which are special kinds of noun phrases, consist of an infinitive and its objects and modifiers. They function, like other noun phrases, in the same slots as nouns:

[To grow old] is what Ambrose most fears.

Ambrose wants [to remain young forever].

Occasionally, an infinitive phrase can be classified as an adverb phrase because it modifies a verb:

He played [to win the big game].

Gerund phrases, which are also special kinds of noun phrases, consist of a gerund with its objects and modifiers:

Sylvia liked [singing all the old songs].

[Climbing trees] was Suzie's favorite sport.

13h.3   Participial Phrases
Participial phrases consist of a verbal adjective (participle) and its modifiers. They function as adjectives, modifying nouns and pronouns:

[Exhausted], Jennifer left the party early.   SINGLE PARTICIPLE

[Walking quickly], she arrived home before midnight.   PARTICIPIAL PHRASE

13h.4   Absolute Phrases
Absolute phrases are like participial phrases except that they contain within themselves a noun or pronoun that the participle modifies. The entire phrase, taken together, then modifies the whole sentence:

The day was dismal, [the clouds [hanging low and dark in the sky]].

13h.5 Prepositional Phrases

Prepositional phrases consist of prepositions with their objects and modifiers. Prepositional phrases can function as either adjectives or adverbs:

ADJ
I saw three movies [about Viet Nam].
(What kind of movies?)

ADV
[After the last movie], we vowed to see no more.
(Vowed when?)

13h.6 Phrases Within Phrases

Phrases often occur within longer phrases. A noun phrase, for example, can be part of a prepositional phrase that is in turn part of a larger noun phrase:

[The student [with [the best grades]]] will win the award.

13i

EXERCISES

Bracket the phrases in the following sentences and indicate what kind each is. Be prepared to discuss the function of each in the sentence.

1. We found a hundred-year-old newspaper in nearly perfect condition.
2. They are planning a trip to Italy in January.
3. Gothic novels are filled with dark castles, handsome strangers, and secret meetings.
4. The old man's tattered hat made him stand out in the crowd.
5. He could have been an officer in the Marine Corps.
6. Some parents have trouble letting go of their children.
7. To see her favorite rock star, she would spend any amount of money.
8. Hearing news from home can be good for a homesick student who wants to leave the dorm.
9. Getting away for the weekend was certainly beneficial.
10. A master's degree is often the prelude to doctoral work.

13i Clauses

A clause is a group of related words with a *subject* and a *complete verb* (either the simple past or present tense, or a participle used with an auxiliary—see **14d**). Clauses are usually divided into two major classes—*independent* and *dependent*. Dependent clauses are subdivided into *subordinate* and *relative*.

13i.1 Independent Clauses

An *independent clause* is not dependent on another clause for its meaning and is therefore *not* introduced by a subordinating conjunction or relative pronoun. The following are independent clauses:

> The attorney was questioning her client.
> And then the attorney questioned her client.
> Finally, the attorney questioned her client.

Note, as in the second sentence above, that an independent clause may be introduced by a coordinating conjunction. It is more common, however, to join such clauses to a previous sentence with a comma or semicolon (see **23a.1**).

The following are not independent clauses:

> who was questioning her client
>
> (*Who* is a relative pronoun referring back to the attorney and therefore needs to be attached to an independent clause that contains the word *attorney*.)
>
> although she was questioning the client
>
> (*Although* is a subordinating conjunction and therefore needs to be attached to an independent clause containing the verb that *although* refers to.)

The following is not a clause at all:

> the attorney questioning her client
>
> (*Questioning* is an incomplete verb form, a participle; it can be used as an adjective, but to be used as a verb it requires an auxiliary.)

An independent clause standing alone is considered a *sentence*; it may also be joined with other independent clauses, with dependent clauses, or with both.

13i.2 Subordinate Clauses

Subordinate clauses begin with a subordinating conjunction like *because*, *although*, or *that*. (A list of the most common subordi-

13i

nating conjunctions is in **13g.3.**) They function as adverbs (marked ADV) or nouns (marked N):

ADV
[*Although* I am a beginner], I can run a mile a day.

ADV
I am going to college [*because* I want to become a doctor].

N
I thought [*that* he was tired].

N
I thought [he was tired].

> (Notice, as in the last example, that the word *that* may be omitted from subordinate clauses.)

13i.3   Relative Clauses

Relative clauses usually begin with a relative pronoun like *who* or *that* (see **13g.5**) and function in the sentence as a noun or adjective:

NOUN CLAUSE
I know [*who* took you to dinner last night].

ADJECTIVE CLAUSE
I know the man [*whom* you were with last night].

ADJECTIVE CLAUSE
The book [*that* is on the table] was written by my mother.

NOUN CLAUSE
I asked [*whose* book it was].

Not every relative clause will begin with a relative pronoun, however. When the relative pronoun is in the object case, it may be deleted and therefore implied (see also **18b.3**):

Paris is the city [*that* I love best in Europe].
Paris is the city [I love best in Europe].

I know the man [*whom* you were with last night].
I know the man [you were with last night].

When the relative pronoun is the object of a preposition (often an indirect object), the preposition may come first in the clause, though it may come later or be deleted altogether:

FORMAL:	That is the person [*to whom* I gave the book].
FORMAL OR INFORMAL:	That is the person [*whom* I gave the book *to*].
INFORMAL OR CASUAL:	That is the person [I gave the book *to*].

Note that the second example, with *whom . . . to*, is a relatively unusual combination of formal and informal, and many writers would consider the mixture inappropriate. It is more common to use the subject case of the relative pronoun when the preposition is moved to the end of the clause:

| INFORMAL OR CASUAL: | That is the person [*who* I gave the book *to*]. |

Notice that the word *that* can be either a relative pronoun or a subordinating conjunction. (See the examples in 13i.2.) When it introduces a subordinate clause, the clause functions as a noun (in the following example, a direct object):

I thought [*that* I would go to Europe next spring break].

When *that* introduces a relative clause, the clause functions as an adjective:

13i

The flowers [*that* bloom in the spring] are my favorites.

EXERCISES

1. In the following clauses, identify the subjects and the verbs, and then indicate whether the clauses are independent or dependent.
   a. which is on the table
   b. Jane Fonda played the leading role
   c. if she wins the award
   d. that I like
   e. because he trained daily
2. Create a new sentence with each of the following dependent clauses by joining it to an independent clause.
   a. although she comes from the South
   b. that he would do it if I begged him
   c. as the student entered the room
   d. who was at the supermarket
   e. which is in the city
3. Change the following independent clauses into dependent clauses by adding subordinating conjunctions or relative pronouns; then create a

new sentence with each dependent clause by joining it to an independent clause.

a. His friends respected his integrity.
b. Helen finished the preparations.
c. They can outplay the veterans.
d. It rains in April.
e. Mike typed the letter quickly.

13j   Basic Sentence Patterns

Every clause and every sentence has both a *subject* (the main word in the subject being a noun or pronoun) and a *predicate* (the main word in the predicate being a verb), although either or both may sometimes be unexpressed (see **13j.4**). All sentences in English, no matter how long or complex, are built on just a few basic patterns. The differences among the patterns are caused by differences in the predicates.

13j

13j.1   With Linking Verbs

The predicate can consist of a *linking verb* (see **13a.3**) and a *complement* (see **13b.2** and **13d**):

SUBJECT (NOUN OR PRONOUN)	PREDICATE (VERB + COMPLEMENT)	
Jeans	are	comfortable.
Bagels	taste	delicious.
She	is	my sister.

Notice that the complement can be either an adjective, as in *comfortable* and *delicious*, or a noun or pronoun, as in *my sister*.

13j.2   With Intransitive Verbs

The predicate can consist of an *intransitive verb* (see **13a.2**):

SUBJECT (NOUN OR PRONOUN)	PREDICATE (INTRANSITIVE VERB)
Students	sleep.
The dog	is growling.
They	have left.

13j.3 With Transitive Verbs

The predicate can consist of a *transitive verb* (see **13a.1**) and an object:

SUBJECT (NOUN OR PRONOUN)	PREDICATE (VERB + DIRECT OBJECT)	
Pavarotti	sings	arias.
The Tigers	beat	the Indians.
She	wrote	that book.

Several variations of this pattern are also common. One includes in the predicate an *indirect object* as well as a *direct object*:

SUBJECT (NOUN OR PRONOUN)	PREDICATE (VERB + INDIRECT OBJECT + DIRECT OBJECT)		
Professors	ask	their students	questions.
Some	give	professors	answers.

Another variation includes in the predicate an *object complement*:

SUBJECT (NOUN OR PRONOUN)	PREDICATE (VERB + DIRECT OBJECT + OBJ COMPLEMENT)		
Sophomores	make	freshmen	angry.
The seniors	elected	Timothy	their secretary.

(Notice that the complement can be either an adjective, like *angry*, or a noun or pronoun, like *president*.)

Another variation includes a verbal noun:

SUBJECT (NOUN OR PRONOUN)	PREDICATE (VERB + VERBAL NOUN + DIRECT OBJECT)		
Pavarotti	likes	to sing	arias.
The Tigers	enjoyed	beating	the Indians.

Finally, another variation of this pattern includes another noun before the verbal noun, which is called the *subject* of the verbal noun:

SUBJECT (NOUN OR PRONOUN)	PREDICATE		
	(VERB +	SUBJECT OF VERBAL NOUN +	VERBAL NOUN +	DIRECT OBJECT)
Professors	want	students	to ask	questions.
Freshmen	like	sophomores	losing	the games.

13j

13j.4 Deleted Subjects and Predicates

While every sentence has a subject and predicate, they may be deleted (unexpressed, or implied) in informal and casual usage, especially in speech:

> Who is your favorite tenor?
> FORMAL: Pavarotti is my favorite tenor.
> INFORMAL
> OR CASUAL: Pavarotti.
>   (Here the entire predicate is unexpressed.)

> What does Pavarotti sing?
> FORMAL: Pavarotti sings arias.
> INFORMAL
> OR CASUAL: Arias.
>   (Here the subject and predicate are deleted, and
>   only the object remains.)

13k Expanding Sentences

13k

All the sentences we have discussed in the basic patterns are *simple* sentences—that is, they consist of one clause only. We can combine sentences with coordinating conjunctions to form *compound* sentences. And we can add modifiers to all of those basic sentence patterns, expanding their meaning and adding depth, richness, and texture. Single words, phrases, and clauses can all be used as modifiers. When only single words or phrases are used, the sentence will remain a *simple* sentence. When clauses are used to modify, the sentence will become *complex*. Notice that linking verb sentences, if the complement is an adjective, have modifiers already in the basic pattern.

13k.1 By Compounding

> My calculus class was tough.
>   (Linking verb sentence with adjective)

> My calculus class was tough but English was easy.
>   (Joined to another LV sentence with *but*)

> I like movies.
>   (Transitive verb sentence)

> I like movies and Jenny does too.
>   (Joined to an intransitive verb sentence with *and*)

13k.2   With Single Words

Roses smell wonderful.
  (LV sentence with adjective)

Roses usually smell wonderful.
  (Adverb added)

Some roses smell wonderful.
  (Adjective added)

Peace roses smell especially wonderful.
  (Adjective and adverb added)

13k.3   With Phrases and Single Words

Jeans are comfortable.
  (LV sentence with adjective)

Jeans are comfortable in the winter.
  (Prepositional phrase added)

White jeans are more comfortable in the summer.
  (Adjective and adverb added)

13k

Jeans are comfortable at any time of year, their cotton fabric warm in winter and cool in summer, their appearance always attractive.
  (Predicate adjective, prepositional phrase, two absolute phrases added)

13k.4   With Adjective and Adverb Clauses

Students sleep.
  (IV sentence)

Students sleep after their exams are over.
  (Subordinate clause functioning as an adverb)

Students who don't study hard rarely sleep before they take an exam.
  (Relative clause functioning as adjective, adverb, subordinate clause functioning as adverb)

Students who stay up all night to study sometimes sleep through the exam.
  (Relative clause functioning as adjective, adverb, prepositional phrase)

13k.5   With Noun Clauses

She knew the reason.
> (TV sentence)

She knew that I was upset.
> (Subordinate clause functioning as noun/direct object)

EXERCISES

1. Make the following sentences compound by adding other independent clauses and suitable coordinating conjunctions.

   a. He looks magnificent.
   b. She is at home.
   c. While they were out, the robber broke in.
   d. Each of us has her doubts.
   e. The clown made everyone laugh.

2. Expand the following sentences through modification with single words and phrases.

   a. The river lay calm, covered with snow.
   b. These trees are planted in the soil.
   c. Whose hat is on the table?
   d. Where did you get that coat and hat?
   e. Which one of you will admit to stealing from the boy?

3. Expand the following sentences through modification with clauses.

   a. I was thinking about my girlfriend.
   b. Teachers need to be given more respect.
   c. Students should be treated with dignity.
   d. I gave him the information.
   e. The clown made everyone laugh.

13k

14

PROBLEMS WITH VERBS

14a Inflections

The *base form* of a verb is its form before anything is added or altered. When a verb is *inflected*, its base is altered to indicate present or past *tense*, singular or plural *number*, and first, second, or third *person*. In the *first person*, the subject of the verb (*I*, *we*) is the speaker or writer. In the *second person*, the subject of the verb (*you*) is the person being addressed. In the *third person*, the subject of the verb is whatever is spoken about or referred to (*he*, *she*, *it*, *they*, and all nouns).

Most verbs follow a *regular* pattern of inflection (*walk*, *walked*, *had walked*); some verbs, though, are *irregular* and follow many different patterns.

14a.1 Present Tense

The present tense of regular verbs and of most irregular verbs is the same as the base form, except in the third-person singular, where *-s* or *-es* is added to the base form (see **22b** for the spelling patterns that govern the *-es* ending):

	SINGULAR	PLURAL
FIRST PERSON	I walk, go	we walk, go
SECOND PERSON	you walk, go	you walk, go
THIRD PERSON	she walks, goes	they walk, go
	the dog walks, goes	the dogs walk, go

There are two important exceptions to this pattern. First, the verb *have* changes to *has* in the third person singular:

	SINGULAR	PLURAL
FIRST PERSON	I have	we have
SECOND PERSON	you have	you have
THIRD PERSON	she has, the car has	they have, the cars have

Second, the verb *be* is the most irregularly inflected of all English verbs. Following are the present tense forms:

	SINGULAR	PLURAL
FIRST PERSON	I am	we are
SECOND PERSON	you are	you are
THIRD PERSON	she is, the woman is	they are, the women are

10a.2 Past Tense

14a

The past tense of *regular* verbs is formed by adding a -*d* or -*ed* to the base form, in all persons, singular and plural:

	SINGULAR	PLURAL
FIRST PERSON	I walked, hoped	we walked, hoped
SECOND PERSON	you walked, hoped	you walked, hoped
THIRD PERSON	she walked, hoped	they walked, hoped
	the dog walked, hoped	the dogs walked, hoped

Instead of using the -*d* or -*ed* ending of a regular verb, the past of *irregular* verbs is formed by changing the spelling and pronunciation of the base form to produce the past tense. The same past-tense form is used in all persons, both singular and plural. A list of the past forms of the most commonly used irregular verbs is given in section **14a.5,** but here are a few examples:

PRESENT	PAST
catch, catches	caught
have, has	had
hide, hides	hid

The verb *be* is the only verb whose past is not the same in all persons. Following are the past tense forms of *be*:

	SINGULAR	PLURAL
FIRST PERSON	I was	we were
SECOND PERSON	you were	you were
THIRD PERSON	he was, the man was	the men were

A few verbs that form the present tense regularly (by adding -*s* in the third person singular) are uninflected in the past tense: I almost always *put* jam on my bread; yesterday I *put* honey. These verbs all end in -*d* or -*t* and include *bet, burst, cut, hit, hurt, let, put, set, split,* and *spread.*

14a.3   Past Participle
The past participle is used either as an adjective (see **13d**) or with an auxiliary in the perfect forms (see **14f**) and the passive voice (see **14h**).

The past participle of *regular* verbs is the same as the simple past tense: -*d* or -*ed* is added to the base form (walk*ed*).

The past participle of *irregular* verbs, like the past tense, is formed differently for each irregular verb. Following are some examples of past participles; notice that some are the same as the simple past tense, and some are different:

14a

PRESENT	PAST	PAST PARTICIPLE
catch, catches	caught	caught
have, has	had	had
hide, hides	hid	hidden

The past participle of the verb *be* is *been.*

14a.4   Present Participle
The present participle is used either as a noun (see **13b**), as an adjective (see **13d**), or with an auxiliary in *progressive* verbs (see **14f**). The present participle of both regular and irregular verbs is formed by adding -*ing* to the base (walk*ing*). (Occasionally some spelling changes occur before adding the -*ing*; see **22b.2, 22b.3,** and **22b.4.**)

14a.5   Principal Parts
The principal parts of all verbs are the ones we have just described: the *base* (which, with a *to* in front of it, is called an *infinitive*), the *present tense,* the *past tense,* the *past participle,* and the *pres-*

ent participle. The following list contains the principal parts of the most common irregular verbs. The present and the present participle have been omitted because they are always the same. (The present always has an *-s* in the third person singular and the present participle always ends in *-ing*; differences in spelling like adding *-es* instead of *-s* or changing a *-y* to *-i* before adding an ending are discussed in 22b).

If you want to find the principal parts of a verb not listed here, you can check the dictionary. If a verb is regular, the dictionary will list only the base; if the verb is irregular, the dictionary will list the base, followed by the simple past, followed by the past participle. If only one form is listed after the base, it is because the simple past and the past participle are the same.

COMMON IRREGULAR VERBS

BASE FORM (INFINITIVE)	PAST TENSE	PAST PARTICIPLE
(to) arise	arose	arisen
(to) awake	awoke	awaked (or awoken)
(to) be	was, were	been
(to) become	became	become
(to) begin	began	begun
(to) bite	bit	bitten
(to) blow	blew	blown
(to) break	broke	broken
(to) bring	brought	brought
(to) buy	bought	bought
(to) catch	caught	caught
(to) choose	chose	chosen
(to) come	came	come
(to) dig	dug	dug
(to) dive	dived (or dove)*	dive
(to) do	did	done
(to) draw	drew	drawn
(to) drink	drank	drunk
(to) eat	ate	eaten
(to) fall	fell	fallen

*Several irregular verbs have alternate past tense and past participle forms which are controversial; see the Glossary of Usage for entries on *dive/dove*, *got/gotten*, *proved/proven*, and *shined/shone*.

BASE FORM (INFINITIVE)	PAST TENSE	PAST PARTICIPLE
(to) feed	fed	fed
(to) feel	felt	felt
(to) fight	fought	fought
(to) find	found	found
(to) fly	flew	flown
(to) forget	forgot	forgotten
(to) forgive	forgave	forgiven
(to) freeze	froze	frozen
(to) get	got	got (or gotten) *
(to) give	gave	given
(to) go	went	gone
(to) grow	grew	grown
(to) hang (suspend)†	hung	hung
(to) have	had	had
(to) hear	heard	heard
(to) hide	hid	hidden
(to) hold	held	held
(to) keep	kept	kept
(to) know	knew	known
(to) lay (see **14b.**)		
(to) lead	led	led
(to) leave	left	left
(to) lend	lent	lent
(to) lie (see **14b.**)		
(to) light	lighted (or lit)	lighted (or lit)
(to) lose	lost	lost
(to) make	made	made
(to) pay	paid	paid
(to) prove	proved	proved (or proven) *
(to) raise (see **14b.**)		
(to) ride	rode	ridden
(to) rise (see **14b.**)		
(to) say	said	said
(to) see	saw	seen
(to) sell	sold	sold
(to) set (see **14b.**)		
(to) shine	shined (or shone) *	shined (or shone) *
(to) shoot	shot	shot
(to) sing	sang	sung
(to) sink	sank	sunk

14a

†The other meaning of *hang,* "to execute," is regular: *hang, hanged, hanged.*

BASE FORM (INFINITIVE)	PAST TENSE	PAST PARTICIPLE
(to) sit (see **14b**.)		
(to) sleep	slept	slept
(to) speak	spoke	spoken
(to) spend	spent	spent
(to) spring	sprang	sprung
(to) stand	stood	stood
(to) steal	stole	stolen
(to) stick	stuck	stuck
(to) sting	stung	stung
(to) strike	struck	struck (or stricken)
(to) swear	swore	sworn
(to) sweep	swept	swept
(to) swim	swam	swum
(to) swing	swung	swung
(to) take	took	taken
(to) teach	taught	taught
(to) tell	told	told
(to) think	thought	thought
(to) throw	threw	thrown
(to) wake	woke	woken
(to) wear	wore	worn
(to) win	won	won
(to) wind	wound	wound
(to) write	wrote	written

14b

EXERCISES

Write sentences using each of the principal parts of the following verbs; you may have to use your dictionary for some of them.

jump	move	bring	shake	talk
put	run	ride	choose	cost

14b LIE and LAY, SIT and SET, RISE and RAISE

Three pairs of intransitive and transitive verbs are often confused: *lie* and *lay*, *sit* and *set*, *rise* and *raise*. *Lie*, *sit*, and *rise* are all intransitive and therefore do not take direct objects. (One trick to remembering them is that the first vowel in each is an *i*, and *intransitive* begins with an *i*.) *Lay*, *set*, and *raise* are all transitive and therefore require a direct object. Here are some examples (the arrows show the relationship between the transitive verbs and their objects):

I *lie* down.	INTRANSITIVE: NO OBJECT
I *lay* the book down.	TRANSITIVE: FOLLOWED BY OBJECT
I *sit* on the chair.	INTRANSITIVE: NO OBJECT
I *set* the cushion on the chair.	TRANSITIVE: FOLLOWED BY OBJECT
I *rise* at seven every morning.	INTRANSITIVE: NO OBJECT
I *raise* the curtain.	TRANSITIVE: FOLLOWED BY OBJECT

Sometimes distinguishing between these pairs is complicated by unfamiliarity with the principal parts. Notice the difference in the principal parts of each pair:

14b

BASE FORM (INFINITIVE)	PRESENT TENSE	PAST TENSE	PAST PARTICIPLE	PRESENT PARTICIPLE
(to) lie (recline)†	lie(s)	lay	lain	lying
(to) lay	lay(s)	laid	laid	laying
(to) sit	sit(s)	sat	sat	sitting
(to) set	set(s)	set	set	setting
(to) rise	rise(s)	rose	risen	rising
(to) raise	raise(s)	raised	raised	raising

Lie is particularly confusing unless you take careful note of several of the principal parts. The simple past of *lie*, which is *lay*, is the same form as the simple present of *lay*:

I *lay* down yesterday for an hour before supper.
I *was lying* down when he came in.
I *lay* the newspaper on my father's bureau every morning.
I *was laying* the newspaper down when he came in.

†The other meaning of *lie*, "to fib," is regular: *lie, lied, lied.*

While *lay* is sometimes used in casual situations to mean *lie,* it is not appropriate in formal and informal use:

CASUAL: A crisis in our economy *lays* just ahead.

INFORMAL OR FORMAL: A crisis in our economy *lies* just ahead.

EXERCISES

Revise any inappropriate verb forms in the following sentences.

1. Instead of just laying in the sun, she decided to help me set out the plants.
2. She lay the hoe down to raise up the azalea, which had been sat crookedly into the hole.
3. Don't just set there! The dog is trying to lie down on top of the tomato plants!
4. Where have you set the fertilizer?
5. If we raise very early in the morning, instead of just laying in bed until all hours, we can get the garden weeded before it gets too hot.

14c

14c Subjunctive Forms

All the verb forms we have studied so far have been in the *indicative mood,* which is used for ordinary questions and statements. Old English had a whole set of inflections in the *subjunctive mood,* used in questions and statements that show possibility, condition, or wish. (Many languages, like French, still use the subjunctive mood extensively.) In modern English, most uses of the subjunctive have disappeared, but in a few special cases, subjunctive forms are still used:

1. In certain clauses that are contrary to fact, especially after *if* and with the verb *wish,* use the subjunctive *were* instead of the indicative *was*:

   If I *were* the boss, I would fire him.
   I wish I *were* a sailor.

   Notice, however, that not all *if* clauses call for the subjunctive. If the clause does not represent a wish or a statement contrary to fact, use the indicative:

If Henry *was* at the party, I didn't see him.

2. In making motions in parliamentary procedure or in making formal demands (with verbs like *move, request,* and *demand*), use the form *be* instead of *is:*

> I move that John *be* the new chairperson.
> I request that Henry *be* invited to the party.
> It is necessary that Isabel *be* fired immediately.

3. Likewise, in making motions or demands with verbs other than *be,* use the uninflected (base) form of the verb instead of the indicative *-s* form:

> I move that John *appoint* the new chairperson.
> It is necessary that Henry *invite* Isabel to the party.

Indicative forms are often used in casual situations, especially conversations. In informal or formal contexts, however, always use the subjunctive forms when appropriate.

CASUAL: If the proposal *was* ready by the first of December, the Board would approve it. I wish Jim Ford *was* here to tend to this problem.

14c

INFORMAL OR FORMAL: If the proposal *were* ready by the first of December, the Board would approve it. I wish Jim Ford *were* here to tend to this problem.

EXERCISES

Underline the subjunctive verbs in the following sentences, and explain why the subjunctive is used in each.

1. I would not send that letter if I were you.
2. I demanded that Poindexter see the chairwoman.
3. Sara often wishes that her job were in New York City.
4. The university requires that each student be responsible for his own work.
5. The dean requested that the valedictorian present the graduation speech.

14d Main Verbs and Auxiliary Verbs

Every clause must have a *main verb*—the verb that carries the primary meaning. If a main verb is in the simple present or past form, it is complete and can stand alone in the clause:

John *gives* a recital on his violin once a year.
Susan *gave* a thousand dollars to the United Fund.

Any other form of the main verb is incomplete and requires an auxiliary ("helping") verb to complete it:

John *was giving* his recital when I walked in.
Susan *had given* a thousand dollars to the United Fund last year.

Three verbs in English can be used either as auxiliary verbs or as main verbs: *be*, *have*, and *do*. (All other verbs in English, except the modals discussed in **14e**, can be used only as main verbs.) It is important to recognize these distinctions:

4d

- *Main Verb* be *(Intransitive)*: *Be* as a main verb often means roughly "to exist" ("I think; therefore, I *am*." "*To be* or not *to be.* . .").
- *Main Verb* be *(Linking)*: When *be* is used as a linking verb, it does not have any meaning in itself but functions something like an equal or identity sign. In "He *is* my brother," the *is* does not mean "exists," but rather establishes a relationship of equality or identity between the words *he* and *brother*.
- *Auxiliary Verb* be: The auxiliary verb *be* also has no meaning of its own, but is used together with the present participle of the main verb to form the progressive tenses (I *am thinking*. He *was swimming*) or with the past participle to form the passive voice (The book *was written*).
- *Main Verb* have *(Transitive)*: *Have* as a main verb means, roughly, "to possess," as in "I *have* five dollars."
- *Auxiliary Verb* have: *Have* as an auxiliary verb has no meaning in itself but is used to form the perfect tenses (I *have driven*. She *had swum*).
- *Main Verb* do *(Transitive)*: *Do* as a main verb means to make, complete, or act, as in "Mary *did* the painting in only an hour."

- *Auxiliary Verb* do: *Do* as an auxiliary verb has no meaning of its own but is combined with the base form of the main verb, either to create emphasis or to form questions and negatives when another auxiliary verb is not present (I *did* walk. *Did* I walk? I *did* not walk).

EXERCISES

1. Underline the forms of *be*, *have*, and *do* in the following sentences. Then indicate whether each is used as a main verb or an auxiliary.

   a. I am taking a dance class.
   b. My partner last night didn't know how to dance very well.
   c. He has only been taking lessons for a week, however, and he did apologize.
   d. He has improved greatly since the course started.
   e. His rhumba has real charm, but his waltz does still need work.

2. Write one sentence using each of the following verb forms as a main verb and one sentence using each as an auxiliary: *am, are, was, were, do, does, did, has, have, had.*

14e

14e Modal Auxiliary Verbs

Nine verbs in English are used only as auxiliary verbs: *can, could, shall, should, will, would, may, might,* and *must.* Each modal functions in a slightly different way, but all of them combine with main verbs to express future time or condition of some sort.

Although modals are used only as auxiliaries, the main verb may be implied rather than stated: "You *can run* really fast. Yes, I *can* [run]." Modals are the only verbs that do not have the *-s* inflection in the third-person singular of the present tense (He *might* go. She *should* win).

14e.1 *Will* and *shall*

Will and *shall* express an intention of something happening, although *shall* is now rare in American English, except in legal documents:

CASUAL, INFORMAL, OR FORMAL:	Tomorrow I *will* sleep late.
FORMAL (LEGAL):	The executor of the will *shall* contact the family of the deceased.

14e.2   *Can* and *may*

Can expresses ability, whether in the present or future. (I *can* sing very well. I *can* get it for you wholesale.) *May* is used to convey permission to do something. (Yes, you *may* go shopping tomorrow.) *May* also indicates possibility. (I *may* go shopping tomorrow.)

   Can is sometimes used in place of *may* to convey permission, but usually only in casual situations:

CASUAL:	I hope I *can* be excused from tomorrow's meeting.
INFORMAL AND FORMAL:	I hope I *may* be excused from tomorrow's meeting.

Some editors and teachers are more accepting of *can* in place of *may* when it is used in a negative contraction after an interrogative pronoun:

CASUAL AND INFORMAL:	Why *can't* we use the new stationery?
FORMAL:	Why *may* we *not* use the new stationery?

14e.3   *Could, would,* and *might*

Could, would, and *might*† all express a conditional happening, and for this reason, they are often used together with an *if* or *when* clause. (*If* I had enough money, I *would* retire early. I *would* go along *if* I were asked. *When* I have finished college, I *might* go to graduate school.)

14e.4   *Must* and *should*

Must and *should*† both express the need for something to be done in the future. *Must* is a little stronger, suggesting there is little choice. (I *must* be at work by 8 a.m. I *must* start my diet tomorrow.) *Should* suggests that one ought to do something. (I really *should* go to class today.)

---

†Be careful not to misspell *might have, should have,* etc., as "might of" or "should of." See **22c**.

EXERCISES

In your daily newspaper or in a weekly news magazine, look for examples of sentences that use the modal verbs: *can, could, shall, should, will, would, may, might,* and *must.* What do you notice about the kinds of articles in which each of these tends to appear?

14f Compound Verb Forms

Since English has only two inflected tenses (present and past), we rely on the auxiliary verbs to indicate other time relationships. The auxiliaries include *be, have, do,* and the modals. (Some verb phrases also act as auxiliary substitutes, like *used to* for *did* and *have to* for *must.*) The auxiliaries are used in combination with main verbs to create a *complete* verb and to indicate time relationships with all forms except the simple present and past. Following are the most common of the combined forms:

14f

1. *Future* (and *Conditional*) = modal + base form of main verb. It is used to show something that will happen in the future:

   I *will go* tomorrow.
   The police *can help*.

When *could, might,* or *should* are used with the base form, they produce *conditional* sentences—that is, statements that have a condition attached to them, expressed in an *if* or *when* clause or in a phrase:

   CONDITIONAL CLAUSE
   He *might cry* [if you say that].
   CONDITIONAL PHRASE
   I *could sing* well [with her coaching].

2. *Present Perfect* = present tense of *have* + past participle of main verb. It is used most commonly for an action that began in the past and continues into the present:

   I *have gone* to the opera many times. [And I still go.]
   He *has cried* for three days now. [And he's still crying.]
   The police *have helped* often. [And they continue to help.]

3. *Past Perfect* = past tense of *have* + past participle of main verb. This form is used for an action that both began and ended in the past:

> The police *had helped* us twice before.
> Harry *had failed* freshman English the previous year, too.

When the past perfect is used in a sentence with another clause that contains a simple past-tense verb, the past perfect indicates an action completed before the action expressed in the simple past:

> [Sam *had gone*] [before Susan *arrived*].
> [He *had finished* college] [before I even *started*].

4. *Present Progressive* = present tense of *be* + present participle of main verb. It is used with a number of meanings: continuous present time, immediate present time, or future time:

> I *am going* to Ohio State because it has a good football team. — CONTINUOUS PRESENT
>
> He *is crying* because he can't go. — IMMEDIATE PRESENT
>
> The police *are helping* us plant the trees tomorrow. — FUTURE

4f

5. *Past Progressive* = past tense of *be* + present participle of main verb. This form is used to show continuous action that occurred in the past:

> He *was crying* all day yesterday.

When the past progressive is used in a sentence with another clause that contains a simple past-tense verb, the past progressive indicates an action that was occurring at the time of the action expressed in the simple past:

> [The police *were planting* trees] [when they *received* an emergency call].

6. *Future Perfect* (and *Conditional*) = modal + *have* + past participle. This form is used for an action that begins and will end in the future: I *will have gone* by midnight. When the future perfect is used in a sentence with another clause that contains

a simple present-tense verb, the future perfect indicates an action completed before the action expressed in the simple present:

[Sam *will have gone*] [before Susan *arrives*].
[He *will have finished* college] [before I even *begin*].

When *could*, *might*, or *would* are used with *have* and the past participle, they produce *conditional* sentences, and they always have an implied or expressed *if* clause or a phrase expressing some condition on which the main clause depends:

[If he had kept his promise], he *would have gone* with me.
I *might have failed* the course [without her help].

7. *Future Progressive* = modal + *be* + present participle. This form is sometimes used to indicate the intention of doing something, as the simple future and present progressive may also do:

Are you going to the party tomorrow night?

Yes, I *will be going.*	FUTURE PROGRESSIVE
Yes, I *will go.*	SIMPLE FUTURE
Yes, I *am going.*	PRESENT PROGRESSIVE

14f

The future progressive is also used to express something that will be happening in the future:

The child *will be growing up* soon.

When the future progressive is used in a clause with a simple present-tense verb, the future progressive indicates action that will be occurring at the time of the action expressed in the simple present:

[She *will be singing* her third aria] {by the time I *arrive*}.

EXERCISES

Underline the compound verb forms in the following sentences. Then indicate what kind of verb each is: present perfect, past perfect, present progressive, past progressive, future, future perfect, or future progressive.

1. P. J. Throckmorton, the famous novelist who writes under the name of Dirk Desire, was celebrating his birthday last week.

2. He had written his first popular novel by the age of sixteen.
3. Throckmorton has written over thirty controversial novels, and he is writing another one now.
4. He will write at least two more formula novels next year, and he will still be writing them when novels with endless scenes of heavy breathing have gone out of style.
5. P. J. Throckmorton will have written over one hundred trashy novels before he dies.

14g   Sequence of Tenses

14g.1   With Dependent Clauses

The verbs in a dependent clause should be logically related to those in the main clause. Notice the following pair of sentences:

> I discovered that Bill *is* a liar.
> I discovered that Bill *was* a liar.

In both sentences, the discovery happened in the past. The first sentence indicates that Bill was a liar at the time of the discovery and still is a liar at the time of the statement. The second sentence states that Bill was a liar at the time of the discovery, but we do not know about the present.

Occasionally, when writing about historical figures, authors will put the verb in the dependent clause into the same tense as the main verb:

> Columbus believed that the earth *was* round.

We know that the author intended to convey Columbus' belief in a constant fact—that the earth was *and* is round—but it could have been expressed more clearly by putting the second verb in the present tense:

> Columbus believed that the earth *is* round.

Here are some more specific guidelines that will help you keep the tenses in dependent clauses logically related to those in the main clause:

1. When the verb in the main clause is past perfect, use the simple past tense in the dependent clause:

CONFUSING: Sam had gone before Susan *had arrived.*

CLEAR: Sam had gone before Susan *arrived.*

> (Sam's going is earlier than Susan's arrival; therefore, the past perfect is used for his action and the simple past for hers.)

2. When the verb in the main clause is future perfect, use the simple present in the dependent clause:

CONFUSING: Sam will have gone before Susan *arrived.*

CLEAR: Sam will have gone before Susan *arrives.*

> (Both Sam's going and Susan's arrival are in the future, after the time the sentence is uttered; the simple present is often used to express future time, although the future, *will arrive*, is also acceptable.)

3. When the verb in either the main clause or the dependent clause is past progressive, the verb in the other clause should be in the simple past:

CONFUSING: The police were planting trees when they *receive* an emergency call.

CLEAR: The police were planting trees when they *received* an emergency call.

CONFUSING: While the police were planting trees, they *receive* an emergency call.

CLEAR: While the police were planting trees, they *received* an emergency call.

14g.2 With Infinitives

Even though infinitives usually function as nouns (see **13h.2**), they are formed from the base of the verb, and like verbs, they convey a sense of time:

> John hopes *to win* next week's game.
> John hoped *to win* last week's game.

To win is called the present infinitve (or just the infinitive). The present infinitive usually expresses a time that is the same as that of the main verb or further in the future. In the first example, John hopes (in the present) to win in the future. In the second example, John hoped (in the past) to win a game that was after his hoping but before the utterance of the sentence.

Now consider the following sentences:

> John hopes *to have won* a game before the end of the season.
> Susan felt proud *to have received* the honor.

The phrases *to have won* and *to have received* are called *perfect infinitives*, because they contain the infinitive form of *have* plus a past participle, *won* or *received*. When the main verb is in the present, the perfect infinitive usually expresses an action that occurs *after* the time of the main verb: John hopes in the present, and the action he is hoping about (winning a game) is in the future but will be completed when the future time arrives. When the main verb is in the past, the perfect infinitive usually expresses an action that occurs *before* the time of the main verb: Susan felt proud in the past, and what she felt proud about (receiving the honor) occurred even further in the past.

When you write a sentence with an infinitive, be sure the tense of the infinitive relates logically to the tense of the main verb. Use a present infinitive if the main verb is perfect, and use a present main verb if the infinitive is perfect:

4g

> CONFUSING: John *had hoped to have won* the chess game.
> CLEAR: John had hoped *to win* the chess game. (or)
>   John *hoped* to have won the chess game.
>   (Either John's hoping preceded the possibility of winning, in which case the present infinitive is used, or John's hoping and the possibility of winning are in the past, in which case the perfect infinitive is used.)

14g.3   With Participles

Use a present participle (*practicing*) to convey an action occurring *at the same time* as the main verb and a perfect participle (*having finished*) to convey action occurring *before* the main verb:

> CONFUSING: *Having practiced* the piano, Peter *became* inspired.
> CLEAR: *Practicing* the piano, Peter *became* inspired.
>   (Peter became inspired *while* he was practicing, not, presumably, *after* he practiced.)

CONFUSING: *Finishing* her novel, Jane *celebrated.*

CLEAR: *Having finished* her novel, Jane *celebrated.*
(We assume Jane celebrated *after* finishing her novel, not *while* she was still finishing it.

14g.4   With Modals

Three modal verbs, *could, would,* and *might* (see **14e.3**), are used to express a conditional action, usually in a sentence with an *if* clause. The sequence of tenses in a sentence can sometimes be confusing if you are not careful about when to use these conditional modals and when to use the equivalent present modals (*can, will,* and *may*). Following are some guidelines that will usually help you choose the appropriate modal form:

1. The verb forms in a conditional sentence should match: use a present modal with other present forms; use a conditional modal with other conditional forms or with past-tense forms:

CONFUSING: If you *slow* down, you *could* get better gas mileage.
                PRES   COND

CLEAR: If you slow down, you *can* get better gas mileage. (or)
                PRES   PRES

If you *slowed* down, you could get better gas mileage.
                COND   COND

CONFUSING: If he *goes,* I *would* be surprised.
             PRES   COND

CLEAR: If he goes, I *will* be surprised. (or)
            PRES   PRES

If he *went,* I would be surprised.
           PAST   COND

CONFUSING: If you *said* yes, I *will* go.
            PAST   PRES

CLEAR: If you said yes, I *would* go. (or)
            PAST   COND

If you *say* yes, I will go.
           PRES   PRES

14g

PAST
CONFUSING: If the temperature *were* to drop too fast, the
PRES
streets *may* ice up.

PAST
CLEAR: If the temperature were to drop too fast, the
COND
streets *might* ice up. (or)

PRES
If the temperature *drops* too fast, the streets
PRES
may ice up.

2. If the *if* clause has a past perfect verb, the result clause should have a conditional modal followed by a present perfect verb:

CONFUSING: If I had known he was in town, I *may* have called him.

CLEAR: If I had known he was in town, I *might* have called him.

4g

3. Do not use a conditional modal with a present perfect verb in the *if* clause; instead, use the past perfect verb alone:

CONFUSING: If the order *would have arrived* on time, we would not have had this problem.

CLEAR: If the order *had arrived* on time, we would not have had this problem.

4. In sentences without an *if* clause but with a noun clause, formal style requires that you use a present modal with a present verb and a conditional modal with a past verb; in informal or casual style, however, it is acceptable to use a past modal with a present main verb:

CASUAL OR
INFORMAL: Yes, I *think* [that] I *might go.*

FORMAL: Yes, I think [that] I *may go.* (or)
Yes, I *thought* [that] I might go.

5. In sentences in which you have both a conditional modal and an infinitive, the tense sequence can be very confusing if you use the present perfect. Use the perfect form of either the modal or the infinitive, but not both:

CONFUSING:	I *would have liked to have made* A's this quarter.
CLEAR:	I would have liked to *make* A's this quarter. (or)
	I *would like* to have made A's this quarter.

14g.5   In Narrative

If you are relating a narrative, you should generally keep the main narrative line either in the simple past or in the simple present. Factual history usually is related in the past (Columbus *discovered* America), and fiction in the present (Othello finally *discovers* Desdemona's faithfulness). You should, of course, use other verb forms logically to indicate events before or after the main narrative line:

> Columbus *discovered* America after he *had obtained* money from Ferdinand and Isabella.
> (Obtaining the money, expressed in the past perfect, is prior to discovering America, expressed in the simple past.)

> Othello finally *discovers* that Desdemona *has been* faithful.
> (Desdemona's faithfulness begins *before* Othello's discovery, expressed in the simple present, and continues to the time of his discovery; hence, it is expressed in the present perfect.)

14g

EXERCISES

In each of the following sentences, underline the verbs. Then revise those verbs that are not in logical sequence with others in the sentence.

1. If you would have won the game, I would have congratulated you.
2. If you would ask, I will tell you.
3. If you were telling the truth, I will believe you.
4. I learned that my best friend was a thief.
5. The students had finished their exams before the class is over.
6. When the jury was entering the room, the defendant suddenly faints.
7. The students wanted to have passed the test.
8. The professor hoped they will pass it.
9. I had thought to have finished the book by today.
10. Hamlet had trouble making decisions, and Ophelia goes mad.

14h   Active and Passive Voice

In sentences in the *active* voice, the subject (marked s) performs the action of the verb (marked v), which in turn affects the direct object (marked DO):

     s   v   DO

The fraternity *brothers brought* all the *food* for the party.

In the *passive* voice, the emphasis is shifted to the object instead of the subject, which is "passive" or acted upon. The object of the active sentence is put in the subject position of the passive sentence, and the subject of the active sentence is made the object of a preposition like *by* (marked OP) or eliminated altogether:

     s   v

All the *food* for the party *was brought* [by the fraternity

 OP

brothers].

Since *by* phrases are often omitted in passive sentences, a sure clue to recognizing a passive construction is the combination of the auxiliary *be* and the *past* participle. In active constructions, as we have shown above, the auxiliary *be* is always used with the *present* participle and the auxiliary *have* is always used with the *past* participle:

ACTIVE:

be + present participle:	The Queen *was stealing* the jewelry.
have + past participle:	The Queen *has stolen* the jewelry.

PASSIVE:

be + past participle:	The jewelry *was stolen* by the Queen. (or)
	The jewelry *was stolen*.

NOTE: Passive constructions are often cumbersome and confusing in writing; see **19d** for a discussion of when to use passive and when to use active forms.

EXERCISES

Underline the verbs in the following sentences, and indicate whether they are passive or active. Then transform each passive sentence into the active voice and each active sentence into the passive voice.

1. Sophia was bitten by a horsefly.
2. Jonathan shot a seagull.
3. Spot caught a dead mouse.
4. My father kicked the bucket.
5. Maureen's bicycle hit a cow.
6. Her bicycle was fixed by the cow's owner.
7. Florence played Beethoven's *Moonlight Sonata* beautifully.
8. The garden was planted by my father-in-law.
9. Gina's father knit the shawl.
10. The furniture was cleaned by a professional.

14h

15

PROBLEMS WITH NOUNS AND PRONOUNS

15a   Inflections of Nouns

An *inflection* is a change in the form of a word to give certain grammatical information. Nouns are inflected for singular and plural *number* and for *relationships* like possession and ownership. Like verbs, nouns can be either *regular* or *irregular* in their inflectional patterns.

15a.1   Plural Forms

Regular nouns have an *-s* or *-es* suffix for the plural (car, car*s*, box, box*es*). The plurals of irregular nouns, however, do not follow that pattern. Some have an irregular plural suffix (child, chil*dren*) and some have a change in the internal spelling (m*ou*se, m*i*ce). Other nouns are the same in both singular and plural forms (one sheep, two sheep), and some have two different plurals (one fish, two fish or fish*es*).

Foreign words usually retain their original plurals until they are completely assimilated into English; even then, they often retain their foreign plurals. The word *curriculum*, for example, has kept its foreign plural *curricula* for a long time but has also acquired an English plural form, *curriculums*. Check the Glossary of Usage for the appropriate plural forms of such words as *data* and *agenda*.

15a.2 Possessive Forms

Nouns are also inflected to show the *possessive case*, used to indicate possession, ownership, or similar relationships. Animate nouns (those referring to people and animals) are usually made possessive by adding an -*'s* (or just an apostrophe, if the noun already ends in an -*s* or -*z* sound): Pattie's tennis racket; Amos' mother. (See **24b** for use of apostrophes.) With inanimate nouns, some writers prefer to show relationship by using a phrase beginning with *of* and followed by the possessive noun ("the cover *of the book*" instead of "the *book's* cover").

There are, however, some situations in which it is preferable to use -*'s* to make inanimate nouns possessive:

1. If the modifying phrase is very short, the -*'s* version is appropriate except in formal writing:

    CASUAL OR INFORMAL: I find this *report's* argument totally unconvincing.

    FORMAL: I find the argument *of this report* totally unconvincing.

2. If the phrase being modified is long enough that the *of* phrase would be awkward, use the -*'s* form even for inanimate nouns:

    AWKWARD: The waste disposal system *of the city* has been totally renovated.

    CLEAR: The *city's* waste disposal system has been totally renovated.

3. If the modifying phrase is very long, use the *of* form :

    AWKWARD: The *Commission on Aid to the Poor's* meeting was boring.

    CLEAR: The meeting *of the Commission on Aid to the Poor* was boring.

4. Both *of* and -*'s* may be used together when necessary to clarify meaning:

    AMBIGUOUS: That is my *brother's* portrait.

    CLEAR: That portrait *of my brother* is a good likeness.

15a

CLEAR: That portrait *of my brother's* cost him a lot of money.

Notice that the possessive noun may come after the word it modifies:

That portrait is my *brother's*.
Is that portrait your *brother's?*

15a.3   Compound Possessive Nouns

If a compound possessive refers to joint possession or relationship, only the last noun in the compound should have an -*'s*:

CONFUSING: We must put another person in Alice*'s* and Barbara*'s* office.
CLEAR: We must put another person in Alice and Barbara*'s* office.
("Alice and Barbara" is considered one unit because the word *office* is singular and therefore must belong to them jointly.)

If a compound possessive refers to individual possession or relation, both possessive nouns should have an -*'s*:

CONFUSING: Have you processed Jim and Martin*'s* expense accounts?
CLEAR: Have you processed Jim*'s* and Martin*'s* expense accounts?
(Since the word *accounts* is plural, we know that Jim and Martin have individual expense accounts, and therefore the *'s* should be used with both names.)

In the case of hyphenated or compound nouns, add the -*'s* only to the last word of the compound: *brother-in-law's* book; *someone else's* problem.

15a.4   Possessive Nouns Before Gerunds

In formal and informal writing, when a gerund is modified by a noun that indicates possession or a similar relationship, the modifying noun is in the possessive case, as it would be before any other noun:

INFORMAL OR
FORMAL: What was the reason for *Henry's* failing?
             (Compare: What was the reason for Henry's
             failure?)

In casual use, the possessive is often omitted:

CASUAL: What was the reason for *Henry* failing?

Sometimes, however, the meaning of a sentence requires a noun without the possessive ending. Compare the following sentences:

I noticed *Henry* falling.
I noticed *Henry's* falling.

In the first sentence, it is Henry who is noticed, and *falling* is a participle modifying Henry. In the second sentence, it is the falling that is the important point, and *Henry's* is the modifier. In most cases, however, such constructions are interpreted as a possessive noun followed by a gerund.

15b

EXERCISES

In the following sentences, circle plural and possessive forms that might not be acceptable in a formal situation. Then revise those forms so that they are both clear and acceptable in a formal situation.

1. I can't remember where John's and Sara's house is.
2. A big fuss was made about the mayor changing his vote.
3. Jean bought a rose for her father's-in-law birthday.
4. The students' advisors have a meeting this afternoon.
5. The childrens' bike was standing out in the rain.
6. The state's budget was in bad shape this year.
7. Please give me Smith and Holland's social security numbers.
8. The central heating system of the house was inefficient.
9. The Research Development and Exchange Foundation's office is on Harding Street.
10. A grade will be given for the student writing.

15b Personal Pronouns and Case Forms

Personal pronouns are almost the only words left in English that have a whole set of inflections (alterations in form). They are inflected for singular and plural *number*, for first, second, and third *person*; for subject, object, or possessive *case*; and for masculine, feminine, and neuter *gender* (in the third-person singular only). Here are the various forms of the personal pronouns:

| | SINGULAR | | | |
	SUBJECT	OBJECT	POSSESSIVE 1	POSSESSIVE 2
FIRST PERSON	I	me	my	mine
SECOND PERSON	you	you	your	yours
THIRD PERSON	she	her	her	hers
	he	him	his	his
	it	it	its	its
	PLURAL			
FIRST PERSON	we	us	our	ours
SECOND PERSON	you	you	your	yours
THIRD PERSON	they	them	their	theirs

The various case forms of personal pronouns have different functions:

15b

1. The *subject case* is used for personal pronouns functioning as subjects or subject complements:

> *She* is a doctor.   SUBJECT
> It is *I.*   SUBJECT COMPLEMENT

When the subject complement follows the linking verb, however, only formal usage requires it be in the subject case. In informal and casual use it would be in the object case (notice that "It is" is always contracted to "it's" when the object case is used):

| FORMAL: | It is *I.* | It is *she.* | It is *they.* |
| INFORMAL OR CASUAL: | It's *me.* | It's *her.* | It's *them.* |

2. The *object case* is used for personal pronouns functioning as direct objects, indirect objects, and objects of prepositions:

> The committee selected *her.*   DIRECT OBJECT
> The president gave *her* the gavel.   INDIRECT OBJECT

I would recommend anyone
but *her*.   OBJECT OF PREPOSITION

The object case is also be used for object complements, objects
of infinitives, and objects of gerunds:

They elected *her* chair-
woman.   OBJECT COMPLEMENT
Jane said she wouldn't want
to be *her*.   OBJECT OF INFINITIVE
Seeing *her* was a surprise.   OBJECT OF GERUND

3. The *possessive case* of pronouns, like possessive nouns, is used
   for noun determiners (a word that signals a noun, like an article), subject complements, or subjects:

Her piano needs tuning.   NOUN DETERMINER
Hers needs tuning.   SUBJECT
That piano is *hers*.   SUBJECT COMPLEMENT

Notice that one form of the possessive is used in the determiner slot, another form in the complement and subject slots.

15b

Choosing the correct case of personal pronouns is sometimes
difficult. Following are guidelines for dealing with the most common problems.

15b.1   After Linking Verbs

In formal situations, always use the subject case for a subject
complement. In casual use, however, the object case is common,
especially when asking or answering a question:

CASUAL: I thought it was *them* I told.
               Officials are certain that the informant is not
               me.

FORMAL OR
INFORMAL: I thought it was *they* I told.
               Officials are certain that the informant is not
               I.

Following the infinitive *to be*, however, the object case is common even in informal use, though not in formal:

| INFORMAL OR CASUAL: | If profits continue to erode, I wouldn't want to be *her* at this time next year. |
| FORMAL: | If profits continue to erode, I wouldn't want to be *she* at this time next year. |

EXERCISES

In the following sentences, the pronouns are acceptable in casual situations and sometimes in informal ones as well. Change them so that they would be appropriate in a formal context.

1. John heard it was *him* who murdered the secretary.
2. But others felt it had to be *her*, because of her obvious motive.
3. The chairwoman asked if it was *us* who had written the proposal.
4. Someone knew it was *me* who was in trouble.
5. Ann thought to be *him* would be a terrible fate.

15b.2   After Prepositions

15b

Always use the object case, even though the subject case might "sound" more formal, especially after prepositions like *but* and *except*:

| NONSTANDARD: | I would recommend anyone but *he*. Between you and *I*, she is not to be trusted. |
| CASUAL, INFORMAL, OR FORMAL: | I would recommend anyone but *him*. Between you and *me*, she is not to be trusted. |

EXERCISES

Underline the correct form of pronoun in each of the following sentences.

1. Katherine asked everyone except he/him what was wrong.
2. Everyone but us/we went to the game.
3. All the students except me/I received A's on the test.
4. Jack brought everyone except they/them a bag of squash.
5. Every one of the dentists in our town except her/she charges outrageous prices.

15b.3 In Elliptical (Shortened) Clauses

When part of the clause is left unstated or "understood," choose the subject case if the pronoun functions as a subject in the shortened clause; choose the object case if the pronoun functions as an object in the shortened clause:

> I am as tall as *he*.
> I like John as well as *she*.

These two sentences are elliptical (shortened) versions of sentences with two full clauses:

> I am as tall as *he* [is].
> I like John as well as *she* [likes John].

Because *he* and *she* are the subjects of *is* and *likes* in the full clauses, they are in the subject case. Sometimes, however, what is left in an elliptical clause is not the subject but the object:

> I like John as well as *him*.

That is an elliptical version of the following:

> I like John as well as [I like] *him*.

In order to decide whether to use the subject or object case after *as* or *than*, therefore, you must mentally fill in the missing part of the second clause.

In casual use, *as* and *than* are often considered prepositions, so that the pronoun following them is in the object case regardless of the elliptical clause. In informal and formal use, however, the case of the pronoun depends on its function in the elliptical clause:

CASUAL:	Rollins seems as likely as *her* to get the uncommitted votes.
	Simpson believes that their research people don't have as much data as *us*.
	I believe John is better qualified than *me*.
INFORMAL OR FORMAL:	Rollins seems as likely as *she* is to get the uncommitted votes.
	Simpson believes that their research people don't have as much data as *we* do.
	I believe John is better qualified than *I* am.

15b

EXERCISES

Underline the appropriate choice of pronoun for formal use in each of the following sentences. In two cases, two interpretations of the elliptical clause are possible. Be prepared to discuss which interpretation fits which choice of pronoun.

1. I am a more agile runner than she/her.
2. Are you as tall as he/him?
3. Richard beat Adrienne more quickly than her/she.
4. Mark cooks better than she/her.
5. He dated Sue as long as her/she.

15b.4   As Noun Determiners

Noun determiners function like the articles *a*, *an*, and *the*. Choose the case the pronoun would be if it were not followed by a noun:

We boys played baseball yesterday.
> (*We* played baseball.)

The Little League championship went to *us* girls.
> (It went to *us*.)

15b

EXERCISES

Underline the correct choice of pronoun in each of the following sentences.

1. We/us women have the championship debating team.
2. The award went to us/we men.
3. We/us five became inseparable friends.
4. The publisher gave us/we apprentices bonuses.
5. We/us runners will try to stay close in the marathon.

15b.5   Before Gerunds

In informal and formal situations, always use the possessive case before a gerund, even when it follows a preposition; in casual contexts, the object case is sometimes used instead:

CASUAL: What was the cause of *him* breaking a leg?
I can give no explanation for *me* refusing to talk to the press.

My employers are quite pleased at *us* getting the contract.

INFORMAL AND
FORMAL:

What was the cause of *his* breaking a leg?
I can give no explanation for *my* refusing to talk to the press.
My employers are quite pleased at *our* getting the contract.

EXERCISES

Underline the appropriate choice of pronoun in each of the following sentences for a formal or informal context.

1. His/Him getting a stress fracture came as a result of swimming.
2. Them/Their winning the award is the satisfying culmination of a great effort.
3. What do you think about our/us getting fined for picnicking on the lawn?
4. My/Me falling overboard was a careless act.
5. Your/You trying for straight A's is praiseworthy.

15b

15b.6 In Compounds

Pronouns used in compounds with *and* or *or* should be in the same case as if they were used alone, even if one member of the compound is a noun:

SUBJECT CASE: *She* and *I* are going to the movies.
(*She* is going; *I* am going)

I can't remember if it was *Johnson* or *he*.
(if it was *Johnson*; if it was *he*)

OBJECT CASE: John has asked *you* and *me* to proofread the report.
(John has asked *you*; John has asked *me*)

John gave the apple to *Ethel* and *me*.
(gave the apple to *Ethel*; gave the apple to *me*)

The supervisor expressed anger toward *her* and *me*.

(anger toward *her*; anger toward *me*)

POSSESSIVE CASE: Those are *Emily's* and *his* coats.
(*Emily's* coat; *his* coat)

EXERCISES

Underline the correct choice of pronoun in each of the following sentences (where more than one possibility exists, choose the one that is most appropriate for *formal* use).

1. She/her and he/him dance with the National Ballet Theatre.
2. Give her essays to I/me or her/she.
3. Either we/us or they/them will assume the open berth on the tournament ladder.
4. Those are he/his and John's books.
5. Is he/him or she/her winning the debate?

REVIEW EXERCISES

Circle the standard pronoun form, or the one appropriate for formal situations, in each of the following sentences.

1. We/Us girls cheered Wonder Woman on to victory.
2. Is that her/she in that wretched picture?
3. What do you think of her/she as a teacher?
4. When they told us/we it was him/he who threw the mimeograph machine out of the window, we couldn't believe it.
5. We were disappointed when the Oscar did not go to her/she.
6. Between you and I/me, let's hope the professor loses those essays.
7. On he/him alone rests responsibility for the sit-in.
8. The account of the murder frightened us/we campers.
9. Give the report to her/she or I/me before you lose it.
10. Why did he choose them/they over us/we?

15c Reflexive Pronouns

Reflexive pronouns are those which refer back to a person mentioned earlier in the sentence:

myself, ourselves
yourself, yourselves
herself, himself, itself, themselves

The reflexive pronoun has two common uses:

1. Reflexives are used in place of the object case of the personal pronoun whenever the object refers to the same person as the subject:

Peter hated *himself* for failing the test.	DIRECT OBJECT
Jean talked to *herself*.	OBJECT OF PREPOSITION
We bought *ourselves* a gallon of ice cream.	INDIRECT OBJECT

2. Reflexives are also used for emphasis, either as appositives or as adverbs (with the *by* frequently omitted):

I *myself* wrote the essay.	APPOSITIVE
I wrote the essay by *myself*.	ADVERB
I wrote the essay *myself*.	ADVERB

In formal and informal situations, use the reflexive only when another noun or pronoun in the sentence refers to the same person. The reflexive is rarely used by itself in place of a personal pronoun, except occasionally in casual speech:

15d

CASUAL:	John will attend the meeting as well as *myself*. The report will be submitted to Whitley and *myself*.
INFORMAL OR FORMAL:	John will attend the meeting as well as *I*. The report will be submitted to Whitley and *me*.

15d Demonstrative Pronouns

The demonstrative pronouns are *this*, *that*, *these*, and *those*. Their function is to point out or define, and to indicate nearness (*this*, *these*) or distance (*that*, *those*). They may be used by themselves in noun slots like personal pronouns (*This* is your life), or as noun determiners (*This* book is yours). When used alone in a noun slot, however, demonstrative pronouns need to have a very clear reference, or they can cause confusion (see **12c.2**).

When a demonstrative pronoun is used before a noun like *kind* or *sort*, it should be consistent in number with the noun and the object of the preposition; all should be plural, or all should be singular:

> If *these kinds* of sales *figures* are maintained, we should be able to pay a dividend this quarter.

> *This* is my favorite *sort* of *book*.

15e   Relative Pronouns

Relative pronouns are used as connectors in relative clauses (see section **13i.3**). They include *who, whomever, whom, whomever, whose, which,* and *that. Whom* and *whose* are inflections of *who*; likewise, *whomever* is an inflection of *whoever*:

SUBJECT CASE:	who	whoever
OBJECT CASE:	whom	whomever
POSSESSIVE CASE:	whose	(no "ever" form; see 4 below)

Which and *that*, however, are uninflected; that is, their forms remain the same whether used as subjects or objects.

The choice of *who, whom,* or *whose,* and of *whoever* or *whomever* depends upon how the word is to function in the relative clause. If a relative pronoun functions as a subject, then *who* or *whoever* is the correct form; if object, *whom* or *whomever*; and if possessive, *whose.* If you are uncertain about which form to use, test it by substituting a corresponding personal pronoun: *he* (for *who*), *him* (for *whom*), and *his* (for *whose*). When the word order has been inverted, as it often is in a relative clause, reverse it while you are testing the pronouns:

> He is the student *who* got the A.   NORMAL WORD ORDER
>
>   (*He* got the A.)
>
> He is the student *whose paper*   NORMAL WORD ORDER
> received an F.
>
>   (*His* paper received an F.)
>
> He is the student *whom* I asked to   INVERTED WORD ORDER
> leave.
>
>   (I asked *him* to leave.)

Following is a discussion of some special problems concerning the use of relative pronouns:

1. In formal and informal written English do not confuse the subject and object forms of *who* and *whom*; in casual speech, however, *who* is sometimes used in an object slot:

   CASUAL: She is the student *who* I noticed first.

   FORMAL OR
   INFORMAL: She is the student *whom* I noticed first.

2. *Whom* is always used in writing if it directly follows a preposition; in formal situations, the preposition comes directly before *whom*, although in informal situations, it may come at the end of the sentence. In casual use, *who* is more appropriate, with the preposition at the end of the sentence:

   CASUAL: She is the student *who* I spoke to.

   INFORMAL: She is the student *whom* I spoke to.

   FORMAL: She is the student *to whom* I spoke.

   Notice that in informal or casual use, the relative pronoun may be omitted entirely:

   INFORMAL
   OR CASUAL: She is the student I spoke to.

15e

3. In determining whether to use *who* or *whom*, *whoever* or *whomever*, do not be misled by the inverted word order of the relative clause or by intervening phrases like "I think," "you said," or "you ask":

   CASUAL: He is the man *who* I think you met.
   You may interview *whoever* you would like.

   FORMAL OR
   INFORMAL: He is the man *whom* I think you met.
   [You met *him*.]
   You may interview *whomever* you would like.
   [You would like to interview *him*.]

4. Since there is no standard possessive inflection of *whoever*, use *whose* instead:

   CASUAL: I wonder *whosever* woods these are.
   I wonder *whoever's* woods these are.

   FORMAL OR
   INFORMAL: I wonder *whose* woods these are.

5. *Who* and *whom* are usually used to refer to humans and sometimes animals, especially house pets. *That* and *which* are usually used to refer to nonhumans, inanimate objects, and ideas, although *that* is often used informally in place of *who* or *whom*:

INFORMAL OR CASUAL: The people *that* I like best are those with a sense of humor.

Jane Adamson wants someone *that* can complete the job with minimal supervision.

Which, however, is almost never used to refer to humans or animate nouns:

NONSTANDARD: The people *which* I like best are those with a sense of humor.

6. In very conservative, traditional usage, a distinction is sometimes made between *that* and *which*, *that* being used exclusively for restrictive (defining) clauses and *which* being used for nonrestrictive clauses (see 23b.4):

CONSERVATIVE: I read the book *that* you recommended.
Jane Eyre, *which* was written by Charlotte Brontë, is my favorite novel.

In contemporary usage, even in formal situations, *which* is equally acceptable for both restrictive and nonrestrictive clauses:

ACCEPTABLE: I read the book *which* you recommended.

7. Because neither *that* nor *which* is inflected for the possessive, use either *whose* or, more formally, *of which* for the possessive form of *that* or *which*:

CASUAL OR INFORMAL: The paper has received copies of the report *whose* authors are believed to be members of the president's staff.

FORMAL: The paper has received copies of the report, the authors *of which* are believed to be to be members of the president's staff.

EXERCISES

In each of the following sentences, underline the pronoun that would be most appropriate in a formal context:

1. Who/whom were you hoping to speak to today?
2. Whoever/whomever eats that pizza will surely get heartburn.
3. I will see whomever/whoever I want to see in the agency.
4. Jonathan was the man who/whom she said was David's good friend.
5. Enlist whomever/whoever you want for the committee.
6. Harry is the student who/that got the highest grade on the exam.
7. The person whom/which I know the best is the division head.
8. The professor who/whom I gave the best evaluation to is Dr. Harris.
9. I heard the symphony whose composer/the composer of which was sitting in the audience.
10. Give the report to whoever/whomever requested it.

15f   Interrogative Pronouns

Interrogative pronouns are used for asking questions. Some interrogative pronouns are identical to relative pronouns: *who*, *whoever*, *whom*, *whomever*, and *whose*. Interrogatives may function as subjects, objects of prepositions, and noun determiners. Here are some examples:

Who gave you that book?	SUBJECT
What is it?	SUBJECT
Whose is that?	SUBJECT
To *whom* were you speaking?	OBJECT
Whose book is that?	NOUN DETERMINER
What time is it?	NOUN DETERMINER
Which one would you like?	NOUN DETERMINER

In formal situations, use *who* and *whomever* in object slots. In casual use, *who* and *whoever* are acceptable:

CASUAL:	*Who* did Sara murder?
	Whoever did she dance with last night?
INFORMAL AND FORMAL:	*Whom* did Sara murder?
	Whomever did she dance with last night?

EXERCISES

Use an appropriate relative or interrogative pronoun in each blank in the following sentences.

1. She is one of those students ——— never have time to study.
2. The university is famous for its biology department, ——— is the best in the country.
3. In his anger, he attempted to find the person ——— was responsible for the theft.
4. Are you the student for ——— I wrote the recommendation?
5. He is the magician ——— I invited to perform at the party.
6. They'll never be sure about the causes ——— led to the disaster.
7. The boy ——— belongings were scattered everywhere couldn't find his keys.
8. The committee couldn't decide ——— deserved the scholarship.
9. He was lecturing on a subject ——— he knew nothing about.
10. Barbara seems to be the candidate ——— is most likely to win.

5g

15g Indefinite Pronouns

Indefinite pronouns include *all, any, each, none, some,* and the following combined forms:

anybody	everybody	nobody	somebody
anyone	everyone	no one	someone
anything	everything	nothing	something

The words with *-one* and *-body* suffixes also have possessive forms (It is *nobody's* house. It is *someone's*).

Indefinite pronouns have functions similar to personal pronouns:

Anybody can do it.	SUBJECT
It is *nobody*.	SUBJECT COMPLEMENT
She gave me *everything*.	DIRECT OBJECT
She gave the book to *someone*.	INDIRECT OBJECT
We could talk about *anything*.	OBJECT OF PREPOSITION

In formal use, indefinite pronouns are considered singular and require a singular pronoun to refer to them. In casual and informal use, however, indefinite pronouns are treated as plural if the context calls for it (see also **16b.5**):

CASUAL AND INFORMAL:	Everyone in class handed in their papers on time.
FORMAL:	Everyone in class handed in his or her paper on time.

(Notice that in the first example, the noun *papers* is also plural.)

15h Personal Pronouns Used as Indefinites

The personal pronouns *you, it,* and *they* are often used in casual situations to indicate an indefinite subject, much as *some, any, one,* and *all* are used (see **15g**). In formal writing, use only indefinite pronouns for indefinite references, or recast the sentence to avoid using *you, it,* and *they* as indefinites. *You* is acceptable in casual or informal use, but *it* and *they* are usually found only in casual use:

15h

CASUAL OR INFORMAL:	*You* never know when inspiration will come. *You* cannot be too careful in a situation like this.
FORMAL:	*One* never knows when inspiration will come. *One* cannot be too careful in a situation like this.
CASUAL:	*It* said in the newspaper that senior citizens will be hit hardest by inflation. *They* had much higher prices on the New York Stock Exchange today.
INFORMAL OR FORMAL:	*The newspaper* reported that senior citizens will be hit hardest by inflation. *Prices* were much higher on the New York Stock Exchange today.

EXERCISES

Rewrite each of the the following sentences to eliminate the indefinite use of *you, it,* and *they,* assuming a formal situation.

1. You never know where or when you will have a flat tire.
2. They have a good safety record in the transportation industry.
3. It says in *The Farmer's Almanac* that we will have Indian summer.
4. You can never know what your blind date will look like.
5. They have high crime rates in metropolitan areas.

5h

16

PROBLEMS WITH AGREEMENT

16a General Rules of Agreement

When words and phrases are combined into clauses and sentences, the inflections of nouns, verbs, and pronouns must all be consistent—that is, *in agreement* with one another. For example, if a noun is plural, the verb should also be plural:

Roses are blooming in my yard.

Most of the rules of agreement have to do with inflections for number (singular and plural); one has to do with gender.

16a.1 Subject and Verb

A subject and its verb must agree in number: singular subjects require singular verbs, and plural subjects require plural verbs.

Remember that singular *verbs* are usually marked with an *-s* or *-es*, while singular *nouns* are *unmarked*:

The boy walk*s*.
The fox run*s*.
The child wish*es*.

Remember too that plural *verbs* are *unmarked*, while plural nouns either have an *-s* or *-es* or have an irregular inflection:

The boy*s* walk.
The fox*es* run.
The child*ren* wish.

16a.2 Pronoun and Antecedent: Number and Person

A pronoun and its antecedent agree in number and person. An *antecedent* is the noun, pronoun, or noun phrase to which the pronoun refers. Remember that first person is the speaker (*I* or *we*); second person is the one addressed (*you*); third person is the person, thing, or idea being talked about (*she*, *he*, *it*, or any noun):

> Jennifer fixed *her* broken bike.
> (*Jennifer* and *her* are both singular and third-person.)

> The parents gave *their* children a party.
> (*Parents* and *their* are both plural and third-person.)

> I bought *my* friend a gift.
> (*I* and *my* are both singular and first-person.)

16a.3 Pronoun and Antecedent: Gender

A pronoun and its antecedent agree in gender. *Gender* refers to whether something is male, female, or neutral. Most nouns in English are neutral, so *it* or *its* would be the appropriate pronoun. But when we refer to individuals or nouns that refer to groups of men or women, we use *he*, *him*, and *his* to refer to male antecedents and *she*, *her*, and *hers* to refer to female antecedents.

When the antecedent is a group of both men and women, or a group of unknown composition, the choice is not so easy. The traditional rule is to use the masculine pronoun whenever the sex of the antecedent is unknown or general:

> TRADITIONAL: Each student passed in *his* paper.

Today, however, many people object to this tradition, arguing that it ignores women and suggesting that masculine and feminine pronouns be used together. Following are some examples:

> ALTERNATIVES: Each student passed in *his or her* paper.
> Each student passed in *her/his* paper.

To avoid the awkwardness of the double constructions, many people when speaking casually use the plural pronoun with a singular antecedent:

CASUAL (SPOKEN):   Each student passed in *their* paper.

In formal or informal situations, however, and even in casual writing, it is still not acceptable to use a plural pronoun with a singular antecedent. Instead, to acknowledge women and men equally, follow one of these guidelines:

1. Use the *her or his, she or he* style:

    TRADITIONAL: Each employee received *his* bonus check, which *he* should cash immediately.

    ALTERNATIVE: Each employee received *his or her* bonus check, which *he or she* should cash immediately.

    (But notice that the sentence becomes a bit clumsy when you have more than one double pronoun.)

2. Put the whole sentence in the plural (including the antecedent pronoun and any related words):

    ALTERNATIVE: *All employees* received *their* bonus checks, which *they* should cash immediately.

3. Get rid of the pronoun in question by rephrasing the sentence:

    ALTERNATIVE: Each employee has received *a* bonus check, *which should be cashed* immediately.

    (But notice that the passive form of the verb, "should be cashed," can be clumsy and confusing in some contexts; see **14h.**)

4. In a long paper, alternate masculine and feminine references (the practice followed in this book), using masculine pronouns in one paragraph or section, feminine ones in the next, and so on. This is not effective in a short paper, however, where such a practice can lead to difficulties with coherence. (See also **20c.**)

16b   Special Agreement Problems

Although the basic agreement rules are fairly simple and straightforward, they are sometimes difficult to apply because it is not always clear whether the subject of the verb or the antecedent of the pronoun is singular or plural. The following principles should help clarify these situations.

16b.1   With Compound Subjects

When a compound subject is joined with *and,* use a plural verb even if one of the subjects is singular; likewise, when a compound antecedent is joined with *and,* use a plural pronoun:

> The [students and their professor] *require* a large room.
> The [students and their professor] left *their* room.

If the compound subject or antecedent is singular in meaning (if it refers to one thing or person), use a singular verb or pronoun:

> The [producer and director] of the movie *is* a genius.
> The [producer and director] loved *her* own latest movie.

6b

When a compound subject is joined with *or* or *nor,* use a singular verb if both parts of the compound are singular; likewise, use a singular pronoun if both parts of the antecedent are singular:

> [Either Susan or Mary] *comes* every Friday to mow my grass.
> But [neither Susan nor Mary] mows *her* own grass.

If both parts of the subject or antecedent are plural, use a plural verb or pronoun:

> [Neither the teachers nor the students] *want* to accept responsibility for what happened.

> [Either the officers or the citizens] should accept it as *their* responsibility.

If one member of the subject or antecedent is singular and one plural, make the verb or pronoun agree with the nearest one:

> [Either John or the other *men*] *are* coming this week.
> [Either John or the other *men*] will bring *their* guitars.
> [Neither the men nor *John*] *is* coming this week.
> [Neither the men nor *John*] likes to play *his* guitar.

16b.2   With Collective Nouns

Use a singular verb with a collective subject and a singular pronoun with a collective antecedent, unless the collective noun refers to the members of the group as individuals rather than to the whole. A *collective* noun or pronoun is one that refers to a *collection* of people or things; usually it refers to the collection or group as a whole and is therefore treated as a singular:

> The choir *gives its* concert this Sunday.

Sometimes, however, the collective subject or antecedent refers to individual members of the group; in that case, it takes a plural verb or pronoun:

> The choir *were* given new robes before *they* presented *their* concert.

16b.3   With Plural-Form Nouns

16b

Nouns that appear to be plural in form but are singular in meaning take a singular verb or pronoun. Nouns of this type include *aeronautics*, *athletics*, *economics*, *electronics*, *mathematics*, *measles*, *mumps*, *news*, *politics*, *physics*, *statistics*:

> *Electronics is* my favorite hobby, but *it is* expensive.

Some of these nouns, however, are used with either a singular or plural meaning:

> *Economics is* a difficult subject.
>   (referring to the subject of economics)

> The *economics* of the situation *require* that we be very careful in spending our money.
>   (referring to economic *facts* or data)

With a plural word spoken of as a word, use a singular verb or pronoun:

> *Children is* an example of an irregular plural in English; *it* reminds us of the complexity of our language.

With a book title that is plural in form, use a singular verb or pronoun, because the book itself is the antecedent:

> *The Hidden Persuaders is* a helpful book; *it* warns us against being manipulated by the world of advertising.

16b.4 With Foreign Plurals

Be sure to use the appropriate verb forms with singular and plural foreign words. Although foreign words adapted into English often change plural forms, a good dictionary will tell you whether current usage considers a word like *data* singular or plural:

> The *data are* ready to be analyzed; *they* may yield some surprising results.

See also **22f** for discussion of foreign noun plurals.

16b.5 With Indefinite Pronouns

Use a singular verb when the subject is an indefinite pronoun; likewise, use a singular pronoun when the antecedent is an indefinite pronoun. Note that prepositional phrases between the pronoun and verb do *not* affect the agreement; see **16b.6.**

> *Neither* of us *was* able to understand the book.
> The maintenance crew reports that *none* of the machines *needs* replacement.
> *Neither* of the companies *is* ready to begin operations.
> Dr. Carmichael wants *everyone* to complete *his or her* report by Friday.

(See **16a.3** for a discussion of how to use the plural antecedent with an indefinite pronoun in order to avoid *his or her*.)

EXCEPTION: A few indefinite pronouns may be treated as either singular or plural, depending on whether they refer to an *amount* of something that is not countable (like ice cream) or a *number* of things that are countable (like ice cubes). When they refer to a number of individual things, use a plural verb with the indefinite subject and a plural pronoun with the indefinite antecedent:

> *Some* of the ice cream *is* melting; put *it* in the freezer.
> *Some* of the ice cubes *are* melting; put *them* in the freezer.

16b.6   With Prepositional Phrases

If a prepositional phrase comes between a subject and its verb or a pronoun and its antecedent, ignore it in deciding whether to use a singular or plural verb or pronoun:

> The *story* [about the Russians] was good; *it* was too long, however.
>
> The *stories* [about the Russians] were good; *they* were too long, however.
>
> The *professor*, [along with his students], *prefers* multiple-choice exams.

(Remember that phrases like *along with* and *together with* are prepositions, not coordinating conjunctions, so they do not affect the agreement of subject and verb.)

16b.7   With Relative Clauses

Agreement in sentences with relative clauses depends on which word in the main clause is being modified by the relative clause. If the relative clause modifies the subject, then make the verb in the relative clause agree with the subject, even if a prepositional phrase or other modifiers intervene :

> It is the *principal*, [not the teachers], who *requires* a final exam.
>
> She is the only *one* [of the teachers] who *requires* a final exam.

If, however, the relative clause modifies the object of a preposition, then make the verb in the relative clause agree with the object:

> She is one [of the *teachers* who *require* a final exam].
>
> The teacher [of the *children* who *sing* well] is very proud.
>
> It's one [of those *things* that *happen*].

16b.8   With Inverted Word Order and Dummy Pronouns

If the word order of the sentence is inverted (so that the subject follows the verb), the verb still agrees with its subject:

16b

Out on the lawn *are* three giant *oaks*.
(*Oaks* is the subject of *are*.)

Out on the lawn *are* a *dogwood* and three *oaks*.
(*A dogwood and three oaks* is the subject of *are*.)

Among the oaks *is* a *dogwood*.
(*A dogwood* is the subject of *is*.)

If the dummy pronoun *there* precedes the verb, the verb still agrees with the subject:

I knew that there *were* several *people* involved.
(*People* is the subject of *were*.)

There *is* a wide *variety* of jobs in the Publications Department.
(*Variety* is the subject of *is*.)

16b.9 With Linking Verbs

16b

In a sentence with a linking verb, the verb agrees with the subject, not with the complement:

The *result* of the fall *was* two broken bones.
(*Result* is the subject of *was*.)

Two broken *bones were* the result of his fall.
(*Two broken bones* is the subject of *were*.)

EXERCISES

1. In each of the following sentences, change one word to make the subject and verb agree.
   a. Neither Sally nor Bill spend much money for entertainment.
   b. If you are observant, you will notice that the leadership style of presidents change.
   c. Of all the activities students may participate in, sports are the most popular.
   d. He is one of those quarterbacks who always manages to complete a crucial pass.
   e. This pile of books need to be shelved.
   f. The committee of department heads meet on Thursdays at noon.
   g. Neither the chairman nor his advisors is sure how the committee should proceed.

h. A great deal of patience, together with strong determination, lead to a correct solution.

i. The kind of tests the teacher uses are multiple choice.

j. She is one of those singers who makes a concert a memorable event.

2. Underline the correct verb form in the sentences below, all of which have indefinite pronoun subjects.

a. Everyone on the team (hope/hopes) to go to the Sugar Bowl.

b. When everyone (do/does) his best, the players feel confident of one another.

c. Any of his books (merit/merits) the award.

d. Both the actors (perform/performs) brilliantly.

e. As soon as everyone (arrive/arrives), we'll begin the bidding.

f. Few students (take/takes) advantage of the library services.

g. Something (tell/tells) me I ought to be careful.

h. She was sure there (was/were) something behind his kindness.

i. I believe that someone (have bugged/has bugged) my telephone.

j. Anything you can imagine (interest/interests) the children.

3. Fill in the blanks in the sentences below with the appropriate possessive pronouns that refer to the indefinite pronoun subjects (antecedents).

a. None of the students knew ——— identification number.

b. Everyone is bringing a couple of ——— favorite recipes to the party.

c. Anyone who cannot find ——— keys will have trouble getting home.

d. No one knew if ——— group would be chosen to go first.

e. Everybody at the restaurant left ——— shoes at the door.

f. When I asked the question, I was surprised that everybody raised ——— hand.

g. Everyone who was at the meeting was interested in discussing ——— hobby.

h. None of the children remembered to bring ——— ticket.

i. Did anyone bring ——— dictionary to class?

j. The hike was a success because everybody brought ———map and compass.

16b

17 _____

PROBLEMS WITH MODIFIERS

17a Confusion of Adjectives and Adverbs

Some adjectives and adverbs have the same form—for example, *early, far, fast, little, only, right,* and *straight.* These words can, of course, be used in either adjective or adverb slots—adjectives to modify nouns or pronouns; adverbs to modify verbs, adjectives, other adverbs, or sentences:

> English was the *only* class in which Peter
> got an A.   ADJECTIVE
>
> If he *only* knew how lucky he was, he would be
> happier.   ADVERB
>
> Maria drives too *fast.*   ADVERB
>
> Maria drives a *fast* car.   ADJECTIVE

Several problems, however, result from failure to distinguish between adjectives and adverbs that are *not* identical:

17a.1 *Well* and *Good*

The word *well* can be used as an adjective or adverb, but with different meanings: the adjective *well* means "healthy," the opposite of "ill"; the adverb *well* means "in a good manner." *Good,* on the other hand, is always an adjective. Compare the following sentences:

Jasper was *sick*, but now he is *well*.
(*Sick* and *well* are both adjectives describing Jasper's state of health.)

Jasper is a *good* writer.
(*Good* is an adjective that modifies *writer*.)

Jasper writes *well*.
(*Well* is an adverb that modifies *writes*.)

In casual speech, the adjective *good* is sometimes used in place of the adverb *well*, but in informal and formal situations, *good* should never be used as an adverb:

CASUAL: For a pitcher, Gomez bats really *good*.

INFORMAL OR FORMAL: For a pitcher, Gomez bats really *well*.

17a.2 Modifiers After Linking Verbs

Linking verbs present special problems in the use of adjectives and adverbs. Linking verbs usually may be followed by adjectives but not by adverbs. The one exception to this rule is that an adverb may follow a linking verb when the adverb itself modifies an adjective that follows it. (Remember that a good way to test whether a verb is a linking verb is to try substituting a form of the verb *be*; see **13a.3**.)

17a

NONSTANDARD: John looks *terribly*.
STANDARD: John looks *terrible*.

NONSTANDARD: Player-spokesman Tony Schmidt told reporters that the whole team felt *badly* about Armstrong's dismissal.

STANDARD: Player-spokesman Tony Schmidt told reporters that the whole team felt *bad* about Armstrong's dismissal.

NONSTANDARD: Susan is *awful* smart.
STANDARD: Susan is *awfully* smart.
(Since *smart* is the adjective that completes the linking verb, it requires an adverb to modify it, not another adjective.)

Remember that *well*, unless it means "healthy," is an adverb and therefore should not follow a linking verb:

NONSTANDARD: Prospects for a speedy settlement look *well*.

STANDARD: Prospects for a speedy settlement look *good*.
(Prospects *are* good.)

17a.3 Adjectives Used as Adverbs

In casual situations, adjective forms are sometimes used in adverb slots, but in informal and formal use a careful distinction is made between adjectives and adverbs:

CASUAL: You will have to move *quick* to get that account.

If the team keeps playing this *bad*, its hopes for another NFL championship are over.

INFORMAL OR FORMAL: You will have to move *quickly* to get that account.

If the team keeps playing this *badly*, its hopes for another NFL championship are over.

17a

Some words, such as *fast*, can be used as both adjectives and adverbs:

She was *fast*.   ADJECTIVE
She ran *fast*.   ADVERB

Many adverbs ending in *-ly* are derived from adjectives (*careful, carefully*; *sad, sadly*). Because some adjectives also end in *-ly*, however, it is not always possible to tell from the suffix alone whether a word is an adjective or an adverb. Some words ending in *-ly* can be used as both adjectives and adverbs:

He was a *kindly* man.   ADJECTIVE
He said it *kindly*.   ADVERB

With a few exceptions like these, when you want to use an adjective ending in *-ly* as an adverb, put it in an adverb phrase; only in very casual speech may it be used as both adjective and adverb:

ADJECTIVE: He was a *friendly* person.

ADVERB, CASUAL
(SPEECH ONLY): He greeted me *friendly*.

| CASUAL, INFORMAL, OR FORMAL: | He greeted me *in a friendly manner*. |

EXERCISES

Some of the following sentences require an adjective and some an adverb. Underline the correct choice for informal and formal contexts.

1. John appeared (indignant/indignantly) when the officer handed him the summons.
2. Because I forgot to put it in the refrigerator, the milk smelled (sour/sourly).
3. Inflation caused the (steady/steadily) rising prices.
4. After I had dieted conscientiously for two weeks, the lemon meringue pie certainly looked (good/well) to me.
5. I hope to do (well/good) on tomorrow's test.
6. The trumpets sounded (flat/flatly) because the recording was (poor/poorly).
7. He accepted the nomination (quick/quickly).
8. My parents always insisted that I do (good/well) in school.
9. My mother did not eat the spinach because it tasted (bitter/bitterly).
10. Searching (careful/carefully) through the debris, the investigators found the missing evidence.

17b

17b Comparative and Superlative Forms

Many adjectives and adverbs are inflected for the *comparative degree* (more of something, or a greater degree of something) and for the *superlative degree* (most of something, or the greatest degree of something). The comparative and superlative degrees of adjectives are often indicated by the inflectional suffixes *-er* and *-est*:

BASE ADJECTIVE/ADVERB	COMPARATIVE DEGREE	SUPERLATIVE DEGREE
loud	louder	loudest
easy	easier	easiest
cute	cuter	cutest
hot	hotter	hottest
fast	faster	fastest

(Notice the double letter in *hotter* and the change from *y* to *i* in *easier*. These spelling rules are explained in **22b**).

Some adjectives and adverbs form the comparative and superlative by using the words *more* and *most* instead of the *-er* and *-est* endings. This is especially true of adverbs ending in *-ly* and of adverbs and adjectives with more than two syllables:

BASE ADJECTIVE/ADVERB	COMPARATIVE DEGREE	SUPERLATIVE DEGREE
beautiful	more beautiful	most beautiful
quickly	more quickly	most quickly

Some adjectives and adverbs have irregular inflections. The most common ones are those following:

BASE ADJECTIVE/ADVERB	COMPARATIVE DEGREE	SUPERLATIVE DEGREE
good	better	best
bad	worse	worst
little	less	least
some	more	most

17b

EXERCISES

1. Change each of the base adjectives below to its comparative and superlative forms.

awful	pretty
delightful	quick
expensive	quiet
fast	rich
mean	wonderful

2. Fill in the blanks in the sentences below with the comparative and superlative forms of the adjectives in the margin, using *-er/-est* endings or *more/most*, whichever is appropriate.

EXAMPLE

happy   Frodo is *happier* than Gollum, but Bilbo is the *happiest* of all.

a. *sunny*   Today was ——— than yesterday; tomorrow's forecast predicts that it will be the ——— day of the year.

b. *lovable*   Dogs are ——— than cats, but skunks are the ——— of all.

c. *bad*   Mortimer is a ——— cook than Algernon, but Oscar is the ——— cook of all the Rover boys.

d. *some*   I brought ——— cookies than Evelyn, but Emily, as usual, brought the ——— cookies.

e. *effective* Hortense has a ——— writing style than Fred, but Hermione has the ——— style of all.

17c Double Comparatives and Superlatives

When forming the comparative or superlative forms of modifiers, use either the *-er* and *-est* endings or *more* or *most*, but do not use both:

NONSTANDARD: That is the *most prettiest* sunset I have ever seen.

Today is the *most humidest* day of the year.

STANDARD: That is the *prettiest* sunset I have ever seen.

Today is the *most humid* day of the year.

17d

EXERCISES

Correct the use of double comparatives and superlatives in each of the following sentences.

1. Our family is more richer than the Joneses.
2. I did worser on the exam than on the midterm.
3. Sue Ellen is the most happiest child I ever saw.
4. Each exercise in this book is more harder than the last.
5. Mary is the most loveliest girl I have ever known.

17d Confusion of Comparative and Superlative Forms

In formal and informal writing the comparative form is used for comparing two things, while the superlative form is used only when comparing three or more things. In casual use the comparative and superlative forms are often interchanged:

CASUAL: We will have to decide at tomorrow's meeting which of these two approaches is *best*.

Detroit has been unable to reach agreement

about which of the three mechanical systems is *more practical*.

INFORMAL OR
FORMAL:

We will have to decide at tomorrow's meeting which of these two approaches is *better*.

Detroit has been unable to reach agreement about which of the three mechanical systems is *most practical*.

EXERCISES

In each sentence below, underline the appropriate comparative or superlative form for formal or informal use.

1. Jack gets to stay up (later/latest) than Joe because he is (older/oldest).
2. Ann, however, has four (older/oldest) sisters and doesn't have to go to bed (earlier/earliest) just because she is the (younger/youngest).
3. All my friends have (more/most) lenient parents; I have the (fewer/fewest) privileges of anyone in my class.
4. Nothing is (more/most) depressing than being treated as if I were the (less/least) trustworthy teenager in town.
5. And Jack complains to our parents that I have (more/most) freedom than he did when he was (younger/youngest)! I do think it's shocking, however, how lax they are with my (younger/youngest) sisters; and Mac, who's the (littler/littlest) of us all, can do anything he wants.

17e

17e Modification of Absolutes

In formal and informal contexts, do not modify absolute adjectives like *perfect, unique,* or *absolute,* since their meanings already carry the notion of "most" of something. In casual speech, such words are often modified, but when they are, they usually mean something different than they seem to mean:

CASUAL: Jennifer is a *more perfect* dancer than Jasper.

INFORMAL OR
FORMAL:

Jennifer is a *better* dancer than Jasper.
(If Jasper were really perfect, Jennifer could not be more perfect.)

CASUAL: James is the *most unique* person I have ever met.

INFORMAL OR
FORMAL:

James is the *most unusual* person I have ever met.

(*Unique* means "one of a kind," so in the strict sense one person cannot be more unique than someone else.)

To convey the idea of one person or thing being closer to perfection or uniqueness than another, either substitute a nonabsolute word (*better* for *more perfect*, *more unusual* for *more unique*) or modify the absolute words with an adverb like *nearly*, which can in turn be modified by *more* or *most*:

CASUAL:

Nothing could be *more perfect* than a week in glorious Saint Lucia.

Experience today the world's *most unique* home climate control system.

INFORMAL OR
FORMAL:

Nothing could be *better* than a week in glorious Saint Lucia. (or)

Nothing could be *more nearly perfect* than a week in glorious Saint Lucia.

Experience today the world's *most unusual* home climate control system.

17f

EXERCISES

Rewrite the following sentences to make them acceptable in formal writing.

1. Every year, late in August, the creek was at its emptiest level.
2. He gave the most complete explanations of any of the job candidates we interviewed.
3. The possibilities for creatively reordering the information are far more infinite with our new computer.
4. It was unquestionably the deadest history class I had ever suffered through.
5. We selected the roundest table we could find for our kitchen.

17f Double Negatives

Negative modifiers include the adjectives *no* and *neither* and the adverbs *not*, *never*, *hardly*, *scarcely*, *rarely*, and *only*. Use only one negative adverb to modify a given word, unless you intend to convey a positive meaning. Be careful also not to use a negative modifier with a negative pronoun like *neither* or *none*:

NONSTANDARD: The accountant could *not* understand the figures *not even* after consulting with the client.

We do *not*, at the present time, appear to have *no* alternatives.

I *can't hardly* understand him when he talks.

I *don't* have *neither* money *nor* time.

STANDARD: The accountant could *not* understand the figures *even* after consulting with the client.

We do *not*, at the present time, appear to have *any* other alternatives.

I *can hardly* understand him when he talks.

I *don't* have *any* money.

17f   When it is used as an adverb, *but*, like *except*, is considered negative. In casual use it is sometimes combined with other negative words, but it should not be used with negative modifiers in formal situations:

CASUAL: I *can't help but* wonder if we made the right decision.

We *didn't have but* a few minutes to decide on a date.

INFORMAL OR FORMAL: I *cannot help wondering* if we made the right decision.

We *did not have more than* a few minutes to decide on a date. (or)

We *only had* a few minutes to decide on a date.

EXERCISES

Correct the use of double negatives in each of the following sentences.

1. We don't hardly know him.
2. We don't want to know him neither.
3. I've never seen no one who was so obnoxious.

4. George didn't see no suspicious characters hanging around the bus station.
5. He didn't have but a few dollars in his pocket.

17g Numerical Modifiers

There are two kinds of numerical adjectives: *cardinal numbers*, which are used to *count* the number of things in a set (*one*, *two*, *three*, etc.); and *ordinal numbers*, which are used to indicate the *order* of things in a series (*first*, *second*, *third*, etc.). The ordinal numbers are already adverbs and do not need the *-ly* ending.

While it is common in casual use to add -ly to ordinal numbers, in formal and informal situations the -ly should never be added:

CASUAL: *Firstly*, we should find out what is playing at the theater; *secondly*, we should make reservations.

INFORMAL OR FORMAL: *First*, we should find out what is playing at the theater; *second*, we should make reservations.

17g

Part Five

EFFECTIVE
SENTENCES

18

CRAFTING SENTENCES

While *grammar* has to do with what is allowable or not allowable within a given language, the *rhetoric* of sentences refers to the choices we have among various grammatical options. The following strings of words are ungrammatical because such patterns are not allowable (they simply do not signal any meaning):

1. *painted John green door the
2. *the painted John green door
3. *door green the painted John

The following are all grammatical sentences among which we make *rhetorical* choices; that is, we can choose the version that has the particular emphasis we want or that best fits the context:

4. John painted the door green.
5. The door was painted green by John.
6. What John painted green was the door.

While there are no meaningful ways to expand examples 1, 2, and 3, there are many ways in which sentence 4 might be expanded to add meaning. Here are two:

7. John painted the door green, balancing himself on a ladder, the paint can dangerously perched on the top rung.
8. John painted the door green, thinking all the time that

*The asterisk in front of a string of words indicates a nonsentence.

he would rather be at the lake swimming or in the woods hiking.

There are also ways to combine example 4 with other sentences, in order to make one longer sentence in place of a number of short ones. For instance, the many short sentences in example 9 below have been combined into one sentence in example 10:

9. John painted the door green. He was tired of the old red color. The old paint was peeling badly. It was faded. He wanted the door to blend with the yard. The yard was green. It had mostly oak trees and Japanese holly bushes.

10. John painted the door green because he was tired of the faded, peeling red and because he wanted the door to blend with the green of the oaks and the Japanese holly in the yard.

While examples 1, 2, and 3 are ungrammatical and convey no meaning to us, the others are all equally grammatical and present real options for a writer. We might argue that example 10 is better than example 9, because the relationships among the items are clearer and more meaningful. But example 9 is just as grammatical, and indeed there could be a situation in which a writer might prefer to write in such a style. In the following sections we will examine ways to combine and expand sentences so they have the effect you want them to have.

18a

18a   Coordination

Coordination is joining two sentences whose meaning is parallel or balanced, using a coordinating conjunction or a semicolon. (See **23b** and **23c** for proper punctuation of coordinate sentences.) Consider the following two sentences:

John was angry.
Mary was happy.

Simply juxtaposed like this, they tell us little, and certainly nothing about a relationship between the two. If we join them with a semicolon or with *and*, the reader can only guess whether a relationship exists between John's anger and Mary's happiness:

John was angry; Mary was happy.
John was angry **and** Mary was happy.

If we join them with *but*, also a coordinating conjunction, the effect is to establish a contrast between them:

John was angry **but** Mary was happy.

Occasionally the use of a group of short, simple sentences, sometimes stopped with periods, sometimes combined by simple coordinating conjunctions like *and* or *but*, can be effective in creating a certain mood or developing a character. The following passage, for example, creates the mood of the speaker reacting to the death of his friend. The coordination is appropriate because in times of emotional stress we are not likely to think or talk in sophisticated sentence patterns, and it is difficult to discriminate between the important and the relatively unimportant. Notice, however, that there are actually three dependent clauses (bracketed in the example) underlying the apparently simple structure:

That was [what you did]. You died. You did not know [what it was about]. You never had time to learn. They threw you in and told you the rules and [the first time they caught you off base] they killed you.   —Ernest Hemingway, *A Farewell to Arms*

18b Embedding

Coordinating is not always the most effective method of crafting sentences, because the reader is left to infer the relationship between clauses. While coordination is effective in certain circumstances, *embedding* one clause in another is often a better way of making clear the relationship between clauses and sentences. The process of embedding includes the use of subordinate clauses, relative clauses, and clauses that have been reduced to phrases or words.

18b.1 Subordinate Clauses

Subordinating conjunctions (see **13g.3**) are used to make an independent clause into a subordinate clause:

John was angry *because Mary was happy.*
Mary was happy *when John was angry.*

Many more variations are possible, but these examples tell us far more about John's and Mary's emotions than does simply coordinating "John was angry" and "Mary was happy."

18b.2   Relative Clauses

Relative pronouns are used to join clauses with a common element. Consider these two pairs of sentences:

> John was angry at his *sister*. His *sister* was late.
> Mary revved up her *motorcycle*. Her *motorcycle* was old and rusty.

The sentences in each pair can be easily combined after converting the repeated nouns into relative pronouns:

> John was angry at his sister, *who* was late.
> Mary revved up her motorcycle, *which* was old and rusty.

It is also possible to combine two sentences with the same subject, by converting the repeated word into a relative pronoun and embedding the resulting clause into the first sentence:

> The *city* attracted many visitors. The *city* is beautiful at night.
> The *city*, [*which* is beautiful at night], attracted many visitors.

18b

18b.3   Reduced Clauses

Relative pronouns and the verbs that follow them can often be deleted, converting the clause into a phrase or just a word. Consider how this is done with the sentences we created in **18b.2**:

> Mary revved up her motorcycle, [which was] old and rusty.
> Mary revved up her motorcycle, old and rusty.

> The city, [which is] beautiful at night, attracted many visitors.
> The city, beautiful at night, attracted many visitors.

Notice that when adjectives are left standing alone after the relative pronoun and the verb have been deleted, they are commonly placed *before* the noun they modify:

> Mary revved up her *old and rusty* motorcycle.

We could place the adjective *beautiful* before *city* only if we deleted the prepositional phrase "at night":

The *beautiful* city attracted many visitors.

EXERCISES

1. Combine the following sentences with coordinating conjunctions. Combine each pair twice, using different conjunctions. Be prepared to discuss the different interpretations possible with each combination.

   a. Pay me what you owe me. Leave the store.
   b. I was amazed at the changes time had etched in her face. I realized that her face mirrored mine in many ways.
   c. Each of us has his secrets. You have so many it scares me.
   d. Give me that bottle. I will take it from you.
   e. A sense of broken dreams and unkept promises pervaded her room. In each dimly lit corner I felt the presence of ghosts.

2. Combine the following sentences with subordinating conjunctions. Combine each pair at least twice, using a different conjunction each time. Be prepared to discuss the varying effects of the different conjunctions. You may have to change or delete some words.

   a. The room had a sinister feeling. John felt his heart quicken.
   b. The Volkswagen was designed to be an affordable, well-built car for the average citizen. Its design reflected the economic conditions in Germany at the time.
   c. The first time many Saudi Arabians saw the wheel, it was attached to an automobile. Many Saudi Arabians are experiencing culture shock.
   d. Beethoven is one of the most renowned composers of all time. Beethoven was poor and unhappy most of his life.
   e. Many artists helped light the fire that sparked the Harlem Renaissance. Langston Hughes helped spark the Harlem Renaissance.

3. Combine the following pairs of sentences by making the second in each group into a relative clause, then embedding the clause in the first sentence, and, finally, reducing the relative clause to an adjective or adjective phrase.

   a. Charlie eats hamburgers. The hamburgers are large.
   b. Bonnie typed that letter. That letter is beautiful.
   c. The grass grew quickly. The grass is green.
   d. Art writes notes. The notes are illegible.
   e. The house is brick. The house will be warm and cosy this winter.

4. For each of the following sentences, write a second sentence that has one noun in common with the first. Then combine the sentences as in the exercise above.

18b

GIVEN SENTENCE	Alice is *friendly* and *outgoing*.
ADDED SENTENCE	Alice greeted her guests at the door.
COMBINED	Alice, *friendly* and *outgoing*, greeted her guests at the door.

a. The night was dark and stormy.
b. The old house at first seemed empty and desolate.
c. The woman who finally answered our knock was very old.
d. Her face was withered and heavily lined.
e. Her eyes were cold and hard.
f. Naturally, Claude and I were fearful.
g. However, all four of our tires were flat.
h. As we walked into the house, our legs were shaking.
i. The woman who awaited us in the library was tall and dark.
j. The two dogs who guarded her chair were huge and ferocious.

5. Of the two groups of information below, which would lend itself better to subordination? Why? Rewrite it in paragraph or extended sentence form. Put the information in the remaining group together by means of coordination.

a. Direct carving is a method of sculpting. The artist begins with a block of wood or stone or metal. The artist chisels. He lets his idea find its shape in the material. Henry Moore was a famous contemporary experimenter with this technique.

b. Mix the yeast with warm water. Let it stand for five minutes. Sift the flour; add the sugar, salt, and spices. Combine this mixture with the yeast. Mix the brown sugar, chopped nuts, and cinnamon together. Spread topping over batter.

18c

18c Cumulative Sentences and Free Modifiers

The *cumulative* sentence† is a stylistic trait of much current written English. A cumulative sentence often begins with a *base clause* (the clause that contains the main assertion of the sentence). If any modifiers precede the base clause, they are relatively few and usually short, so if the base clause is not first, it is very near the front. The base clause is followed by a series of *free modifiers*—phrases or clauses that point backward either to the base clause or to another clause that precedes them. The placement of free

†The cumulative sentence as a common form in modern English was first described and analyzed by Francis Christensen.

modifiers is flexible, as long as it does not cause ambiguity or confusion. The cumulative sentence, then, gives the impression of a person in the process of thinking, adding modifiers to the base clause and to other modifiers, until the full effect the author wants to create has been achieved. Following is an example by one of the masters of the cumulative sentence:

> He [the writer] must teach himself that the basest of all things is to be afraid; and, teaching himself that, forget it forever, leaving no room in his workshop for anything but the old verities and truths of the heart, the old universal truths lacking which any story is ephemeral and doomed—love and honor and pity and pride and compassion and sacrifice.
>
> —William Faulkner, Nobel Prize Acceptance Speech

We can use the idea of levels of abstraction (**6c**), of coordination (**18a**), and embedding (**18b**) to diagram the way this sentence works. We will assign a number (1) to the base clause, a (2) to anything subordinate to it and a (1) to anything coordinate with it (or a restatement of it); we will assign a (3) to anything subordinate to (2); and so on.

(1) He must teach himself
    (2) that the basest of all things is to be afraid;
    (2) and, teaching himself that,
(1) forget it forever,
    (2) leaving no room in his workshop for anything but
        (3) the old verities and truths of the heart,
(3) the old universal truths
           (4) lacking which any story is ephemeral and doomed—
        (3) love and honor and pity and pride and compassion and sacrifice.

One characteristic common to many cumulative sentences is the *absolute phrase*, which has a noun modified by an adjective or participle; the entire absolute phrase modifies the entire phrase, clause, or sentence preceding it (see **13h.4**). Consider the following descriptive passage:

> After all these years I can picture that old time to myself now, just as it was then: the white town drowsing in the sunshine of a summer's morning; the streets empty, or pretty nearly so; one or two clerks sitting in front of the Water Street stores, with their splint-bottomed chairs tilted back against the walls, chins on breasts, hat

slouched over their faces, asleep—with shingle-shavings enough around to show what broke them down; a sow and a litter of pigs loafing along the sidewalk, doing a good business in watermelon rinds and seeds . . . the great Mississippi, the majestic, the magnificent Mississippi, rolling its mile-wide tide along, shining in the sun; the dense forest on the other side; the "point" above the town, and below, bounding the river-glimpse and turning it into a sort of sea, and withal a very still and brilliant and lonely one.

—Mark Twain, *Life on the Mississippi*

Although this is a long sentence, the absolute phrases and other modifiers are placed so skillfully that the sentence reads easily, gradually building up the visual impression of the town. Examples of absolute phrases are "the white town drowsing in the sunshine of a summer's morning," "the streets empty," and "one or two clerks sitting." The participle *drowsing* modifies *town*, but the entire phrase modifies "that old time"; likewise, *empty* modifies *streets* and *sitting* modifies *clerks*, while both phrases modify "that old time."

One other thing to notice about this pasage: it begins not with the base sentence, but with a modifier, so that there is a level (2) phrase before the base sentence:

　　(2) After all these years
(1) I can picture that old time to myself now,
　　(2) just as it was then:
　　　　(3) the white town drowsing in the sunshine of a summer's morning; . . .

The effect of a cumulative sentence can be created even when a passage is not punctuated as a single sentence. The following passage, for example, has the effect of a single cumulative sentence even though it is punctuated as a series consisting of a sentence and several fragments:

That's what it was to be alive. To move about in a cloud of ignorance; to go up and down trampling on the feelings of those about you. To spend and waste time as though you had a million years. To be always at the mercy of one self-centered passion, or another.

—Thornton Wilder, *Our Town*

The fact that there are only two levels of subordination (the base sentence and the series of infinitive phrases) and the fact that each phrase is punctuated like a sentence gives the effect of stopping after each added thought, much like the halting style of the Hemingway passage. This passage also illustrates how effectively repetition of pattern (see **18e**) can be combined with the cumulative structure to produce emphasis, in this case emphasis on the activities of "being alive" expressed in the infinitive phrases (*to be alive, to move, to go, to spend, to be*).

Cumulative sentences can be created by combining sentences as well as by adding free modifiers to a base clause. Take the following group of sentences:

> Bagels taste delicious.
> They have raisins.
> They have cream cheese.
>
> The cheese oozes.
> It oozes into the hole.
> It runs over the sides.
> It gets all over my face.
>
> The raisins explode one by one.
> They explode as I chew.
>
> Their juice is sweet.
> It complements the taste of the cream cheese.

The sentences to be combined comprise four groups, according to the subject of the sentences: bagels (the first three sentences), cream cheese (the next four), raisins (the next two) and juice (the last two). Combine them a group at a time: turn each sentence after the first in a group into a clause or reduced clause (phrase or word); then attach the reduced sentences to the first sentence. In the following examples, the italicized words are those that have been reduced:

> *Raisin* bagels taste delicious *with cream cheese*.
> The cheese oozes *into the hole*, *runs over the sides*, and *gets all over my face*.
> The raisins explode one by one *as I chew*.
> Their juice is sweet and *complements the taste of the cream cheese*.

18c

Now you have four sentences to combine. One of the best ways to combine long sentences like this is to make the sentences that follow the main sentence into absolute phrases:

> the cheese *oozing* into the hole, *running* over the sides, and *getting* all over my face
>
> the raisins *exploding* one by one as I chew
>
> their sweet juice *complementing* the taste of the cream cheese

Now add these three absolute phrases as modifiers at the end of the first sentence, which now becomes the base clause:

> Raisin bagels taste delicious with cream cheese, the cheese oozing into the hole, running over the sides, and getting all over my face, the raisins exploding one by one as I chew, their sweet juice complementing the taste of the cream cheese.

Remember that when you combine sentences, just as when you expand them, there is no single effective way; you want to place the most important words in the most effective slots in the sentences, considering your purpose and your audience. In the following sections we will look at some specific devices that are effective in combining or expanding sentences, whether with coordination, embedding, or free modifiers.

EXERCISES

18c

Combine the following sentences by turning all the sentences after the first in each group into free modifiers and then attaching them to the first sentence (which becomes the base clause).

1. I have always liked the Beatles. Their music is original and dynamic. It is constantly changing. It is always satisfying.
2. Humphrey Bogart was fantastic in *Casablanca*. He was thick-skinned yet soft-hearted. He was a loner who was capable of love. He was wise to life's delusions but not a cynic.
3. Chief Joseph loved his tribe. His tribe was the Nez Perce. He provided them with a model of courage, sacrifice, and dignity.
4. Buddy Holly was one of the first great rock and rollers. There was a movie made about him. He helped change the sound of popular music.
5. Attitudes toward the CIA have changed a great deal since the 1950s. The public knows more about its dealings now. The CIA is facing closer scrutiny and greater regulation in the 1980s.

18d   Periodic Sentences

In a periodic sentence, the main clause is withheld until just before
the period. Its effect is the opposite of the cumulative sentence.
In a cumulative sentence, the main clause is at or near the beginning of the sentence, and the modifiers pile up after it, so that our
impression of the main subject is gradually shaped and altered;
in a periodic sentence, the modifiers—whether phrases or clauses—
are placed at the beginning, creating a kind of suspense with the
main clause held until the end. In a cumulative sentence, the
movement of the modifiers is backward, pointing to the main
clause or subordinate modifiers; in a periodic sentence the movement is forward, toward the main clause at the end. The effect of
the cumulative sentence is a kind of loose thinking out of a subject; the effect of the periodic sentence is a carefully planned climax.

One of the most common patterns in a periodic sentence is the
repetition of a series of *if* clauses. The following sentence illustrates this pattern:

> If we wish to be free; if we mean to preserve inviolate those inestim-
> able priveledges [*sic*] for which we have been so long contending; if
> we mean not basely to abandon the noble struggle in which we have
> been so long engaged, and which we have pledged ourselves never
> to abandon until the glorious object of our contest shall be obtained—
> we must fight! I repeat it, sir, we must fight! An appeal to arms, and
> to the God of hosts, is all that is left us.
>
> —Patrick Henry, Speech in Virginia Convention

18d

When periodic sentences are combined with balance (see **18e**),
the effect is even stronger. In the following selection, Thomas
Wolfe uses a series of three periodic sentences, which in turn build
to a climax, producing a kind of periodic paragraph; in addition,
each *if* clause has balanced coordinate direct objects of the verb
has:

> If a man has a talent and cannot use it, he has failed. If he has a
> talent and uses only half of it, he has partly failed. If he has talent
> and learns somehow to use the whole of it, he has gloriously suc-
> ceeded, and won a satisfaction and a triumph few men ever know.
>
> —Thomas Wolfe, *The Web and the Rock*

Finally, let us look at an example of how effectively a cumulative sentence can be combined with a periodic sentence—to build

to a climax first and then to get the reader more involved by adding phrases that describe the action we should take. The main clause is italicized, so you can see where the movement in the sentence shifts from forward (periodic) to backward (cumulative):

> With malice towards none; with charity for all; with firmness in the right, as God gives us to see the right, *let us strive on to finish the work we are in*; to bind up the nation's wounds; to care for him who shall have borne the battle, and for his widow, and his orphan— to do all which may achieve and cherish a just and lasting peace among ourselves, and with all nations.
>
> —Abraham Lincoln, Second Inaugural Address, 1865

EXERCISES

Using the first sentence in each group as your base clause, construct periodic and cumulative sentences. Draw ideas and phrases from the modifiers listed below each sentence, or create your own.

1. Lightning pierced the sky and the clouds burst.
   * we were traveling along a dirt road approaching Canyonlands National Park
   * we had just stopped to examine some petroglyphs
   * thunder raged

2. The Vietnam Veterans Memorial is a moving reminder of the thousands who died in a war many Americans would like to forget.
   * it is black like the earth itself, and half buried
   * it contains no slogans, only a numbing list of name upon name
   * its polished surface reflects the faces of those who have come to read the names and to mourn or to remember

18e

18e   Repetition of Words, Patterns, and Sounds

One of the most basic of all sentence techniques is repetition— the repetition of a word for emphasis or special effect; the repetition of a pattern to produce parallel or balanced phrases, clauses, and sentences; and the repetition of sound and rhythm to reinforce patterns.

We have already seen how repetition of words provides cohesion, but repetition can also be used with special rhetorical effect.

The following excerpt is an especially good illustration of how effective the repetition of key words (*monotonously* and *falls*) can be in setting a mood:

> Monotonously the lorries sway, monotonously come the calls, monotonously falls the rain. It falls on our heads and on the heads of the dead up the line, on the body of the little recruit with the wound that is so much too big for his hip; it falls on Kemmerich's grave; it falls in our hearts.
>
> —Erich Maria Remarque, *All Quiet on the Western Front*

Repeating patterns in a sentence, often along with the repetition of key words, produces *parallelism* and *balance*. Parallel sentences or phrases are like parallel streets: they run in the same direction and follow similar patterns of turns and curves. The effect of parallel *structure* is to emphasize the parallel *function* of words, phrases, or clauses—whether in a pair or in a series of three or more. Parallel structure also emphasizes the connection of ideas in different parts of a sentence or paragraph by phrasing them in a parallel manner. The following quotation exemplifies both of these effects, in the parallel series of noun phrases which are all direct objects of the word *loves*, and in two pairs of parallel phrases: "*he means* not only . . ." / "*He means* . . ." and "an inner light *in which*" / "*and in which*."

> When an American says that he loves his country, he means not only that he loves the New England hills, the prairies glistening in the sun, the wide and rising plains, the great mountains, and the sea. He means that he loves an inner air, an inner light in which freedom lives and in which a man can draw the breath of self-respect.
>
> —Adlai Stevenson, Speech in New York City

18e

Another kind of repetition of pattern is the *balanced* sentence, in which two parallel parts, usually expressing a contrast or contradiction or qualification, are balanced against each other much as the two sides of a scale or seesaw are balanced, usually with a coordinating or correlative conjunction acting as the fulcrum does on a balance scale:

> There never was a good war or a bad peace.
>
> —Benjamin Franklin, Letter to Josiah Quincy

> We must all hang together, or assuredly we shall all hang separately.
>
> —Benjamin Franklin, spoken at the signing of
> The Declaration of Independence

Notice that in the first example the balance is between two noun phrases, both of which are complements of the verb *was*; the fulcrum that balances them is *or*. The sentence might be visualized this way:

There never was

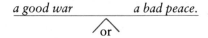

a good war   *a bad peace.*
or

In the second example, two entire clauses are balanced against each other, with the conjunction *or* and the adverb *assuredly* acting as the fulcrum:

We must all hang together,   *we shall all hang separately.*
or assuredly

One of the most effective techniques is to combine balance with the repetition of words and patterns:

> To every thing there is a season, and a time
>   to every purpose under the heaven:
> A time to be born, and a time to die;
>   a time to plant, and a time to pluck
>   up that which is planted;
> A time to kill, and a time to heal;
>   a time to break down, and a time to build up;
> A time to weep, and a time to laugh;
>   a time to mourn, and a time to dance . . .
> A time to love, and a time to hate;
>   a time of war, and a time of peace.
> —Ecclesiastes 3:1-8

18e

Now the trumpet summons us again—not as a call to bear arms, though arms we need; not as a call to battle, though embattled we are; but as a call to bear the burden of a long twilight struggle, year in and year out, "rejoicing in hope, patient in tribulation," a struggle against the common enemies of man: tyranny, poverty, disease and war itself.   —John F. Kennedy

The repetition of pattern is often reinforced by the use of *sound* repetitions—especially *alliteration* (the repetition of similar consonant sounds) and *rhyme*, as well as the rhythm that is set up by repeating parallel structures:

Early to bed and early to rise makes a man healthy, wealthy, and
wise.   *—Poor Richard's Almanack*

If you would not be forgotten, as soon as you are dead and rotten,
either write things worth reading, or do things worth the writing.
                                                           —Poor Richard's Almanack

Notice in the second example how Franklin breaks the rhythm in
the second half of the sentence, in order to give a note of serious-
ness to what started out as humorous rhyme.

18f   Rhetorical Questions

Rhetorical questions are used for a special effect, with no answer
expected. An author may, for example, use a rhetorical question
in place of a thesis or topic sentence, in which case the essay or
paragraph develops an answer to the question or develops an
argument in support of the answer. See, for example, the paragraph by Malinowski in **13b.2** and the speech of Shylock from
The Merchant of Venice in Exercise 2 following **6g.** A writer may
also leave readers with a question at the end of a piece of writing,
to get them to project beyond the essay and think about wider
issues or about the future and perhaps to move them to some
kind of action.

Rhetorical questions can also be used to create mood and to
establish a relationship between an author and his readers, as in
the next passage (notice the use of repetition in the pattern of the
questions):

> Which of us has known his brother? Which of us has looked into
> his father's heart? Which of us has not remained forever prison-
> pent? Which of us is not forever a stranger and alone?
>   —Thomas Wolfe, *Look Homeward, Angel*

18f

EXERCISES _____

Identify the predominant rhetorical pattern in each of the following sentences, and consider how the sentence structure reinforces the meaning.

1. We ought to remain a little aloof and take pleasure in this aloofness
   while at the same time we keenly enjoy—passionately enjoy, enjoy
   with tears and shivers—the inner wave of a given masterpiece.
                                                      —Vladimir Nabokov, in *Esquire*

2. I saw on that ivory face the expression of sombre pride, of ruthless power, of craven terror—of an intense and hopeless despair.

—Joseph Conrad, *Heart of Darkness*

3. He believed himself thus at the centre of life; he believed the mountains rimmed the heart of the world; he believed that from all the chaos of accident the inevitable event came at the inexorable moment to add to the sum of his life.   —Thomas Wolfe, *Look Homeward, Angel*

4. Sons rarely get to know their fathers very well, less well, certainly, than fathers get to know their sons.

—Larry King, in *The Washington Post*

5. On sweltering summer days and crisp autumn mornings I have looked at the South's beautiful churches with their lofty spires pointing heavenward. I have beheld the impressive outlines of her massive religious-education buildings. Over and over I have found myself asking: "What kind of people worship here? Who is their God? Where were their voices when the lips of Governor Barnett dripped with words of interposition and nullification? Where were they when Governor Wallace gave a clarion call for defiance and hatred? Where were their voices of support when bruised and weary Negro men and women decided to rise from the dark dungeons of complacency to the bright hills of creative protest?"

—Martin Luther King, Jr., "Letter from Birmingham Jail"

18g   Variations in Word Order

18g

In addition to combining sentences, there are many other ways to vary the basic sentence patterns to create the meaning and emphasis you want. Following are some of the most common variations, and while there are often good reasons for using them, they should be used sparingly, because they often are less clear and more wordy than the standard patterns.

The most important effects to be gained by varying standard sentence patterns are clarity and emphasis, although sometimes writers vary sentences simply to avoid monotony. If you want your sentences to be as emphatic and clear as possible, you need to remember the following general principles:

1. Generally, the end of a clause or sentence is the strongest position, so the word or words you want to emphasize are best placed there; the beginning of a sentence or clause is usually the second most emphatic position, and the middle is weakest.

2. A complement following a linking verb is usually stronger than a direct object (see **18g.2** and **18g.3**).
3. But active verbs will often make a sentence more powerful than linking verbs (See **19e** and **20b.1**).
4. The subject position is usually stronger than the object position following a preposition (see **18g.1**).
5. Usually the material in dependent (subordinate and relative) clauses is weaker than material in main clauses (see **18g.2**).
6. Any unusual inversion will place emphasis on the elements that are not in their normal position (see **18g.4**).
7. If following any of these principles produces ambiguity or confusion in one of your sentences, ignore it and choose a sentence pattern that makes your meaning as *clear* as possible.

18g.1   Passive Voice

Most sentences in which the predicate contains a transitive verb (see **13j**) can be expressed in the passive voice, in which the object of the active sentence becomes the subject of the passive sentence, and the subject of the active sentence is placed in a prepositional (*by*) phrase:

ACTIVE: *Terrorists* bombed *the embassy* last night.
PASSIVE: *The embassy* was bombed *by terrorists* last night.

The effect of the passive sentence is to weaken the emphasis on the original subject by burying it in the prepositional phrase: It is also possible, in a passive sentence, to drop the *by* phrase altogether. If one's purpose is to hide the agent (the active subject) or to deemphasize it as much as possible, one can simply leave the original subject out of a passive sentence:

18g

PASSIVE: *The embassy* was bombed last night.

In casual use, a form of the verb *get* is sometimes used in place of the verb *be*:

FORMAL OR
INFORMAL: The embassy *was* bombed last night.
CASUAL: The embassy *got* bombed last night.

Sometimes the passive voice can be used to hide the truth, and it can often become clumsy and tedious if overused (see **19d**). But when the agent is less important than the thing affected, as in these two sentences, then the passive is appropriate:

PASSIVE: My dog was run over by a truck last week.
PASSIVE: My aunt was stricken with cancer.

It is not necessarily a direct object that becomes the subject of the passive sentence; it may also be an indirect object:

ACTIVE: Professors ask their students questions.
PASSIVE: Students are asked questions by their professors.
           (or)
           Questions are asked of students by their professors.

Depending on what you want to emphasize, one passive version might be more effective than the other.

EXERCISES _____

1. Rewrite the following active sentences in the passive voice.
    a. Harry gave me a great deal of advice on buying my house.
    b. My mother gave me nothing but grief about it.
    c. Instead of lessening my confusion, the real estate agent added to it.
    d. He told me to be wary of such an old house and suggested a newer one farther down the road.
    e. An old woman inhabited it.
    f. Her children were sending her to a nursing home.
    g. My visit upset her.
    h. She politely told me and the real estate agent to leave.
    i. She wrote her children a nasty letter.
    j. She made them feel very guilty.
2. Which sentences are more effective in the passive voice? How does the context affect their effectiveness?

_____

18g.2   *It* Pattern

Almost any sentence can be converted to another sentence in which *it* acts as a kind of "dummy subject" followed by a linking verb:

James left early.
It was James who left early.

The original subject (*James*) becomes the complement followed by a relative clause that includes the original verb (*who left early*). Since the relative clause is dependent on the main (*it*) clause, the verb and its complement in that clause are deemphasized while the original subject is emphasized, because it comes at the end of the main clause and because it follows a linking verb, a position of strength in most sentences. Compare, for example, an altered version of a verse from Psalm 100 with the original word order of the Authorized (King James) Version:

NORMAL WORD ORDER: He has made us and not we ourselves.

INVERTED ORDER: *It is* He *that* hath made us, and not we ourselves.

The rhythm of the *it* construction puts the emphasis on *He*. Likewise, in the next set of sentences, the second version would be stronger than the first if the writer wanted to emphasize *Pavarotti* rather than *lullabies*:

NORMAL WORD ORDER: Pavarotti sings his daughter lullabies.

INVERTED ORDER: *It is* Pavarotti *who* sings his daughter lullabies.

Notice that passive sentences can also be converted to the *it* pattern:

NORMAL PASSIVE
WORD ORDER: Students are asked questions by their professors.

INVERTED ORDER: *It is* students *who* are asked questions by their professors.

18g

When used with the passive voice, the *it* pattern can be used to deceive or protect, by omitting the subject:

ACTIVE: Three of your coworkers have suggested that you be fired.

PASSIVE: It has been suggested that you be fired.

EXERCISES _____

Choose any five sentences from the previous exercise and convert them to the *it* pattern. Are they more or less effective than before the shift?

_____

18g.3 *There* Pattern

Another way of varying sentence structure to produce a desired emphasis, in sentences with a linking verb, is to put the "dummy" pronoun *there* at the beginning, followed by the linking verb already in the sentence. The effect of this shift is to put into complement position what was originally the subject:

NORMAL ORDER: Three people were on the bus.
INVERTED ORDER: There were three people on the bus. (or)
There were three people who were on the bus.

The difference in emphasis is sometimes minimal, but one advantage of the inverted order, aside from adding variety to normal sentence patterns, is the possibility of dropping the modifier ("on the bus") if it is unimportant. You can say "There were three people," but you would not say "three people were" except in an elliptical sentence as an answer to a question. The passive can also be inverted in this manner:

NORMAL ORDER: Three people were killed.
INVERTED ORDER: There were three people killed. (or)
There were three people who were killed.

The emphasis in the original passive sentence is on *killed*, while in the inverted sentence the emphasis is on *three people*, since those words immediately follow the linking verb.

But it is a good idea to avoid using sentences beginning with *there* too often, particularly when using *there* would cause you to choose a linking verb over an active verb; see **19e**.

EXERCISES _____

1. Change the emphasis in the following sentences by adding or eliminating a *there*.

   a. There were no nurses on duty in that wing.

b. Nobody can answer that question.

c. There are many interesting sharks in the New England Aquarium.

d. Five deer were killed on the parkway during the first week of November.

e. There were no dogs in the kennel.

f. Few people are willing to donate their spare time to volunteer organizations.

g. Several of us knew him well and admired his work.

h. There are a lot of leftovers in the refrigerator.

i. Five people actually witnessed the murder, yet the jury ruled that the evidence was inconclusive!

j. No one can do that as well as you can.

2. Which version of each sentence is more effective? In what context?

18g.4 Other Variations in Word Order

In addition to the patterns we have discussed, which all involve adding words, and sometimes phrases and clauses as well, English allows a fair amount of variation just by moving parts around without adding anything. For example, a direct object or modifier can be shifted to the front of a sentence for special emphasis:

NORMAL ORDER:	I hate cauliflower, cabbage, and carrots, but I detest broccoli.
INVERTED FOR EMPHASIS:	I hate cauliflower, cabbage, and carrots, but *broccoli* I detest.
NORMAL ORDER:	She knocked haltingly and tentatively at the door of his house.
INVERTED FOR EMPHASIS:	*Haltingly and tentatively*, she knocked at the door of his house.
NORMAL ORDER:	The lorries sway monotonously. The calls come monotonously. The rain falls monotonously.
INVERTED FOR EMPHASIS:	*Monotonously* the lorries sway, *monotonously* come the calls, *monotonously* falls the rain.

18g

—Erich Maria Remarque,
All Quiet on the Western Front

Notice in the last sentence not only how the adverb has been shifted to the beginning of each clause, but how in the second and third clauses the verb and subject have also been reversed.

The use of *not* in English often requires an auxiliary verb (some form of *do*); but if you drop the *do*, you can place more emphasis on the negative word:

NORMAL ORDER: Do not ask . . .

INVERTED FOR
EMPHASIS: And so, my fellow Americans, *ask not* what your country can do for you; ask what you can do for your country.
                —John F. Kennedy, Inaugural Address, 1961

Finally, modifying phrases are often used to interrupt the normal forward movement of a sentence in order to place special emphasis where the writer wants it. The sentence just quoted from John F. Kennedy's inaugural address illustrates this principle well, with his interpolation of "my fellow Americans." Here are some other examples:

NORMAL ORDER: When it becomes necessary . . .

INTERRUPTED
FOR EMPHASIS: When, *in the course of human events*, it becomes necessary . . .   —Thomas Jefferson
                The Declaration of Independence, 1776

NORMAL ORDER: All poets who experience a choked feeling when reading from their own works are major.

INTERRUPTED
FOR EMPHASIS: All poets who, *when reading from their own works*, experience a choked feeling, are major.   —E. B. White

All of these techniques should be used sparingly. The reason that they work so well to create emphasis is that they are unusual: they shake readers out of their normal expectations. If these techniques are overused, they no longer have the effect of creating the unusual. And if they are used awkwardly or self-consciously by the writer, they will draw attention to themselves and thereby defeat the purpose of using them at all—which is to draw attention to the ideas or words placed out of normal order, not to the technique by which that is done.

EXERCISES

1. Create as many variations as you can for the following sentences. Remember to maintain meaning and standard English grammar even though you will be shifting the emphasis.
   a. If I could be granted only one wish, I'd ask for there to be no more wars.
   b. She apologized, but he was angry nonetheless.
   c. Slowly and stealthily, the murderer ascended the steps to the bedroom in which she slept.
   d. Not spending time with our children, not reading to them, not playing with them, not teaching them—these are the true roots of violence in our society.
   e. Need your words be always dramatic?
   f. With reluctance she agreed to marry him.
   g. Is it truly possible that a nuclear war could begin by error?
   h. You will note, however, that this is not the case.
   i. Do not speak of such disloyalty!
   j. I love the springtime.
2. Discuss the effect of each variation. Which would be most effective in which contexts?

18g

19

REVISING SENTENCES

Although the effectiveness of any piece of writing should be judged in context, it is possible to describe some of the common problems writers have in making sentences effective. All effective sentences demonstrate three principles that weak or ineffective sentences sometimes lack: clarity, emphasis, and variety. We will keep all three in mind in discussing the following sentence problems and ways to revise them.

19a   Problems in Coordination

Be sure that coordinate structures are genuinely coordinate in content. Sometimes sentences are written in a coordinate structure when their parts are not really coordinate, making the writing unclear as well as deemphasizing the relatively more important ideas. The following sentence, for example, says six things about red maples without indicating what their relationship is to each other:

> Red maples make good ornamentals *and* they give a lot of shade *and* they grow fast. They are *also very* easy to find *and* inexpensive *and* they are really beautiful.

All six statements are made to seem parallel with each other by the use of *and* and *also* and by the division of the statements into two sentences. Instead, the writer needs to give proper emphasis to the value of red maples as ornamentals and to make clear that the other characteristics contributute to their making good ornamentals. She should therefore subordinate the reasons to the central point in the main clause, with a conjunction that makes the relationship clear—a conjunction like *because*:

> Red maples make good ornamentals *because* they give a lot of shade, they grow fast, they are easy to find and inexpensive, and they are beautiful.

Notice that the four clauses which are subordinate to the main clause are actually more parallel than they were before, emphasizing their relationship to one another as well as their causal connection to the main clause; furthermore, *easy to find* and *inexpensive* are linked because they are so closely related.

The next sentence also links, in coordinate clauses and phrases, three events that are not in reality coordinate:

> I was practicing the piano *and* someone came to the door *and* told me I was making too much noise.

In revising this sentence, a conjunction like *while* or *when* will make the time sequence clear; and changing *told* to the infinitive *to tell* will make clear what the reason is for the person coming to the door. Not only are the following versions clearer, but they also put the emphasis in appropriate places (depending of course on the context):

> I was practicing the piano *when* someone came to the door *to tell* me I was making too much noise. (or)
>
> *While* I was practicing the piano, someone came to the door *to tell* me I was making too much noise.

The following sentences use the conjunction *so*, a coordinating conjunction with the effect of making two clauses parallel:

> The murderer left a hole in his alibi, *so* he was discovered.
> This book is dull, *so* I'm not going to finish it.

But *so* is a weak connector; various kinds of emphasis can be created by using other conjunctions to clarify the causal connection between the clauses:

19a

Because the murderer left a hole in his alibi, he was discovered.

I'm not going to finish this book *because* it's so dull.

Another connector that does not usually provide the clarity and emphasis a writer needs is *then* or *and then*. *Then* is an adverb which expresses a time relationship, but it does so without subordinating the appropriate clause for proper emphasis:

It started lightning *and* thundering *and* just *then* the murderer took her opportunity to shoot.

Consider how much more concise, clear, and emphatic this version is:

Just *when* it started lightning and thundering, the murderer took her opportunity to shoot.

Coordinated sentences can be tedious in a piece of writing where there is almost no texture—no embedding of subordinate clauses or phrases, no attachment of free modifiers. Variety, then, is an important consideration as well.

19b   Problems in Subordination

19b

Be sure that subordinate structures are also subordinate in content and that the appropriate conjunction is used. A lack of clarity results from subordinating a part of the sentence that is not logically subordinate, as in this example:

A grenade exploded [*when* several soldiers were killed].

If the writer wants to emphasize that the soldiers were killed, he could make it clearer by putting that fact in the main clause rather than a subordinate clause:

Several soldiers were killed [*when* a grenade exploded]. (or)
[*When* a grenade exploded], several soldiers were killed.

Confusing subordination can also occur when one uses the wrong subordinator. In the following sentence, for example, the writer probably does not really mean *after*:

The picnic was canceled [*after* it rained].

Notice how much clearer the sentence is with *when* or *because*:

> The picnic was canceled [*when* it rained]. (or)
> The picnic was canceled [*because* it rained].

EXERCISES

Revise the following sentences by using the most effective combination of coordination and embedding. Remember that effectiveness involves emphasis, clarity, and variety.

1. She plays baseball very well, and she has talent but she works hard and she has played since she was old enough to hit a ball.
2. You can plant tomatoes in that soil and you can plant corn in that soil; however, don't plant them next to each other because side-by-side planting encourages certain pests.
3. Writing essays requires time and it's not easy even though writing essays is sometimes pleasurable.
4. Of all aquariums, the one in Boston is my favorite since it has a coral reef, a tremendous variety of tropical fish, and a dolphin show.
5. A higher court ruled that his sentence had been much too severe and it was reduced by ten years.
6. The best pizza place in town is on North Main Street because it has good atmosphere and great pies.
7. World War II ended when there was a baby boom.
8. Henry Fonda and Katharine Hepburn co-star in a film and it's bound to be a success.
9. You want to emphasize your positive qualities so discuss your ability to write coherently and cogently.
10. The train was delayed when there were tornado warnings.

19c

19c Problems in Modification

Be careful to use modifiers to create the clarity and emphasis you desire. Modifiers are the words that flesh out a sentence, adding depth and texture. But used carelessly, they can cause confusion instead of clarity and emphasis.

19c.1 Overuse of Modifiers

Use adjectives and other modifiers with restraint. Too many adjectives directly in front of the noun they modify, for example, can weigh down a piece of writing and cause a failure to discriminate between levels of abstraction or between the relatively important and the relatively unimportant. The following sentence is a good example of this problem:

> The tall, green, lush, sweet corn in the garden was ready to harvest and cook.

With a minor revision in the placement of the adjectives, the sentence is clearer as well as more emphatic:

> The sweet corn in the garden—tall, green, and lush—was ready to harvest and cook.

Too many prepositional phrases piled on top of one another can be not only distracting, but confusing. Like the child's singing game, "There's a Hole in the Bottom of the Sea," any sentence in English can be infinitely expanded with modifying phrases, but not always effectively. Take the following sentence as an example:

> The picture was in a beautiful frame of oak veneer with elaborate filigree representations of birds of different types.

But the number of prepositions can be reduced from five to two, the structure tightened, and the emphasis placed more effectively:

> The picture had a beautiful oak-veneered frame, decorated with filigree representations of various birds.

19c

19c.2 Split Infinitives

Be cautious about splitting infinitives—that is, inserting a modifier between *to* and the main verb. Traditional advice has been, "Never split an infinitive." For good modern English, more appropriate advice would be to split an infinitive only when you have a good rhetorical reason for doing so. Consider the following three examples; each of them is grammatical English, so the questions involve their effectiveness (their clarity and emphasis):

1. If you want *to* really *know* what happened, read Smith's article.

The writer's placement of *really* emphasizes *to know*; she probably intended *really* to modify *want* or *happened*; if the adverb were placed directly in front of the word it modifies, the sentence would be clearer:

> If you want to know what *really* [happened] . . . (or)
> If you *really* [want to know] what happened . . .

2. It is necessary *to* thoroughly *consider* the alternatives.

In this example, there is no ambiguity about what *thoroughly* modifies; since it is an adverb, it cannot modify *alternatives*. Moving the adverb to a position before or after the infinitive, in fact, would make the sentence sound rather formal, even stilted:

> It is necessary *thoroughly* [to consider] the alternatives. (or)
> It is necessary [to consider] *thoroughly* the alternatives.

If, however, we moved the adverb to the end of the sentence, we would avoid any objections to the split infinitive and also produce a lighter sentence:

> It is necessary [to consider] the alternatives *thoroughly*.

3. His job is *to* quickly, smoothly, and efficiently *straighten* our accounts.

In this example the split between the infinitive marker *to* and the infinitive *straighten* is wider than in the other two examples, and moving the adverbs to the end would put greater emphasis on them:

> His job is [to straighten] our accounts *quickly, smoothly, and efficiently*.

The decision about whether to split an infinitive should be based, like all other rhetorical decisions, on the effectiveness with which you get your point across.

19c.3   Placement of Prepositions

When placing a preposition at the end of a sentence, be sure the emphasis is where you want it. Another old schoolbook rule says, "Never end a sentence with a preposition." That too is a generalization with a germ of truth; whether or not to end a sentence with a preposition should depend on the effect you want to achieve

19c

in your writing. Because they are normally unstressed, prepositions can create a falling rhythm at the end of a sentence, which
usually should be the strongest position. Consider the following
examples:

> Increased unemployment is a condition the country will have
> to live *with*.

> The supervisor tried to deal with the problem the man was
> complaining *about*.

In the first sentence, if the writer's purpose is to emphasize the
country's *living* with something, it would be more emphatic to
put *live* at the end of the sentence:

> Increased unemployment is a condition *with which* the
> country will have to live.

Notice that we had to insert a *which*; that is because the original
phrase, "a condition the country will have to live with," is a
shortened form of "a condition *which* the country will have to
live with."

In the second sentence, a revision to get the preposition away
from the end would probably be less effective than in the first
example and would be used only in very formal situations:

> The supervisor tried to deal with the problem *about which*
> the man was complaining.

19c

It would be more effective to get rid of the preposition altogether:

> The supervisor tried to deal with the man's complaint.

19c.4 Placement of Adverbs

Be careful to place adverbs where their meanings will be as clear
as possible. Words like *only*, *even*, *hardly*, *just*, *nearly*, and *almost*
can cause ambiguity if they are not placed carefully. Consider the
following sentence:

> The director *only* has one year left in her term.

We might interpret the sentence to mean it is only the director
who has one year left; but it might also mean that she has *only*
one year left. To avoid the ambiguity, *only* should be placed closer
to the noun it modifies:

Only the director has one year left. (or)
The director has *only* one year left in her term.

19c.5 Misplaced Modifiers

When there are several modifying phrases or clauses in a sentence (especially prepositional phrases and relative clauses), place the modifiers as close as possible to the words they modify, in order to avoid ambiguity.

Misplaced Prepositional Phrases

AMBIGUOUS: Sebastian asked me to go for a ride *on the telephone.*

> (Does "on the telephone" refer to the asking or the ride?)

CLEAR: Sebastian asked me *on the telephone* to go for a ride. (or)

> *On the telephone*, Sebastian asked me to go for a ride.

Misplaced Relative Clauses

AMBIGUOUS: Is that the professor with the new assistant *who gave you the F?*

> (Does "who gave you the F" refer to the professor or the assistant?)

CLEAR: Is the professor *who gave you the F* the one with the new assistant? (or)

> Is the professor with the new assistant the one *who gave you the F?*

19c

Misplaced Subordinate Clauses

AMBIGUOUS: The board of directors sold the company to a large corporation *before it went bankrupt.*

> (Does "before it went bankrupt" refer to the company that was sold or the corporation that bought it?)

CLEAR: *Before the company went bankrupt*, the board of directors sold it to a large corporation.

Misplaced Single-word Modifiers

AMBIGUOUS: You told me you bought that house *already.*

> (Did you tell me already, or did you buy the house already?)

CLEAR: You *already* told me you bought that house. (or)
You told me you *already* bought that house.

19c.6 Squinting Modifiers

Be careful not to create ambiguity with squinting modifiers. Squinting modifiers are those that come in the middle of a sentence and appear to look ("squint") both forward and backward, modifying in both directions. If we had corrected the example above in the following way, we would have created a squinting modifier:

AMBIGUOUS: You told me *already* you bought that house.

Because *that* has been omitted from the noun clause ("that you bought that house"), it is possible to interpret "already" as referring to either clause—"You" or "you bought that house." By restoring *that*, the ambiguity is eliminated:

CLEAR: You told me already *that* you bought that house.

Most squinting modifiers occur with single words or prepositional phrases, and especially with adverbs of time:

AMBIGUOUS: The president promised *every day* to get some exercise.
The president promised *on Saturday* to get some exercise.
(Do the phrases "every day" and "on Saturday" refer to promising or getting exercise?)

CLEAR: *Every day* the president promised to get some exercise. (or)
The president promised to get some exercise *on Saturday*.

19c.7 Dangling Modifiers

Be sure your modifiers are attached to a word they modify. Dangling modifiers have nothing to modify, often because the subject is buried in a passive construction or in the direct object slot. Following are the most common kinds of dangling modifiers:

19c

1. *Dangling Participial Phrases*: These are especially common when the modified word appears somewhere in the sentence other than in the subject slot:

> AMBIGUOUS: *Having finished her aria*, we saw the singer collapse.
>
> > (The word modified by *having finished her aria* is *singer*, but at first glance, the phrase seems to modify *we*.)

To clarify the meaning in a sentence like this, make the subject of the modifying phrase the grammatical subject of the sentence:

> CLEAR: *Having finished her aria*, the singer collapsed.

Or make the dangling phrase into an absolute phrase. Remember that an absolute phrase has a noun within it for the participle to modify, and the whole phrase then modifies the sentence:

> CLEAR: The singer *having finished her aria*, we saw her collapse.

2. *Dangling Prepositional Phrases*: These occur most often with the prepositions *before* and *after*:

> AMBIGUOUS: *After signing the treaty*, the troops stopped fighting.
>
> > ("After signing the treaty" appears to modify "the troops.")
>
> CLEAR: *After signing the treaty*, the president commanded the troops to stop fighting. (or)
>
> > *After the president signed the treaty*, the troops stopped fighting.

19c

Quite often the cause of a dangling prepositional phrase is that the sentence is in the passive voice, thus burying the subject that the phrase is supposed to modify:

> AMBIGUOUS: *Before agreeing to the terms*, a discussion was held.
>
> CLEAR: *Before agreeing to the terms*, the seller and buyer held a discussion.

3. *Dangling Infinitive Phrases*: These too are caused either by

burying the subject of the modifier in a passive construction or by switching to another subject:

AMBIGUOUS: *To alter the payment schedule*, the board's approval is required.

CLEAR: *To alter the payment schedule*, the customer must have the board's approval.

4. *Dangling Elliptical Clause*: An elliptical clause is one in which something is left out. Quite often, when the subject is left out, the clause will dangle because the subject of the clause is needed to make the connection with the main clause:

AMBIGUOUS: *While waiting for the bus*, my knees collapsed.

CLEAR: *While I was waiting for the bus*, my knees collapsed.

EXERCISES

1. Revise each of the misplaced, squinting, and dangling modifiers in the following sentences so that the ambiguity is eliminated and the meaning is perfectly clear.

   a. Forgetting that it was a holiday, the empty mailbox surprised me.
   b. Having lasted three months, the children were still disappointed that their vacation was over.
   c. Tanned and well rested, the school bus deposited the students at the main entrance of the building.
   d. Having begun a new job, the pay was much better.
   e. To make a good cake, the ingredients must be fresh.
   f. Before assigning grades, the students wrote their term papers.
   g. While still a student, a job offer was received.
   h. John wrote a letter about the trip to his friend.
   i. I saw the movie about the dog that won the award.
   j. The teacher told me yesterday she was ill.

2. Revise the following sentences for more effective modification.

   a. The black, long-haired, green-eyed cat stood in my path.
   b. I want to better understand the language and culture of Portugal.
   c. The cake had six layers with lemon custard between them which was covered by a creamy chocolate frosting which was covered by frosting "flowers" and decorations on the top.
   d. She brought cookies to the school board meeting on a redwood tray.
   e. Wagging his tail, John walked his new dog down Main Street.

19c

f. I made that cake for the boys on the table.

g. I only asked for one thing for my birthday, but I didn't get it.

h. Jennifer found a dog that had mange that had to be taken to the pound which took the responsibility for putting the big, brown dog to sleep.

i. The chief cause of the accident was a big guy in a little car with a big mouth.

j. I want to always, at least while I'm young, be able to run three miles a day.

19d Problems with Passives

Use the passive voice only when it creates the emphasis you need and when it is clear. As we saw in **18g.1**, the passive voice can be used effectively to create the emphasis a writer wants. But if it is overused, as it is in some professional writing and research reports where convention does not allow the writer to use the first person or even to refer to himself in the third person, then it becomes not only very tedious but very difficult to understand. Following is an example:

> During the winter, a variety of entertainment has been provided by the Fine Arts Department to the local community. Concerts were given by the university orchestra, a ballet was performed by the dance department, woodworking and ceramics were displayed by faculty craftspeople, and a play was produced by the drama group. Almost all of this entertainment was received with enthusiasm by the community.

Consider the same passage written in the active voice:

> During the winter, the Fine Arts Department has provided a variety of entertainment to the local community. The university orchestra gave concerts, the dance department performed a ballet, faculty craftspeople displayed woodworking and ceramics, and the drama group produced a play. The community received almost all of this entertainment with enthusiasm.

Other problems with passives occur when a writer gets the emphasis in a place where it does not belong, as in the following:

The bill was paid by my boss.

19c

Unless the writer means to emphasize that it was the bill, rather than something else, that the boss paid, he will probably make the meaning clearer by using the active voice:

My boss paid the bill.

Likewise, the following example puts the emphasis in the wrong place and even omits the subject of the underlying sentence:

The pennant was won last night.

One change would be to reinstate the *by* clause:

The pennant was won by the Yankees last night.

Although that change tells us who won the pennant, it does not place the emphasis where most baseball fans are going to be interested. The following version does:

The Yankees won the pennant last night.

EXERCISES

Revise the following sentences so they are in the active instead of the passive voice. Discuss their effectiveness. In what circumstance might the passive sentences be more effective?

19d

1. The novel was written by the famous Russian dissident, Aleksandr Solzhenitsyn.
2. The speech was given by Andrei Sakharov only a few days before his arrest.
3. Aleksandr Ginsberg was granted asylum by the United States.
4. For many years journalists, novelists, and poets have been persecuted by the Soviet government.
5. Some of the inhumane treatment was meted out by Stalin's henchmen.
6. There have been many times when news of such persecution was received with a deaf ear by the West.
7. There have also been countless cases of political persecution when the West was given no clue of such activities by Tass or other foreign news agencies.
8. News of the recent defection by four Soviet journalists was read with satisfaction by many U.S. citizens.
9. Writers in the West have not been made aware of what they might do to help their colleagues behind the Iron Curtain.

10. And dissident Russian writers have not been given much opportunity to meet with Western journalists.

19e   Problems with Inversions

Do not invert the word order of sentences unless it is necessary to create special emphasis. We have discussed (**18g**) some of the rhetorical effects of inverting word order, but like all other stylistic techniques, this one can be ineffective if used in the wrong context. It can cause either inappropriate formality or lack of clarity, as in the following sentences:

> Racquetball I never play.
> Jeans she would never wear to dinner.

Unless the context demanded this kind of inversion, the sentences are much clearer in normal word order:

> I never play racquetball.
> She would never wear jeans to dinner.

A special problem with inversions concerns the "dummy" pronouns or placeholders *it* and *there* (see **18g.2** and **18g.3**). While it is often useful to be able to invert the word order by putting an *it* or *there* at the beginning of a sentence, doing so can weaken your sentences. Consider the following sentences:

19e

> 1. There will be many problems as a result of this new legislation.
> 1a. This legislation will cause many problems.
> 1b. Many problems will result from this legislation.
>
> 2. It is sure to be a successful opening night.
> 2a. Opening night is sure to be a success.

Sentences 1a and 1b are both stronger than 1 because they put the key words (depending on the author's intention, either *legislation* or *problems*) near the front of the sentence, where they receive more emphasis. Likewise, both 1a and 1b put the action into the verb *(will cause, will result)* instead of into a linking verb plus noun *(will be . . . as a result)*. (See **20b.1**.) Sentence 2a puts the emphasis on *opening night* by moving it to the front of the sentence.

EXERCISES _____

Rewrite the following sentences to eliminate the inversions of normal word order. Which version is most effective?

1. There were dishes on the counter I never washed.
2. The moon's surface they walked on.
3. There are some new magazines on the table.
4. It was raw clams he could not eat without problems.
5. Her silk brocade pillow I would never put my head on.
6. Whose woods these are I think I know.
7. There were millions of spectators watching the Super Bowl.
8. There are twenty-seven students in my class.
9. It is too far to bicycle from New York to Los Angeles.
10. His problems I sure wouldn't want to have.

19f   Problems with Predication

19f

Be sure that predicates are logically related to their subjects. Problems with predication arise when there is a mismatch between the subject and its predicate. English has built-in constraints on the use of certain kinds of verbs with certain kinds of subjects. When a mismatch occurs, it causes lack of clarity—either ambiguity or serious confusion about the author's intention. Consider the following sentences:

> The ERA does not believe in the family.
> The most important ingredient is to add the yeast.

In the first example, the problem arises because a cause, the ERA or any other, is an abstract entity, of which one does not ordinarily predicate *belief*; belief is something predicated only by humans. What, then, does the writer mean? That the stand ERA takes on women's rights will disrupt the family? That the ERA will weaken the sociological institution known as the family or weaken individual families?

In the second example, the problem is that *ingredient is* requires a noun that fits into the category of things one can put into bread.

The mismatch here results from an attempt to complete a linking verb with an infinitive, when the subject it is being linked to requires a different kind of noun.

In both of these cases the solution is for the writer both to be more specific and to match a subject with its predicate so that the meaning is as clear as possible. Without knowing the context of the sentences or the authors' intentions toward their audiences, we cannot easily judge the effectiveness of the following revisions, but they will at least give you an idea of the kinds of solutions that exist:

> One possible *result* of passing the ERA is *that the American family will become a weaker institution.*
>
> (The subject, *result*, is linked to a noun clause through the verb *is*).

> The most important *ingredient* is the *yeast.* (or)
> The most important *step* is *to add* the yeast.
>
> (In the first, the subject, *ingredient*, is linked to a noun, *yeast*; in the second, the subject, *step*, is linked to an infinitive noun that is an appropriate completer of the subject.)

While most problems of predication depend on the particular sentence in which they occur, a few recur frequently. Most of them occur in sentences with linking verbs. Following are some examples:

> I *read* in today's paper *where* a woman in Arizona trains snakes.
> This *paragraph* is *where* the mistake was made.
> The most exciting *part* was *when* the hero cut through the barbed wire and escaped.
> The *reason* we are marketing it now is *because* Smith and Bradley are developing a similar device.

The problem with the first sentence is that traditionally a transitive verb (*read*) requires a direct object; a noun clause can fill the object slot, but not an adverb clause (*where a woman . . .*). The solution, then, is to substitute a noun clause:

> I *read* in today's paper [*that* a woman in Arizona trains snakes].

Or, since the object of a transitive verb may be implied, it is possible to follow it with a prepositional phrase:

> I *read* in today's paper *about* a *woman* in Arizona who trains snakes.

In the other three sentences, the problems all arise from following a linking verb with an adverb clause, since a linking verb should be followed by a noun or adjective. All of them would be appropriate in casual writing, but the following versions would be better in informal or formal writing. One solution is to substitute a noun plus "in which . . . ," a prepositional phrase that functions as an adjective:

> This *paragraph* is the *place in which* the mistake was made.
> The most exciting *part* was *the scene in which* the hero cut through the barbed wire and escaped.

Another solution is to substitute a noun clause:

> The *reason* we are marketing it now is *that* Smith and Bradley are developing a similar device.

Often a more effective solution is to substitute an action verb for the linking verb (since an action verb is modified by an adverb) and to rearrange the sentence to eliminate the linking verb:

> The mistake *was made* in this paragraph.
> The most exciting part *occurred* when the hero cut through the barbed wire and escaped.
> We *are marketing* it now because Smith and Bradley are developing a similar device.

EXERCISES

Revise the following sentences for more accurate and effective predication. Why are the revised versions better?

1. The part I like best is when the villain ties the heroine to the railroad tracks.
2. Freedom is when you can say what you want without fear of reprisal.
3. This country knows a lot about the problems of urban decay.
4. At the third stop sign is where he turned.
5. Until recently Congress had a growing number of representatives from the Sun Belt each year.

6. San Francisco is where some of the best seafood can be found.
7. The Civil War era gives me more perspective on our country's history.
8. Topkapi Palace was where many sultans lived.
9. Democracy is when everyone has the right to vote.
10. Etching is when you cut deep grooves into the surface of the printing plate.

19g   Problems with Parallel Structure

Be sure that parallel ideas are stated in parallel structures. Two kinds of problems with parallelism (or the lack of it) occur frequently; one is the obscuring of parallel ideas by not expressing them in parallel fashion, as in the following sentence:

> Abraham Lincoln has long been an American hero because he so perfectly exemplifies the American dream: he grew up in a one-room cabin but came to inherit the White House, and he was wise even though he didn't have any formal education.

Two ideas in this sentence support the assertion that Lincoln exemplifies the American dream: the first, "he grew up in a one-room cabin but came to inherit the White House," states his boyhood first and the contrast in his adult life second. The second idea, however, states first that he came to be wise and then contrasts the outcome with the fact that he had no formal education, obscuring the parallelism in ideas between this and the previous clause. Consider how much clearer as well as more emphatic this revision is:

> Abraham Lincoln has long been an American hero because he so perfectly exemplifies the American dream: he grew up in a one-room cabin but came to inherit the White House, and he received his only education by reading from borrowed books but came to inherit the wisdom of great men.

A greater problem arises when correlative conjunctions are placed so as to confuse the parallelism. Usually it is most effective to keep the elements following each part of a correlative conjunction equivalent (though when *not only . . . but also* is used in clauses, there is an exception, as explained below). Consider the following sentences:

> The new product *not only* is better than the old, *but* cheaper.
> The manager should *either* resign *or* he should be fired.

The first sentence might be more effective if made strictly parallel. In the original, *not only* is followed by a linking verb and a complement, *is better*; *but* is followed by a complement only, *cheaper*. If the linking verb *is* is to cover for both parts of the parallel complement, it should come before the first correlative:

> The new product *is not only* [better] than the old, *but* [cheaper].

Or the linking verb should be repeated:

> The new product *not only* [*is* better] than the old, *but* [*is* cheaper]. (or)
> [*is also* cheaper].

The same thing holds true in the second sentence: the sentence parts that come after each of the correlatives should be equivalent for strict parallelism. *Either* is followed by the verb *resign*, while *or* is followed by an entire clause. To revise it, we could either make *manager should* work for both parts of the verb or put the *either* before the beginning of the first clause:

> The manager *should either* [resign] *or* [be fired]. (or)
> *Either* [the manager] *should* [resign] *or* [he] should [be fired].

19g Most correlative conjunctions come directly in front of the structures they correlate, as in the examples of *either . . . or*, *neither . . . nor*, and *both . . . and*, above. *Not only . . . but also* follows this rule when it joins words or phrases, but when it joins clauses, as in the second example below, the word order is different. The first half of the conjunction, *not only*, comes at the beginning, followed by the verb + subject (inverted from the normal subject + verb order); *but* comes at the beginning of the second clause, but the *also* is placed after the verb (with linking verbs) or after the subject (with other verbs). Notice the difference between the conventional word order of the first version, using the simple coordinating conjunction *and*, and the word order with the correlative *not only . . . but also*:

> [He was my best friend] *and* [he was my husband].
> *Not only* [was he my best friend], *but* [he was *also* my husband].

EXERCISES

Revise the following sentences so that parallel ideas are stated in parallel structures.

1. Not only did I flunk the history test, but the calculus test too.
2. The history professor should either resign or she should learn to teach history better.
3. Calculus and history are my worst subjects along with English.
4. The new dormitory building is dark where it should be light, as is the study lounges, and where it should be cool, as in the bedrooms, it is overheated; it is also cramped in the cafeteria where there needs to be more room.
5. The river that Mark Twain described was not only the mighty Mississippi but mysterious and fascinating as well as the most direct means of transportation from north to south.
6. Either we should get a raise or fewer work hours.
7. The speaker both muffled his words and he was long-winded and boring.
8. Not only did I fall asleep but snored.
9. Anne both got a new job and she came into a great fortune.
10. I want to learn how to swim and dive as well as doing water ballet.

Part Six

WORDS

20

CHOOSING EFFECTIVE WORDS

Learning to use words so that they achieve your purpose and produce the effect you want is something that comes with experience. The more you write, and the more you get other people's reactions to your writing, the more you will become aware of the power of words. A few basic principles, however, will help you make those choices that with practice will come more naturally.

20a   Choosing Words for Clarity

20a.1   Specific and Concrete Words

Use specific, concrete words in place of vague, abstract, or general ones. But do not forget that specific details need to *work*: they should support a generalization, develop an idea, persuade an audience of the truth. Data without the generalizations that give meaning to them are as meaningless as generalizations without details to support them. (See **6c.**)

In a review, for example, you might very well begin with a generalization:

> Last night's concert by the Detroit Symphony was wonderful.

But you must go on to support that statement, to give your readers a precise idea of what the concert was like. It is tempting just to vary the general words: the concert was *great, terrific, fantas-*

tic, really first-rate, absolutely superb. But none of these gives your reader any more exact idea of the concert than *wonderful* does. Instead, you must be at once more specific and more concrete:

> The orchestra began by playing the Second Symphony of Johannes Brahms, with a balanced sense of Brahms' romantic melody lines and his precise tonal colors.

All the nouns, verbs, and adjectives in English exist at various levels on the abstraction ladder (see **6c**), and it is almost always possible to move down the ladder to find more specific and concrete terms than the ones that first come to mind. Here are some examples:

> person
>
> man
>
> young man
>
> young man of about twenty-five
>
> young man of twenty-five with pale complexion, gray-green eyes, and light brown hair.
>
> going down the street
>
> walking down the street purposefully
>
> marching down the street
>
> marching down the street toward the drugstore
>
> marching hurriedly, with his eyes fixed straight ahead on the door of the drugstore at the far end of the street
>
> marching hurriedly, with his eyes fixed on the shiny glass door of Hamilton's drugstore about five hundred yards away at the far end of the street

20a

The need for specific language is just as important in nondescriptive kinds of writing. Contrast the following two sentences:

> Our need for anti-inflationary measures is strong and immediate.
>
> The U.S. Congress must enact a bill before the end of the year that will provide wage and price controls, as well as penalties for credit-spending by consumers and by the state and federal governments.

The second sentence could be an elaboration of the first; but the first by itself is so general it would have very little impact on its readers.

20a.2 Nouns as Modifiers

Nouns used to modify nouns, called *nominal attributes*, are fairly common in English (*tomato soup*, *auto mechanic*, *cement walk*, and *garage door*). Some are so well established that they have come to be written as one word: *sailboat*, *moonlight*, *pancake*. Except in established usage like this, however, nominal attributes are often criticized by good writers, particularly in a string of more than two nouns.

Use nouns to modify other nouns only when they do not cause confusion or difficulty in reading. Here are several examples:

> We have set up a *task force* to deal with the problem.
>
> I recommend that we establish a committee to investigate new *business development opportunities* in Latin America.
>
> The flood was of *disaster proportions*.
>
> He lost his job for *health reasons*.

Task force is a good example of a noun phrase that has come to be almost as widely accepted as *tomato soup*, even though some people still criticize it simply because it is new.

In the second example, the string of three nouns can make the sentence hard to read. The sentence would be stronger if the writer focused on "new opportunities" instead of burying them in a string of nouns:

> I recommend we establish a committee to investigate new *opportunities for developing business* in Latin America.

The other two examples, *disaster proportions* and *health reasons*, have become clichés and can easily be avoided:

> The flood was *a disaster*.
> He lost his job *because of his bad health*.

Your decision to use or not use nominal attributes must be made within the wider context of your writing; but generally, your sentences will be more vigorous and easier to read if you avoid long strings of nominal attributes.

20a

20a.3   Using the Exact Word

You will find, as you write more and get people's response to your writing, that there are certain words you may confuse with one another, and they will confuse the reader. The Glossary of Usage contains the most frequently misused ones, including pairs like *imply/infer* and *disinterested/uninterested*. Other words often confused are *homonyms* (words spelled differently but pronounced the same), like *site/cite* and *who's/whose*, along with words derived from the same root but with different meanings (*healthy/healthful*). Such words are listed in **22d**.

Other words that are often used in a less than exact sense are *idioms*—word combinations that are peculiar to a language and whose meaning cannot be entirely predicted from the words that make up the combination. Expressions like *polished it off* and *got what it takes* are examples of idioms that every native speaker of English knows but which would be difficult to understand just by analyzing the individual words. The ones that cause the most trouble are those that include prepositions or particles. *Turn in* means either "go to bed" or "turn and go into" a house or driveway. But when do you say *different from* rather than *different than*? Is *center around* as acceptable as *center on*? Since these phrases must be taken whole, not by looking at their parts, logic will not always answer such questions. It is always a good idea to check your dictionary (idioms are usually listed at the end of the entry for the most important word in the phrase). You will find the most common ones in the Glossary of Usage.

EXERCISES

20a

1. In the following passage, Annie Dillard enables the reader to see with her eyes, hear with her ears, and smell with her nose. How does she achieve such startling precision and grace? How many abstractions do you find in the following paragraph? How many specific and concrete terms? List seven or eight of Dillard's best word choices. Do they fall into any particular category? How many of them contain more than three syllables?

One night a moth flew into the candle, was caught, burnt dry, and held. I must have been staring at the candle, or maybe I looked up when a shadow crossed my page; at any rate, I saw it all. A golden female moth, a biggish one with a two-inch wingspread, flapped into the fire, dropped abdomen into the wet wax, stuck, flamed, and frazzled in a second. Her moving wings ignited like tissue paper, like angels' wings, enlarging the circle of light in the clearing and creating out of the darkness the sudden blue sleeves of my sweater, the green leaves of jewelweed by my side, the ragged red trunk of a pine; at once the light contracted again and the moth's wings vanished in a fine, foul smoke. At the same time, her six legs clawed, curled, blackened, and ceased, disappearing utterly. And her head jerked in spasms, making a spattering noise; her antennae crisped and burnt away and her heaving mouthparts cracked like pistol fire. When it was all over, her head was, so far as I could determine, gone, gone the long way of her wings and legs. Her head was a hole lost to time. All that was left was the glowing horn shell of her abdomen and thorax—a fraying, partially collapsed gold tube jammed upright in the candle's round pool.   —Annie Dillard, "Death of a Moth"

2. Pick a moving object that you can observe closely—an insect, clouds on a windy day, a sailboat, a fish, a small child playing alone. Describe it with all the concreteness that Annie Dillard does the moth, trying to recreate for your reader all the senses that come into play—sight, hearing, smell, perhaps even taste and touch.

3. All of the following sentences contain one or more nominal attributes. Identify the nominal attributes and decide if their use is appropriate. If not, rewrite the sentences to exclude them.

   a. This permanent position offers an excellent opportunity for substantial earnings and an attractive commission arrangement.
   b. Fall is porch enclosure season.
   c. This company offers fine executive positions, ample possibilities for career achievements, and a location in an area with great recreation opportunities.
   d. The real estate company advertised a waterfront liquidation sale.
   e. Energy independence is vital to us all.

4. Following is a list of frequently confused words. Explain the meaning of each word of the pair, and use them both in context to demonstrate their unique function in our language. Which of these distinctions do you think are important? Which useless? Check **22d**, the Glossary of Usage, or your dictionary for any words you are not sure about.

   a. artful/artistic   f. literally/virtually
   b. decide/opt   g. plus/and
   c. eager/anxious   h. use/usage
   d. fortuitous/fortunate   i. viable/reasonable
   e. implement/use   j. void/devoid

20a

20b Choosing Words for Emphasis

20b.1 Using Emphatic Verbs

Prefer verbs to nouns, and prefer verbs of action to verbs of being. Compare the following sets of sentences:

> The company *put the blame* on Congress.
> The company *blamed* Congress.

> Dorothy *made a request* to take her vacation early.
> Dorothy *requested* to take her vacation early.

> She *does exercises and goes jogging* every morning.
> She *exercises and jogs* every morning.

> The coach *is afraid that* her team will lose.
> The coach *fears* her team will lose.

> Joan *has the responsibility for the determination of* the sales goals.
> Joan *must determine* the sales goals.

Not only does the second sentence in each pair eliminate unnecessary words, but it also avoids the pileup of prepositional phrases that can make reading very difficult.

20b.2 Using Fewer and Shorter Words

Prefer one word to several, and prefer short words to long ones. Sometimes you will be faced with a choice of one word that is long or several that are short, so you will not always be able to follow both parts of this principle at once. *Redundant* phrases (in which the same meaning is conveyed by more than one word) are often used when writers feel the need for more words, as though saying something directly and simply were the mark of a poor stylist.

Following are some examples of both wordy and redundant phrases; notice that the revised versions are clearer and more concise:

> I am writing *in regard to* your advertisement in the March 12 *Wall Street Journal.*
> I am writing *about* your advertisement in the March 12 *Wall Street Journal.*

20b

He failed the test *because of the fact that* he didn't study.
He failed the test *because* he didn't study.

There is no *reason why* we cannot repair the table for her.
There is no *reason* we cannot repair the table for her.

The board has been unable to reach a *consensus of opinion*.
The board has been unable to reach a *consensus*.

(The word *consensus* means "agreement of opinion.")

There are many other phrases for which fewer and shorter words could easily be substituted. Following is a list of conjunctions and prepositions that can easily substitute for these longer phrases:

- **about** (**concerning, regarding**): in connection with, in reference to, in regard to, in relation to, in respect to, pertaining to, referring to, relative to, with regard to, with respect to
- **because** (**since**): as a consequence of, as a result of, because of the fact that, for the reason that, inasmuch as, owing to
- **by** (**through, via**): by means of, by way of
- **during** (**throughout, while**): all during the time that, as long as, at the same time as, during the period of, during the time that, for the period of, in the time of, throughout the time of
- **for** (**to**): for the purpose of, in order that, in order to, so that, with the intentions of
- **if**: in case, in the case of, in the event that
- **like**: as though, correspondent with, of a kind with, of a like mind with, similar to
- **now**: at present, at this moment, at this time, at this point in time, at this very moment, in this day and age
- **then**: at that point in time, at that time, in that day and age, in the far distant past

20b

20b.3 Slang, Dialect, Jargon, and Euphemism

Use special vocabulary words—especially slang, dialect words, jargon, and euphemisms—very carefully. *Slang* words are created to fit the need of a particular group of people at a particular time. They are created to define an in-group, and as they are adopted by society at large, the in-group members must develop new slang in order to maintain a distinction between themselves and the out-group. When high school students begin to pick up college slang, for instance, college students will begin to use new expressions.

Slang is usually appropriate only in casual writing, since formal and even informal writing are aimed at communicating with people who very likely are *not* in the writer's social group. To pretend that the audience is in the writer's group, as advertising copywriters do, is offensive to many people; normally we do not like being made to feel intimate with a stranger, and any attempt by a writer to create an intimacy by using slang words and expressions is more likely to create barriers than to build bridges. Slang words that may be considered vulgar or obscene pose a special problem; it is extremely important to know who your readers are and how they will react to what you have written.

Like slang, *dialect words* mark a writer as the member of a particular geographical region or social group. To use such words and pronunciations deliberately is often a way of creating character, of showing a reader concretely how a person speaks. In Mark Twain's *Adventures of Huckleberry Finn*, for example, the different social classes, levels of education, and racial groups are defined through the careful way the author has recorded the speech of people living beside the Mississippi River before the Civil War. The differences between Huck, Miss Watson, Pap, and Jim are dramatized through their speech. You should not overlook, even in writing essays, the value of using special dialect words. But you should also be aware that your readers may not understand you if you choose words that are not widely known and recognized.

Jargon has traditionally meant the special language of a trade or discipline, but it has come to mean more often the language of science, politics, business, or academe used out of context or used inappropriately—to make a minor issue sound major, to cloak something subjective in the language of scientific objectivity, to make something sound more important than it really is.

Euphemisms are polite ways to refer to things that are normally taboo except in closed circles of family and friends. Words for sex, bodily elimination, social differences, death, and anything that reminds us of death are all subjects we are very sensitive to. We rarely say, for example, that someone died; he *passed away*, *went home*, *fell asleep*, or *passed over*. Undertakers are euphemistically known as *funeral directors*, cemeteries as *memo-*

20b

rial gardens, funeral homes as *memorial chapels*, and the dead person as *the loved one*. Euphemistic language is often a sign that we are avoiding something.

While our society has become less sensitive about bodily functions, it has become more sensitive to political realities. Some of the worst political atrocities in the last generation have been cloaked in euphemistic jargon: *pacification*, *resettlement*, and other such words have come to hide from us the reality of military action. (See **5g.12**.)

What should you do about euphemisms in your writing? In order to be sensitive to your readers, use euphemisms when they help you avoid offending your audience, but do not use them to hide the truth.

20b.4 Mixing Levels of Formality

Be consistent in the kinds of words you use, particularly in not mixing slang with more formal expressions. Slang is often inappropriate in writing because it is incongruous with its environment. So too are very informal expressions (including dialect terms and informal euphemisms) in an otherwise more formal piece of writing. On the other hand, a formal-sounding euphemism will be out of place in an informal piece of writing.

Such uses of words call attention to themselves, while normally words should point beyond themselves to the ideas they represent. For example, using slang words in formal contexts creates the same effect as wearing tennis shoes with a cocktail dress or a suit and tie to a party. And to put quotation marks around the word, as though to excuse it, merely draws attention to it and makes the incongruity more obvious—like apologizing to your host for forgetting to change your shoes, instead of keeping your feet under the dinner table where no one will notice them.

Consider the following examples:

> The Boston Celtics played hard to *ameliorate* their losses in the first half, but the Cleveland Browns *slammed* them anyway.
>
> The purpose of the agency is to *ameliorate* the living conditions of retirees.

20b

In the first example, the word *ameliorate* is clearly inappropriate in the same sentence with *slammed*. (It is even inaccurate, since *ameliorate* does not mean "improve" in the sense of that sentence.) The incongruity between *ameliorate* and the less formal context of the sentence is a good example of what can happen when you use a thesaurus in the wrong way; it is wiser to use a good dictionary of synonyms, which would make it clear that *ameliorate* was inappropriate in the first example (see **21d.3**). In the second sentence, *ameliorate* is appropriate, not only because the meaning is just right, but also because the formal tone is consistent with the words of Latin origin. (Words of Latin origin tend to be used in more formal situations than Anglo-Saxon words; see **20b.5**.)

20b.5 Unnecessary Variety

Aim for variety in your writing but be careful of using empty or "fancy" words and variation for their own sake. A thesaurus or dictionary of synonyms (see **21d.3**) can be helpful in finding fresh ways of expressing ideas for which you have used the same word too many times. But remember that fancy or unusual words used for their own sake are likely to be distracting rather than helpful to the reader, and too much variation can cause confusion rather than clarity.

This problem is most obvious when a writer tries to find enough synonyms to avoid ever repeating a word. Imagine in an article on thinking, for example, using this list of synonyms, most of them Latin in origin, in place of the simple Anglo-Saxon *think*:

cogitate	excogitate	ratiocinate	ruminate
cerebrate	introspect	reflect	speculate
deliberate	meditate	retrospect	theorize

20b

One place in which writers are obsessed with this kind of variety is in the sports pages of daily newspapers. How many words can you think of for *beat*? Any sports page is a resource for innumerable ways to say it without saying it.

Every writer has to find the right balance between too much and too little variety, between too much fancy language and too many one-syllable Anglo-Saxon words. And remember, above all, that too much variety will weaken the coherence of your writing, which depends on a certain amount of repetition (see **12d**).

20b.6 Figurative Language

Use figurative language with restraint. Figurative language makes a comparison between two things we would not ordinarily think to compare—often between an abstract idea and something concrete. The purpose of figurative language is to illuminate and clarify something the writer wants to say.

An *analogy* helps to make the unfamiliar understandable by comparing it to something familiar, or to make the commonplace interesting. See **4f** for an example in which Sigmund Freud compares the elements of the personality to a horse and its rider.

A *metaphor*, like an analogy, makes a comparison, but it is usually brief (an "extended metaphor" is really an analogy), and the comparison is *implied*—it does not say explicitly that one thing is *like* another—as an analogy may, and as a simile always does. The following sentences exemplify the use of a well-known metaphor, comparing experience to a lamp:

> I have but one lamp by which my feet are guided, and that is the lamp of experience. I know no way of judging of the future but by the past. —Patrick Henry, Speech in Virginia Convention

A *simile* is like a metaphor, in that it compares one thing with another in order to illuminate the first, but it does so *explicitly*, usually with the words *like* or *as*. In the following quotation, the speaker is describing a jeweler he meets in a shop:

> His hair was parted in the center. The part ran up into the bald spot, like a drained marsh in December.
> —William Faulkner, *The Sound and the Fury*

In the following example, Benjamin Franklin begins with a simile and expands it so that it almost has the force of an analogy:

> The body of Benjamin Franklin, Printer (like the cover of an old book, its contents torn out and stripped of its lettering and gilding), lies here, food for worms; but the work shall not be lost, for it will (as he believed) appear once more in a new and more elegant edition, revised and corrected by the Author.
> —Benjamin Franklin, "Epitaph on Himself"

20b

Another common figure of speech is *personification*, in which an abstract idea, inanimate object, or animal is spoken of as though it were a person.

Figures of speech should be used, however, with restraint. Trying too hard to be clever or original can strain your writing and make your reader more aware of the trick you are playing with language than of the point of what you want to say.

20b.7 Clichés and Trite Expressions

Use sparingly figures of speech or other expressions that have become clichés. A *cliché* is an expression that has been overused and therefore has come to be the opposite of what it was intended to be: a way of giving a reader a fresh view of something. Often clichés are worn-out metaphors, like "You can't teach an old dog new tricks" or "Kill two birds with one stone." But other trite expressions are also abundant in writing we read every day. (*Trite* comes from a Latin verb, *tritus*, and means "worn out.") Phrases like *viable alternative*, *feasible plan*, and *at this point in time* are common in newspapers, business reports, government documents—almost everywhere.

One of the major difficulties in avoiding clichés is recognizing them for what they are. Quite often, something that seems original to you may very well have come to mind because it was lodged somewhere in your memory. The best way to recognize clichés is to read widely. If you read regularly in current newspapers and magazines, you will recognize many clichés before you are tempted to use them in your own writing.

EXERCISES

1. The Indian guru, Meher Baba, is famous for his advice, "Don't worry; be happy." Because of the simplicity and brevity of this statement, some people have regarded it as ridiculous, others as sublime. What is your opinion? Discuss an alternative way of giving the same advice.

20b

2. Rewrite the following sentences until you have pared them down to their most direct, concise form, while keeping their meaning intact.

   a. She borrowed the programming information with intentions of putting it to use only on her own project and then returning it to its original location as expeditiously as possible.

   b. I will personally see to it that each person is able to understand all the information pertaining to her particular area of responsibility.

   c. At this point in time, we are unable to reach a consensus of opinion on the necessity for a standing committee to take responsibility for the social gatherings of the department.

d. We are in agreement on the necessity of shorter, more concise sentences in order to achieve writing characterized by vigor.

e. Due to the fact that in this matter a dictionary might be of better service to you than a thesaurus, it would be wise to rely more heavily on the former.

3. Read the following memo, which is filled with jargon and other unnecessary words. Rewrite it as concisely as possible, using the fewest words without sacrificing the meaning of the original.

DATE: February 10, 1988
TO: All employees
FROM: Your eminent president
SUBJECT: De-institutionalization of escalating disarrayed report framework

    I speak to the issue of the overwhelming negatively factored vocabulary syndrome that afflicts our company. It seems that a multitude of employees hypothecate a miscertified, counterfactual envisionment that the dialoging of pseudo-sophisticated reports will enhance chances for promotion. I intend to deactivate the habitual abuse of the English linguistic system within our institution expediently.

    Fully integrated, multidisciplinary procedures will be taken to circumvent and option out individuals who cannot rectify their counter-productive heuristically related English skills. Further, only upper-sectored managers and politicians should implement the utilization of trivialized, multimodulated, quasi-deregulated executory lexicon. More concisely, employees who continue to write in this framework will encounter a zero-based compensation level.

4. With the other members of your class, make up a list of your favorite slang and informal expressions. For each item on the list, decide whether the usage is current, or speculate on the time period when the word or phrase was in use. Provide a meaning for as many as you can, and identify which items you consider to be informal and which slang. You may be surprised to find that a good college dictionary may contain many of them.

5. The following sentences are written with mixed levels of formality. Rewrite each one twice: once so it reflects a consistent formal or informal level, and once so it reflects a consistent informal or casual level.

20b

a. It was an auspicious reenactment of a totally awesome drama.

b. My friend Steven got pretty bent out of shape ruminating on examples of current slang.

c. A major desideratum for our department is a lounge or commons room where we can be laid back and let it all hang out.

d. Sober, responsible columnists may brood about the status of female newscasters and their inability to compete effectively for prime jobs, but what really grabs me is how these women get themselves up.

e. The pious and gentle St. Francis of Assisi had birds hanging off him all the time.

20c Choosing Words That Do Not Discriminate

Avoid words that discriminate by sex, race, social class, or age. Recently we have become more and more aware of the racism and sexism inherent in our language. We can hardly avoid, perhaps, all the metaphoric meanings of black and white or male and female that might inadvertently offend, but we can do a lot to be sure we use our language to foster social equality rather than to prevent it.

One way to avoid discriminatory language is to be aware of qualifiers. For instance, you should not identify a "woman judge" unless the gender is relevant, because the implication is that it is surprising to find a woman who is a judge. A situation in which gender might be relevant, however, would be in a report of a study on differences in sentencing by male and female judges (in which case both female judges *and* male judges would be identified by gender); it would *not* be relevant, however, in an article about severity of sentencing by judges in general.

You must also be careful about the terms you use for referring to groups of people by race, sex, or age. The word *Negro*, for instance, was once a polite euphemism for *colored person*, but during the civil rights movement it gained negative connotations and was replaced by the term *black*. Likewise, as the image of women has changed so have the connotations of terms used to refer to women. *Baby, sweetheart*, and *honey*, once considered flattering, are now more often considered insults. Similarly, *senior citizens*, which was originally a euphemism for the elderly, has come to have negative connotations to some people who regard it as condescending.

Terms for referring to people change rapidly in a changing society, but that is a relatively minor problem, one that can be handled easily enough with a little care and sensitivity on the part of the writer. A more difficult problem, because it is inherent in the structure of our language, is the problem of sexist references.

20c

Our present pronoun system, with *he*, *him*, *his*, and *she*, *her*, *hers*, presents us with all kinds of difficulties when we want to refer to an individual either without knowing the sex or without wanting to make a specific gender designation when the reference is indefinite (like *anyone*, *everybody*, *person*, etc.).

The most difficult problem occurs with pronoun-antecedent agreement, since many people still consider it ungrammatical to use *their* to refer to a single indefinite pronoun. Of the various solutions mentioned in **16a.3**, the ones I have used in this book are, first, to use the plural whenever possible, and when not, to alternate male and female references. It is, of course, easier to alternate references in a long work like a book. In a short essay, such a solution could prove distracting and it might be necessary, occasionally, to use combination forms like *his or her*.

Gender also presents a problem with nouns that refer to human beings. The word *lady* is considered an unfavorable euphemism by many women, since it originated as a term referring to a specific social class in an age when social hierarchies were much more important than today. While most younger females prefer to be called *women*, the history of the word *woman* is itself an example of how deeply *man* is entrenched in our language. The word *mann* in Old English denoted either "man" or "person," and the word *wifmann* meant "female person." Our word *woman* comes from *wifmann*, so in theory *woman* ought to be as unacceptable as *lady* (which comes from Old English *hlaefdig*, "kneader of bread"). The truth is, however, that words mean what we want them to mean and at the moment the connotations of *woman* are acceptable to almost all women, while the connotations of *lady* are not.

Consider the following sentences:

> We are looking for a good *man* to fill the position. (referring to male or female)

> A university *spokesperson* told reporters that the Board of Visitors had appointed Samuel Delaney acting chancellor.

> All requests for information are to be sent to *Ms.* Jackson.

20c

Many readers would reject the use of *man* to refer to male or female. The word *spokesperson*, on the other hand, is acceptable to most people, as is *Ms.* as a form of address. Unless you know better, it is safest to address a woman as *Ms.* Use *Miss* or *Mrs.* when you know the woman prefers one of these.

A word similar to *spokesperson* that has caused some controversy is *chairperson* or, simply, *chair.†* Almost all business and educational institutions use these forms instead of *chairman* when the person could be a woman as well as a man, and it is best to use these forms unless you are referring to a particular person who you know is offended by the newer form.

Because we are living in a period of transition, questions of sexism in language are particularly controversial and difficult. In general, the best advice is to try to be sensitive to the feelings of your audience. In academic and business settings, the newer non-discriminatory forms are the safest to use; in more informal and personal situations, you may have to depend on what you know about the preferences of your readers.

EXERCISES

1. In its guidelines on avoiding language that discriminates, the National Council of Teachers of English provides the passage below as an example of words, ideas, and phrases to rethink and revise. Rewrite the entire passage to eliminate anything discriminatory. Remember that this may necessitate omitting details, as well as changing words.

O'CONNORS TO HEAD PTA

Jackson High School PTA members elected officers for the 1975-76 school year Wednesday night at the school cafeteria.

Dr. and Mrs. James O'Connor were elected co-presidents from a slate of three couples. Dr. O'Connor, a neurosurgeon on the staff of Howard Hospital, has served for two years on the PTA Budget and Finance Committee. Mrs. O'Connor has been active on the Health and Safety Committee.

Elected as co-vice-presidents were Mr. and Mrs. Tom Severns; secretary, Mrs. John Travers; and treasurer, Mrs. Edward Johnson. Committee chairmen were also selected. Each chairman will be briefed

20c

---

†Although some people object to the metaphorical use of *chair* to refer to a person, it is interesting that the word *board* has been accepted for years as a metaphor for the people who sit around that board (table) to make important decisions. If we have a board, why not also a chair of the board?

on his responsibilities at a special meeting on June 3. The revised budget will be presented at that meeting.

Principal Dick Wade announced that Mrs. Elizabeth Sullivan had been chosen Teacher of the Year by the Junior Women's League. She was nominated in a letter written by ten of her students. Each student discussed how she had influenced him.

Mrs. Sullivan, an English teacher at Jackson for ten years, is the wife of Joseph Sullivan, a partner in the law firm of Parker, Sullivan and Jordan, and the mother of two Jackson students.

Smartly attired in a blue tweed suit, Mrs. Sullivan briefly addressed the group, expressing her gratitude at receiving the award.

2. In the following sentences, identify all the words that suggest ways in which language can misrepresent, mislead, or mistreat; then rewrite the sentences to correct any prejudice.

   a. It was one small step for a man, one giant leap for mankind.
   b. He who hesitates is lost.
   c. It is her responsibility to man the computer every Thursday.
   d. They regarded him as a great womanizer.
   e. Each child has his part rehearsed perfectly.
   f. It is customary for advertisers, salesmen, and politicians to use euphemisms.
   g. All employees are invited to bring their wives and children.
   h. This purse is manufactured from the finest quality man-made materials.
   i. The traitress was convicted and sentenced.
   j. The female dentist found two cavities in his wisdom teeth.

3. To what extent do the following words convey precisely equal meaning, except for the matter of gender? Consult your dictionary if necessary.

   a. waiter/waitress   d. warlock/witch
   b. tailor/seamstress   e. dairyman/dairymaid
   c. porter/portress

4. Why, do you think, are there no equivalent words referring to the opposite sex for the following terms?

   a. laundress   d. ladies' man
   b. fishwife   e. maitre d'[hotel]
   c. rake

20c

21

WORDS AND
MEANINGS

21a The Roots of Our Language

Language is a social phenomenon: it exists primarily for the purpose of communication. Without language, we would not be able to carry on the activities of a civilized culture. Consequently, language is influenced by all the forces that affect the lives of the people who speak it: geographic location, political power, social prestige, economic advantage.

English is the descendant of an ancestor language called *Indo-European*, which was probably spoken by a group of tribes living in central Europe in the late Stone Age, or about the fifth millennium B.C. We assume that those tribes, probably for economic reasons, moved out from their common location to find sources of food. As they did so, they became separated by geographical barriers (rivers, lakes, mountains, and sheer distance) and probably also by tribal rivalries. Since all living languages constantly change, and since change occurs differently among groups no longer in contact with each other, we assume that the Indo-European language spoken by the separated tribes must have developed differently in different places.

At first, the changes would have been minimal—a shift in the meaning of a word here, a slight change in pronunciation there. After a period of years in which the different groups had little or no contact with each other, their respective versions of the language would come to be recognizably different—but still varieties of the original language and still intelligible to speakers of the other groups. In other words, *dialects* of the original language had developed.

But when the speakers of the various dialects lived away from each other long enough, the changes in vocabulary, pronunciation, and grammar would have become so great that speakers of one dialect could no longer understand speakers of other dialects. In other words, the various speech patterns had become separate *languages* rather than dialects of a single language. We assume that each of these dozen or so distinct languages in turn produced various dialects which themselves evolved into separate languages. Through the continuation of that process, scores of separate languages have developed—most of those spoken in Europe, in India, and in the Americas. Thus English, French, Spanish, German, Polish, Russian, and many others have all evolved from a common source.

We do not, of course, have any written records of the Indo-European language, since it was spoken long before the invention of writing. How, then, do we know there was such a thing? One source of evidence is the multitude of *cognates*—words that mean roughly the same thing in different languages, that derive from common sources, and that have similar though different forms. For example, by comparing cognates like Sanskrit *trayas*, Greek *trias*, Latin *tres*, and English *three*, scholars have been able to infer the characteristics of the ancestor language and through this process reconstruct an approximation of Indo-European.

Scholars have divided Indo-European into a number of language families; you can think of each family as an offspring of the original, which in turn had descendants of its own. Five of these families have produced languages that are known to most Americans:

21a

Balto-Slavic: the Baltic branch, including *Latvian* and *Lithuanian*, and the Slavic branch, including *Polish*, *Slovak*, *Czech*, *Bulgarian*, *Ukrainian*, and *Russian*.

Italic: the ancestor of *Latin*, which produced local dialects that in turn developed into the modern "romance" languages, including *Italian*, *French*, *Romanian*, *Spanish*, and *Portuguese*.

Hellenic: the ancestor of classical and modern *Greek*.

Celtic: the languages of the earliest known inhabitants of the British Isles—*Welsh*, *Irish Gaelic*, and *Scottish Gaelic*.

Germanic: The ancestor of *English* as well as of *German*, *Dutch*, and the Scandinavian languages—*Swedish*, *Norwegian*, *Danish*, and *Icelandic*.

English descended from the West Germanic branch of Indo-European, but before 450 B.C., the British Isles were inhabited by the *Celts*, who spoke several languages in the Celtic family of Indo-European. With the collapse of the Roman Empire and the return of Roman soldiers (who had occupied England for several hundred years) to their homeland, the native Britons were left vulnerable to the attacks of several Germanic tribes—the Angles, the Saxons, and the Jutes—who came from the North Sea coasts of northern Germany and southern Denmark. These tribes spoke slightly different dialects of West Germanic, but when the tribes settled in the British Isles, their dialects evolved into a language that we now call English, after the Angles. (Old English is sometimes called Anglo-Saxon.)

The Old English period lasted roughly from A.D. 450 to 1100, and during this period the language remained very much a Germanic language. With the invasion of England by William the Conqueror in 1066, however, the English came under the rule of a foreign power: Norman French became the official language of government, commerce, and the upper classes, while English was spoken primarily by the peasants.

During the Middle English period (roughly 1100 to 1500), many native words were replaced or supplemented with French words, and the language underwent important shifts in pronunciation. In contrast to the Old English period, especially in the ninth century under King Alfred, who encouraged the creation of literature in English, the first few centuries after William's invasion saw very little written in English. By the middle of the fourteenth century, however, authors were beginning to write serious literature in English again, culminating in Chaucer and his contemporaries in the latter half of the century.

21a

By the time of Chaucer, the political center of England had shifted from the West Saxon area, where Alfred had held court, to the East Midland area, around London, where the French kings had held court and where their English successors continued to rule. As a result, the dialect that became standard for literature, government, and commerce was the East Midland dialect. What is considered standard today, in England, the United States, and

Canada, descended from that dialect. If it were not for those political events that established London as a center of government, trade, and learning, the language we speak today might be quite different.

What we call Modern English began around 1500, when the changes in pronunciation caused by French influence were almost complete and English, rather than French, had again become the language of the educated. And largely because of the genius and popularity of Shakespeare, Spenser, and Milton, English became a major literary language.

But the history of the English language does not stop with Shakespeare and Milton. The language has continued to grow and change during the last four hundred years. As England became a great colonial power, and as her colonies, like the United States and Canada, have themselves become major world powers, the English language has been influenced by languages from all over the world. The modern variation of dialects in the United States and Canada is partially due to the patterns of settlement and migration of the colonists from England, but contact with innumerable languages of immigrants (both voluntary immigrants from Europe and forced immigrants from Africa) and the native Americans has enriched our vocabulary and sometimes affected the grammar and pronunciation of our language as well.

EXERCISES

Following are four versions of the first two lines of the Lord's Prayer. How do you explain the differences among them? How do these versions compare with the one you know? Look carefully at the letters and words themselves, as well as the spelling and word order.

Old English (sixth century):
   Faeder ure þu þe eart on heofonum . . .

Middle English (twelfth century):
   Our fadir that art in heunes . . .

Early Modern English (1611):
   Our father which art in heaven . . .

Contemporary English (1960):
   Our father in heaven . . .

21a

21b   Increasing Your Vocabulary

The best writers always seem to have just the word needed to convey their intentions. Sometimes that skill seems to come from an inherited good ear and good memory, but almost all effective writers have had to work consciously to develop a vocabulary they can draw on with insight and ease. The best way to develop that kind of vocabulary is by wide and varied reading and writing, but some knowledge of the origins and relationships of words will help you as well.

21b.1   Native Words and Borrowed Words

English has a rich store of words that have descended from Old English and ultimately from Germanic and Indo-European. Most of our *function* words (pronouns, conjunctions, prepositions) and most of our words for common, everyday things come from the native Old English word stock (words like *honey, board, stool, cow, work*).

Many of our words have been borrowed from other languages, and much of the richness and flexibility of the language is due to this vast store of loan words. Some words were borrowed very early, when missionaries from Ireland and Rome began to Christianize the Anglo-Saxons in the sixth century; these include many words relating to religion, like *bishop, creed, deacon, disciple, martyr, mass, monk, priest, pope,* and *synod,* which were all borrowed from Latin.

In the early ninth century, when the Danish Vikings invaded the British Isles, they contributed to English some of our most basic words, including the pronouns *them, their,* and *they*. Occasionally words from Scandinavian and Old English existed side by side (the Scandinavian *skirt,* for instance, originally meant the same as Old English *shirt*). Also during this period, English borrowed a number of words from the Celtic languages spoken by the native inhabitants of the British Isles. Some of them, like *shamrock* and *leprechaun,* relate to Celtic culture, while others have been more widely used (like *bog, clan, plaid, slogan,* and *whiskey*).

In the thirteenth and fourteenth centuries, English went through its first major stage of borrowing: under the influence of the Norman French, scores of new words entered the language, many of them co-existing with Old English words that had similar if not identical meanings. Compare these words:

OF FRENCH ORIGIN	OF ENGLISH ORIGIN
act	deed
appear	seem
chair	stool
cycle	wheel
edifice	building
finish	end
labor	work
multitude	crowd
table	board
vision	dream

The second period of major borrowing occurred in the sixteenth and seventeenth centuries, during the English Renaissance, when many words were borrowed from classical Greek and Latin. Some words were borrowed from Latin at different times, and thus English sometimes has two words with similar meanings but different forms. The word *chalk*, for instance, came into early Old English through Latin, and the word *calcium* was borrowed in Modern English. And some words were borrowed from Latin and used alongside native words with similar meanings, as in the following examples (sometimes the native word is a noun form and the borrowed one an adjective, but not always):

OF LATIN ORIGIN	OF ENGLISH ORIGIN
aural	ear
corpulent	fat
dental	tooth
fraternal	brother
illumination	light
malignant	evil
maternal	mother
ocular	eye
oral	mouth
paternal	father

21b

The third great borrowing has taken place over the last two centuries, during which the growth of science and technology has caused the development of an international set of shared words, varying only in minor ways from each other. Much of the borrowing has been of Greek roots that have been combined into new words to describe new scientific discoveries—words like *bacteriology*, *barometer*, *telegraph*, and *telephone*. English has continued to borrow words from French and from other European languages as well, especially in North America, where the great flood of immigration in the seventeenth century and again in the late nineteenth and early twentieth centuries enriched our stock of words. For instance, from French we borrowed *brochure* and *chaperone*; from Portuguese, *veranda*; from Spanish, *cafeteria and marijuana*; from Italian, *serenade* and *umbrella*; from Swedish, *ski*; from Dutch, *cookie*; from German, *hamburger* and *kindergarten*; from Arabic, *algebra*; from Persian, *paradise*.

English in North America has also been strongly influenced by Native American Indian languages and by the various African dialects spoken by slaves brought to the American colonies. In addition to hundreds of American place-names, Native American languages have bequeathed us many other words, many of them referring to things in nature, like *chipmunk*, *pecan*, and *hurricane*. Likewise, many of the words English has borrowed from African languages include natural objects like *banana* and *cola* as well as musical terms like *jazz*.

21b.2 Compounding

Compounding creates new words by joining two words or a word and a borrowed root. Compounds are usually spelled as two separate words when they are new; hyphenated when used as adjectives or when they begin to be better known; and finally, when they have been fully accepted into English, usually spelled as one word (see **24a.1**). Some examples of words created by compounding are *bedroom*, *bookcase*, *cookbook*, *input*, *roommate*, *singsong*, *sit-in*, *space-age*.

New words created from Greek or Latin roots also represent a kind of compounding (for example, *telephone*). A *root* is the base part of a word, the part that carries the central meaning. Roots borrowed from Latin or Greek can sometimes stand alone as words in English (*phone*, for instance), but usually are combined with prefixes or suffixes or, as in the list below, with other roots.

21b

Following is a list of Greek and Latin roots that have been used in creating English compounds. Studying the roots and their meanings will help to increase your recognition vocabulary and, eventually, your working vocabulary as well.

GREEK ROOTS	MEANING	EXAMPLES
anthropos	man	anthropology, misanthropy
arkhow	rule, highest rank	matriarch, architect
archaeo	early, old	archeology, archaic
auto	self	autograph, automatic
bios	life	biology, biography
biblion	book	bibliography, bibliophile
cracy, crat	rule, supporter of a rule	democracy, bureaucrat
demos	people	democracy, demagogue
eu	good, well	eulogy, euphemism
graphein	write	graphic, lithograph
khroma	color	monochrome, chromatic
latreia	worship, service	idolatry, bibliolatry
logos	word	catalog, geology
lithos	stone	lithograph, monolith
megas	great	megaphone, megacycle
monos	one	monorail, monophonic
morphe	form, shape	morphogenesis, anthropomorphic
neos	new	neologism, neoclassical
pan	all	panhellenic, pantheism
philos	loving	philosophy, audiophile
phone	sound, voice	phonograph, telephone
phot, phos	light	photograph, photosynthesis
pseudein	lie	pseudoscience, pseudonym
sophos	skilled, clever	sophisticated, sophomore
techne	art, skill	technical, architecture
typos	impression	typewriter, archetype

21b

LATIN ROOTS	MEANING	EXAMPLES
audire	hear	audible, audience
bene	good, well	beneficial, benediction
cedere	go	proceed, decease
claudere	close	include, conclude
clinare	lean, bend	incline, recline

LATIN ROOTS	MEANING	EXAMPLES
dicere	say	diction, predict
ducere	lead	induction, ductile, reduce
facere	do	fact, manufacture
gramma	something written	telegram, gramophone
magnus	great	magnify, magnanimous
manus	hand	manuscript, manufacture
malus	evil	malady, malfeasance
mobilis	move	mobile, automobile
multus	much	multitude, multiply
omnis	all	omnibus, omnipotent
semi	half, part	semicircle, semicolon

21b.3 Derivation

Derivation is the process of creating new words by adding prefixes and suffixes to the root, whether that root is an English word or a Latin or Greek single root or compound. Derivational suffixes often, but not always, change the part of speech when added to a root. Following is a list of the most common suffixes. While many suffixes are used with only one part of speech, some of them are used with more than one (*-ly*, for example, can be either an adjective or an adverb marker).

VERB-MAKING SUFFIXES	MEANING	EXAMPLES
-ate	to make	automate, duplicate
-en	or	soften, fasten
-fy	to cause	satisfy, pacify
-ish	to be	finish, polish
-ise, -ize, -yze		advise, realize, analyze

NOUN-MAKING SUFFIXES	MEANING	EXAMPLES
-ance, -ence	state of	abundance, independence
-ancy, -ency	state of	flippancy, currency
-dom	state of	kingdom, wisdom
-ee	person who	employee, payee
-eer	person who	profiteer, auctioneer
-er, -or	person who	employer, debtor
-ery	quality of	bravery, forgery
-hood	state of	womanhood, childhood

21b

NOUN-MAKING SUFFIXES	MEANING	EXAMPLES
-ian	person who	librarian, veterinarian
-ice	quality of	cowardice, prejudice
-ion, -sion, -tion	act of	rebellion, domination
-ism	act of	capitalism, baptism
-ist	person who	physicist, capitalist
-ite	person who	parasite, anchorite
-ment	act of	government, argument
-ness	state of	kindness, happiness
-ship	state of	friendship, worship

ADJECTIVE-MAKING SUFFIXES	MEANING	EXAMPLES
-able, -ible	capable of	capable, possible
-al	related to	ational, social
-an, -ian	related to	Scandinavian, Shakespearean
-ant, -ent	having	significant, intelligent
-ate	having	affectionate
-en, -in	like	wooden, elfin
-escent	full of	luminescent, effervescent
-ful	full of	careful, wonderful
-ic	having	ironic, energetic
-ish	like	British, foolish
-less	without	careless, helpless
-like	like	childlike
-ly	like	womanly, friendly
-ous	full of	humorous, delicious
-some	being	fulsome, tiresome
-y	having	witty, funny

ADVERB-MAKING SUFFIXES	MEANING	EXAMPLES ·
-fold	number	twofold
-ly	like	wisely, fondly
-ward		forward, upward
-ways	direction	sideways, always
-wise		lengthwise, cornerwise

21b

Because the addition of derivational endings is a common way of creating new words in our language, we should not be surprised to see the process going on continually. Quite often, however, new words are rejected by people who are not used to them or who feel uncomfortable with them. Three suffixes have been particularly controversial in recent times: the adjective endings *-wise* and *-type*, and the verb ending *-ize*. The following sentences illustrate the process of derivation:

> He described it as a *concrete-type* surface.
> *Productionwise*, we are four days behind schedule.
> Government mediators expect the new contract to be *finalized* this week.

One reason many writers and editors object to the use of words like *concrete-type* is that English already has an adjective-making suffix that does the same thing as *-type*, namely *-like*. We do, however, have other duplications of suffixes (like *-ly* and *-like*); the real reason that many *-type* words have been rejected is that they are new and therefore jar our notions of what is right in the written language.

The suffix *-wise*, in the second sentence, would be rejected by most writers and editors as artificial and strained. Consider this variation:

> We are four days behind in our production schedule.

The third sentence is more acceptable to many writers, though some still object. Perhaps because *finalize* has become so widespread in the written language, and has been around longer than either *concrete-type* or *productionwise*, it feels more "natural."

English also uses a large number of prefixes to form new words. Following are the most commonly used prefixes, taken from Latin, Greek, and Old English. The words used here as examples have been formed at every stage of the history of our language.

21b

GREEK PREFIXES	MEANING	EXAMPLES
a-	without	amoral
ambi-, amphi-	around, on both sides	ambidextrous, amphibious
ana-	back, opposite	anachronism
anti-	against	antibody
cata-	down	cataclysm
dia-	through	diatribe
dys-	bad	dysfunction

GREEK PREFIXES	MEANING	EXAMPLES
epi-	upon	epigraph
ex-	out	exercise, exegesis
hyper-	beyond, excess	hypertension, hyperthyroid
hypo-	under	hypothyroid, hypotension
meta-	beyond, changed	metamorphosis, metaphysics
para-	side by side, near	paraphrase, paragraph
peri-	around	perimeter
proto-	first	prototype
syn-, sym-	together	synchronize, symphony

LATIN PREFIXES	MEANING	EXAMPLES
ab-	away, from	absent, abdicate
ac-, ad-, ag-, at-†	toward, near	accuse, adverb, aggregate, attack
ante-	before	antedate, antebellum
bi-	two	bicycle, biennial
circum-	around	circumstance, circumnavigate
col-, com-, con-†	with, similar	colleague, community, conceive
contra-	against	contradiction, contrary
de-	reverse, down, remove	degrade, define
dis-	apart, away, reversal	disappoint, distrust
ex-	out	exceed, exit, ex-president
extra-	outside	extracurricular, extrapolate
in-, en-	in	inside, intuition, enclose, entrance
il-, im-, in-, ir-†	not	illicit, immature, inhuman, irrational
inter-	between	intercede, interracial
intra-	within	intramural, intra-office
intro-	within, inside	introspection, introvert
juxta-	near	juxtapose
non-	not	nonsense, nonconformist

21b

†These variations are caused by a process called *assimilation,* by which the original spelling of a prefix is changed to fit the pronunciation of the root to which it is attached.

LATIN PREFIXES	MEANING	EXAMPLES
ob-, oc-, of-, om-†	against, opposite	obstacle, occasion, offend, omit
per-	through	perforate
post-	after	postoperative, postdoctoral
pre-	in front of, before	prevent, predict
pro-	forward	project, progress
pro-	away	prodigal
pro-	in front	prohibit
pro-	before, in anticipation	provide, proceed
re-	again, back, restore	repeat, receive, recognize
retro-	backward	retrogress, retroactive
sub-, suc-, sup-†	under, less, in place of	subcommittee, succeed, support
super-	over	supernatural, supersede
trans-	across, beyond	transcribe, transfer, transatlantic
uni-	one	uniform, unity, unique

OLD ENGLISH PREFIXES	MEANING	EXAMPLES
a-	on	aboard, ashore
be-	near	bemoan
for-	wrong, destruction, prohibition	forswear, forbear
mis-	error, wrong	mistake, misfortune, misfire
out-	beyond	outlaw
over-	too much	overeat
un-	not	unclean, unbalanced, unfit
under-	under	underwear, underage
with-	against	withstand

21b

21b.4   Other Sources of New Words

Back-formations are words that have been created by eliminating a derivational ending that was part of the word when it came into English. It is a kind of reverse derivation. For example, the word *edit* was formed from *editor*, *educate* from *education*, and *televise* from *television*. Just as people frequently object to new derivations, so they also object to some new back-formations; see, for example, *enthuse* in the Glossary of Usage.

Shortening is a process similar to back-formation; it seems particularly popular today, although it has gone on throughout the history of the language. Some shortenings that have been around for a long time, like *piano* from *pianoforte*, are perfectly acceptable in both formal and casual writing. Others, however, like *exam* (from *examination*) and *dorm* (from *dormitory*), are more appropriate in casual and informal writing.

Some scientific and literary terms are formed from the names of inventors and discoverers or from characters in literary works. The word *volt*, for example, comes from Count Volta, who formulated that unit of measurement; similarly *ampere* is after Andre Marie Ampere. *Quixotic* and *lilliputian* describe qualities characteristic of literary figures (the hero of *Don Quixote* and the little folk of *Gulliver's Travels*). Forming *acronyms* is becoming a more and more common way of inventing new words, so that sometimes we forget the words are based on the initials of other words (VISTA, for example, which is from "Volunteers in Service to America," or CORE, the "Congress on Racial Equality"). Some words are apparently blends of two or more words whose meanings they reflect (*flaunt* from *flout* and *vaunt*, *slide* from *slip* and *glide*). And some words, including some of the earliest words in our language, are imitative of the thing they refer to (*splash*, *whack*, *zip*).

EXERCISES

1. The Pittsburgh Steelers derived their name from the main product of Pittsburgh. Is this derivation logical? Comment on the derivational process that must have occurred to yield the following team names:
   a. San Francisco 49'ers
   b. New York Mets
   c. Green Bay Packers
   d. Los Angeles Lakers
   e. Houston Oilers

2. Consider the names of your college and high school teams. What are their sources?

3. Choose a hobby, sport, or special interest of yours and make a list of at least twenty words that relate to it. Look those words up in a college dictionary (or better yet, in the *Oxford English Dictionary*) to see what their origin is and whether there is any pattern to their etymologies. Were many of the words, for instance, borrowed from a particular foreign language, or are most of them native? Were many of them borrowed at one period in the history of English? Were many of them

21b

borrowed from another field of interest? What can you tell about the history of your special interest from the history of the words that are common to it? Write an essay in which you relate the origin of the words to the social and national origins of the subject you have chosen.

4. The names of the astrological signs come from Latin; use your dictionary to answer the following questions:

   a. The word *Capricorn* comes from the Latin for "goat." What words that begin the same way as *Capricorn* might be related to qualities we associate with goats?

   b. What does *Taurus* mean? Can you find any related words?

   c. The word *Aquarius* is related to a great many other words through the root *aqua*. What does *Aquarius* mean? Find five words with related meanings.

   d. *Gemini* was the name of a recent spacecraft. You may need to use an encyclopedia to help you discover how this name is related to the astrological sign. What does this tell you about the sign of the zodiac with the same name?

   e. *Pisces* comes from the Latin *piscis*, meaning "fish." What words can you find having the beginning *pisc-* that share meaning with *Pisces*?

5. The following words are all taken from proper names. Check your college dictionary for the meanings of any of the words you are not familiar with and for the origins of all of them. Then take one of the groups and check the *Oxford English Dictionary* to discover as much as you can about how the words first came to be used. Write an essay in which you report your findings.

   a. *Science*: angstrom units, curies, ohms, roentgen rays, watts

   b. *Flowers*: dahlia, forsythia, fuchsia, poinsettia, wisteria

   c. *Cloth*: calico, cashmere, lisle, madras, worsted

   d. *Personality Traits*: cupidity, jovial, lunatic, mercurial, saturnine

   e. *Miscellaneous*: babel, dunce, jeremiad, pander, tantalize

21c

21c   Changes in Words

Not only does our language constantly add new words and throw off old ones, but the meanings of those words also change over time. We can distinguish between two kinds of meaning—denotative and connotative. *Denotative* meanings are what words refer to. *Red* denotes (refers to) a certain range of color, *chair* denotes a certain class of furniture, and *run* denotes a certain kind of action. *Connotative* meanings are the *values* and *emotions* we attach to words. After the Second World War, the word *red* took on both a new denotation ("communist") and a strong negative connotation, as expressed in the slogan of the time, "Better dead than red." To call someone a *red* was to attach to that person a value (evil) and an emotional reaction (fear and hatred), all related to the notion of "communist." When words change, they change not only in denotation but in connotation as well.

21c.1 Functional Shift

One of the most common changes in our language is the shift in the function of a word (that is, its part of speech). For instance, a word that was once a noun, denoting an object or idea, can come to be a verb as well, denoting an action or a state of being. The word *contact* was once a noun, denoting "touch" or "connection"; it later came to be used as a verb, denoting "get in touch with"; and recently, it has come to be used as an adjective (though not without some controversy) denoting a purpose or quality of being in touch, as in "contact person" or "contact disease." Sometimes a verb is simply shifted to a noun function while another noun with a somewhat different meaning is created with a derivational suffix, as in pairs like *combine / combination*; *move / movement*; *meet / meeting*. And sometimes a shift in pronunciation occurs when a verb becomes a noun. Consider the difference in pronunciation in these pairs:

> to *abuse* someone / physical *abuse*
> to *use* something / put to *use*
>> (shift from final *z*-sound to *s*-sound)

> to con*duct* a meeting / someone's *con*duct
> to per*fume* the house / someone's *per*fume
>> (shift in stress from second syllable to first)

21c

Some adjectives that become verbs also have a derivational form: for example, *rough, roughen*; *loose, loosen*; *black, blacken*.

Functional shift, along with other kinds of language change, is often open to criticism while it is happening, although we do not think to criticize the same phenomenon when it has already occurred. A number of shifts are sharply criticized in contemporary English, and these are included in the Glossary of Usage.†

21c.2   Other Changes in Denotation

Extension occurs when the area of meaning of a word is enlarged. The word *ticket*, for example, referred once to admission to a theater; now it means any piece of paper used for a purpose of admission, or it can denote a means of achieving something (as in, "He is our ticket to success"). *Chest* originally referred to a coffin and now denotes any kind of a large box or container (as in "chest of drawers"). *Companion* was once a person who shared bread, but now means someone who shares time, entertainment, or almost anything else.

A special kind of extension occurs when brand names come to represent a whole class of things: *band-aid*, *jello*, *kleenex*, and *xerox*, for instance, are no longer limited to the brand they originally named and consequently are often not capitalized.

Semantic extension, like functional shift, often causes controversy when a word is in the process of changing. Controversial uses of semantic extension are included in the Glossary of Usage.*

Restriction is the opposite of extension; it occurs when a word's meaning is narrowed. The word *starve*, for instance, once meant "to die"; later it came to mean specifically "to die of hunger," and now it has come to mean "to suffer severely from hunger." The word *meat* once meant any food (as it still does in our word *mincemeat*), the word *corn* any grain, *liquor* any liquid, and *deer* any animal.

Transfer occurs when a word takes on a nonliteral meaning. Metaphors and other figures of speech are examples of transfer; *frozen metaphors* are those which have become so much a part of our language that we no longer regard them as metaphors. Many frozen metaphors originally referred to parts of the body: the *mouth* of a river, the *hands* of a clock, the *teeth* of a gear, the

21c

†These include *above, author, chair, critique, impact, said, same, some,* and *such.*

*These include *aggravate, alibi, amount, angle, anticipate, anxious, any, apt, awfully, balance, between, bimonthly, contact, disinterested, expect, factor, farther, feedback, figure, fine, further, gotten, hopefully, in back of, individual, infer, input, less, liable, party, plus, utilize.*

jaw of a vise, and the *foot* of a table (or chair). Some Latin borrowings that originally denoted physical conditions now denote abstract ones: *depressed* came from a Latin word denoting "pushed down," *inspire* meant "breathe in," *intact* meant "not touched," and *insist* meant "stand on." Some native English words have undergone a similar evolution: *upset*, *breakdown*, *insight*.

Another kind of transfer is seen in the figure of speech known as *synecdoche*, in which a part of something comes to denote the whole: a field *hand*, counting *noses*, a *transistor* (radio). *Metonymy* is another figure of speech, in which a closely related object comes to denote something else. The word *candidate*, for example, once referred to a person seeking initiation or office who wore a white gown (from the Latin word *candidus*, "white"); the word *chair* has come to denote a committee chairman or chairwoman; and *board* has come to denote a governing body or payment for meals (as in "room and board"), by association with the table around which these activities are carried out.

21c.3   Changes in Connotation

Not only do words change in their denotative meanings, but the values or emotions we associate with them also change.

Elevation occurs when a word that once had a negative or neutral connotation comes to have a positive one. *Enthusiasm*, for instance, meant "fanaticism" in the eighteenth century, with a strong negative connotation; the word *minister* once meant "servant" and has moved from the negative connotation of that meaning to the positive connotations associated with a minister of state or a minister of the church; and the words *pretty*, *nice*, and *fond*, which now all have positive connotations, once had negative associations (*pretty* meaning "sly" and the other two "foolish").

Degradation occurs when a word that once had a positive or neutral connotation comes to have a negative one. The word *lust*, for instance, once meant "pleasure"; *immoral* meant "not customary"; *hussy* meant "housewife"; *libel* meant "writing"; and *reek*, *stink*, and *stench* meant simply "smell."

21c

EXERCISES

1. Following are examples of words that are undergoing a functional shift at the present time. For each, identify the part of speech traditionally attributed to the word. Then see if you can think of an example of current usage in which the word assumes another function.

access	feedback	mire	strike
baseline	freeze	pamper	summit
distance	information	panic	toy
doctor	jump	read	trial
end	key	stress	waffle

2. Suppose you heard the following statement on the news: "The Dow Jones Industrial Average gained a fraction in heavy trading today." Would you assume the "fraction" was closer to 1/8 or 7/8? Why? Include a discussion of the denotative and connotative meanings of *fraction* in your answer.

3. Compare the word choices used in the following descriptions of Mark Chapman:

   a. His eyes vacant, his hands toying with a tissue, a pudgy, 25-year old amateur guitar player and former mental patient whom police described as a "wacko" was charged yesterday with the murder of ex-Beatle John Lennon. He was sent to Bellevue Hospital for psychiatric tests. —Alton Slagle, "Charge Ex-Mental Patient as Killer,"
   New York Post, December 10, 1980

   b. Mr. Chapman had played the guitar in a rock band in high school in Georgia and had often expressed his love for the Beatles. Herbert J. Adlerberg, Mr. Chapman's court-appointed lawyer, said his client had attempted suicide in Honolulu in 1977, after which he was institutionalized, and in New York City two weeks ago. At the arraignment yesterday there were moments of confusion when the office of the Manhattan District Attorney mistakenly introduced the long criminal record of another man as Mr. Chapman's.—Paul L. Montgomery, "Police Trace Road to Lennon's Slaying,"
   New York Times, December 10, 1980

21c

4. The following sentences contain words used in archaic, obsolete, and rare senses. Provide the meaning of each underlined word as used in the context below; you will probably have to consult a college dictionary with etymological information or the *Oxford English Dictionary*. Then provide the current, central meaning of the word, again consulting a dictionary as necessary. Finally, determine what kind of change has occurred in denotation or connotation.

   a. He praised her with the most *violent* emotion.
   b. I was delighted by her *condescension* and grace.
   c. They attributed the victory to the king's divine *majority*.

    d. He traced the meteor's *career* through the solar system.

    e. It was an altogether *curious* work, a fitting tribute to her art.

5. All of the words underlined in the following sentences reflect the process of change in language. For each, provide an example of a use of the same word in a different context, and compare that use with the one provided. Identify the type of change that has occurred in connotation or denotation or both. Consult a dictionary as needed.

    a. Responsibility for the attack fell on a radical *arm* of the liberation front.

    b. She is a collector of rare, *vintage* automobiles of the 1920s.

    c. The only thing he could do to ease the pain was to take two *aspirin*.

    d. The bar was well stocked with over one hundred bottles of *rum*.

    e. The *coke* temporarily satisfied their need to replenish bodily fluids.

21d   Dictionaries and the English Lexicon

The *lexicon* of English—that is, the total words in the language that are available for our use—is constantly changing as new words come into the language, old words disappear from active use, and meanings of words shift. To define that lexicon is virtually impossible. Linguists estimate that the lexicon of English includes upwards of two million words. The largest unabridged dictionary in English has about 500,000. (It is "unabridged" in relation to shorter versions of the dictionary, not in relation to the lexicon of the language.)

On the other hand, we use only a small proportion of the total words available in the lexicon, and so for the purposes of most of us, an unabridged dictionary is more than adequate. And while it is handy to have such dictionaries available in a library, the best dictionary for use at home or at work is an abridged (*desk* or *college*) dictionary: one with roughly 100,000 to 150,000 entries.

The earliest collections of English words were published in the seventeenth century. These books were not meant to define common words, but were intended to be *glosses*: explanations of foreign and other unfamiliar or difficult words that a reader might come across. The first dictionary to resemble modern ones was written by Samuel Johnson in 1755 and called *A Dictionary of the English Language*. Johnson was concerned (as many are today) that our language was changing too rapidly and often in a way he considered confusing. His dictionary, Johnson said, was meant to "retard what we cannot repel": by writing down "correct" meanings and pronunciations, he hoped at least to slow the tide of change.

The first modern dictionary and the first in America was published by Noah Webster in 1828. Webster's work was based on his belief that languages constantly change, that the purpose of a dictionary is to reflect the way our language is actually used and to keep up with changes, and that the purpose of an *American* dictionary (as opposed to Johnson's *English* dictionary) is to record the language of Americans and not to try to force British patterns on American speakers.

Following Webster's example, modern dictionaries attempt to record the way language *is* used. Modern dictionaries are more like histories or biographies than like law books; they give us the story of words and describe how contemporary writers and speakers use them rather than tell us how we *ought* to use them.

If dictionaries base their definitions and other information on the actual use of words, how do they get this information? The most important step in the making of a dictionary is gathering *cite slips*, that is, recording on individual slips of paper the different uses of a word in different contexts, in both speech and writing. Editors sort and classify the cite slips, noting the different *areas* of meaning or *senses* in which a word can be defined. The definitions that we read in a published dictionary, then, are the result of a long and painstaking process of observing the language, gathering data about it, classifying those data, and writing up definitions, each of which is a generalization of the various ways in which a word is used.

21d

21d.1   Unabridged and Historical Dictionaries
Webster's Third New International Dictionary of the English Language. (G. & C. Merriam Co., 1981) is the best-known of all unabridged dictionaries. It caused a controversy when first published because it dropped almost all restrictive usage labels (like *nonstandard, colloquial, informal*) on the grounds that a dictionary's job is to describe the language, not to provide a book of

linguistic etiquette. (It does use the label *slang*, but only very occasionally.) So users of this dictionary, while they will be likely to find more words in it than in any of the other unabridged dictionaries, will not receive much guidance about the social status of various words or definitions. *Webster's Third* includes over 450,000 words. Although it does not include any proper names, it does include words used in all English-speaking countries, not just the United States. This is the dictionary on which *Webster's Ninth New Collegiate Dictionary* is based (see **21d.2**).

The Random House Dictionary of the English Language (Random House, 1973) is perhaps the only affordable dictionary for those who want an "unabridged" dictionary in their homes. It contains about 260,000 words, including names of persons and places, and is the book on which the *Random House College Dictionary* is based. Random House designed this dictionary partly in response to the "permissiveness" of *Webster's Third*, and so it includes restrictive usage labels to let a reader know when a particular word, spelling, or pronunciation is acceptable, and it includes comments on the usage of controversial forms (like, for instance, the difference between *uninterested* and *disinterested*).

Funk and Wagnalls New Standard Dictionary of the English Language (Funk and Wagnalls, 1963) is not as widely known as the first two, but it is an excellent dictionary, more inclusive than the Random House though not so recently revised. It is the dictionary on which *Funk and Wagnalls Standard College Dictionary* is based. Its roughly 450,000 entries include 65,000 proper names of persons and places.

The Oxford English Dictionary (The Clarendon Press, 1933, 1972, 1977) takes up twelve volumes, though there is a popular two-volume edition, photographically reduced from the original and published in 1971. This dictionary was originally entitled *A New English Dictionary on Historical Principles* and was issued one volume at a time between 1888 and 1933, with later supplements. It is most valuable for its detailed word histories, which trace the uses of each word from the time of its first recorded use in English (sometimes as far back as the eighth or ninth century) up until the time of publication. Nowhere is the history of word meanings so clear as in this dictionary, and perhaps in no other place can you gain such a clear idea of how our language is con-

21d

stantly changing. For that reason, the OED (as it is abbreviated) has influenced other dictionaries to place more emphasis on *etymology* (the history of words).

The *Dictionary of American English on Historical Principles* (University of Chicago Press, 1940), in four volumes, was planned on the same principles as the *Oxford English Dictionary*, but for American English. It traces the use of words by American writers from 1620 to 1900 and so is a good supplement to the OED, although it has not been updated with supplements.

21d.2 College Dictionaries

The most dependable abridged dictionaries are from publishers with a large enough editorial staff and a sufficiently scholarly approach to lexicography to insure that definitions and other information are based on reliable evidence. The dictionaries listed below have somewhat different features and different emphases, but owning and consistently using any one of these dictionaries will go a long way toward giving you strong control over your working vocabulary:

The American Heritage Dictionary, Second College Edition (Houghton Mifflin, 1982).

Funk and Wagnalls Standard College Dictionary (Funk and Wagnalls, 1974).

Random House College Dictionary, Revised Edition (Random House, 1982).

Webster's New World Dictionary, Second College Edition (William Collins and World, 1980). Also published in a paperback edition (complete) by Simon and Schuster, 1983.

Webster's Ninth New Collegiate Dictionary (Merriam-Webster, 1983).

21d

Anything smaller than these dictionaries will not be very helpful. If you do need a small paperback to carry with you, you should buy an abridgment of one of the college dictionaries, so that you can trust the data on which it is based; it will be helpful for checking spelling and some general word meanings when you do not have access to a better dictionary, but you should not try to make a paperback do the work of a good college dictionary. (And beware of supermarket "Websters" and other "home and office dictionaries," which are likely not to be worth the money you pay for them.)

Because dictionaries compress a large amount of information into a very small space, they use many abbreviations and conventions that you must understand in order to use them efficiently. We will use *Webster's Ninth New Collegiate* to illustrate the basic principles of a college dictionary. For more specific information about using your own dictionary, you should go to the user's guide at the front.

Webster's Ninth New Collegiate Dictionary (abbreviated WNC in the discussion below) is based on *Webster's New International Dictionary*, abridged from about 450,000 entries to roughly 160,000, but with all the scholarship and extensive data of the unabridged to support it. Figure 21.1 will show you most of the typical features of this dictionary and of most dictionaries. Each of the letters refers to the discussion below:

a. *Entry words* are listed in strict alphabetical order. Spaces and hyphens are ignored in alphabetizing: *dish* precedes *disheveled*, which in turn precedes *dish out*. (Names of persons, names of places, and abbreviations appear in separate lists at the end of the dictionary.) *Centered dots* indicate where a word may be divided (hyphenated) at the end of a line.

b. A *superscript* (a number raised slightly above the line) indicates two words that are spelled alike but have different meanings, as with the two different entries (one a verb, one a noun) for *disinterest*. (Closely related meanings of words are listed under the same entry word; see item g.)

c. *Spelling variants* are separated by the word *or* if they are considered roughly equivalent choices but by *also* if the first is preferred to the second.

d. *Pronunciation and stress* are indicated in back slashes (\ \). Stress is indicated differently in the Merriam-Webster dictionaries than in most others—that is, by a small vertical mark just before the stressed syllable (upper marks indicating primary stress and lower marks secondary stress). Variations in pronunciation are presumed to be roughly equal unless the second is preceded by *also* or a restricting label: notice that three different pronunciations are given for *dishabille*, although in each case only the last syllable of the word varies.

21d

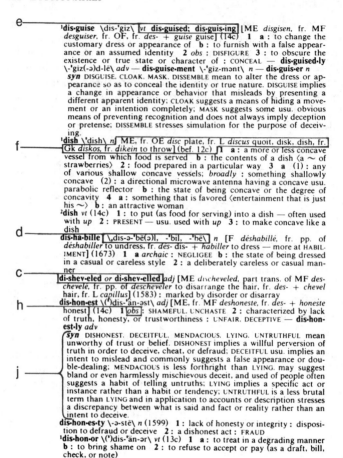

¹dis·guise \dis-'gīz\ *vt* dis·guised; dis·guis·ing [ME *disgisen,* fr. MF *desguiser,* fr. OF, fr. *des-* + *guise* guise] (14c) 1 a : to change the customary dress or appearance of   b : to furnish with a false appearance or an assumed identity   2 *obs* : DISFIGURE   3 : to obscure the existence or true state or character of : CONCEAL — dis·guised·ly \-'gīz(-ə)d-lē\ *adv* — dis·guise·ment \-'gīz-mənt\ *n* — dis·guis·er *n*
syn DISGUISE. CLOAK. MASK. DISSEMBLE mean to alter the dress or appearance so as to conceal the identity or true nature. DISGUISE implies a change in appearance or behavior that misleads by presenting a different apparent identity; CLOAK suggests a means of hiding a movement or an intention completely; MASK suggests some usu. obvious means of preventing recognition and does not always imply deception or pretense; DISSEMBLE stresses simulation for the purpose of deceiving.

¹dish \'dish\ *n* [ME, fr. OE *disc* plate, fr. L *discus* quoit, disk, dish, fr. Gk *diskos,* fr. *dikein* to throw] (bef. 12c) 1 a : a more or less concave vessel from which food is served   b : the contents of a dish ⟨a ~ of strawberries⟩   2 : food prepared in a particular way   3 a (1) : any of various shallow concave vessels; *broadly* : something shallowly concave   (2) : a directional microwave antenna having a concave usu. parabolic reflector   b : the state of being concave or the degree of concavity   4 a : something that is favored ⟨entertainment that is just his ~⟩   b : an attractive woman
²dish *vt* (14c) 1 : to put (as food for serving) into a dish — often used with *up*   2 : PRESENT — usu. used with *up*   3 : to make concave like a dish

dis·ha·bille \ˌdis-ə-'bē(ə)l, -'bil, -'bēl\ *n* [F *déshabillé,* fr. pp. of *déshabiller* to undress, fr. *des-* dis- + *habiller* to dress — more at HABILIMENT] (1673) 1 a *archaic* : NEGLIGEE   b : the state of being dressed in a casual or careless style   2 : a deliberately careless or casual manner

di·shev·eled *or* di·shev·elled *adj* [ME *discheveled,* part trans. of MF *deschevele,* fr. pp. of *descheveler* to disarrange the hair, fr. *des-* + *chevel* hair, fr. L *capillus*] (1583) : marked by disorder or disarray

dis·hon·est \(')dis-'än-əst\ *adj* [ME, fr. MF *deshoneste,* fr. *des-* + *honeste* honest] (14c) 1 *obs* : SHAMEFUL. UNCHASTE   2 : characterized by lack of truth, honesty, or trustworthiness : UNFAIR. DECEPTIVE — dis·hon·est·ly *adv*
syn DISHONEST. DECEITFUL. MENDACIOUS. LYING. UNTRUTHFUL mean unworthy of trust or belief. DISHONEST implies a willful perversion of truth in order to deceive, cheat, or defraud; DECEITFUL usu. implies an intent to mislead and commonly suggests a false appearance or double-dealing; MENDACIOUS is less forthright than LYING. may suggest bland or even harmlessly mischievous deceit, and used of people often suggests a habit of telling untruths; LYING implies a specific act or instance rather than a habit or tendency; UNTRUTHFUL is a less brutal term than LYING and in application to accounts or description stresses a discrepancy between what is said and fact or reality rather than an intent to deceive.

dis·hon·es·ty \-ə-stē\ *n* (1599) 1 : lack of honesty or integrity : disposition to defraud or deceive   2 : a dishonest act : FRAUD

¹dis·hon·or \(')dis-'än-ər\ *vt* (13c) 1 a : to treat in a degrading manner   b : to bring shame on   2 : to refuse to accept or pay (as a draft, bill, check, or note)

FIGURE 21.1. Sample Page from *Webster's New Collegiate*

²**dishonor** n [ME *dishonour*, fr. MF *deshonor*, fr. *des-* + *honor* honor] (14c) **1** : lack or loss of honor or reputation **2** : the state of one who has lost honor or prestige : SHAME ⟨would rather die than live in ∼⟩ **3** : a cause of disgrace ⟨became a ∼ to his family⟩ **4** : the nonpayment or nonacceptance of commercial paper by the party on whom it is drawn ⟨*syn* see DISGRACE⟩— **dis·hon·or·er** \-'än-ər-ər\ n

dish out vt (1641) : to give freely ⟨the blatant picturing of crime and disorder *dished out* by the cinema —R. T. Flewelling⟩

dish·pan \'dish-,pan\ n (1872) : a large flat-bottomed pan used for washing dishes

dishpan hands n pl but sing or pl in constr (1944) : a condition of dryness, redness, and scaling of the hands that results typically from repeated exposure to, sensitivity to, or overuse of cleaning materials (as detergents) used in housework

dish·rag \'dish-,rag\ n (1839) : DISHCLOTH

dish·ware \'dish-,wa(ə)r, -,we(ə)r\ n (1946) : tableware (as of china) used in serving food

dish·wash·er \-,wȯsh-ər, -,wäsh-\ n (15c) **1** : a worker employed to wash dishes **2** : a machine for washing dishes

dish·wa·ter \-,wȯt-ər, -,wät-\ n (15c) : water in which dishes have been or are to be washed

dishy \'dish-ē\ adj **dish·i·er; -est** chiefly Brit (1961) : ATTRACTIVE

¹**dis·in·ter·est** \(')dis-'in-trəst; -'int-ə-,rest, -ə-rəst, -ərst; -'in-,trest\ vt (1612) : to divest of interest

²**disinterest** n (1658) **1** : lack of self-interest : DISINTERESTEDNESS **2** : DISADVANTAGE **3** : lack of interest : APATHY

dis·in·ter·est·ed adj (1612) **1 a** : not having the mind or feelings engaged : not interested ⟨telling them in a ∼ voice —Tom Wicker⟩ ⟨Introverted. Unsocial . . . *Disinterested* in women —J. A. Brussel⟩ **b** : no longer interested ⟨husband and wife become ∼ in each other —T. I. Rubin⟩ **2** : free from selfish motive or interest : UNBIASED ⟨a ∼ decision⟩ ⟨∼ intellectual curiosity is the lifeblood of real civilization — G. M. Trevelyan⟩ *syn* see INDIFFERENT — **dis·in·ter·est·ed·ly** adv — **dis·in·ter·est·ed·ness** n

usage *Disinterested* and *uninterested* have a tangled history. *Uninterested* orig. meant impartial, but this sense fell into disuse during the 18th century. About the same time the original sense of *disinterested* also disappeared, with *uninterested* developing a new sense — the present meaning — to take its place. The original sense of *uninterested* is still out of use, but the original sense of *disinterested* revived in the early 20th century. The revival has since been under frequent attack as an illiteracy and a blurring or loss of a useful distinction. Actual usage shows otherwise. Sense 2 of *disinterested* is still its most frequent sense, esp. in edited prose; it shows no sign of vanishing. A careful writer may choose sense 1a of *disinterested* in preference to *uninterested* for emphasis ⟨teaching the letters of the alphabet to her wiggling and supremely *disinterested* little daughter —C. L. Sulzberger⟩ Further, *disinterested* has developed a sense (1b), perhaps influenced by sense 1 of the prefix *dis-*, that contrasts with *uninterested* ⟨when I grow tired or *disinterested* in anything, I experience a disgust —Jack London, letter, 1914⟩ Still, use of senses 1a and 1b will incur the disapproval of some who may not fully appreciate the history of this word or the subtleties of its present use.

e. Following the pronunciation is an abbreviation for the *part of speech*, along with *inflected forms*. (All abbreviations are listed in the "Explanatory Notes" in the front.)

f. *Etymology* follows the part-of-speech label and inflections. Numerous abbreviations are used, listed in the front matter. The abbreviation *fr* is used to indicate "comes from." In the etymology of *dish*, we learn that the word came from a Middle English (*ME*) word (since the Middle English word is not given, we assume it has the same spelling as Modern English *dish*), which came from the Old English (*OE*) word *disc*, meaning "plate," which came from the Latin (*L*) word *discus*, meaning "disk" or "dish." That word in turn came from the Greek (*Gk*) word *discos*, which came from the word *dikein*, meaning "to throw." (Since no language is specified for *dikein*, it is the same as the previous language, Greek.) Notice that some words, like *disinterested*, do not have an etymology, because the meaning of the word is made up of the prefix *dis-* and the root *interested*. You can find the etymology by looking up those two parts. Immediately before the definitions for some words are given the dates of their first recorded use in English. *Dishabille*, for instance, was used as early as 1673, and *disinterest* was used as early as 1612 with the first meaning and 1658 with the second. When no date is given for a word, that is because it is not possible to determine the earliest use of the word.

g. The use of *definitions* in WNC is illustrated by the words *disinterest* and *disinterested*. Since the etymology comes early in the entry, it seems natural that in WNC the oldest definition should come first; thus, the first meaning of *disinterest* is "not interested," while the second is "unbiased." The editors often provide a quotation using the word, to help define it in its natural context. When contexts are given, the swung dash (∼) stands for the main entry word, as, for example, in the contexts for *disinterested*: "husband and wife become *disinterested* in each other" or "*disinterested* intellectual curiosity is the lifeblood of real civilization."

h. All dictionaries use *restrictive labels* of some sort, but WNC is unusual in that it uses very few labels that restrict the use of a word to certain contexts. The only usage label is *slang*. WNC does

21d

use temporal and regional labels, however, as in the abbreviation *obs.* (obsolete) for the first definition of *dishonest* and the abbreviation *chiefly Brit.* (chiefly British) before the first meaning of *dishy.* While many dictionaries also have some label to show when foreign words should be italicized in print or underlined in manuscript (those foreign words that have not been naturalized or "Anglicized"), WNC has no distinguishing marks; instead it lists foreign words in the special section at the back of the dictionary.

i. Usage paragraphs discuss controversial word uses, as in *disinterested.*

j. Synonomy notes and paragraphs provide guidance on varying shades of denotations and connotations, while in other cases WNC indicates just a brief synonym or two, or a cross-reference like the one for *dishonor* ("see *disgrace*").

21d.3 Dictionaries of Synonyms

Although all the reliable college dictionaries have synonyms scattered throughout their definitions, most writers find eventually that they need to have the more detailed information found in a good dictionary of synonyms or thesaurus. The classic example of a dictionary of synonyms is *Roget's Thesaurus* (the title comes from the Latin word for "treasure"), but a number of variations of Roget have also developed, along with other dictionaries of synonyms and thesauruses:

The New Roget's Thesaurus in Dictionary Form, edited by Norman Lewis, 1978.

Roget's International Thesaurus, 4th ed., edited by Robert L. Chapman, 1977.

Roget's II: The New Thesaurus, by the editors of the *American Heritage Dictionary*, 1980.

Webster's Collegiate Thesaurus, by the editors of *Webster's New Collegiate Dictionary*, 1976.

Webster's New World Thesaurus, by the editors of *Webster's New World Dictionary*, 1983.

21d

21d.4 Specialized Dictionaries

In addition to dictionaries of synonyms, there are many other useful and interesting dictionaries that specialize in a particular area of language. Following are some that you might find helpful from time to time:

Bernstein, Theodore M. *The Careful Writer: A Modern Guide to English Usage*. New York: Atheneum, 1965.

Bliss, A. J. *A Dictionary of Foreign Words and Phrases in Current English*. London: Methuen, 1983.

Follett, Wilson. *Modern American Usage: A Guide*, ed. Jacques Barzun. New York: Hill & Wang, 1966.

Fowler, H. W. *A Dictionary of Modern English Usage*, rev. Sir Ernest Gowers, 2nd ed. Oxford University Press, 1983.

Freeman, William. *A Concise Dictionary of English Idioms*. London: English Universities Press, rev. ed., 1976.

Klein, Ernest. *A Comprehensive Etymological Dictionary of the English Language*, 2 vols., Elsevier, 1971.

Morris, William and Mary. *Morris Dictionary of Word and Phrase Origins*. New York: Harper & Row, 1977.

Newmark, Maxim. *Dictionary of Foreign Words*. Westport, CT: Greenwood Press, 1965.

Onions, Charles T., et al. *The Oxford Dictionary of English Etymology*. Oxford University Press, 1966.

Partridge, Eric. *Dictionary of Clichés*. London: Methuen, 5th ed., 1978.

Partridge, Eric, ed. *A Dictionary of Slang and Unconventional English*. New York: Macmillan, 9th ed., 2 vols., 1985.

Partridge, Eric. *Origins: A Short Etymological Dictionary of Modern English*, 4th ed., 1966.

Shipley, Joseph T. *Dictionary of Word Origins*. Totowa, NJ: Littlefield Adams, 1979.

Wentworth, Harold and Stuart Flexner. *Dictionary of American Slang*. New York: Crowell, 2nd supplemented ed., 1975.

Whitford, Harold C. and Robert J. Dixson. *Handbook of American Idioms and Idiomatic Usage*. New York: Regents, 1973.

Wright, Thomas. *Dictionary of Obsolete and Provincial English*, 1967.

21d   EXERCISES

1. Use your college dictionary to look up the following words:

credit	mulberry	stomach
high	orient	will
lather	plot	
liaisons	plus	

Explain the meaning of each descriptive label in the definitions.

2. Compare entries for the following words in an unabridged dictionary,

a college dictionary, and a thesaurus. Which entry do you prefer? Which do you think would be more useful? For what purposes? Explain.

city	lively	shirt
circulate	peddle	trauma
deserve	pattern	
hop	rake	

3. Look up the following words in five dictionaries, being sure to consult at least one unabridged and one college dictionary. For each, provide the most descriptive definition you find and the most prescriptive. Decide which definition you prefer and consider which entry is easiest to read, is arranged most logically, and provides the most information for your usual purposes. What can you tell about the social history of the word from its etymology?

bad	gyp	squeeze
beat	hit	waste
dump	junk	
grind	kill	

4. Trace the etymology and usage of the following words in the *Oxford English Dictionary*. Identify functional shifts, changes in denotation, and changes in connotation.

aggravate	host	squeeze
career	liable	virgin
curious	liquor	
fool	majority	

21d

22

SPELLING

22a Coping with English Spelling

The famous British playwright George Bernard Shaw once complained that English spelling was so unpredictable that it would be perfectly reasonable to spell the word "fish" as *ghoti*. As Shaw pointed out, we often use the spelling *gh* to represent the sound of "f," as in the word *rough*; the letter *o* can represent a short "i" sound, as in the word *wo*men; and the spelling *ti* can represent the "sh" sound in a word like *acti*on.

Why is English spelling so troublesome and unpredictable? There are at least two reasons. First, spelling was originally a way to represent speech in writing. As pronunciation changed over the centuries, so did spelling, so that our spelling system was, up until about the fifteenth century, roughly phonetic. When manuscripts had to be copied by hand, each scribe would spell the words as they represented the sounds of his particular regional dialect, and as manuscripts were copied, the scribes changed the spelling to reflect the changes that had occurred. With the invention of printing, however, written texts were given a permanency and distribution they had not had before. Many copies could be made at once, distributed throughout the country and different dialect areas, and saved for many generations. Eventually, the spelling of English as it was spoken in the London area came to be standard, and because words became "frozen" in print, it took much longer for a change in pronunciation to be reflected in the spelling. That explains why words like *rough*, *women*, and *action* are spelled in a fashion that appears irregular. It also explains why today we have words like *knight* that are spelled with so many silent letters. At one time all its letters were pronounced.

The second reason English spelling is so confusing is that we have borrowed words from hundreds of other languages with different spelling systems and then have gradually changed the spelling and pronunciation. *Marriage*, for instance, was borrowed from Old French, but both the spelling and pronunciation have changed. Because of these borrowings and changes, we have many combinations of letters in English that represent one sound (*ie*, *ee*, and *ea*, for instance, can all represent the long *e* sound, as in *wield*, *feet*, and *real*). Likewise, one combination of letters can represent more than one sound (*ea*, for instance, represents the long *e* sound in *real* but an *ah* sound in a word like *heart*). For these reasons, it is often difficult to tell from the pronunciation of a word how it ought to be spelled, or vice-versa.

There are, however, some regularities in English spelling that you can learn, and some of the apparent exceptions in fact follow patterns of their own, as the following sections will show. But it is also a good idea to get in the habit of doing some things to help yourself wherever you have problems. Try keeping a spelling notebook, for instance: each time you have to check the spelling of a word in the dictionary, write it down and underline the troublesome part of the word. You might also note the origin of the word (Greek and Latin roots, for instance, have a great deal of regularity in their spelling; see **21b.2**) and the pattern (or exception) that explains its spelling (see **22b**). Even if you do not regularly go back to the notebook, the act of writing it down will help you remember. In any case, keeping your own notebook of words that are troublesome to *you* will be far more beneficial than sitting down and memorizing lists of commonly misspelled words.

22b   Common Spelling Patterns

22b

22b.1   *Ie* and *ei*
If the vowel rhymes with *be*, write i before e except after c:

IE:	believe	pierce
	chief	relief
	field	thief
	grief	wield
	niece	yield

EI: ceiling   perceive
       conceit   receive
       conceive   receipt
       deceive

EXCEPTIONS:

IE: financier

EI: caffeine   protein
       either   seize
       leisure   weird
       neither

(Note that *either* and *neither* are often pronounced with a long I sound, and *leisure* is often pronounced to rhyme with *pleasure*.)

When the vowel sounds rhyme with *pay*, write e before i:

EI: beige   sleigh
       eight   veil
       freight   vein
       neighbor   weigh
       reign

When the sound is neither *ee* nor *ay*, the vowel will usually be written with e before i:

EI: counterfeit   heifer
       fahrenheit   height
       forfeit   heir
       foreign   stein

EXCEPTIONS:

IE: friend
       mischief

22b

22b.2 Final *e* Before a Suffix
Drop the final silent e before adding a suffix that begins with a vowel but NOT before one that begins with a consonant. There are many exceptions, but the majority of words will fit the pattern:

	SILENT E DROPPED BEFORE A VOWEL	SILENT E KEPT BEFORE A CONSONANT
excite	exciting, excitable	excitement
double	doubly	
guide	guidance, guided	guidebook
like	likable, liking	likely
probable	probably	
love	loving, lovable	lovely
use	usable, usually	useful

(But note that *likeable* is also an acceptable spelling for *likable*.)

Some words drop the final e before the suffixes *-dom*, *-ful*, *-ly*, *-ment*, and *-y*:

-DOM:	wise	wisdom
-FUL:	awe	awful
-LY:	due	duly
	true	truly
	whole	wholly
-MENT:	abridge	abridgment
	argue	argument
	judge	judgment

The e is also dropped in three numbers (notice that in two of them, the v also changes to an f):

five	fifth
nine	ninth
twelve	twelfth

The e is usually retained before suffixes beginning with a or o if the preceding consonant is a soft c or g (pronounced like "s" or "j"); but the e is dropped, following the usual pattern, before i:

22b

	SILENT E KEPT BEFORE A AND O	SILENT E DROPPED BEFORE I
change	changeable	changing
notice	noticeable	noticing
revenge	vengeance	revenging
engage		engaging
rage		raging
advantage	advantageous	

courage	courageous
marriage	marriageable
outrage	outrageous
service	serviceable

Finally, a few other words retain the e before a vowel:

acre	acreage
dye	dyeing
(note the contrast with the words *die* / *dying*)	
here	herein
hoe	hoeing
line	lineage
mile	mileage
shoe	shoeing
singe	singeing
there	therein

22b.3   Changing *y* to *i*

If a word ends in a consonant followed by y, change the y to i before adding a suffix beginning with any letter EXCEPT i:

CONSONANT + Y	CHANGE Y TO I:	KEEP Y:
apply	applied	applying
carry	carries	carrying
cry	cried	crying
defy	defiance	defying
forty	fortieth	
happy	happiness	
lovely	lovelier	
ninety	ninetieth	
party	parties	partying
study	studious	studying

If a vowel precedes the y, keep it:

VOWEL + Y

day	days
dismay	dismayed
joy	joyful
lay	layperson
pay	payment
play	player

A few common exceptions are these words that retain the y:

baby	babyhood
lady	ladylike
shy	shyness

And finally, if a proper name like *Mary* or *Patty* is made plural, the y remains:

Mary	Marys
Patty	Pattys

22b.4   Doubling of Final Consonants

Double the final consonant before adding a suffix if the final consonant follows a *single vowel* and if it ends on an *accented syllable*. (Note that all one-syllable words are accented.)

ONE-SYLLABLE WORDS

drag	dragged
hid	hidden
kid	kidded
sit	sitting
wrap	wrapping

TWO-SYLLABLE WORDS WITH ACCENT ON THE LAST SYLLABLE

abhor	abhorred
admit	admitted
begin	beginning
occur	occurring
regret	regrettable

If more than one vowel precedes the final consonant, the consonant will NOT be doubled:

appear	appearing
rain	raining
feed	feeding

22b

If the last syllable is not accented, the consonant will NOT be doubled:

consider	considered
reckon	reckoned

EXCEPTION:

| benefit | benefited | (*or*) benefitted |

Notice that the accent shifts in some words when a suffix is added, so that the same word may have a single consonant with some endings and a double consonant with others:

FINAL SYLLABLE ACCENTED		FINAL SYLLABLE UNACCENTED
confer	conferring	conference
defer	deferred	deference
infer	inferring	inference
prefer	preferring	preference
refer	referred	reference

If the final consonant follows another consonant, it will not be doubled:

insist	insistent
turned	turning

The only common exception to the doubling pattern is the word *questionnaire*, in which the final consonant is doubled even though it is preceded by a double vowel. (But other forms of *question* follow the standard pattern, like *questioning*.)

22b.5 Doubled Letters with Prefixes and Suffixes

If a prefix ends with the same letter the word begins with, or if a suffix begins with the same letter the word ends with, be careful NOT to drop one of the doubled letters:

book	+	keeper	=	bookkeeper
clean	+	ness	=	cleanness
dis	+	satisfied	=	dissatisfied
mis	+	spell	=	misspell
pre	+	eminent	=	preeminent
				(or pre-eminent; see **24a.1**)
un	+	necessary	=	unnecessary
wool	+	ly	=	woolly

22b.6 *-able* and *-ible*

If the root of a word is itself an independent word, the suffix will usually be spelled *-able*:

accept	+	able	=	acceptable
comfort	+	able	=	comfortable

profit	+	able	=	profitable
tax	+	able	=	taxable

Some of these words are complete except for the dropped final *e*:

believe	+	able	=	believable
like	+	able	=	likable (or) likeable
size	+	able	=	sizable (or) sizeable

If the root of a word does not exist as an independent word, the ending is usually *-ible*:

compat	+	ible	=	compatible
cred	+	ible	=	credible
ed	+	ible	=	edible
vis	+	ible	=	visible

EXCEPTION:

cap	+	able	=	capable

The ending will usually be spelled *-ible* if the word ends in a double consonant that includes at least one *-s*. (This is true even if the double consonant is followed by a silent e that is dropped.)

collapse	+	ible	=	collapsible
defense	+	ible	=	defensible
response	+	ible	=	responsible
resist	+	ible	=	resistible

admiss	+	ible	=	admissible
permiss	+	ible	=	permissible
transmiss	+	ible	=	transmissible

Notice that if you listen to the pronunciation of *flexible*, it follows the pattern of consonant pairs with *-s*, since the *x* is pronounced like *ks*:

flex	+	ible	=	flexible

22b

A few words that do not have independent roots nevertheless add an *-able* because they were originally independent words whose final syllable is dropped when the *-able* ending is added:

irritate	+	able	=	irritable
separate	+	able	=	[in]separable
tolerate	+	able	=	[in]tolerable

Finally, a few words are exceptions to all the patterns:

> gullible
> discernible
> formidable
> durable
> flammable

22b.7   Distinguishing -*ally* and -*ly*

Another pair of suffixes that are often confused are -*ly* and -*ally*. The suffix -*ly* is added to adjectives to form adverbs:

fair	+	ly	=	fairly
usual	+	ly	=	usually
swift	+	ly	=	swiftly
sincere	+	ly	=	sincerely

The suffix -*ally* is added to adjectives ending in ic to form adverbs:

academic	+	ally	=	academically
basic	+	ally	=	basically
scientific	+	ally	=	scientifically

EXCEPTION:

| public | + | ly | = | publicly |

22b.8   Plural and Present Tense -*s* and -*es* Endings

The normal ending for regular noun plurals is -*s*:

| dog | dogs |
| cake | cakes |

Likewise, the regular ending for the third-person singular present tense of the verb is usually spelled -*s*:

| walk | he walks |
| make | she makes |

However, when a noun or verb ends in ch, s, sh, x, or z, an -**s** ending alone would be difficult to pronounce, and so an -*es* is added instead:

| NOUNS: | church | churches |
| | kiss | kisses |

22b

	wish	wishes
	box	boxes
	buzz	buzzes
VERBS:	latch	she latches
	pass	he passes
	fish	she fishes
	fix	he fixes
	whizz	it whizzes

Words that end in o sometimes add -s and sometimes -es to form the plural of the noun or present tense of the verb. Some words are acceptable either way:

	-s ENDING	-es ENDING
auto	autos	
Latino	Latinos	
memo	memos	
piano	pianos	
pimento	pimentos	
pro	pros	
buffalo		buffaloes
echo		echoes
hero		heroes
mosquito		mosquitoes
Negro		Negroes
potato		potatoes
tomato		tomatoes
veto		vetoes
motto	mottos	mottoes
no	nos	noes
zero	zeros	zeroes

22b.9   Changing *f* to *v*

With most nouns that end in f or fe, change the f or fe to v and add -es to form the plural. But notice that not all words that end in f are changed; to be sure you choose the right ending, check your dictionary:

	CHANGE FROM F TO V	NO CHANGE
leaf	leaves	
life	lives	
thief	thieves	

wolf	wolves	
hoof	hooves (*or*)	hoofs
roof		roofs

Notice that some nouns will change form, while the correspond-ing verb will not:

| knife | knives | he knifed |

EXERCISES _____

Decide whether each of the following spellings is correct. Determine which pattern governs this spelling, and tell whether the spelling is consistent with that pattern or an exception to it.

automaticly	inscrutable	objectionable	siege
clutches	ironicly	plainness	shelved
deductable	magically	rein	sinuses
gracious	manageable	roguish	surveillance
grovelling	mementoes	seive	wearisome

22c   Problems with Pronunciation

Because spelling changes more slowly than speech, certain mis-spellings are the result of common (and completely acceptable) variations in pronunciation. Notice in the following words the letters that are frequently omitted in spelling because they are commonly omitted in pronunciation:

Arctic	literature
accidentally	maladjusted
aspirin	mathematics
bachelor	parliamentary
boundary	primarily
business	privilege
criminal	probably
February	sophomore
incidentally	temperature
interest	temperament
laboratory	veteran
literacy	

Be careful not to leave an *-ed* ending off a verb when the verb precedes *to*. Because *-ed* is pronounced like *t* before the word *to*, it merges with the *to* in pronunciation and is easy to forget in spelling:

supposed to   used to

Likewise, do not confuse *of* with *have*. The word *have* is often pronounced like *of* when it follows certain words (especially modals ending in *d* or *t*), so it is easy to misspell:

could have   might have

Because people frequently add syllables in pronunciation that are not represented in spelling, the spelling may be incorrect, as in the following words:

athletics   (*not* atheletics)
disastrous   (*not* disasterous)
grievous   (*not* grievious)
mischievous   (*not* mischievious)
similar   (*not* similiar)

EXERCISES

Following is a list of words frequently misspelled because we glide over sounds and syllables when we pronounce or because we pronounce a sound which in fact is not included in the spelling. Decide which ones are misspelled and correct all errors.

extrordinary	maintainence	particuliar	reminiscience
govenor	mavrick	pecular	rigamarole
horscope	monsterous	penitentiary	salve
ingenius	omniscient	prepostrous	sociable
magnificence	ostentatious	pyrmid	vegtable

22d

22d Frequently Confused Words

Many words are misspelled in English because they are *homonyms* (spelled differently but pronounced alike) or because they are spelled similarly to other words. Studying the following list will help you to become aware of whether you frequently confuse such words. Remember to use the list for reference whenever you are unsure.

accept	verb, "to take"
except	verb, "to leave out"
	preposition, "leaving out"
access	noun, "a way in"
excess	noun, "too much"
addition	noun, "increase"
edition	noun, "issue of a book"
adapt	verb, "to adjust"
adept	adjective, "skilled"
adopt	verb, "to take as one's own"
advice	noun, "guidance"
advise	verb, "to guide"
affect	verb, "to influence"
	noun, "an emotion"
effect	verb, "to bring about"
	noun, "result"
aid	noun, "help"
aide	noun, "helper, assistant"
aisle	noun, "a space between rows"
isle	noun, "island"
alley	noun, "a back street"
ally	noun, "a supporter"
allude	verb, "to refer"
elude	verb, "to avoid"
allusion	noun, "reference"
illusion	noun, "mistaken belief"
already	adverb, "previously"
all ready	pronoun/adverb, "everyone (or everything) prepared"
altar	noun, "table, place of sacrifice"
alter	verb, "to change"
altogether	adverb, "completely"
all together	pronoun/adverb, "everyone (or everything) in one place"

22d

angel	noun, "supernatural messenger"
angle	noun, "corner"
appraise	verb, "to determine the worth of"
apprise	verb, "to inform"
arc	noun, "curve"
ark	noun, "boat"
ascent	noun, "rising"
assent	noun, "agreement"
	verb, "to agree"
assistance	noun, "help"
assistants	noun, "helpers," plural of "assistant"
bazaar	noun, "fair"
bizarre	adjective, "strange"
bare	adjective, "naked"
bear	noun, "animal"
	verb, "to carry"
birth	noun, "to be born"
berth	noun, "sleeping place"
board	noun, "piece of wood"
	noun, "food" (as in "room and board")
bored	adjective, "uninterested"
born	adjective, "alive"
borne	adjective or verb, "carried"
breath	noun, "air taken in through the lungs"
breathe	verb, "to take in air"
canvas	noun, "cloth"
canvass	verb, "to poll"
Calvary	noun, "hill on which Jesus was crucified"
cavalry	noun, "regiment of soldiers on horseback"
capital	adjective, "upper case" or "major"
	noun, "top of an architectural column"
	noun, "wealth, net worth"
	noun, "major city" or "seat of government"
capitol	noun, "building which houses state or national government"
censor	verb, "to not allow"
censure	noun, "condemnation"

choose	verb, "to pick"
chose	verb, "picked," past tense of "choose"
cite	verb, "to acknowledge or point out"
site	noun, "a place"
	verb, "to locate"
sight	noun, "ability to see"
coarse	adjective, "not fine"
course	noun, "path" or "unit of study"
complement	noun, "completer"
	verb, "to provide balance"
compliment	noun, "flattery"
	verb, "to flatter"
conscience	noun, "inner sense of right and wrong"
conscious	adjective, "aware"
corps	noun, "military group"
corpse	noun, "dead body"
council	noun, "legislative body"
counsel	noun, "advice"
dairy	noun, "place to manufacture milk products"
diary	noun, "daily journal"
dam	noun, "barrier to hold back water"
damn	verb, "to consign to hell"
defer	verb, "to put off"
differ	verb, "to disagree, be dissimilar"
deference	noun, "respect, yielding"
difference	noun, "lack of similarity"
diffidence	noun, "lack of confidence"
descent	noun, "the way downward"
dissent	noun, "disagreement"
desert	verb, "to leave"
	noun, "dry land"
dessert	noun, "sweet course at end of meal"
device	noun, "a machine or implement for getting something done"
devise	verb, "to create or think up"
dully	adverb, "in a boring manner"
duly	adverb, "in a proper manner"

22d

| dyeing | verb, "coloring" |
| dying | verb, "losing life" |

| envelop | verb, "to enclose" |
| envelope | noun, "enclosure for a letter" |

| fair | adjective, "objective" or "pale" |
| fare | noun, "food" or "entrance money" |

| formerly | adverb, "before" |
| formally | adverb, "not casually" |

| forth | adjective, "forward, ahead" |
| fourth | adjective, "number four" |

| gorilla | noun, "jungle animal" |
| guerilla | noun, "soldier who works through surprise raids" |

gild	verb, "to cover with gold"
guild	noun, "organization of craftspeople"
guilt	noun, "responsibility, remorse"

| hear | verb, "listen and understand" |
| here | adverb, "in this place" |

| heard | verb, past tense of "hear" |
| herd | noun, "group of animals" |

| hole | noun, "gap" |
| whole | adjective, "in one piece" |

| holy | adjective, "sacred" |
| wholly | adjective, "completely" |

| human | noun or adjective, "Homo sapiens" |
| humane | adjective, "acting like a human" or "kind" |

incidence	noun (singular), "frequency of an occurrence"
incident	noun, "occurrence, happening"
incidents	noun, plural of "incident"

| its | pronoun, possessive of "it" |
| it's | pronoun/verb, contraction of "it is" |

| later | adverb, "after a while" |
| latter | adjective, "last mentioned" |

lead	noun (pronounced to rhyme with *head*), "a metal"
	verb (pronounced to rhyme with *seed*), "to guide"
led	verb (pronounced to rhyme with *head*), past tense of "lead"

lesson	noun, "something to learn"
lessen	verb, "to cause to be less"
lightning	noun, "electricity caused by a storm"
lightening	verb, "making (or becoming) lighter"
lose	verb, "to misplace"
loose	adjective, "not tight"
maybe	adverb, "perhaps"
may be	verb, "might be"
miner	noun, "one who works in a mine"
minor	adjective, "small or insignificant"
	noun, "someone under age"
moral	adjective, "good"
	noun, "lesson"
morale	noun, "state of mind"
passed	verb, past tense of "pass"
past	adjective, "previous"
patience	noun, "quality of being patient"
patient	adjective, "steadfast and uncomplaining"
	noun, "person under treatment"
patients	noun, plural of "patient"
peace	noun, "absence of war"
piece	noun, "part, section"
personal	adjective, "intimate"
personnel	noun, "employees"
	adjective, "pertaining to employees"
plain	adjective, "without decoration"
plane	noun, "surface" or "aircraft"
	verb, "shave off wood"
playwright	noun, "maker of plays"
play writer	noun, "one who writes plays"
precede	verb, "to go before"
proceed	verb, "to continue"
presence	noun, "being present"
presents	noun, "gifts"
principle	noun, "moral conviction"
principal	adjective, "major"
	noun, "head of a school"

2d

prophecy	noun, "prediction"
prophesy	verb, "to make a prediction"
purpose	noun, "aim"
propose	verb, "to suggest"
quiet	adjective, "silent"
quit	verb, "to stop"
quite	adverb, "very"
respectfully	adverb, "with respect"
respectively	adverb, "in reference to"
right	adjective, "correct"
rite	noun, "ceremony"
stationary	adjective, "not moving"
stationery	noun, "paper for writing letters"
statue	noun, "sculpture"
stature	noun, "height" or "influence"
statute	noun, "law"
straight	adjective, "without curves"
strait	noun, "narrow passage, especially in water"
taut	adjective, "tight"
taught	verb, past tense of "teach"
taunt	verb, "to tease"
than	preposition, "besides"
	conjunction, "as"
then	adverb, "at that time"
their	pronoun, possessive form of "they"
there	adverb, "in that place"
they're	pronoun/verb, contraction for "they are"
through	preposition, "in and out"
	adjective, "finished"
thorough	adjective, "complete"
to	preposition, "toward"
too	adjective or adverb, "also"
two	adjective, "one plus one"
track	noun, "course or road"
tract	noun, "pamphlet"
weather	noun, "atmospheric conditions"
whether	conjunction, "if"

22d

wear	verb, "to have clothes on"
were	verb, past tense of "be"
we're	pronoun/verb, contraction of "we are"
where	adverb or conjunction, "in what place"

who's	pronoun/verb, contraction of "who is"
whose	pronoun, possessive form of "who"

your	pronoun, possessive form of "you"
you're	pronoun/verb, contraction for "you are"

EXERCISE

Provide meanings for the following pairs of frequently misspelled words.

aught / ought
confident / confidant
disburse / disperse
exercise / exorcise
extent / extant
flout / flaunt
grisly / grizzly
knave / nave
inequity / iniquity
magnate / magnet

marital / martial / marshal
mote / moat
mute / moot
peak / peek / piqué
pendant / pendent
populace / populous
prodigy / protege
shear / sheer
track / tract
vial / vile / viol

22e Differences in British and American Spelling

Be aware of differences in British and American spelling. Most of these differences have come about because spelling of words has changed more quickly in America than in Great Britain, particularly under the influence of Noah Webster's first American dictionary in 1828 (see **21d**).

1. American English has e in words where British usage retains the older Latin and Greek spellings ae and oe:

AMERICAN:	anemia	BRITISH:	anaemia
	anesthetic		anaesthetic
	encyclopedia		enyclopaedia
	fetus		foetus

2. The prefixes meaning "in" or "toward" are usually spelled *im-* and *in-* in American usage, *em-* and *en-* in British usage:

| AMERICAN: | impanel | BRITISH: | empanel |
| | inquire | | enquire |

But notice that some words still have the older *en-* prefix in American English as a variation of *in-*, while others have only the *en-* form:

AMERICAN:	enclose	OR	inclose
	entomb	OR	intomb
	entrust	OR	intrust
	enlarge		
	enlist		
	engrave		

3. The prefixes *-ize* and *-yze* are often spelled *-ise* and *-yse* in British usage:

AMERICAN:	analyze	BRITISH:	analyse
	apologize		apologise
	criticize		criticise

But notice that some words still have the older *-ise* suffix in American English as a variation of *-ize*, while others have only the *-ise* form:

AMERICAN:	advertise	OR	advertize
	apprise	OR	apprize
	exercise		

4. In words borrowed from French, the American *-or* ending corresponds to the British *-our* ending:

AMERICAN:	armor	BRITISH:	armour
	clamor		clamour
	color		colour
	flavor		flavour
	labor		labour
	odor		odour
	vigor		vigour

22e

5. Likewise, the American o in the middle of words is often spelled ou in British:

| AMERICAN: | mold | BRITISH: | mould |
| | smolder | | smoulder |

6. When the ending *-tion* follows a c, it is spelled *-xion* in British:

| AMERICAN· | connection | BRITISH: | connexion |
| | inflection | | inflexion |

7. Words that end in el often double the l before adding a suffix in British, whereas the l remains single in American:

AMERICAN:	leveled	BRITISH:	levelled
	quarreling		quarrelling
	traveler		traveller

8. While the e is omitted before a suffix is added in certain words in American usage, British usage keeps the e

| AMERICAN: | acknowledgment | BRITISH: | acknowledgement |
| | judgment | | judgement |

EXERCISES

Which of the following are not correct American spellings? Correct them.

authorise	inlist
candour	inrage
contour	recognise
complexion	reconnoitre
convexion	subpoena

22f   Foreign Plurals

Many foreign words retain their foreign plurals when they come into English, although as they become assimilated they tend to develop regular English plural forms. Following are some of the most common foreign nouns with their foreign plural forms and, where appropriate, their newer English forms. Whenever both forms exist, you will be safest using the foreign plural in formal writing:

	FOREIGN PLURAL	ENGLISH PLURAL
agendum	agenda	agendas
alga	algae	
alumna (female)	alumnae	alums
alumnus (male)	alumni	alums
analysis	analyses	
appendix	appendices	appendixes
basis	bases	
crisis	crises	
criterion	criteria	
curriculum	curricula	curriculums
datum	data	datums
focus (noun)	foci	focuses
hypothesis	hypotheses	
index	indices	indexes
memorandum	memoranda	memorandums, memos
phenomenon	**phenomena**	
radius	radii	radiuses
stratum	strata	stratums
syllabus	syllabi	syllabuses

Note that in some uses, English plural forms (like *datums* and *indexes*) have a slightly different meaning from the foreign plurals.

EXERCISES

For the following words, provide the foreign plural and, if you can verify its existence in a good college dictionary, the English plural also.

antenna	parenthesis
chateau	sanctum
delirium	sanitarium
matrix	scapula
momentum	solarium

22f

Part Seven

PUNCTUATION AND MECHANICS

23

PUNCTUATING SENTENCES

The purpose of punctuation is to set off the various elements in a sentence or paragraph in order to make the meaning clear. In speech, we convey punctuation through pauses, inflection of voice, and even gestures. In writing, we communicate punctuation through space left on the page, upper-case letters, and special marks of punctuation. For example, we indicate the beginnings and ends of words by leaving space between them; we mark off a sentence with a capital letter at the beginning and a period at the end; and we signal new paragraphs either by skipping a line on the page or by indenting several spaces or both.

Punctuation is *conventional*: that is, a mark of punctuation signals whatever people in general agree it should mean; so using a period where your readers conventionally expect a comma can lead to confusion. While punctuation often reflects the pauses and gestures of speech, there is not a one-to-one correspondence between pauses in speech and commas or periods in writing. Punctuation marks serve the same purpose in writing that pauses and gestures do in speech, but one cannot always be easily translated into the other, and pauses in speech are not a safe guide to written punctuation.

23a   End Punctuation

23a.1   Periods
Periods are used to mark the ends of sentences that are statements or commands:

It's raining.
Please shut the door.
He wondered whether she had heard the news.

Use a period to end one sentence before a second sentence starting with a coordinating conjunction only if you want to cause a sharp break in order to emphasize the second sentence. Otherwise, join such sentences into one, with a comma or semicolon before the coordinating conjunction (see **23b.1** and **23c.1**). Compare the effect of the following sentences:

I wanted to go to the movie. But I did not want to go with my brother.
I wanted to go to the movie, but I did not want to go with my brother.

A period is also used occasionally when the writer wants something less than a full sentence (a phrase or word) to be sharply separated from other sentences:

Oh no—another blizzard on the way.
What did you eat for supper? A delicious steak and a rotten potato.

But be cautious about using periods in this way (see **23f**).

23a.2   Question Marks

Use question marks at the end of sentences that ask direct questions, but not at the end of indirect questions:

DIRECT QUESTIONS:	Is it raining outside?
	She asked, "Do you like war movies?"
INDIRECT QUESTIONS:	I wonder whether it's raining outside.
	She asked if I like war movies.

The subject and verb of the direct questions are inverted from the order they would follow in a statement: *do you* rather than *you do* and *is it* rather than *it is*. And when the direct question is part of dialogue, it is enclosed in quotation marks. Indirect questions are embedded in a subordinate clause, usually beginning with *whether* or *if*, and the subject and verb of the indirect question are in normal subject-verb order. The direct question requires a question mark and the indirect question a period. Question marks

23a

may also be used after just a word or phrase, particularly when indicating conversation:

> "I heard Janine was in the hospital."
> "Really?"
> "But she doesn't want anyone to know."
> "Why?"

23a.3 Exclamation Marks

Exclamation marks are used to mark the ends of sentences that express surprise or other strong emotion. They may also be used after a word or phrase that expresses a single thought or emotion, to separate it from sentences before and after:

> Watch out for the ice!
> I hate this class!
> The Redskins won in the second half after a really bad start!
> Hurray!

Exclamation marks should be used sparingly; overusing them is like beating your reader over the head with how surprising or amazing a situation is. Consider this paragraph:

> After I had arrived at college, I was amazed to see how small my dorm room was! My room at home had been more than twice as large! And I was distressed to hear that I would have to share my dorm room with a roommate!

Consider how the following revision sounds less hysterical; the italicized words add the details that create a sense of surprise or distress—without ever using an exclamation mark:

> After I had arrived at college, *leaving my spacious home behind*, I was amazed to see how small my dorm room was: *it measured only 8 x 6*. My room at home had been more than twice as large *and I had it all to myself*. I was *even more* distressed to hear that I would have to share this *tiny cell* with a *very large* roommate *who had an even larger wardrobe*.

Because readers will not be overwhelmed by the exclamation marks, they are more likely to concentrate on what the writer is saying.

23a

EXERCISES

1. Determine whether each of the following requires a period, question mark, or exclamation mark. Provide a brief justification for each choice.
   a. I wonder if he ever received that check
   b. Thousands of activists chanted, "Give peace a chance"
   c. Do you know the zip code for Hanksville
   d. Are these the negatives you wanted to discard
   e. Gentlemen may shout peace, peace—but there is no peace
   f. Would you be willing to advise him to seek psychological help
   g. Not in a million years
   h. If she's so sure of herself then why did she make that alternate plan
   i. What makes me so mad is her insistence on correctness in speech
   j. I asked whether it was possible to access another terminal
2. In the following example, where has the writer placed exclamation marks to the greatest effect? Where should the exclamation marks be changed to periods?

   I had always dreamed about visiting the Everglades, and finally I was taking my first trip there! With a park ranger, I waded through knee-deep water half the afternoon. Then I saw it—right in front of me! A mother alligator not two feet away! I remember those teeth—the biggest teeth I think I've ever seen! I screamed and tried to turn to run, but it's hard to run in water!

23b Commas

23b.1 With Coordinating Conjunctions

Use a comma to join coordinate clauses only if a coordinating conjunction precedes the second clause. (If you use a comma *without* a coordinating conjunction, you will create a comma splice; see **23g**.) The coordinating conjunctions are *and*, *but*, *so*, *yet*, *for*, *or*, and *nor*.

> The professor could not understand why her students failed, *and* the students couldn't either.
> I would have gone with you, *but* I wasn't feeling well.
> I have often wondered why she came, *yet* I would never ask.

23b

Notice, however, that *short* coordinate clauses may be joined with only a coordinating conjunction, without a comma:

> Henry ate steak and Diane ate clams.

Notice also that a comma is *not* used when the coordinating conjunction introduces a predicate instead of an entire clause. In the sentences below, the comma joins a compound predicate that has one subject:

UNCONVENTIONAL PUNCTUATION:

The dean gloomily explained next year's budget, and told the faculty that the university could afford no raises.

The attorney explained that he would take the case if he was convinced of the client's honesty, and if he was sure the client was innocent.

The incorrect punctuation can be fixed either by omitting the comma or by giving the second predicate a subject, so that the comma joins two clauses instead of two predicates (phrases):

NO INTERNAL PUNCTUATION:

The dean gloomily explained next year's budget and told the faculty that the university could afford no raises.

The attorney explained that he would take the case if he was convinced of the client's honesty and if he was sure the client was innocent.

COMMA JOINING TWO CLAUSES:

The dean gloomily explained next year's budget, and *he* told the faculty that the university could afford no raises.

(There is no effective way to break the second sentence into two independent clauses.)

23b.2   In Series

Use commas between the items in a series of words, phrases, or clauses of roughly equal importance, along with a coordinating conjunction (usually *and, but*, or *or*) before the last item in the series:

This term I'm taking calculus, introductory sociology, Spanish, and freshman composition.

Next summer I plan to fly to Mexico City, find a cheap place to stay, get a job washing dishes or waiting tables, and practice my Spanish.

The picnic was wonderful because Gertrude brought home-

23b

made banana bread, Jill brought fresh shrimp, and Harry brought his famous chicken quiche.

In casual or informal writing, the comma is omitted before the last item in the series. In formal writing, however, the comma is usually included:

CASUAL OR INFORMAL: We drove through Ohio, Pennsylvania and West Virginia.

FORMAL: We drove through Ohio, Pennsylvania, and West Virginia.

Use commas to separate a series of *coordinate* adjectives:

The movie was funny, poignant, and brilliantly acted.
We went to see a funny, poignant, and brilliantly acted movie.

Notice that each of the three adjectives is *coordinate* because each modifies the noun *movie*; notice that you could substitute *and* for the commas—a clue that the words are coordinate. In the following sentence, however, a comma is not used because the adjectives are not coordinate; *wonderful* modifies the whole phrase that follows it, "war movie," and you would not use an *and* between *wonderful* and *war*:

We went to see a wonderful war movie.

Use commas to separate a series of independent clauses with a coordinating conjunction before the last clause:

When we took our fast trip through England we ate breakfast in London, we ate lunch in Windsor, and we ate dinner in Oxford.

Occasionally the coordinating conjunction is omitted before the last clause, particularly in fiction or in informal situations where you want to create a sense of movement or immediacy:

The dancing kept up, the drinking kept up, the noise went on.
—Ernest Hemingway, *The Sun Also Rises*

23b.3 With Introductory Modifiers

23b

Use a comma between an introductory modifier and the rest of the sentence. Introductory modifiers may be single words, phrases, or clauses, and they may act as either adverbs or adjectives:

Afterwards, I went to bed.	ADVERB
In the morning, I was amazed.	PREPOSITIONAL PHRASE
	SERVING AS ADVERB

| Because the professor arrived look-ing unusually haggard and tense, I knew something was wrong. | ADVERB CLAUSE |

| Tired, I went quickly to bed. | ADJECTIVE |

| Wondering why you came, I decided to ask you. | PARTICIPIAL PHRASE |
| | SERVING AS ADJECTIVE |

It is not necessary to put a comma after a very short introductory clause:

> After you arrived I knew something was wrong.

Be careful not to confuse a gerund phrase that functions as the subject of the sentence with a participial phrase. Since a subject should never be separated from its verb with a comma, you should not use a comma after a gerund phrase:

| PARTICIPIAL PHRASE: | Seeing him so sick, I decided to send for the doctor. |

| GERUND PHRASE, UNCONVENTIONAL: | Seeing him so sick, worried me. |

| GERUND PHRASE, CONVENTIONAL: | Seeing him so sick worried me. |

23b.4   With Nonrestrictive Modifiers

Use commas to set off nonrestrictive modifiers, but do not use them with restrictive modifiers. A *restrictive* modifier is one that helps to *define* or *limit* the word it modifies, while a *nonrestrictive* modifier is one that adds information that is interesting but not necessary to understand the word in question. The following examples should illustrate the difference. Both the restrictive and the nonrestrictive modifiers are enclosed in brackets.

23b

Relative Clauses:

| RESTRICTIVE: | Books [that are too long] are not likely to be read. |

NONRESTRICTIVE: The book, [which is about the first woman paratrooper], is not yet in the book stores and must be ordered from the publisher.

Prepositional Phrases:

RESTRICTIVE: The old houses [at the far end of the street] were demolished.

NONRESTRICTIVE: The old houses, [in various states of decay], were demolished.

Adverb Clauses:

RESTRICTIVE: The professor would never fail a student [because his homework was late].

NONRESTRICTIVE: The professor would never fail a student, [because she was too soft-hearted].

Verbal Phrases:

RESTRICTIVE: The students [making the highest grades] have the best chance to get into medical or law school.

NONRESTRICTIVE: Amanda, [making the highest grades in her class], is sure to get into her choice of medical school.

Appositives:

RESTRICTIVE: My brother [John] is the youngest of all my brothers.

NONRESTRICTIVE: My youngest brother, [John], is a wonderful singer.

23b.5 With Absolute Phrases

Always separate absolute phrases from the main clause with commas. An *absolute* phrase (see **13h.4**) is a participial phrase with its own subject; in the following examples, the absolute phrases are enclosed in brackets:

The murderer looked insanely jealous, [her hand gripping the knife with desperation].

[His lecture notes yellowed and his eyes dull], the professor seemed to have been teaching for centuries.

23b

23b.6   With Transitional Expressions
Use commas to separate conjunctive adverbs and other transitions from the rest of the sentence, regardless of where in the sentence they appear. A transition in the middle of a sentence must have a comma on both sides:

> Nevertheless, he won the race.
> The day was extremely dull, however.
> The neighbors, needless to say, were angry.

23b.7   With Contrasting Expressions
Use commas to set off phrases that indicate the contrast of one thing with another. When they come in the middle of a sentence, such phrases should have a comma on both sides:

> Unlike you, I detest apples.
> Oranges, not apples, are the tastiest fruit.

23b.8   In Direct Address
Use commas to set off the names of people being addressed:

> You know, Patricia, how difficult that is.
> Ms. Jensen, will you please step over here?
> Have you ever met Patricia, Ms. Jensen?

23b.9   With Interjections
Use commas to set off interjections (you can also sometimes use exclamation marks; see **23a.3**):

> Oh dear, I forgot the salt.
> Good heavens, the roast tastes awful!

23b.10   In Titles, Addresses, and Dates
When a person's name is followed by a degree or other indication of title, the title should be set off with commas:

> Donald M. Perry, Jr.
> J. R. Smith, III
> Alberta Sexton, Ph.D.

23b

When a name with a title is part of a sentence, use a comma after the title as well:

> Alberta Sexton, Ph.D., will be the luncheon speaker.

Use a comma between the day of the month and the year:

> January 23, 1984

If the date is part of a sentence, a comma may or may not follow the year:

> January 23, 1984, is the Bradleys' fiftieth anniversary.
> January 23, 1984 is the Bradleys' fiftieth anniversary.

The comma is omitted if only the month and year are used:

> The Bradleys will celebrate their fiftieth wedding anniversary in January 1984.

Commas are also omitted if the date-month-year order is used:

> The Bradleys will celebrate their fiftieth wedding anniversary on 23 January 1988.

Use commas to separate the elements in an address (except the zip code, which is never preceded by a comma) when they are run together rather than set off on separate lines as on an envelope:

> London, England
> 2115 Irene Rd., Cleveland, Ohio 44124

When an address is included in a sentence, the last element should be followed by a comma:

> He lived in London, England, for three years.
> She moved to 2115 Irene Rd., Cleveland, Ohio 44124, last year.

23b.11 To Prevent Misreading

Even if it means violating one of the previous principles, use a comma where you need it to prevent misreading. Quite often, these uses of commas will reflect a pause in speech:

CONFUSING: Soon after she arrived home.

                  (On first reading, one expects something to fol-
                  low, since the whole sentence reads like an intro-
                  ductory adverb clause. A comma would prevent
                  this misreading.)

CLEAR: Soon after, she arrived home.

CONFUSING: Those who prefer to take geology instead of
                  chemistry.

                  (Here too a first reading misleads the reader to
                  expect something to follow, because the whole
                  sentence sounds like a complex subject that
                  requires a predicate.)

CLEAR: Those who prefer to, take geology instead of
                  chemistry.

EXERCISES

Do the following sentences require commas? Provide a brief justification
for each comma you insert, referring to the rules above.

1. Teratology the study of deformities derives its name from the Greek
   word for monster.
2. Hearing the train whistle caused Zach to look up in anticipation and
   delight.
3. The blues is a distinctly American sound yet it has often received
   more attention in Paris than New York.
4. All roads may lead to Rome but my mother and I got hopelessly lost
   trying to drive there from Naples.
5. The Gamble House one of the finest examples of the arts and crafts
   architecture in America is located in Pasadena California.
6. The most hard working of all the students in the class she despaired
   when others received substantially higher grades.
7. Their new mailing address is 1735 E. 19th Street Brooklyn New York
   11229 and their phone number is 212-929-8771.
8. You know I can't tolerate such behavior Susan.
9. Exhausted and penniless he stared at the brightly lit interior imagining a warm fire a table laden with delicious hot food and large beds
   with clean white linen.
10. It was a charming older home whose turn-of-the-century decor
    enhanced its character.

23c Semicolons

Semicolons share something with both commas and periods. They are like commas in the sense that they are used to separate elements *within* a sentence, but they are like periods in that they sometimes separate independent clauses. There are only two situations in which they are normally used.

23c.1 To Separate Independent Clauses

Use a semicolon to join two main clauses when there is no coordinating conjunction:

> Sally joined the aerobics class a week late ; she found the rest of the class was far ahead of her.

> Freshmen begin the fall term on September 1 ; other students don't have to come until September 5.

Use a semicolon with a coordinating conjunction if the clauses are long or if there are many commas within the clauses:

> After the beautiful sunset, the swim in the lake, and the walk along the beach, there was little to say ; but each knew how the other felt.

> (A comma could be used in place of the semicolon, but because the first clause is long and has a number of internal commas, the semicolon more clearly separates the two main clauses.)

> The office workers decided to strike against the university for better pay ; and after a long and bitter debate that lasted three hours, the faculty agreed to support them.

> (Here too a comma could be used in place of the semicolon, or the semicolon could be used without the conjunction *and*; with both the semicolon and the *and*, however, the sentence reads more clearly and emphatically.)

Use a semicolon between independent clauses whenever the first clause starts with a conjunctive adverb. Inexperienced writers sometimes neglect to do this because they confuse conjunctive adverbs (words like *however* and *nevertheless*) with coordinating conjunctions. While a coordinating conjunction can be used after

23c

a comma, a conjunctive adverb cannot without creating a comma splice (see **23g**):

> She learned how to play the piano when she was only five; however, at age twenty-five she could hardly remember anything about it.

Contrast this sentence with the following one, which uses a comma and a coordinating conjunction:

> She learned how to play the piano when she was only five, but at age twenty-five she could hardly remember anything about it.

21c.2   To Separate Items in Series

Although commas are normally used to separate items in a series (see **23b.2**), use a semicolon when the items in the series have internal commas:

> Jonathan has lived in Des Moines, Iowa; Orange, California; Houston, Texas; and Blacksburg, Virginia.

> Wayne brought the egg-drop soup; Ken, the orange-flavored chicken; Connie, the stir-fried broccoli; Deborah, the fried rice; Carl, the wine; and Josie, the dessert.

EXERCISES

Which sentences below require semicolons? (Other punctuation may also be missing.) Provide a brief justification for each semicolon you insert, referring to the rules above.

1. Many labels suggest the products are "natural" nevertheless, they often contain lots of sugar, salt, and other considerably less than healthy ingredients.
2. Hall defines "the hidden dimension" in human interaction as our need for a certain amount of personal space a measurement which will vary from individual to individual situation to situation and culture to culture.
3. Because this is a delicate variety, cover the plants carefully before the first frost be sure not to remove the cover prematurely in the spring.
4. I was put off by their tasteless advertising campaign but I bought the car.
5. Many top executives in our company do not have college degrees

23c

however, this is a trend which has been reversing itself in the last two decades.

6. The most memorable sights were the Palace of Versailles the chateaux of the Loire Valley and the Cathedral of Notre Dame.
7. Sow the seeds for both perennials and biennials in the nursery bed they can be moved in the fall or transplanted in the spring.
8. The participants in the final drawing were John Cummings, a lawyer from Quincy, Massachusetts, Janet Baldoch, a pediatrician from Augusta, Georgia, and Phil Costantino, a welder from Albany, New York.
9. I have seen at least thirty films in the last year not one has had half the impact on me that this one has.
10. He graduated *magna cum laude* moreover he was perhaps the most popular member of his class.

23d   Colons

23d.1   Between Independent Clauses

Use a colon to separate two independent clauses when the first one points ahead to the second and when the second one explains or amplifies the first. While a semicolon acts like a substitute for a coordinating conjunction, a colon usually acts like a substitute for the phrase "that is." If you cannot decide whether to use a semicolon or a colon between two independent clauses, ask yourself whether a coordinating conjunction or "that is" would be more appropriate:

> There were many things wrong with the car when she took it in for the first check-up: the water pump needed to be replaced, the brakes had to be adjusted, the oil needed changing, and about half a dozen other adjustments were needed.

Often the second clause will be a quotation:

> I always remember the beginning of the Gettysburg Address: "Fourscore and seven years ago . . ."

23d

23d.2   Before Lists

While the part of the sentence before the colon must usually be a complete independent clause, the second part can be simply a list:

According to her shopping list, she needed mostly dairy products: milk, cheese, yogurt, and ice cream.

But notice that occasionally a list may precede a colon, providing that what comes after it is an independent clause with a word that refers to the list before the colon, as *these* refers to the list in the sentence below:

Milk, cheese, and yogurt: stacks of these filled her arms.

Do not use a colon before a list if what precedes it is not a complete independent clause:

UNCONVENTIONAL:	After school she had to: go to the bank, mail a package at the post office, and pick up her boots at the shoe repair shop.
CONVENTIONAL:	After school she had to do several errands: go to the bank, mail a package at the post office, and pick up her boots at the shoe repair shop. (or)
	After school she had to go to the bank, mail a package at the post office, and pick up her boots at the shoe repair shop.

23d.3 Other Uses

Use a colon between a title and subtitle of a book or article:

The Art of Fishing: How to Become an Expert in Three Days

Use a colon to separate the hour from the minutes:

7:23 P.M.
10:30 A.M.

When citing a reference to a book of the Bible, use a colon to separate the chapter from the verse or verses:

Genesis 40:1-10
John 3:16

EXERCISES

Are the following colons used correctly? If they are, explain why, citing the relevant guideline. If not, rewrite the sentence using conventional punctuation. Are any of these questions of punctuation dependent on the context?

1. Save a life: give blood.
2. He had just one thought in mind: to get into the burning building quickly and to get his girlfriend out even faster.
3. The company is trying to: increase productivity to record levels during the second quarter, expand its subsidiaries in Canton, Ohio, and increase its efficiency through new uses of robotics.
4. Researchers have barely scratched the surface: genetic engineering is a newborn, and no one can be sure what it will grow up to be.
5. I am tired of your constant jokes and pranks: so I'm going home now.
6. Toyota recently set up two new companies: one is a relatively small operation in Paducah, Kentucky; the other, in Wytheville, Virginia, rivals some of Ford's largest operations in Dearborn.
7. I decided to try the roquefort: but I found it was inferior in taste and texture to the blue cheese.
8. Few people in the United States concern themselves with hunger in the Third World: far more are conscious of the latest fad diet.
9. My copy of *Milton: Complete Poems and Major Prose* has a thick layer of dust on it.
10. Please think about your decisions carefully: this will help you to make the right choice.

23e Dashes and Parentheses

Dashes are sometimes used like commas and parentheses to set off nonrestrictive modifiers, and sometimes they are used like colons. They have the effect of making the sentence seem more emphatic and less formal than commas or colons do, often suggesting an abrupt shift in thought.

Be sure to distinguish between a dash and a hyphen. A dash is *sentence* punctuation; it is used to set off elements within a sentence. A hyphen, on the other hand, is *word* punctuation and is used to break words at the end of a line or to join compound words. When writing, your dash should clearly be longer than a hyphen; otherwise, especially when it comes at the end of a line, it can be mistaken for a hyphen. On the typewriter, use two hyphens, with no spaces before, between, or after, to make a dash.

23e.1 Dashes with Nonrestrictive Modifiers

Use dashes to set off nonrestrictive modifiers when you want to create more dramatic emphasis than commas would create:

> Her favorite color—a pale, rather washed-out blue—was predominant in every room.

> The students came to class—completely unprepared—the Monday after homecoming.

23e.2 Dashes to Set Off Independent Clauses

Use dashes sparingly to set off independent clauses in the middle of other sentences:

> The book he was reading—I found it to be terribly written—has been open to the same page for at least three months.

23e.3 Dashes Before Interjections and Brief Comments

In casual or informal contexts, it is appropriate to use a dash after interjections and brief comments:

> Oh nuts—I've lost my glasses again.
> Poor Sam—I knew this would happen.

In dialog, use a dash to indicate a break in speech or thought:

> "Where's Herman?"
> "I think he's—oh—he's here."
> "How are you?"
> "I'm—uh—well—I guess I'm OK."

23e.4 Dashes Before or After Lists and Summary Statements

In casual or informal contexts, use a dash when you want to begin a statement with a list or summary and want that part of the sentence to point ahead to the rest of it. (In formal contexts, you would use a colon in such situations; see **23d.2.**)

> Geology, biology, and chemistry—all he was taking this year was science.

> A city full of contrasts between rich and poor—that was how London impressed me.

23e

23e.5   Parentheses

Use parentheses to set off nonrestrictive modifiers when you want to de-emphasize the modifier in relation to the rest of the sentence. (Parentheses tend to highlight or emphasize less than commas and considerably less than dashes.)

> The ERA (Equal Rights Amendment) has caused controversy not just in the United States but around the world.
>
> The milk you are drinking (which is very old) is not healthy.

EXERCISES

In the following sentences, would you place the italicized words in parentheses or between dashes? Why?

1. My friend Margaret *the least likely of all my friends to find happiness in a career* just got a wonderful job.
2. Five key companies dominate business as well as research *not only in the U.S. but throughout the world.*
3. Many important chemicals could be manufactured *cheaply and easily* through gene-splicing.
4. The Rockville *Maryland* plant is now the number one producer of the drug.
5. A new Japanese company expects to quadruple profits *from $10 million to $40 million* within two years.
6. Lubrizol, a corporate investor in Genentech, owns about one-fifth *actually 17 percent* of this new and rapidly growing company.
7. Most of the company's employees *about 90 percent* are shareholders.
8. Scientists are learning not only how to read DNA *deoxyribonucleic acid* but also how to write it.
9. The discovery of oncogenes, interferon, and growth hormones *these are only the beginning.*
10. He gingerly took the first step *his heart pounding with fear and glory* onto the lunar surface.

23f   Sentence Fragments

A *sentence fragment* is part of a sentence that has been punctuated as though it is a complete sentence, with a period, exclamation mark, or question mark at the end. While some sentence fragments are acceptable, especially to create emphasis in informal writing (see **23a.1**), generally you should be sure that when you use end punctuation, you really are marking the end of a complete sentence. The most common kinds of fragments result from punctuating phrases or dependent clauses as though they were full sentences. In the following sentences, a period separates a complete sentence from phrases or dependent clauses. In order to make the punctuation conventional, either change the period to a comma or eliminate the punctuation altogether (and change the capital letter that follows to a small letter). In some cases, the modifying phrase or clause will read more clearly if it comes before instead of after the independent clause:

UNCONVENTIONAL: I asked to take Professor Nelson's course. Because I had heard he was so good.

Because is a conjunction that introduces a subordinate clause, which must be attached to an independent clause (see **13g.3** for other subordinating conjunctions):

CONVENTIONAL: I asked to take Professor Nelson's course, because I had heard he was so good. (or)
Because Professor Nelson was so good, I asked to take his course.

UNCONVENTIONAL: Janie won the first-place trophy. Being the best golfer on the team.

Being is a participial adjective (see **13d**) and introduces a participial phrase (see **13h.3**), which is not conventionally punctuated as a sentence. You can either attach it to the sentence that has the words it modifies (in this case, *being* modifies *Janie*), or you can use an independent form of the verb *be* and attach the clause to the first sentence with a subordinating conjunction:

CONVENTIONAL: Being the best golfer on the team, Janie won the first-place trophy. (or)
Because she was the best golfer on the team, Janie won the first-place trophy.

UNCONVENTIONAL: I noticed, after an hour or so, his strange look. Which seemed to indicate that he had removed himself a long way from his surroundings.

23f

Which is a relative pronoun that introduces a relative clause, which must be attached to an independent clause (see **13g.5** for other relative pronouns):

CONVENTIONAL: I noticed, after an hour or so, his strange look, which seemed to indicate that he had removed himself a long way from his surroundings.

23g   Comma Splices

A comma splice is created when you join two independent clauses with a comma. They need to be either clearly joined with a coordinating conjunction or clearly separated, with a period ending the first and a capital letter beginning the second. You can also correct a comma splice by using a semicolon between the two clauses, which has the effect of clearly setting them off yet establishing a logical connection between them.

UNCONVENTIONAL: I asked the accountant if he would explain exactly why I had underpaid my taxes, he couldn't do it.

CONVENTIONAL: I asked the accountant if he would explain exactly why I had underpaid my taxes, **but** he couldn't do it. (or)
I asked the accountant if he would explain exactly why I had underpaid my taxes. He couldn't do it. (or)
I asked the accountant if he would explain exactly why I had underpaid my taxes; he couldn't do it.

UNCONVENTIONAL: Kim wanted to see the new group playing at After Sundown, so did I.

(Notice that in this sentence, *so* is not a coordinating conjunction, but an adverb that means "also" or "too.")

CONVENTIONAL: Kim wanted to see the new group playing at After Sundown, **and** so did I. (or)
Kim wanted to see the new group playing at After Sundown. So did I. (or)

23g

> Kim wanted to see the new group play-
> ing at After Sundown; so did I.

Commas are often used between independent clauses to emphasize balance and parallelism (even in formal writing; see examples in **18e**). Sometimes, comma splices can also be used effectively
in fiction and in informal writing when you want to join short
sentences together to create an effect of immediacy:

> You understand me, he made some reservations, but on the whole
> the book to him was sound.—Ernest Hemingway, *The Sun Also Rises*

> It was not only a popularity contest, it was a *cosmetic* popularity
> contest.   —Tom Wolfe, *The Right Stuff*

> I was carried out later on a stretcher, an x-ray showed a minor crack
> and a small split in the girdle of the pelvis.
>   —Norman Mailer, *An American Dream*

But use this technique cautiously.

23h   Fused Sentences

In a fused sentence, two independent clauses have been run together
with no punctuation. In order to correct it, use any of the methods described above for commas splices: join them with a comma
and a coordinating conjunction; join them with a semicolon; or
separate them with a period and a capital following:

UNCONVENTIONAL: He asked me a question I didn't answer
                  it.

CONVENTIONAL: He asked me a question, but I didn't
                  answer it. (or)
                  He asked me a question. I didn't answer
                  it. (or)
                  He asked me a question; I didn't answer
                  it.

EXERCISES ───────────────────────────

Revise the following fragments, fused sentences, and comma splices by
rewriting them or inserting the necessary punctuation.

1. Although he was clearly capable of understanding differential calculus.

23h

2. When my cat got hit by a car, I took him to a veterinarian, two days and $120 later the cat was fine again.
3. He asked me a question he had no business asking me it was so personal and pointed.
4. Just for your information, Pa.
5. In that scene Peter shows that he doesn't care about people he is an animal just like everyone else.
6. Since we all know the difference between premeditated murder and manslaughter.
7. To what extent you answer these questions is your business, my business is to make judgments based on what you say.
8. We had a good dinner later we went dancing.
9. No matter what your justification was.
10. To err is human, to forgive is divine.

24
PUNCTUATING WORDS

24a Hyphens

24a.1 To Join Compound Words

Use a hyphen to join two words in making a new word. Throughout the history of English, new words have been formed by joining two older words. When the words are first used together, they are written as two separate words, but as they come to be thought of as a single unit, they are hyphenated: eventually, the hyphen will disappear and the words will be written together. For example, before the word *roommate* was written as a single word, it was written *room mate* and later *room-mate*.

A hyphenated word, then, is in transition from two separate words to a single word. Consequently, it is often difficult to know whether to write a word as two words, as one hyphenated word, or as a solid (unhyphenated) word. Since the status of hyphenated words changes so quickly, it is best to consult your dictionary. (Most dictionaries indicate hyphenated words by using a hyphen in the main entry instead of the dot that is usually used to show a syllable break.) For instance, the following word is used in all three ways at the moment:

head waiter
head-waiter
headwaiter

The word *pancake* has come to be written as a single word, while *pan-broil* is usually hyphenated and *hot cake* is still written as two separate words.

Use a hyphen to join two words used as a single modifier before a noun:

He is well dressed.
He is a well-dressed man.
We ate a lot of ice cream last summer.
We had an ice-cream cone on the way home every night.

If the compound modifier includes a word ending in -*ly*, the hyphen is *not* used:

He was handsomely dressed.
He was a handsomely dressed man.

When using two or more hyphenated words with a common base, leave a space after each hyphen except the last:

The university offered two-, three-, and four-credit courses.

Use a hyphen between some prefixes and the words they are attached to. Particularly with *re-*, the hyphen is often necessary in order to distinguish one word from another that would otherwise look just like it. Compare the following pairs; notice that the *first* syllable is stressed in the words on the left, while the last is stressed in the words without the hyphen. The hyphen, then, indicates where you should put stress so that you know which meaning of the word is intended:

re-form (form again)   reform (improve)
re-creation (new creation)   recreation(fun and games)
re-cover (cover again)   recover (get better)

Some other common prefixes that are usually followed by a hyphen are *anti-*, *pro-*, *self-*, and *ex-*. The suffix *-elect* is also usually separated by a hyphen from the word it modifies:

anti-aircraft
pro-communist
self-made
ex-president
governor-elect

24a

Hyphens are sometimes also used to separate a prefix from its root when the prefix ends in the same vowel as the root begins, although when the word is very common, the hyphen is not used. Compare:

pre-engineered reelection
co-opt   cooperation

24a.2 To Divide Words

Hyphens are used to divide words at the end of a line when there is not room for the whole word on one line. Words should only be divided between syllables (use the main entry in a dictionary to see where the syllables are divided), and they should never be divided so as to leave only a single letter on a line:

UNCONVENTIONAL: a-butment
      quarr-y
      he-avenly
CONVENTIONAL: abut-ment
      quar-ry
      heaven-ly

Hyphenate between letters that have been doubled by the addition of a suffix, but do not hyphenate between double letters that are part of the root word:

run-ning *but* will-ing

If you have to divide a compound word at the end of a line, always divide it at the point where it is already hyphenated:

UNCONVENTIONAL: sis-ter-in-law
CONVENTIONAL: sister-in-law (or)
      sister-in-law

24a.3 Minor Uses

Use hyphens as substitutes for the word *to* in phrases showing inclusive time or place:

1929-1935 (from 1929 *to* 1935)
pp. 25-34 (pages 25 *to* 34)

Use hyphens when spelling out compound numbers from 21 through 99:

24

forty-five
seventy-third

24b Apostrophes

Apostrophes are used to indicate possession or other relationship, in a few cases to form the plural, and to form contractions.

24b.1 For Possession
Use an apostrophe followed by an *s* to indicate possession or
relationship:

Paula's problem
the cat's pajamas

If a singular word already ends in an *s* or *z* sound, use either an
apostrophe followed by an *s* or an apostrophe alone:

for appearance's sake	(or)	for appearance' sake
Cass's house	(or)	Cass' house

If a plural word ends in -*s*, use only an apostrophe to make it
possessive:

the girls' teacher
the Joneses' car

But if a plural word does not end in -*s*, use an apostrophe together
with an -*s* to make it possessive:

the children's book
the men's room

For further information on possessive forms, including compounds, see **15a.2**.

24b.2 For Plural
An apostrophe may be used with an *s* to form the plural of numbers and abbreviations, but an *s* alone is equally acceptable. You
should, however, be consistent.

Each of the children was asked to write ten 2's and ten 3's.
(or) Each of the children was asked to write ten 2s and ten
3s.

The Meyers invested in three IRA's last year. (or)
The Meyers invested in three IRAs last year.

Do *not* use an apostrophe to make the plural of proper nouns; add just an *s* or, if the pronunciation requires, an *es:*

I have taken my vacation for three Septembers in a row.
The Joneses are our next-door neighbors.

Do, however, use an apostrophe followed by *s* with abbreviations that are followed by periods and whenever the phrase would be confusing without it:

The university awarded more B.A.'s than B.S.'s last year.
He helped the children learn their abc's.

24b.3   For Contractions

Use apostrophes to make contractions and other shortened forms. (But see **24g** for advice on using abbreviations.)

couldn't
Ass't Professor
the class of '55

Contractions are acceptable in casual or informal writing, but not in formal situations:

CASUAL OR   I'm not going.
INFORMAL: She can't read that.

FORMAL: I am not going.
   She cannot read that.

24c   Underlining (Italics)

Printers set certain words in *italic* (slanted) type in order to emphasize them for one purpose or another. When you type or handwrite, you should *underline* anything that a printer would set in italics.

24c.1   Published Works

Underline (italicize) the titles of newspapers, magazines, books, pamphlets—everything that is published as a separate work rather than as part of a larger work. (Sections of these larger works are enclosed in quotation marks; see **24d.3**.)

NEWSPAPERS: *The Detroit Free Press*
MAGAZINES: *Newsweek*
BOOKS: *A Tale of Two Cities*
PAMPHLETS: *Understanding the Metric System*

(Note that the names of sacred books are not italicized when used in a generic sense—for example, when referring to the Bible in general. Only when you are citing the exact title of a particular edition should you italicize it: *The Holy Bible*, King James Version, 1611.)

24c.2 Other Media

Underline (italicize) the titles of films, of television and radio programs, of paintings and other works of art, of major musical works, and of record albums. (But note that individual songs on an album are enclosed in quotation marks like chapters of books; see **24d.3**.)

FILMS: *Modern Times*
TV PROGRAMS: *60 Minutes*
WORKS OF ART: *Mona Lisa*
MUSICAL WORKS: *Appalachian Spring*
RECORD ALBUMS: *Graceland*

24c.3 Ships and Other Vehicles

Underline (italicize) the names of ships, aircraft, and other well-known vehicles, including trains and racing cars:

SHIPS: SS *Queen Elizabeth II*
AIRCRAFT: *Hindenburg*
TRAINS: *Orient Express*

24c.4 Foreign Words and Phrases

4c

Underline (italicize) foreign words that have not yet been "naturalized" into English:

They visited the beautiful *hôtel de ville* in Calais.

Often you may not be sure whether a word is fully accepted as an English word; a good college dictionary will indicate (usually by italicizing the main entry) whether a word is still considered foreign enough that it should be underlined.

24c.5 Letters, Numbers, and Words Under Discussion

Underline (italicize) letters and numbers when you refer to them as words:

> The Germans and French pronounce their *r*s very differently from English speakers.

> In this card game, the *5*s are wild.

Underline (italicize) words that you are discussing as words:

> The word *kiosk* was borrowed from Swedish.

24c.6 For Emphasis

Occasionally (but only very occasionally), underline (italicize) words that you want to stress. If you do this too often, you will tire your reader and lose much of the emphasis you want to create:

> I will *not* vote to reinstate capital punishment, because it is the *worst* thing that could *possibly* happen to *anyone*: death is *too final*.

If the writer were more careful about her choice of words, she could create just as much emphasis without making her readers feel beaten over the the head:

> I will never vote to reinstate capital punishment: nothing is so final as death.

24d Quotation Marks

Quotation marks are used primarily to indicate that you are quoting words from another source or to indicate parts of published books and music, although there are a few other minor uses as well. (Be careful not to be confused when reading books

24

printed in Great Britain, since British use of quotation marks is considerably different from American.)

24d.1 For Speech in Narrative

Use quotation marks to enclose the words spoken by characters in a narrative:

> Then Pete said, "Stop! I can't listen to this any more."
> "How strange," Jane thought.

24d.2 Quoting from Outside Sources

Whenever you are reporting someone else's words, whether they were originally spoken or written, you should put quotation marks around them to distinguish them from your own words:

> According to my professor, "Haste makes waste but get your papers in on time."

> It was Abraham Lincoln who described a democracy as a government "of the people, by the people, and for the people."

See also **9b.3** and **9b.4**.

24d.3 To Cite Parts of Larger Publications

Use quotation marks for chapters of books, essays, short stories, and songs:

> Guy de Maupassant wrote the famous short story "The Necklace."

> My favorite song on that album is "The Sound of Silence."

24d.4 For Words Used in a Special Sense

Use quotation marks around words that you are using in a special sense, to let your reader know you are not referring to the more general meaning of the word:

> Henry calls that abomination he painted "art."

4d

But do *not* use quotation marks around slang words as though to excuse them. See **20b.3**.

24d.5   Quotation Marks with Other Punctuation

Many writers get confused about where to put punctuation marks when quoting. Actually, the rule is easier than you may realize:

Periods and commas *always* go before the closing quotation mark:

> I heard him say, "nevermore."
> "Yes, I would like to go," she said, "if you don't mind."

Colons and semicolons *always* go outside quotation marks:

> According to the Declaration of Independence, "All men are created equal"; did the founding fathers have women in mind too?

> "All men are created equal": does that mean women too?

Other marks of punctuation go inside or outside quotation marks depending on whether they are part of the quoted material:

> "May I come along?" she said.
>
> (What is being quoted is a question; therefore, the question mark is placed within the quotation marks. Notice that the customary comma after the quotation is omitted when another mark of punctuation occurs.)

> Did she say, "I'd like to come along"?
>
> (The quotation is a sentence, but it is contained in the speaker's question; therefore, the question mark comes after the closing quotation marks.)

24d.6   Single Quotation Marks

Use single quotation marks to set off a quotation within a quotation:

> I heard the teacher say, "Children, please don't say 'I ain't'; instead, say 'I'm not.'"

EXERCISES

Some of the words in the following sentences require hyphens, apostrophes, underlining (italics), or quotation marks. Rewrite each, making all necessary changes.

24d

1. The reviewer said Hill Street Blues was the best show on TV.
2. It was with a lump in my throat that I bid au revoir to my French friends.
3. The Beatles first American release album, Meet the Beatles, is now a collectors item.
4. When Kennedy said in 1961, ask not what your country can do for you, he struck a chord of patriotism which may not have reverberated in quite the same way in the 1980s.
5. Does Faulkners treatment of time in The Sound and the Fury remind you at all of Salvador Dalis painting The Persistence of Memory?
6. I was hoping for an A in Calculus this semester, but when I scored 15 on the first test, I decided to readjust my goals.
7. When the Rolling Stones twenty third album was released, reviewers devoted more comments to the longevity of the group than to the quality of the music.
8. In his collection of essays entitled Hens Teeth and Horses Toes, Stephen Jay Gould quotes Vilfredo Pareto: Give me a fruitful error any time, full of seeds, bursting with its own corrections. Keep your sterile truth for yourself.
9. Critics labeled the defense plan the Star Wars initiative.
10. One of the seven year olds, who was having an understandably hard time learning the Beatitudes, said, Blessed are the poor in spirit, for they shall inhabit the earth.
11. I cant tell you what folly I think it is to try to turn a novel like Ulysses into a made for TV movie.
12. The word teriyaki comes from two Japanese words: teri, meaning sunshine or flame, and yaki, which means to broil.
13. If this is truly the winter of our discontent, then I don't hold out much hope for this spring.
14. We ate at L'Auberge, a gourmets dream restaurant.
15. The Los Angeles Times gave the incident front page coverage.

24e   Ellipses and Brackets

Ellipses and brackets are both used when a writer alters quoted material for some reason. Ellipses indicate that something has been omitted; brackets indicate that something has been inserted by the writer.

24e.1   For Omissions

Use an ellipsis (made with three *spaced* periods) to indicate that something has been left out of quoted material. When the ellipsis comes in the middle of a sentence, use a space on either side:

> "Fourscore and seven years ago our fathers brought forth upon this continent a new nation . . . dedicated to the proposition that all men are created equal."

If the ellipsis in the quoted material comes at the end of your own sentence, use a sentence period and then the ellipsis:

> Thomas Jefferson began the Declaration of Independence with words few people remember today: "When in the course of human events. . . ."

24e.2   For Insertions

Use brackets when you insert an editorial comment or a clarifying word into a quotation, so that the reader can distinguish your words from those of the person you are quoting:

> According to the Declaration of Independence, "All men [not women?] are created equal."

> "Soon after, they [Hermione and Frances] began to question whether they were on the right road."

EXERCISES _____

Select a quotation from E. B. White's short definition of democracy below, and follow these directions:

1. Introduce its author and title within the same same sentence.
2. Select a part of the sentence and integrate it into the beginning, middle, or end of one of your own.
3. Modify the quote by inserting an editorial comment.
4. Leave something out of the middle of the quote.

DEMOCRACY

July 3, 1943

    We received a letter from the Writers' War Board the other day asking for a statement on "The Meaning of Democracy." It presumably is our duty to comply with such a request, and it is certainly our pleasure.

Surely the Board knows what democracy is. It is the line that forms on the right. It is the don't in don't shove. It is the hole in the stuffed shirt through which the sawdust slowly trickles; it is the dent in the high hat. Democracy is the recurrent suspicion that more than half of the people are right more than half of the time. It is the feeling of privacy in the voting booths, the feeling of communion in the libraries, the feeling of vitality everywhere. Democracy is a letter to the editor. Democracy is the score at the beginning of the ninth. It is an idea which hasn't been disproved yet, a song the words of which have not gone bad. It's the mustard on the hot dog and the cream in the rationed coffee. Democracy is a request from a War Board, in the middle of a morning in the middle of a war, wanting to know what democracy is.　　　—E. B. White

---

24f   Capitalization

24f.1   In Sentences and Titles

Begin the first word of each sentence (like this one) and each line of traditional poetry with a capital letter. When transcribing poetry, always follow the capitalization, spacing, and punctuation exactly as they were originally printed.

> To see a World in a Grain of Sand
> And a Heaven in a Wild Flower,
> Hold Infinity in the palm of your hand
> And Eternity in an hour.
> 　　　—William Blake, "Auguries of Innocence"

Note that some modern poetry is not written with capital letters at the beginnings of lines. The following opening stanza of a longer poem uses lines that do not begin with capitals as well as some that do:

> is an enchanted thing
> 　　like the glaze on a
> katydid-wing
> 　　　subdivided by sun
> 　　　till the nettings are legion.
> Like Gieseking playing Scarlatti;
> 　　—Marianne Moore, "The Mind Is an Enchanting Thing"

24f

When a full sentence follows a colon, it may begin with a capital letter, especially if you want to create emphasis:

Follow these directions carefully: Go directly to jail; do not pass Go; do not collect two hundred dollars.

Always capitalize the pronoun *I* and the interjection *O* (but not the interjection *oh*):

She always cared what I thought.

> Yet once more, O ye laurels, and once more
> Ye myrtles brown . . .
> > —John Milton, "Lycidas"

She lost the match, but oh, how exhilarated she felt.

Begin the first and last words of a title with capitals, as well as all other words except articles, conjunctions, and short prepositions (four letters or fewer):

Much Ado About Nothing
"The Fall of the House of Usher"

24f.2   In Proper Nouns

Proper nouns are those that name particular persons, places, organizations, and groups (Susan, Detroit, West End Literary Society, Washington Redskins). *Common* nouns are those that name general classes (woman, city, club, team).

As a general rule, capitalize the first letter of proper nouns but do not capitalize the first letter of common nouns. Most of the time it is very clear which nouns are proper and which common, but sometimes it can be confusing. The following principles will cover most situations, but when you are in doubt, check your dictionary. If it is common practice to capitalize a particular noun, the main dictionary entry for that word will begin with a capital letter. (Note that rules of capitalization hold for fictional and mythical proper names as well as real ones.)

NAMES OF PEOPLE:

Letitia Simms

PERSONIFICATIONS:

Uncle Sam
Winnie the Pooh

24f

TITLES:

> Jennifer Smith, Dean of the College of Engineering
> Dean Smith
> Rabbi Dimmesdale

But note that when a title word is used to refer to a general class rather than as a term of address, it is *not* capitalized:

> Jennifer has become a dean.
> Our new rabbi came from St. Louis.

NAMES OF FAMILY MEMBERS:

> Uncle John is a great guy.
> Mom and Dad are coming to visit.

But note that when names for family members are not used as an immediate title, they are *not* capitalized:

> John, my uncle, is one of my best friends.
> I want you to meet my mom and my dad.

NAMES OF LANGUAGES:

> English   Swahili

NAMES OF NATIONAL, ETHNIC, OR RACIAL GROUPS:

> the French   Jews   Blacks

(But note that in combination with "whites" the term "blacks" is not usually capitalized.)

NAMES OF REGIONS AND CONTINENTS:

> the Orient   Africa

Note that points of the compass are *not* capitalized unless they refer to specific regions:

> We plan to go south this winter.
> The Middle East and the Midwest are thousands of miles apart.

NAMES OF COUNTRIES:

> Poland

24f

NAMES OF STATES, PROVINCES, AND COUNTIES:

> Ohio   Ontario   Washington County

NAMES OF CITIES AND TOWNS:

Philadelphia   Blacksburg

NAMES OF NEIGHBORHOODS, PARKS, AND STREETS:

Cicero   Central Park   Park Avenue

NAMES OF BODIES OF WATER:

the Atlantic Ocean   Lake Michigan

NAMES OF ASTRONOMICAL PLACES AND OBJECTS:

the Milky Way   Halley's Comet

NAMES OF GEOLOGICAL FEATURES:

the Sierra Nevada   the Grand Canyon
Mount St. Helens

NAMES OF TRAINS, SHIPS, AND SPACECRAFT (which are also italicized):

the *Orient Express*
the *Monitor* and the *Merrimac*
Voyager II

NAMES OF RELIGIONS AND RELIGIOUS GROUPS (including their members and the adjectives derived from their names):

Christianity, a Christian, Christian doctrine
Buddhism, a Buddhist, Buddhist practice

NAMES FOR THE SUPREME BEING AND OTHER RELIGIOUS TERMS:

God
the Madonna

NOTE: Older style required capitalizing pronouns used to refer to God, but that is no longer necessary except to avoid ambiguity:

Our Father, who art in heaven . . .
St. Paul was sent by God to preach to His people.

NAMES OF SACRED BOOKS:

the Bible   the Torah

(Note that the names of these books are not italicized; see **24c.1.**)

24f

HISTORICAL PERIODS, EVENTS, AND DOCUMENTS:

the Renaissance

the Battle of Hastings
the Magna Charta

NAMES OF POLITICAL GROUPS AND BODIES (including their members and the adjectives derived from their names):

the Republican Party, a Republican, the Republican platform
the United States Senate

But note that when words like *democratic* and *republican* are used to describe general beliefs and practices rather than a specific party, they are not capitalized:

Ancient Rome followed a republican form of government.
The schools try to train children in democratic procedures.

NAMES OF LODGES AND CIVIC ORGANIZATIONS:

the Masons   Rotary Club

NAMES OF COMPANIES AND CORPORATIONS:

East Ohio Gas Co.   Burlington Industries, Inc.

NAMES OF EDUCATIONAL AND CULTURAL INSTITUTIONS:

The University of Minnesota
Museum of Modern Art

Note that when words like *high school* or *university* are used without reference to a specific institution, they are *not* capitalized:

Oscar graduated from high school before I was born.
But we're both attending college this year.

But if someone refers to "the University," meaning a particular university, the capitalization is appropriate:

[In a letter to alumni and alumnae from a university president:] Centennial gifts to the University will be most appreciated.

24f

TITLES OF COURSES:

Freshman English 102   Principles of Psychology 200

But note that general disciplinary areas, when they are not the names of particular courses, are *not* capitalized, unless the area of study is a proper noun:

> Next semester I have to take courses in calculus, chemistry, art history, and French.

MONTHS, DAYS, HOLIDAYS, HOLY DAYS, AND HOLY SEASONS:

June	Hannukah
Tuesday	Lent
Martin Luther King Day	

But note that the seasons of the year are *not* capitalized:

> We plan to go to Florida in the winter.

24g Abbreviations

Generally speaking, the more formal the writing, the fewer abbreviations are used, and some abbreviations are never acceptable in writing. The following principles will give you some general guidelines.

24g.1 In Titles and Forms of Address

The following abbreviations are almost always used in front of a name. Rarely will you see their full forms spelled out when used as a form of direct address:

Mr.   Ms.   Mrs.   Dr.   Prof.
St. (Saint)   **Hon.** (Honorable)   **Gen.** (General)

On the other hand, never use such abbreviations to refer to a profession or to a person without the person's name following the abbreviation:

UNCONVENTIONAL: Dear Dr.:
Paul is my favorite St.
Paula is a prof.

CONVENTIONAL: Dear Doctor: (or)
Dear Dr. Smith:

24g

> Paul is my favorite saint.
> Paula is a professor.

Avoid redundant titles; if you list an academic degree after the name, omit the title in front of the name, or vice versa:

UNCONVENTIONAL: Dr. Sarah B. Hayden, Ph.D.
CONVENTIONAL: Dr. Sarah B. Hayden (or)
Sarah B. Hayden, Ph.D.

24g.2   In Other Situations

In written-out text (as opposed to bibliographical citations and other shorthand forms), use the full forms of streets, states, countries (except USA and USSR), months, days, and units of measure:

UNCONVENTIONAL: Next month I will be visiting clients on Fifth Ave. in N.Y.C.
CONVENTIONAL: Next month I will be visiting clients on Fifth Avenue in New York City.

UNCONVENTIONAL: Each Tues. during the month of Sept., we will receive five free lbs. of ground beef.
CONVENTIONAL: Each Tuesday during the month of September, we will receive five free pounds of ground beef.

Except in footnotes and other special situations, spell out *page, chapter, volume,* and *line* when citing references:

UNCONVENTIONAL: The most important images are in ll. 35 and 36.
CONVENTIONAL: The most important images are in lines 35 and 36.

UNCONVENTIONAL: I read the whole chap. in thirty minutes; it was only fifteen pp.
CONVENTIONAL: I read the whole chapter in thirty minutes; it was only fifteen pages.

24g

Do not abbreviate the words *company, corporation,* or *incorporated* or use an ampersand (&) unless the official title of the company is written that way:

Lord and Taylor   W. W. Norton & Company, Inc.

Do abbreviate words used with numerals (as opposed to written-out numbers; see **24h**). Several of the common abbreviations for time and date have different forms, with or without periods, with or without capitalization; all are equally acceptable, but if you have occasion in your manuscript to refer to times or dates often, be sure to be consistent:

No. 17	(or)	no. 17		
2:45 AM	(or)	A.M.	(or)	a.m.
12:00 EST	(or)	E.S.T.	(or)	e.s.t.
500 B.C.	(or)	500 BC		
A.D. 1500	(or)	AD 1500		

Note that while BC comes *after* the date, AD comes *before* it. While BC means "before Christ," AD stands for the Latin *anno domini*, "in the year of our Lord."

Acronyms (words that have been made from abbreviations) never include periods:

NATO   (*not* N.A.T.O.)

If you are using an unfamiliar acronym in your writing, use the full name the first time with the acronym in parentheses, in order to establish a definition of it for your reader; then in subsequent references to it, you can simply use the acronym:

The first meeting of Students for a Democratic Society (SDS) on our campus was not held until the 1970s.

Certain Latin abbreviations are perfectly acceptable in all kinds of writing. Notice that they are not italicized and be sure you do not confuse one with another:

ca.	"about," "approximately,"
cf.	"compare"
e.g.	"for example"
et al.	"and others"
etc.	"and so forth"
i.e.	"that is"
viz.	"in this way"
vs.	"versus"

24g

24h   Numbers

Spell out numbers that are under one hundred or that take no more than two words to write. Note the difference in journalistic style, in which you write out only numbers under ten:

ACADEMIC STYLE:	five	fifteen	twenty-three	179
JOURNALISTIC STYLE:	five	15	23	179

But if you have a series of numbers of varying sizes, keep them consistent—either all numbers or all words:

The winning numbers were 506, 100, 323, 10, and 53.

Note that it is not necessary, in the middle of your own text, to put periods at the end of dollar amounts, although it is a good idea to use commas to set off every third digit, for ease of reading: $1,278,369.

There are a number of cases in which figures are used instead of spelled-out words:

TIMES:

> 2 a.m.   (or)   2:35 p.m.
> 2:00   (or)   14:35

DATES:

> September 5, 1985 (or)
> 5 September 1985
>   (Notice there is no comma in this form.) (or)
> September 5th (but *not* September 5th, 1985)

STREET NAMES:

> E. 30th St. (or)
> East Thirtieth Street
>   (Note that figures are used with abbreviations and spelled-out numbers with the full street names.)

TIME PERIODS:

> the 1920's (or)
> the 1920s (or)
> the twenties

24h

IDENTIFICATION NUMBERS:

> Channel 13
> Route 114

ACTS, SCENES, AND LINES IN DRAMA:

> Act II, scene iv (or)
> Scene 4, lines 40-76

DECIMALS AND FRACTIONS:

> 2.5 million
> 1/3 cup

EXERCISES

Edit the following sentences for conventional capitalization. Also revise any use of abbreviations and numbers that would not be acceptable in formal writing.

1. during the fall and winter, he used to rise each day at five a.m., gulp down 3 cups of coffee while reading his bible for 25 mins., take the route 1 bus to williams hall, and work for several hours on his m.a. thesis on "the democratic ideals of the saint louis city planners."

2. she was influenced by nietzsche's *will to power* and kant's *critique of pure reason*, and she very nearly decided to become a professor of philosophy.

3. while attending cornell university in ithaca, new york, my cousin pierre studied physics, chemistry, french, and jewish history.

4. he lived at 1770 east twenty-second st., apt. 7, for 6 mos. but later moved to gov't. subsidized housing.

5. the gold acupuncture needle, measuring 6.5 cm, was unearthed on dec. 7th 1968 as part of a large archeological project in the people's republic of china guided by chairman mao.

6. the art historian dated the vase ca. 2500 bc, suggesting it was a rare relic of the shang dynasty.

7. he hoped to finish work in sept. on his paper on the failure of nuclear disarmament negotiations, eg., s.a.l.t. and s.t.a.r.t., etc.

8. he paid $50000 for one of f. scott fitzgerald's early manuscripts, written during the twentys, which the author had originally sold to scribner's for $25.

9. it is hard to say when we crossed the international date line; it was either apr. 11 or april 12.

10. dr. j. ogburn, m.d., runs the pediatric assoc. in nashville, tenn.

24h

PROFESSIONAL WRITING

The choices you must make when writing business letters, memoranda, and such specialized forms as resumes are similar to those for any other kind of writing. Your freedom will be restricted by the conventions of the medium and by the expectations of your audience, but you will still have to decide how best to fulfill the purpose of each communication.

One constant in all these forms of writing is that you are writing for a busy audience. People in business need to know right away what they should do with a particular letter or memo—file it, pass it on to the appropriate person, respond to it in some specified way. For this reason, writing in the business world needs to include clear information about routing, about subject matter, about desired actions; and that information needs to come early. In business writing, suspense is not a virtue.

Aa Business Letters

Business letters normally use a standard format regardless of their content, though there is some room for variation. This uniformity of appearance helps people in reading and responding to letters, because it makes vital information easy to find.

The usual business letter is typed on standard size (8½ × 11-inch) white typing paper. It consists of five main divisions. (See figure A.1 for a common letter form.)

Aa.1 The Heading Block

The *heading block* may be lined up with either the right margin or the left margin. If you are using letterhead stationery, most of the heading block is already printed. In that case, all you add is the date. If you are using plain paper, type in your return address (without your name), then skip a line and type in the date:

This chapter was written for the first edition by Donna J. Hudelson and has been revised for the second edition by Constance J. Gefvert.

8333 North Main Street
Crossroads, VA   24060

March 8, 1987

Timothy Cross, Catalog Manager
Jones and Marley, Inc.
4200 Olive Street
St. Louis, MO   63103

Dear Mr. Cross:

We wish to order twenty-five (25) long-sleeved
sweatshirts, as advertised in your direct mailing of
February 15. A check for $325.00 is enclosed.

Specifications for these sweatshirts are as follows:

>   Red with white lettering, lettering to read
>   "Rho Chi Rho Spring Celebration, May 18-20."
>
>   All sweatshirts are to be size "Large."

We understand that we are to allow six weeks for delivery
and therefore expect to receive the shirts about April
19.

Sincerely,

Thomas Renfrew

Thomas Renfrew
Secretary
Rho Chi Rho Fraternity, Inc.

Encl.:   check for payment: $325.00

FIGURE A.1. Business Letter: Modified Block Style

8333 North Main Street
Crossroads, VA 24060

March 8, 1987

The lines of the heading are punctuated internally just as any address and date would be (see **23b.10**), but there should be no punctuation at the ends of lines.

Aa.2 The Inside Address and Salutation Block

The *inside address and salutation block* consists of two elements. Skip two or three lines after the date. Then, aligned with the left-hand margin, type the name and address of the person or company to whom you are writing, exactly as it appears on the envelope; then skip a line and type in the salutation.

The salutation of a business letter is always followed by a colon. Salutations are sometimes tricky. If you know the name of the person to whom you are writing, your job is fairly easy. You say "Dear Mr. Jones:" or "Dear Mrs. (or Miss or Ms.) Brown:" If your addressee is a woman and you do not know how she prefers to be addressed, "Ms." is safest. If your addressee has a title, you can avoid the Mrs./Miss/Ms. problem altogether by saying, for example, "Dear Dr. Brown:"

If you do not know the gender of the person to whom you are writing—your addressee might be named Leslie or Lynn, for example—you may address the person by his or her full name: "Dear Leslie Brown:" or "Dear Lynn Jordan:" If you do not know name or gender, you may use the person's title: "Dear Director:" or "Dear Registrar:"

Some years ago, the all-purpose opening was "Dear Sir:" which assumed that all anonymous business people were men. You might still use "Dear Sir:" if you know your addressee is a man, but you are more likely to know and use his name. "Dear Sir or Madam:" is still a possibility.

If you are writing to a company rather than to an individual, you can no longer safely use the once-prescribed "Gentlemen:" unless you know the company has no women. You can safely use "Dear Gentlemen or Ladies:" or, logically enough, the name of the company: "Dear Thompson Company:" or "Dear Wilson and Daughters:" A modified form of business letter, akin to a memorandum, has been developed to avoid problems of how to address the person to whom you are writing. This form substitutes for the salutation a subject line (for example, "RHO CHI RHO SWEATSHIRTS"). Because it is less common, some people consider this kind of letter less formal than a letter with a more conventional salutation.

Now skip a line, and you are ready for the body.

Aa.3 The Body

The *body* is the main message of your letter. It is usually typed single-spaced, with double-spacing between the paragraphs. If you are lining up all the blocks of your letter with the left margin, the paragraphs will *not* be indented. They are already marked, after all, by the double spacing. If you are lining up the heading and signature blocks with the right margin, you may decide to indent paragraphs, but you need not.

Make the nature of your letter clear in the opening paragraph. Are you ordering something? complaining? asking for information? introducing an accompanying report? applying for a job (see **Ac.1**)? In the rest of the letter, give whatever information the recipient will need in order to respond usefully to your letter. Maintain a formal, courteous tone throughout, even if your letter is a complaint. Sweet reason is usually more effective in a letter than is name-calling or abuse.

Aa.4 The Signature Block

The *signature block* comes next. Skip a line and type in the complimentary close, followed by a comma. Here are some common closes:

Sincerely,	Yours truly,
Sincerely yours,	Very truly yours,

After the complimentary close, skip three or four lines (four if you have space) and type your name. You may want to add a title on the next line, if the title is relevant. In full form, with a title, the signature block would look like this:

Sincerely yours,

Jacob Marley
Adjustments Manager

The extra space, of course, is for your signature.

Aa.5 Miscellaneous Information

Possible *miscellaneous information*, if any, would come after the signature block, lined up with the left margin. Three kinds of information are commonly included in business letters:

- An indication of the author and typist of the letter, usually shown by initials—the author's first, the typist's after the slash: (AB/rs or AB:rs).
- An indication of which other people will be receiving copies of the letter:

Copies to: Eula Blankenbaker, Legal Department
Leslie Jones, Quality Control
Rafael Hernandez, VP Marketing

Sometimes the list is introduced by the letters *cc*, thus:

cc: Johanna Bjorklund, Sales Manager
Eula Blankenbaker, Legal Department

• An indication that other material is enclosed:

Enclosures, 2: resume, writing sample
Encl.: photocopy of canceled check

Ab   Memos

Memoranda (memos for short) differ from regular business letters in that they are normally internal communications. They are often short, even less than half a page, though they may be longer: some reports in memorandum form can run to many pages. Some companies have printed forms on which to write memos. In the absence of a printed form, a memo has three basic parts. See figure A.2 for a common memo form.

Ab.1   The Heading Block

At a minimum, the *heading block* contains TO, FROM, and SUBJECT indications, usually written in all capital letters and followed by a colon and two spaces. TO and FROM indications will give the names of sender and recipient(s) and usually their titles as well. The sender usually signs or initials a memo next to the FROM indication rather than signing at the end, as with a letter.

The SUBJECT indication tells what the memo is about. It should be brief (usually no more than a line and a half) and should begin with the most important noun. Avoid long beginnings like "A study of the feasibility of building a new picnic shelter in the town park." Say instead, "Picnic shelter: results of feasibility study." This second form lets a reader see more quickly what the memo is about. Furthermore, memos are often kept on file, and a memo filed under "Picnic shelter" will be much easier to find later than one filed under "Study."

The *date* of a memo is extremely important. It normally appears early, either before anything else or immediately after the SUBJECT indication. To leave the date off a memo is inefficient, especially since some memos supersede or contradict others. People need to know what information is in force.

```
                                    April 25, 1987

     TO:   William LaRosa
           Pizza Committee

     FROM:  Walter Fan
            President, Athletic Association

     SUBJECT:  Pizza preferences of softball team

     REF:  Your memo of April 15 (on anchovies)


     Sandy Hernandez has polled the softball team and
     has found that, of the 12 members, only 2 like
     anchovies,  Your order for the year-end dinner
     should therefore include no more than one pizza
     with anchovies.


     WF/akp
```

FIGURE A.2. Memo

Ab.2 The Body
The *body* is normally exactly like the body of a letter, since a memo is essentially an internal letter. Like the body of a letter, it will vary according to what the memo is meant to accomplish, but in any case it should get quickly to the point and include no unnecessary information.

Ab.3 Miscellaneous Information
The *miscellaneous information* in a memo is like that of a letter. When people other than the primary recipient are to receive copies of the memo, a distribution list may appear at the bottom; or the memo may show the initials of author and typist; or it may indicate that there are enclosures or attachments. References to other communications and related projects may also be included. This information may go at the bottom with the miscellaneous information block. Or it may go near the top, immediately after the SUBJECT indication. Here are some examples:

    REF: Biological control of Drosophila
         (March 10, 1978)

REF: Project Z225J

REF: Your memo of April 15 (on anchovies)

Ac   Letters of Application and Résumés

Letters of application and the résumés that accompany them are special business communications. The object of both letter and résumé is to get you an interview with an organization for which you may want to work. The letter tells what job or kind of job you are applying for and highlights your strongest qualifications; the résumé is an advertisement for you, and the letter is an advertisement for the résumé.

Ac.1   Letters of Application

The physical form of a letter of application is exactly like that of any business letter. The body usually has from three to five paragraphs, arranged as follows (see figure A.3):

Paragraph 1: Indicate what job you are applying for. If you are answering an advertisement, say so, and indicate where that advertisement appeared. If Professor Whitney suggested that you write, say so. If you have a name to drop, drop it in this paragraph if you can. And be sure to mention your strongest qualification.

Paragraph 2: Expand on your strongest qualifications or on those that relate most closely to this job. If your strongest qualification is education, you will have mentioned your degree and your college in paragraph 1. If your strongest qualification is experience, you will have mentioned that, citing a specific job or specific duties. In paragraph 2 you expand on these things. Cite other related jobs, for instance, or give more of the details of your education. If you are fluent in one or more foreign languages, this paragraph is a good place to say so (if it is relevant; otherwise, save it until later).

Paragraph 3: This is for your next strongest qualification. If you have been emphasizing experience, this may be the paragraph in which to deal with education. If you have been emphasizing education, this may be the place for experience. If you have been emphasizing education and have little experience but responsible extracurricular activities, the activities go here. If you have experience *and* responsible extracurricular activities, your letter will probably run to five paragraphs.

Paragraph 4: This may be your closing paragraph. If it is, indicate where and when you may be reached to schedule an interview, refer the recipient(s) to the enclosed resume, say something polite, and close. If

1501 South Oak Street
Apartment 12A
Fickle, IN   47947

January 10, 1988

William Johnson
Operations Manager
Consolidated Bottle Caps, Inc.
Romney, IN   47974

Dear Mr. Johnson:

When I worked in your department last year in
connection with the cooperative education program at
Purdue, you said that I should get in touch with you when
I was ready to work on a permanent basis. Since I will
receive my B.S. degree in statistics from Purdue this
coming year, that time has now arrived.

During my senior year, I have been able to continue
the work on quality control sampling begun at your plant
in 1986. The sampling model is now much more refined than
we were able to make it at that time. A senior seminar in
statistical methods of quality control has given me the
opportunity to find tests that are both more efficient and
more sophisticated than the ones with which we began.

As you will remember, before working for your company
I spent a co-op term with the Fancy Farms Poultry Company,
where I gained hands-on experience with computerized
records. This experience supplements the training I had
already received. I will be continuing that training this
term in an integrated block of courses in computerized
statistical methods.

You may reach me by mail at the address listed above
or by telephone at (317) 333-3333. Since Romney is within
easy driving distance, I could come for an interview at
any time. Thank you for your time. I look forward to
hearing from you.

Sincerely yours,

Harriett Sisson

Harriett Sisson

Encl.:   resume

FIGURE A.3. Letter of Application

paragraph 4 has been discussing, say, activities, then this closing information goes in paragraph 5.

Following are some guidelines for writing application letters:

- DO make clear in paragraph 1 what job or kind of job you are applying for, and state it in terms of the specific organization you are applying to. If you are applying to several companies or organizations, a word processor will enable you to customize each application letter without having to retype each time.
- DO be specific. "I organized the parts inventory and was promoted to parts manager after six months" is much better than "I have an organized mind and can work well with detail."
- DO emphasize your strengths. Try to arrange your paragraphs so that your strengths are easy to find in the letter.
- DO NOT bad-mouth anybody. If you say negative things about a former employer or about your school, your prospective employers will be reluctant to hire you. You might, after all, be the kind of person who would say negative things about *them*.
- DO NOT describe yourself with a lot of vague adjectives. Do not just say, "I am thrifty, clean, brave, and reverent." Give concrete evidence based on concrete achievements.
- DO NOT handicap yourself from the start by making negative assertions about yourself. Do not start, as one person did, "When I recovered from my heart attack. . . ." Do not start with "Although I do not have the qualifications you ask for, I feel. . . ."
- DO NOT talk about your religion, your politics (unless one of your qualifications is, say, your work organizing Senator X's successful campaign), or personal matters such as height, weight, age, marital status, or children.

Always remember when writing this letter that the people reading it are interested in what you can do for the organization, not what the organization can do for you.

Ac.2 Résumés

Résumés display your qualifications in easy-to-read summary form. They come in two basic models—the chronological summary (often called *curriculum vitae*, Latin for "course of life") and the summary arranged by function. Either type of résumé can be useful to you, depending on which will display more clearly your own qualifications for a given job.

Before starting to construct a résumé, or even deciding which form will do most for you, you will need to call to mind, and probably get into a set of notes, just what your qualifications are. Consider all your education, all the jobs you have had, all the offices you have held, all your extracurricular activities, all your special skills. At this stage, write down everything, as you do when you brainstorm (see **2b.1**). You can select and arrange later. You *will* have to select, because unless you have years of experience at many jobs a résumé should not run to more than one or two pages (one is sufficient for most entry-level jobs).

Now begin to select and arrange. Your résumé should have the following categories: your name, address, and telephone number; the kind of job you are applying for; education; and experience. The categories, especially education and experience, are not always treated in the same order, as you will see. In addition, the résumé may include such categories as honors and awards, offices and activities, publications, artistic exhibitions, or others that fit your circumstances. Be concise, getting the relevant information across as economically as possible, but do not skimp on the information.

1. Your résumé will always start with your *name, address, and telephone number*. It need not have any title. It need not have any of the information about height, weight, age, marital status, state of health, and so on that some people group under "personal data." If you want to put such information on your résumé, it certainly does not go first. If you put it first, you are asking to be judged on it, and you surely have more interesting qualifications than being twenty-three years old, with one child (unless you are applying for a job in which parental experience is relevant).

2. As in the letter, the first item in the résumé is some indication of *the kind of job you are applying for*. If you are sending the same résumé to more than one organization, do not make this job objective too narrow. Try to state it so that it will mention one of your top qualifications. If you have a word processor, you can easily vary the résumé as needed for each job you apply for.

3. Next, in a chronological summary, list either *education or experience*, whichever is stronger, generally starting with the most recent schooling or job and working backwards. If you are looking for jobs that require a college degree, you need not (probably should not) mention high school.

In listing *education*, start each entry with your degree or the name of the college, depending on which one you think will be more impressive. If you have been to more than one college, list them in consistent form; that is, you should start each entry with the degree or each one with the name of the college. Here are some samples of ways to present your education:

a. Western University, City, State, BSEE "with distinction," 1983. Specialization in electronic communication, including honors seminar in communications satellites and senior design project in which submitted design for satellite ground station. Regional Community College, City, State, 1978-79 academic year. Freshman year studies in calculus, English, and French.

b. BS *summa cum laude*, Animal Science (preveterinary option), State Technical University, City, State, 1983. Field work in poultry pathology with Fancy Farms, Inc., summer session 1982; senior seminar in turkey management.

If your training has been scattered over time or over several kinds of institutions or if it represents more than one specialty, you may want to consider arranging this section of your resume by function, grouping education into two or more blocks governed by the kind of education discussed, as in the following example:

c. Education:
    IN WRITING: University of North Carolina,
                       Greensboro, North Carolina, MFA 1983.
                       University of Virginia,
                       Charlottesville, Virginia, BA 1973.
    IN EDUCATION: Radford University,
                       Radford, Virginia, M.Ed., 1976.

4. Put *experience* before or after education depending on which seems stronger or more relevant. List your experience in a chronological summary, again starting with your most recent experience and working backwards (see figure A.4). Entries about jobs need the names of the organizations, the job titles, and the dates. If your job titles are more impressive or show your qualifications more clearly than the names of the organizations, start your entries with your job titles. If the organizations are more impressive or show your qualifications more clearly, start your entries with them. If there is no clear advantage either way, you may start your entries either way, but be consistent.

Do not just list job titles. Indicate, at least for important jobs, what your duties were. One way of doing so is to put the duties in an indented block directly under each job entry. Here are two sample job entries:

a. In this entry, the order probably does not matter much. The writer has elected to put the organization first:

Pete's Shoe Store, Lafayette, Indiana. Salesperson, summers, 1978-1982.

```
                                     Harriett Sisson
                                     1501 South Oak Street
                                     Apartment 12A
                                     Fickle, IN    47947

                                     Telephone (317) 333-3333

JOB OBJECTIVE

Position that will use expertise in statistics,
particularly statistical methods of quality control.

EDUCATION

Purdue University, West Lafayette, Indiana.   B.S. in
statistics expected June 1989.
     Concentration in industrial applications.   Senior
     seminar in statistical methods of quality control.
     Design project developed quality control sampling
     plan for Consolidated Bottle Caps, Inc., Romney,
     Indiana.

EXPERIENCE

Consolidated Bottle Caps, Inc., Romney, Indiana, 1987-88
     academic year.   Junior Statistician.
     Developed and supervised prototype sampling plan for
     quality control, began project for computerization
     of sampling plan.

Fancy Farms Poultry Company, Yorktown, Indiana, 1985-86
     academic year.   Computer Operator.
     Kept records of egg production, time in production
     of hens, casualty losses of chicks.

OFFICES AND ACTIVITIES

Treasurer, Statistics Club.
Captain, Women's Crew.

HONORS AND AWARDS

Member, Academic Honor Society for College of Arts and
 Sciences.
Recipient of Jelmer T. Fogburn Scholarship, 1988


REFERENCES

Available upon request.
```

FIGURE A.4. Résumé: Chronological Summary

Fitted and sold children's shoes, kept track of inventory. Introduced system to speed inventory checking and was promoted to Assistant Manager, 1982.

b. Notice that in the next entry, the job title more clearly indicates qualifications than does the name of the organization:

Computer Programmer, Billy's Better Burgers, Blacksburg, Virginia, 1981-83.
Supervised computerization of payroll and inventory control for chain of 15 hamburger shops in southwestern Virginia.

If you have decided on a functional summary for your experience, you will classify that experience into categories that will pull it together and make clear its relevance to the kind of job you are applying for (see figure A.5). These categories may be as closely related as Sales Promotion, Sales Management, Market Research, and Direct Sales or as oddly scattered as Management, Education, Nursing, Photography, and News Reporting (an actual person's list). Find the categories that fit your situation.

The *appearance* of both application letter and résumé is extremely important. When you have found what seems to be the best arrangement and have typed both neatly on high-quality paper, get someone to proofread both for typographical and other errors. If you are sending out several applications, you may want to have the résumé reproduced. (A word processor and printer are ideal for insuring neat, good-quality copies.) Go to a printer who will use good photocopying equipment or an offset press. Do not send out carbon copies, mimeographed copies, copies from a spirit duplicator, or copies from most coin-operated machines.

EXERCISES

1. You ordered an assortment of bulbs (advertised as good for indoor forcing) from a reputable mail-order plant company. When the bulbs arrived, you followed the directions that came with them, but only half the bulbs sprouted. Write to the company about this situation. You will have to make up its name.
2. Look in the want ads of your local paper, the notices posted in your placement office, or some other reliable source, and construct a letter of application and a résumé applying for a job for which you qualify.
3. Construct a letter of application and a résumé for a job teaching the course in which you are using this book or for a job as dean of your college. Use the qualifications you actually have, rather than making up new ones.
4. Construct two résumés covering your qualifications—one a chronological summary and one with either education or experience or both presented according

WILLIAM HARRISON CONKLIN, JR.

Until June 6, 1989
8333 Telegraph Avenue
Berkeley, CA 94704
Telephone (415) 951-1597

After June 6, 1989
Route 3, Box 364
Pearisburg, PA 17012
Telephone (814) 673-4567

Job Objective: Sales or management position with potential to use training and experience in administration and accounting.

Experience: ADMINISTRATION
               Proprietor of house painting business from spring 1983 until fall 1985. Supervised six two-person painting crews, prepared estimates, handled inventory and billing. Financed 100% of education.

               ACCOUNTING
               Treasurer, Rho Chi Rho fraternity, 1987-89. Standardized accounting procedure for house expenses and membership dues.

               Payroll Accountant, Conklin's Hardware Company, 1984-85.

               SALES/PUBLIC RELATIONS
               Chairman, Rho Chi Rho popcorn sales committee, 1988.
               Popcorn sales at football games financed gift of $5,000 to local Volunteer Rescue Squad.

               Publicity Chairman, Rho Chi Rho Spring Celebration 1988 and Fall Fling 1987. Designed multifaceted publicity campaign, including radio spots, posters, buttons, and sweatshirts, for formal dances held in student center ballroom with admission charge of $15 per couple.

Education: University of California at Berkeley. Expect bachelor's degree in June 1989. Major, Accounting. Secondary concentration, Business Administration.

               County Community College, Pearisburg PA. Associate in Business Administration, 1985.

References: Available on request.

FIGURE A.5. Résumé: Functional Summary

to function. Write a brief essay in which you discuss which of these arrangements seems best for your purpose.

5. Write a memorandum to the head of your major department in which you suggest some action by which the department can help its students. Be reasonable. Make a serious suggestion, not a frivolous one.

GLOSSARY OF USAGE

The glossary that follows contains words that present special problems to writers, either because they are commonly misused or because professional writers and editors disagree about their appropriate use. The advice given for each word or phrase in this glossary is based on careful research of college dictionaries, handbooks of usage, and especially on the usage survey conducted in preparation for this book (see "Usage Survey" in the Introduction). The labels *casual*, *formal*, and *informal* are the same as those used in the rest of the book and are explained in the Introduction. Whenever there is serious controversy about the appropriateness of a word or words, you can be confident that the advice in this glossary, as in the book as a whole, is based on the results of research and is not merely the author's whim. Further, the advice is based on practices common in business, industry, and government; and it reflects what is considered appropriate and inappropriate in the kinds of jobs most students go into after college graduation.

The advice offered in this glossary about a particular word or phrase is seldom absolute, unless it is something that almost all writers agree about. With controversial usage, however, which includes most of this glossary, we describe the conditions under which our sources believe a particular word or phrase to be appropriate. It is up to you, then, the writer, to decide how closely you want to follow the opinion of the dictionary writers, the authors of the handbooks of usage, and the survey participants.

above: *Above* is considered acceptable by most writers when it comes before the word it modifies (**the *above* figures**), but it is often considered more graceful to put *above* after the noun it modifies (**the figures *above*;** compare **the figures *below***). *Above* used as a noun is also accepted by many writers, though not as often as the adjective form: **Based on the *above*, I recommend a complete reassessment of the problem.**

ad: As a short form of *advertisement*, *ad* is accepted by most writers in all situations, though some writers prefer to use the full form in formal writing.

agenda: In Latin, *agenda* is the plural form of *agendum*, which means "something to be done"; but as it has been assimilated into English, *agenda* has come to mean "list of things to be done" and is considered singular. The new and commonly accepted plural form is *agendas*, meaning "lists of things to be done."

aggravate: *Aggravate* was once used to mean "intensify" or "make worse": **His letter only served to *aggravate* an already bad situation.** But it is now also used to mean "anger" or "annoy": **The neighbors were *aggravated* by the noise and traffic associated with the fraternity house.** Some writers, however, prefer to restrict the meaning of the word to "intensify."

alibi: Most writers restrict the use of *alibi* to a legal defense: **The defendant could provide no *alibi* for the crucial hour.** In the following example, then, it would be best to substitute *explanation* or *excuse* for *alibi*: **When I confronted Butler with his failure to complete the report by the deadline, his *alibi* was that his secretary had been ill and there was no one else to type it.**

alot, a lot: The correct spelling is always in two words, *a lot*, whether you mean "a great deal of" (*a lot* of money) or "often" (**My friend screams *a lot***).

alright, all right: Here too the correct spelling is always in two words, *all right*, whether you mean "everything correct" (**The students' answers were *all right***) or "OK" (**I guess I feel *all right***).

amount, number: Almost all writers reject the use of *amount* to mean *number*. The word *number* should always be used with countable nouns and *amount* should be used with mass nouns: **a large *number* of people; a large *amount* of food.**

and/or: *And/or* meaning "both or either" is commonly found in legal and commercial writing, though it is quickly becoming acceptable in other kinds of writing as well: **Please make selections from Group A *and/or* Group B.** Some writers, especially in formal non-legal writing, prefer paraphrasing such sentences: **Please make selections from Group A, Group B, or both.**

and, but: *And* and *but* at the beginning of a sentence are always grammatically acceptable, although not necessarily rhetorically effective, especially in formal writing. See 23a.1.

angle: When it means "point of view" or "personal interest," the word *angle* is acceptable by most writers in a casual context. In a formal or informal context, **I don't understand her *angle*** would be best written, **I don't understand her *point of view*.**

anticipate: To *anticipate* sometimes means to "foresee an action and act ahead of it": **Her resignation *anticipated* her being asked to leave.**

But in current American usage the definition has broadened and now most frequently means to "expect something to happen": **The mayor *anticipates* strong dissension over the proposed tax increase.**

anxious: The word *anxious* once meant primarily "nervous or fearful," but in current American usage, it more commonly means "eager." While some writers accept that use of *anxious* only in colloquial use, most find it acceptable in any situation: **We were *anxious* for the party to start.**

any: Some writers do not accept *any* to mean "all" when it is used in a formal context: **Harrison has the best organization of *any* candidate.** Most writers find this use of *any* to be totally acceptable, though others prefer in formal situations to say **Harrison appears to have the best organization of *all* candidates** or **Harrison appears to have a better organization than *any other* candidate.**

apt: The word *apt* often means "inclined or disposed": **He is *apt* to lose his temper when he doesn't get his way.** A broadening of the meaning has occurred so that now it is acceptable in colloquial and informal situations to use *apt* to mean "likely" (but still not entirely accepted in formal use): **He is *apt* to be unhappy when he learns of the decision.**

around: Using *around* to mean "about" or "approximately" is appropriate in colloquial situations: **Tell her I can see her *around* the middle of next week.** In formal or informal use, it is best to use *about* instead: **Tell her I can see her *about* the middle of next week.**

as, as if, like: While many writers accept *like* as a conjunction when it is used in informal or casual situations, the great majority of writers insist that in formal situations *as* or *as if* be used as conjunctions and *like* as a preposition: **It looks *as if* (not *like*) it's going to rain; Bozo behaves *as* every good dog should.**

as, so, than: A few very conservative writers prefer *so* to *as* when used as the first item in a negative comparison: **Jan is not *so* tall as Lynn.** It is much more common, however, and just as appropriate to use *as*: **Jan is not *as* tall as Lynn.**

When you have a comparison with *as . . . as* and also a comparison with *than*, be sure to complete the first comparison with *as*: **Pete is *as* short as if not shorter than Joe** (not **as *short* if not *shorter than***).

as to: *As to* meaning "about" or "concerning" is considered stilted by many writers. A sentence like **I will notify you *as to* Ferguson's response** can be written more gracefully **I will notify you *about* Ferguson's response.**

author: *Author* is a controversial word when used as a verb to mean "write." Since so many writers find it objectionable, you will find that it is shorter and less stilted to write **The new president *wrote* the report** than **The new president *authored* the report.**

awfully: While *awfully* meaning "very" is widely accepted, it is most common in casual writing. In a sentence like **Personnel directors are awfully confused about the effects of the new law on their procedures,** the *awfully* seems out of place because a casual word is being used in a more formal context.

bad, badly: Except in extremely casual use, *badly* is the adverb and *bad* the adjective: **If the team keeps playing this badly** (not **bad**), **their hopes for another NFL championship are over.** While *badly* is often found after a linking verb, many writers still insist that the adjective form should follow linking verbs: **The whole team felt bad** (rather than **badly**) **about Armstrong's dismissal.**

back of, in back of: Most writers consider *behind* more concise and direct than *in back of* when it is used metaphorically: **Senator Torres confirmed at today's news conference that he is behind** (not **in back of**) **the attempt to remove Senator Strong as chairman.**

balance: The word *balance* is an accounting term referring to the amount of money in an account after credits have been added and debits subtracted. The extended use of the word, to mean any *remainder*, is controversial; it is probably best to use *remainder* rather than *balance* in a sentence like the following: **The remainder of the commission disagreed with the two members' findings.**

between: When more than two things are being compared, most writers prefer *among* to *between*: **We are working to reconcile the differences among** (not **between**) **the three estimates.** *Between* is appropriate only when comparing two things: **We had to choose between the two estimates.**

bi-: The prefix *bi-* has traditionally meant "every other" while *semi-* meant "twice in." Recently, however, the terms have become almost interchangeable. While most writers prefer the traditional distinction, a word like *bimonthly* might mean either "every other month" or "twice in a month." **The magazine is published bimonthly,** therefore, might more clearly be expressed **The magazine is published every other month** (or **twice a month**).

but: For *but* at the beginning of sentences, see *And, but*.

But with negatives is considered unacceptable to most writers because *but* itself, when used as an adverb, has a negative meaning. A sentence like **We didn't have but a few minutes** really contains a double negative. You can rewrite it without the negative *didn't*: **We had but a few minutes** or, less formally, **We only had a few minutes.** (See also *can't help but*.)

but that, but what: Most writers consider these phrases wordy and roundabout ways of expressing a positive statement by way of two negative ones. A sentence like **I don't know but that the professor is correct** could be written more clearly **I believe the professor is correct.**

can, could: The verb *could* is always used with a conditional or past meaning. If another verb in the sentence is in the present tense, use *can* instead of *could*; see **14g.4**.

can, may: Many writers still prefer to use *can* to mean "able to" and *may* to mean "have permission to." A sentence like **I hope I *can* be excused** is more acceptable in casual or informal situations than in formal ones. The negative contraction of *can*, however, is accepted by a majority of writers in questions, perhaps because it is awkward to make *may* negative in a question form: **Why *can't* we submit the report a day late?**

can't help but: Because *can't help but* contains a double negative (see *but*, above), most writers prefer alternative phrasing in all but casual situations. The verb that follows *can't help but* can be placed immediately after *help* and often changed to an -*ing* form. Thus, **I *can't help but* wonder** can be rewritten, **I *can't help wondering*** or simply **I *wonder*.**

center around: Since *center around* seems a logical contradiction (*around* refers to the circumference), most writers prefer the phrase *center on* except in casual situations: **The defense's argument will *center on* the lack of motives.**

chair: *Chair* used as a verb is now accepted by the vast majority of writers: **Jane Maxwell will *chair* the group's meeting.**

Chair used as a noun, designating a person who chairs a meeting, is widely used as a substitute for *chairman*, *chairwoman*, or *chairperson*, yet it is still controversial. See **20c**.

chairman, chairwoman, chairperson: The first of these, *chairman*, is commonly rejected unless you know the person is male. The second, *chairwoman*, is often used when you know the person is female. *Chairperson* is more widely accepted than *chair* when the sex of the leader is unknown. But all these variations are still controversial; see **20c**.

consensus of opinion: Most writers reject this phrase because of its redundancy. *Consensus* means "agreed opinion," so it is best used by itself.

contact: Used as a verb, to mean "get in touch with," *contact* is almost universally accepted, though some writers dislike it because it is not specific. In a sentence like **Sally Martin *contacted* Jack Whitley about the position,** you can often find a more specific substitute, like *telephoned* or *wrote to*.

could: See *can, could*.

critique: Most writers accept the use of *critique* as a verb, as in the following sentence: **Please *critique* the attached report.**

A good number of people, however, still prefer to use *critique* only as a noun. If you want to be conservative, you can rewrite the previous sentence this way: **Please *write a critique of* the attached report.**

data: Unlike *agenda*, a Latin plural form that has been almost completely accepted as a singular noun in English, the use of *data* in the singular is still controversial. In informal or casual use, especially when *data* is thought of as a mass noun like *evidence*, the use of *data* with a singular verb is acceptable. But in formal writing and especially in scientific writing where *data* usually refers to discrete, countable units, it is best to use a plural verb: **So far, the *data* are inconclusive.**

different from, different than: While usage guides have argued for decades about which form of these phrases is best (*different from* is the traditional choice), both forms are widely acceptable today. The best guide is to use *different from* when a pronoun, noun, or noun phrase follows: **The pitching style of the Indians is very *different from* the Yankees'.** Use *different than* when a clause follows: **The new team looks *different than* the old team did.**

disinterested, uninterested: While many people use *disinterested* to mean the same thing as *uninterested*, most writers still make a distinction, using *disinterested* to mean "objective, unbiased" and *uninterested* to mean "not caring." A sentence like **John was *disinterested* in the outcome of the election** should probably be rewritten **John was uninterested in the outcome . . .**

dove: While the historic past form of *dive* is *dived*, a more recent variation is *dove*. It is still controversial in formal writing, though it is coming to be more and more widely used.

due to: Some writers prefer to use *due to* only when *due* is an adjective following a linking verb and *to* is a preposition: **His failure was *due to* poor study habits.** But when *due to* comes at the beginning of a sentence or follows any verb except a linking verb, the whole phrase is considered a preposition and some writers prefer substituting *because of*. Thus, a sentence like **Prices have increased *due to* pressures from the European markets** can be rewritten **Prices have increased *because of* . . .** Most writers, however, accept *due to* either as an adjective or as a preposition. See also *the fact that*.

enthused: Most writers dislike the verb *enthuse* because it has developed connotations of insincere or overstated feelings. In most sentences the word *enthuse* could be replaced by *said enthusiastically*, unless the writer intends to make the subject look insincere or silly. Thus the sentence **"The group has a great future," music critic Matt Olsen *enthused* after the performance Thursday night** could be written **. . . Matt Olsen *said enthusiastically*. . .**

expect, figure: While *expect* and *figure* with the meaning of "think" are becoming more common, even in formal writing, most writers object to them because they are less clear and specific than the word *think*. **He** *expected* that they were aware of his plans could be rewritten **He *thought* that they were aware of his plans.**

the fact that: *The fact that* can often result in unnecessarily wordy constructions, especially when combined with *due to*. A sentence that begins *Due to the fact that* could more concisely start with *because*: **Because she was ill she could not get to work on time** is much more direct than *Due to the fact that* she was ill . . . But in some cases, when you cannot use *because*, the phrase is useful. Most writers accept its use in sentences like the following: **The fact that he used to work for IBM should not enter into the decision.**

factor: While most writers accept *factor* as a general word that means "thing," most often you can find a more specific word. **We have to take a number of *factors* into consideration** could be rewritten **a number of *problems*, a number of *possibilities*, a number of *people*,** and so forth.

farther, further: While these two words are commonly interchangeable in casual use, most writers make a distinction in formal and informal writing, using *farther* to refer to literal distance and *further* to mean metaphorical distance. Thus you would say **Our new airplane flies *farther* on less gasoline than any other,** but **We have agreed to go no *further* with our investigation.**

feedback: A relatively new word that has come into common use through the computer revolution, *feedback* is accepted by most writers as a synonym for "opinion" or "contribution": **We need as much *feedback* as possible from our readers.**

fewer, less: Traditionally *fewer* has been used before nouns that can be counted (**John has *fewer* books than Mary**), while *less* has been used before nouns that represent volume or mass of something (**Mary puts *less* sugar in her coffee than John does**). While some people now use *less* as a synonym for *fewer*, most writers prefer to continue the distinction.

figure: See *expect, figure.*

finalize: While some writers find this relatively new verb objectionable, most writers accept it as a shorthand way of saying "make final": **Government mediators expect the new contract to be *finalized* this week.**

fine: As an adjective meaning "good," *fine* is widely accepted: **Martinez has been doing a *fine* job as acting manager.** As an adverb, however, many writers prefer to substitute *well* in formal and informal writing. Thus, **The new guidelines are working *fine*** could be rewritten **The new guidelines are working *well*.**

firstly, etc.: Ordinal numbers (first, second, etc.) may be used as adjectives or adverbs, so adding an *-ly* is redundant. Most writers prefer *first* to *firstly, second* to *secondly,* etc.

further: See *farther, further.*

gentleman, lady: Since the word *gentleman* is rarely used any longer, except in formal address ("Ladies and Gentlemen"), the word *lady* is also best not used, since many women consider it an unflattering euphemism. The best guide is not to use *lady* unless it is paired with *gentleman*.

get: The uses of *get* and its inflected forms to mean something other than "receive" are often controversial, although most of them are well-established idioms. One of the most common idiomatic uses of *get* is as an auxiliary verb. Except in casual situations, many writers reject sentences like **Do you think he will *get through* typing the report before the meeting?** and **She just *got* finished in time.** In a sentence like **Tom *has gotten* tired of all the delays,** most writers would prefer *has become,* except in casual use.

When *get* is used to mean "arrive," as in **I *got home* after dark,** it is almost always acceptable.

The phrase *have got to,* meaning "must," is common in informal and casual writing but not in formal.

Finally, there are many other idiomatic uses of *get* which are too numerous to comment on here but can be found in any college dictionary. They include phrases like *get to* (do something), *get away with*, *get back at* someone, *get to me* (meaning "annoys"), and *get away with* something. Most of them are widely accepted in casual use; the only use of *get* that is almost universally rejected by writers and editors is *got* used alone to mean "have," as in **I *got* lots of friends.**

got, gotten: In American usage, *gotten* is the more common past participle form when the word is used to mean "receive": **The university has just *gotten* a large grant.**

he, she; his, her: Phrases combining male and female references are widely used in formal writing as well as in informal and casual in order to avoid using the male pronoun alone when women may be among those referred to. The slash forms (*she/he, his/her*) are just as acceptable to most writers as the "or" forms (*he or she, her or his*), although the "or" form is somewhat more common. In either case, it is best to avoid long strings of these compound pronouns if you don't want to make reading difficult; see 20c for alternative suggestions.

hopefully: Conservative writers insist that *hopefully* must have a specific word in the sentence to modify, as in **He asked the question *hopefully*,** that is, "in a hopeful manner." Such writers consider *hopefully* a dangling modifier in sentences like ***Hopefully,* it will rain tomorrow,** preferring to rewrite it **I hope it will rain tomorrow.** Nevertheless, *hopefully* has come, in modern American usage, to be widely accepted as a sentence modifier; that is, you do not have to think of it as a dangling modifier if you consider that it modifies the entire sentence (as the adverb *fortunately* often does). Most writers, therefore, consider *hopefully* acceptable as a sentence adverb in casual or informal writing if not in formal.

human: See *man, person, human.*

if, whether: Traditionally, *if* has been used to express uncertainty (**I wonder *if* I can pass the test**) and *whether* has been used to express alternatives where an *or* is present (**He doesn't know *whether* he will go tomorrow or Wednesday**). In modern usage, however, the two words are largely interchangeable; only in the most formal writing is the older distinction maintained.

impact: *Impact* is one of those words whose use is rapidly changing. While it traditionally was used only as a noun (**The *impact* of the new law was questionable**), it now is often used as a verb, followed by *on*, meaning "have an impact on": **The new poverty program *impacts* especially on one-parent families.** Even more recently, *impact* has come to be used as a transitive verb without the *on*, meaning "affect": **The raise in tuition will *impact* low-income families the hardest.** In spite of its gradually increasing use, most writers still prefer not to use *impact on* or *impact* as a verb, so it is safest for you to substitute *affect.*

imply, infer: While *infer* is sometimes used to mean *imply* in casual situations, most writers prefer to distinguish between the two meanings. Use *imply* to mean "hint": **Do you mean to *imply* that I have not fulfilled my half of the bargain?** Use *infer* to mean "draw a conclusion": **I *inferred* from the expression on his face that I had angered him.**

in back of: See *back of, in back of.*

individual, party, person: Some writers do not accept *individual* as a synonym for *person*, maintaining that *individual* should be used only when you are referring to a single unit within a larger group (**We sampled forty-five *individuals* for the study** or **Each student in this class is an *individual***). Today, however, most writers accept the two words interchangeably: **That *individual* is crazy** or **That *person* is crazy.**

Many writers prefer to use the word *party* only when it refers to a group or to someone(s) who could be single or a group: **Will the *party* who asked for a window table please step forward.** With the advent of the telephone, *party* came to be used more widely, since a telephone could belong to either a family or an individual. Therefore, most writers accept the singular use of *party* as a synonym for *person*, at least in informal and casual use: **I have been unable to reach the *party* who called earlier.**

The effect of both of these extensions of meaning—to use *individual* and *party* to mean any person—is to make your prose sound more aloof, formal, and impersonal. Except when their special senses are needed or in extremely formal situations, it is most effective to use *person.*

infer: See *imply, infer*.

input: *Input* is a relatively new word borrowed from computer language. While *input* can often be replaced by *opinion* or *contribution*, the great majority of writers consider *input* perfectly acceptable in informal and casual use, and most consider it acceptable even in formal situations: **We need the *input* of all employees before we make the decision.**

is when, was where: Most writers accept the use of adverbs like *when* and *where* after linking verbs, especially in informal and casual situations. Many writers, however, prefer the older rule that only nouns or adjectives can follow linking verbs. In that case, the sentence **The most exciting part *was when* the hero cut through the barbed wire and escaped** could be rewritten **The most exciting part *occurred* when . . .** (changing the linking verb to an intransitive verb that can be followed by an adverb). Similarly, **This paragraph *is where* the mistake was made** could be rewritten **This paragraph *is the place where* the mistake was made.**

it: While *it* is sometimes used as an indefinite place-holder at the beginning of a sentence, most writers consider it inappropriate in almost all kinds of writing to use *it* in a sentence like **It said in the newspaper that senior citizens will be hit hardest by inflation.** That sentence can be more concisely written **The newspaper said . . .**

kind of, sort of: These words are perfectly acceptable in a phrase like **that *kind of* man** or **those *sorts of* movies.** But almost all writers insist that the number should be consistent. A phrase like **these *kind* of sales figures** should be rewritten **these *kinds* of sales figures.**

When they are used to mean "somewhat" or "rather," most writers prefer restricting them to casual use. A sentence like **The company is *kind of* well known** would be written preferably **The company is *rather* well known.**

lady: See *gentleman, lady*.

lay: *Lay* is the present tense of the transitive verb *to lay* (**The dog *lays* the newspaper next to the bed every morning**) and the past tense of the intransitive verb *to lie* (down) (**The singer *lay* down to take a nap before the concert**). Almost all writers agree that *lay* should never substitute for *lie*. See 14b for a complete explanation.

less: See *fewer, less*.

liable: While *liable* once referred strictly to legal responsibility (**He is *liable* for damages**), it is now often used to mean "probably" or "likely": **Cavanaugh's resignation is *liable* to complicate union negotiations with City Council.** Most writers, however, prefer to use another word in such sentences: **Cavanaugh's resignation is *likely* to complicate union negotiations.**

like: See *as, as if, like*.

man, person, human: It would be ludicrous to tell Billie Jean King and Bobby Riggs "May the best man win." Likewise, in most academic, business, and technical writing, it is no longer acceptable to use *man* to refer to a person or group that may include both sexes. Thus, **We are looking for a good *man* to fill the job** would be rewritten **We are looking for a good *person* to fill the job**. Likewise, a phrase like **the history of *mankind*** would be rewritten **the history of *humankind*** or **the history of the *human* race**. See **20c** for a more complete discussion.

may: See *can, may*.

may, might: The verb *might* is always used with a conditional or past meaning. If another verb in the sentence is in the present tense, use *may* instead of *might*; see **14g.4**.

more, most: *More* is traditionally used when comparing two things (**John is *more* understanding than Mary**), while *most* is traditionally used when comparing three or more things (**Mary is the *most* intelligent of all the students**). For more information, see **17d**.

more perfect, most unique: Words like *perfect* and *unique* are words that traditionally cannot be modified since their meaning is "absolute"— logically, if something is perfect, it cannot be more or less perfect. In casual use, however, people use words like *perfect* and *unique* in a non-absolute sense and then modify them: ***more perfect*** often means "closer to perfection" and ***most unique*** often means "most unusual." Except in casual use, however, most writers do not like attaching *more* and *most* to these kinds of words. See **17e** for a fuller explanation.

Ms.: The great majority of writers accept *Ms.* as a term of address for all women, married or single, particularly when a woman's preferred form of address or her marital status is not known.

myself: *Myself*, like other reflexive pronouns, is traditionally used only when *I* or *me* is already present in the same clause and the writer wants to indicate that both refer to the same person: **I will wash the car *myself*; I will wash *myself***. Many people use the word *myself* in place of *I* or *me* because they are uncertain about which pronoun is appropriate. In the following two sentences, however, there is no previous reference to the speaker and therefore almost all writers agree that *I* or *me* should be used instead of *myself*: **John will attend the meeting as well as *I*** (not *myself*). **The report will be submitted to Secretary Whitley and *me*** (not *myself*).

not even: While *not even* is often used in an already negative sentence to create emphasis, the majority of writers still reject it as an unnecessary double negative. Thus, the sentence **The accountant couldn't understand the figures, *not even* after consulting with the client** would be rewritten **The accountant couldn't understand the figures, *even* after consulting with the client**.

not un-: *Not un-* negatives are often used to create a weak positive statement. In a statement like **The meeting was *not* unproductive,** the writer seems to suggest that while the meeting was not a total waste of time, neither was it clearly productive. Most writers, however, still prefer to avoid the often confusing *not un-* construction and modify the positive form with an adverb instead: **The meeting was *somewhat* productive.**

number: See *amount, number.*

OK, O.K., okay: All three spellings are equally acceptable. When *OK* is used as an adverb (**The movie was *OK***), it is almost universally acceptable, although it is often replaced in formal writing by *all right* or another adverb. When *OK* is used as a noun, most writers also accept it in casual or informal writing, though in formal writing it is often replaced with *approval* or a similar noun: **As soon as we have Jack's *OK,* we'll submit the bid.**

party: See *individual, party, person*

per: When *per* is used to mean "a," or "each," it is accepted by almost all writers: **Profits in the electronics industry are growing at a rate of 9% *per* year.** When *per* is used to mean "according to," it is more controversial; while still acceptable to most writers, it sounds stilted in all but the most formal and technical of contexts: **I have notified the architects of the specifications *per* your memorandum of April 3.** While *according to* is longer than *per,* its effect is to make the writing seem less impersonal and stilted: **I have notified the architects of the specifications *according to* (or simply *in*) your memorandum of April 3.**

As per, while occasionally used, is an unnecessary combination: **as per your memorandum** could be written either **as your memorandum states** or simply **per your memorandum** (or, in a less stilted fashion, **according to your memorandum**).

person: See *individual, party, person.*

plus: *Plus* used as a noun, meaning "asset" or "addition," is frequently used in casual writing but rarely in informal or formal: **Suzie was a real *plus* at the party.**

When *plus* is used as a conjunction to join two words or phrases, it is widely accepted in all but the most formal writing. Note that *plus,* unlike *and,* does not require a plural verb because the two nouns or phrases it joins are usually interpreted as a single unit: **John *plus* Mary is a great singing combination.**

Most writers disapprove of *plus* used to join two clauses in all but the most casual situations. Thus a sentence like **I admire her work, *plus* I enjoy her personality** can be rewritten **I admire her work, *and* I also enjoy her personality** or **I *both* admire her work and enjoy her personality.**

proved, proven: *Proved* and *proven* are both accepted by most writers as the past participle form of *prove*, although *proved* is the more traditional form. *Proved* is slightly more common when used as a verb (**The process has *proved* to be more efficient than we expected**) and *proven* slightly more common when used as a participial adjective (**It was a *proven* fact**).

provided, providing: Traditionally, *provided* was the form to use to mean "if" or "on the condition (that)." Today, however, both forms, along with the combination *provided that*, are widely used, although some writers still prefer *provided*: **They will lease the building, *provided* we renovate the interior.**

quick, quickly: Almost all writers still insist on a distinction, using *quick* only as an adjective and *quickly* as the adverb form: **You will have to move *quickly* to get that account.** See 17a.3.

reason . . . because, reason why: Traditionally, *because* and *why* are both considered redundant, since *reason* already carries in it the notion of "why" and "because." Most writers reject *because*, suggesting that *that* is a better conjunction to use, and many writers reject *why* as simply unnecessary. Thus, **The *reason why* we are marketing it now is *because* Smith and Bradley are developing a similar device** could be rewritten **The *reason* we are marketing it now is *that* Smith and Bradley are developing a similar device.**

regarding: Most writers consider that *regarding* and its near cousins (*as regards, in regard to, with regard to*) could more simply be stated *about*. Thus, a sentence like **We need to talk *regarding* that option** could be more simply stated **We need to talk *about* that option.**

said: Most writers consider *said* used as an adjective to be overly formal or even legalistic in informal and casual writing. Thus a phrase like **in *said* example** could be less formally written **in *that* example** or **in *the* example *above*.**

same, such: Almost all writers reject the use of *same* and *such* as pronouns. The sentence **She sold her boat because her friends did not care for *same*** can be rewritten **. . . did not care for *it*.** *Such* will usually work if the word it modifies is added. Thus **Cal told me yesterday that he enjoyed the tennis matches, but Fred had no use for *such*** could be rewritten **. . . had no use for *such sports*** or **. . . had no use for *them*.**

she, he: See *he, she*.

shined, shone: While *shined* is always acceptable as the past and past participle of *shine*, most American writers prefer to restrict *shone* to intransitive uses of the verb. Thus **The sun *shined*** or **The sun *shone*,** but **Jackie *shined*** (not *shone*) **our shoes.**

so: See *as, so, than*.

slow, slowly: Almost all writers still insist on a distinction, using *slow* only as an adjective and *slowly* as the adverb form: **The board seems to be acting as *slowly* as possible.** See 17a.3.

some: While *some* is commonly used in speech as an adverb, most writers reject it. Thus, **The new technique will allow us to cut costs *some*** would be rewritten . . . **cut costs *a little*** or . . . **cut costs *somewhat*.**

sort of: See *kind of, sort of.*

spokesperson: Almost all writers accept *spokesperson* as a substitute for *spokesman* because it includes both males and females. Some writers, who find *spokesperson* too formal, substitute *representative* or a similar word.

such: See *same, such.*

than: See *as, so, than.*

that, which: While a few very conservative writers prefer to use *that* for restrictive clauses and *which* for nonrestrictive (see **15e** and **23b.4**), the majority of writers accept *which* in either situation: **I read the book *which*** (or *that*) **you recommended.**

that, who: While *that* is frequently used to refer to both human and non-human antecedents, most writers prefer to use *who* to refer to humans. Thus, **I need someone *that* can complete this job quickly** would be rewritten **I need someone *who* . . .**

their, them, they: While these pronouns are frequently used to refer to singular antecedents, especially in speech and casual writing where they provide a less wordy substitute for frequent *his/her*, *she or he* references, most writers still insist that *these* and *they* are singular only. Thus, **Everybody should complete *their* reports by Friday** would be rewritten **Everybody should complete *her or his* report by Friday.** See **16b.5.**

these, they: While *these* and *they* are often used without a specific antecedent, many writers prefer to rephrase a sentence to create a definite antecedent. Thus **I like this university because *they* really care about students** could be rewritten **I like *the professors at* this university because *they* really care about students** or **I like this university because *the professors* really care about students.** See also **12c.2.**

try and: Most writers reject *try and* as an inaccurate substitute for *try* followed by an infinitive: **Martin feels sure that they will *try to get*** (not *try and get*) **the account away from us.**

-type, -wise: Many writers reject *-type* and *-wise* as suffixes meaning "like" and "manner" because these relatively new additions to the language duplicate endings we already have. Particularly in formal situations, a sentence like **He described it as a *concrete-type* surface** could be rewritten **He described it as a *concrete-like* surface** or . . . **a *surface similar to concrete*.** Similarly, the sentence **Financewise, he is not doing well** can be rewritten **Financially, he is not doing well.** When a substitute word is not available, you can still usually rewrite the sentence to be much more specific. Thus, *Timewise, I can't permit you to take a vacation* can be rewritten *There is not enough time for you to take a vacation.*

uninterested: See *disinterested, uninterested.*

utilize, utilization: While most writers accept *utilize*, the word can almost always be replaced by the simpler *use*: **He wants the agency to *use* every resource available.** The noun *utilization* is clumsier and can easily be replaced by *use*: **The commission measured the *use* (not *utilization*) of the new highway.**

was, were: Most writers still prefer to use *were* for the subjunctive form of *be*: **He felt sure that if the proposal *were* (not *was*) ready by the first of December, the board would approve it.** See 10c for a more complete discussion of the subjunctive.

was where, is when: See *is when, was where.*

where: Almost all writers reject the use of *where* as a subsitute for *that*: **I read in today's paper *that* (not *where*) a woman in Arizona trains snakes.**

whether: See *if, whether.*

which: When *which* is used to refer to an entire clause, some writers object though most accept it provided there is no ambiguity. Thus the following sentence is perfectly clear: **I want to insulate the attic, *which* should reduce our utility bills.** See 12c.2 for a discussion of how to revise sentences with ambiguous references.

which, that: See *that, which.*

who, that: See *that, who.*

who, whom, whoever, whomever: While *who* and *whoever* have virtually replaced *who* and *whom* in speech, most writers still take care to distinguish between subject and object forms in all but casual writing: **The key question is *whom* the governor wants to appoint to the post; You may interview *whomever* you would like.**

-wise: See *-type, -wise.*

would have: Almost all writers agree that if you have *would have* in one clause, you should not use it in the other: **If the order *had arrived* (not *would have arrived*) on time, we would not have had this problem.** See 14g.1.

you: Most writers accept *you* as a substitute for *one* in informal and casual writing: **You can't be too careful in my situation.**

you and I: Many people, because they have somehow gotten the idea that *I* is better than *me*, use *I* inappropriately, especially in the phrase *you and I. I* is always used for the subject case and *me* is always used for the object case: **John has asked *you and me* (not *you and I*) to proofread the report.**

INDEX OF GRAMMATICAL TERMS

INDEX

CONTENTS